HISTORY OF ARCHITECTURE

STONEHENGE TO SKYSCRAPERS

DORA P. CROUCH

School of Architecture
Rensselaer Polytechnic Institute

McGraw-Hill Publishing Company

New York St. Louis San Francisco Auckland Bogotá
Caracas Hamburg Lisbon London Madrid Mexico Milan
Montreal New Delhi Oklahoma City Paris San Juan
São Paulo Singapore Sydney Tokyo Toronto

HISTORY OF ARCHITECTURE
STONEHENGE TO SKYSCRAPERS

567890 HDHD 99876543210

ISBN 0-07-014524-5 SC

ISBN 0-07-014531-8 HC

Library of Congress Cataloging in Publication Data

Crouch, Dora P.
History of architecture.

Includes bibliographies and index.
1. Architecture—History. I. Title.
NA200.C76 1985   720′.9   84-7900
ISBN 0-07-014531-8
ISBN 0-07-014524-5 (pbk.)

This book was set in Optima by Black Dot, Inc. (ECU).
The editors were Anne Murphy and David A. Damstra;
the designer was Joan E. O'Connor;
the production supervisor was Charles Hess.
Halliday Lithograph Corporation was printer and binder.

Cover Photograph Credits
Front cover photograph by Dora P. Crouch;
back cover top photograph by R. Hummel;
back cover bottom photograph by D. Gardner.

CONTENTS

CONTENTS

CONTENTS

CONTENTS

CONTENTS

ACKNOWLEDGMENTS

This book is dedicated to Spiro Kostof, Norma Evenson, Henry Millon, and Roger Conover, without whose example and encouragement at crucial points it could not have come into being. It is also dedicated to the many fine architects (for example, Louis Kahn) and buildings (for example, Salisbury Cathedral) left unmentioned in the drastic simplification of architectural history set forth here.

I have also to thank Cynthia Field, who read the entire manuscript and made numerous invaluable suggestions for its improvement. My son Marshall Crouch has read the chapters from a student's point of view and saved me from many obscurities and irrelevancies. Shirley Weiner has typed and retyped with almost endless patience. The School of Architecture at R.P.I., in the person of its dean, David Haviland, has released me from other duties to work on the manuscript, a boon of great value to me. Other persons have read individual chapters, but I refrain from mentioning them lest the residual errors embarrass them; they have my thanks.

The style for capitalization follows McGraw-Hill standards. Persons raised on Henry Russell Hitchcock, who may expect to find a term such as "high Victorian gothic" completely capitalized, will be disappointed.

Dora P. Crouch

INTRODUCTION

In any field, the answers discovered correspond to the questions asked. New facts or new relations are rarely uncovered in the absence of penetrating questions. As an example of this process, consider the problem of cholera epidemics, as described by Benevolo in *The Origins of Modern Town Planning*. During the early years of the nineteenth century, one cholera epidemic after another swept the city of London. People were living in crowded and filthy conditions, the population having increased rapidly as a result of the industrial revolution. Water supply remained what it had been in the seventeenth century, and drainage was inadequate. Cholera thrives in such conditions. While each epidemic was going on, doctors sacrificed themselves to save human lives but were frequently defeated and oftentimes succumbed to the disease. How the disease was carried was still not known, but the worst outbreaks were certainly in the most crowded, filthy, and ill- drained areas. As long as cholera was thought of as a medical problem, given the existing physical circumstances, no solution was possible. When cholera began to be thought of as an engineering problem, however, a solution was possible. By an increase in the amount of pure water brought to the city in new pipe systems and by the design and installation of new drainage pipes that were both more efficient and cheaper, problems of filth and poor drainage in the most crowded areas were greatly alleviated. With fewer pools of stagnant water for germs to breed in, and with pure water for drinking and bathing, the entire population of London was free at last from the danger of cholera epidemics. With the right kind of question having been asked and addressed, a comprehensive solution could be found.

In architecture the nature of the questions frequently determines the nature of the answers. Architects, patrons, historians, and ordinary people may well ask separate sets of questions; even when they use the same words, they may be looking for different sets of truths, because of their different needs. For a comprehensive understanding of architecture, we must ask as many different sorts of questions as we can, recognizing the mutual interactions of the many factors that determine what is built.

In this book, to simplify learning, one question will be matched with one monument. A glance at the Contents will reveal at once the major questions to be considered. For each question, one particular monument is examined in enough depth to make clear how the question and the monument illuminate one another. Because such pairing is arbitrary, after a few chapters, we will stop and pair the monuments with other questions, stating explicitly that all questions are assumed to apply to all monuments in some degree. Having originally paired Egyptian pyramids with *economics*, we will find it illuminating to consider them again with *social context*. Students are then encouraged to repeat the process with the pyramids as they learn about structures, materials, motivations, and so on.

At the end of the book, all the major monuments will be examined again in the light of one question—the question of light—and all the questions will be used to examine one monument—the World Trade Center. By this time the student will be prepared to see the great complexity of architecture. Its constraints come from physics and politics, as well as from the creative imagination and the organization of the building industry. Architecture is both a matter of utility and a matter of art, its complexities exceeding our expectations for the merely useful or merely artistic.

Because the author is a historian, questions of the relation between architecture and history are very seriously taken in this book. From the beginning of the publication of histories of architecture (about 1750), questions of style, form, and aesthetic meaning have been asked by historians and critics. These questions have been significant, having held the interest of many scholars in architectural history for the past 100 years or more. The study of symbolism (iconography) and biographies of artists, along with style and period, has been fruitful in that the material turned up has enriched our understanding of the art of the past. More recently, these questions have been joined by many others taken from the adjacent disciplines of sociology and psychology and from intellectual and economic history. Studies of the development of knowledge in engineering and technology have generated another group of questions for the history of architecture. Increased consciousness of the historiography (the principles, theories, and history of historical writings) of architectural history has made the teachers of architectural history aware that conventional teaching methods are inadequate with respect to the desire for knowledge that their students and they themselves have about architecture.

Architects now realize that the history of architecture is incredibly rich. From 1750 until even as late as 1950, the past was seen as a great mine of motifs that architects could copy for the decoration of their structures. For practicing architects in the nineteenth century, it was difficult to manage the possibilities offered by the greatly expanding awareness of historical styles. No one could reasonably expect the first generation to penetrate beyond the fascinating surface of the historical differences. Then the second generation had a revulsion against this visual richness—hence the austerities of the modern movement. It was left to the third generation—ourselves—to begin to achieve a new synthesis of our own needs and what the past has to offer—a synthesis that goes far beyond appearance and yet includes it.

Architects now have different uses for history—both practical and intellectual ones. If architecture as built is the tightly interlocking set of solutions to the problems of housing human activities, then the more examples an architect is familiar with, the richer, potentially, are his or her solutions. Just as the case study method has proved so successful in schools of business administration, so can the case study method in architecture be useful. By studying particular solutions, architects gain better understanding of how their own problems differ or might be solved. By understanding the complexity of past architectural problems, today's architects will be less inclined to simplistic solutions that leave out important human and architectural factors.

A beginning in developing the method of this book was made in 1970 and 1971 when the author taught at Berkeley with Norma Evenson and Spiro Kostof. It was further developed in classes taught at Dominguez Hills State College (now University) in southern California (1972 to 1975), where the high level of curiosity among students was paired with a complete range of abilities and skills, making teaching there a supreme challenge. Finally, the method matured at Rensselaer Polytechnic Institute, where since 1975 the author has taught mostly architecture students, but also engineers and humanists. The method is suitable for all who want to know about the physical expression of culture in buildings and cities, whether they be students of art appreciation, professional architecture students, art history majors, or liberal arts students. Teachers who use the book will want to supplement its materials or contradict the author altogether, thus demonstrating to their students that architecture is even more complex and controversial than the author has been able to show.

1
STONEHENGE
A MEASURE OF TIME

Architecture, which exists in time, is a record of the passage of time. There is no question about which came first; time has the position of primacy. History is an account of the doings of people during the passage of time, and the history of architecture is the history of their buildings. The shape of time (see Kubler, *The Shape of Time*) has changed drastically during the twentieth century and with this change so has our understanding of the shape of architectural history changed.

Figure 1-1 shows time lines that correspond to history as it was commonly conceived before 1930 by western Christian society and history as it is now commonly conceived. Note that geography has changed as well. In the earlier version of human history, creation took place about 4000 B.C. The first humans were Adam and Eve, who lived somewhere in the Middle East. Their sons

Figure 1-1   Time lines of two scenarios for the history of humankind (facing page).

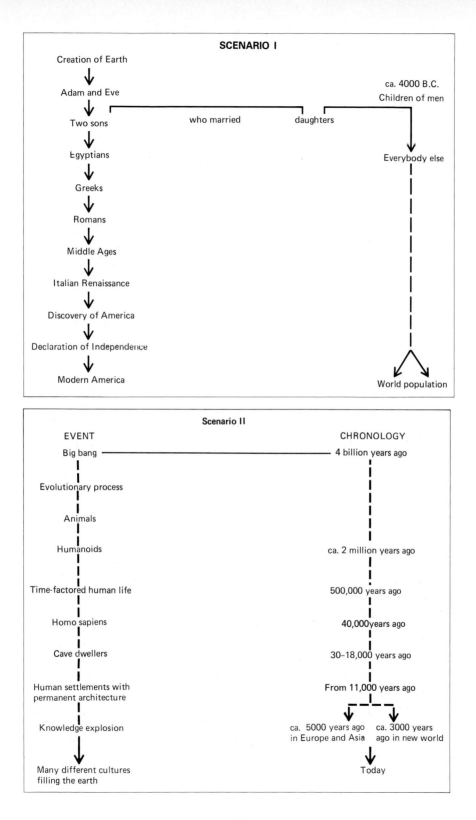

married daughters of men whose origin is not clear. Perhaps a thousand years later the Egyptians appeared on the scene, to be followed by the Greeks, the Romans, the Christians of the Middle Ages in western Europe, and the intellectual and artistic Italians of the Renaissance. Finally, America was discovered and the Declaration of Independence was signed; and by the inevitable processes of history, the United States of America stood forth as the culmination of human development. It was true that the world did contain others, but since they were living in such far off and unknown places as China, they were not then taken seriously as part of human history.

The newer theory is more inclusive with respect to both chronology and geography. It posits a beginning of 4 billion years ago or more that started with a big bang. Once the solar system had settled down to spin and the planet had cooled off, life began. To us, the process seems still homocentric, for we understand it to be aimed at producing humanoids and finally our own species: Australopithecines 4-5 million years ago; Homo Erectus 1 million years ago; Neanderthals 100,000 years ago; Homo sapiens 40,000 years ago. About 500,000 years ago human beings began leading a time-factored existence; that is, they made careful note of when in the spring the salmon would run and when in the fall it was time to make warm winter clothes (see Marshak, *The Roots of Civilization*). After a long period of more careful observation, people began keeping calendars perhaps as early as 30,000 to 27,000 years ago. That is, they began to record the changing phases of the moon. Each lunar month was recorded on a separate counter. What we realize is that keeping track of time—recording history—is an intrinsically human activity. In fact, one might define humans as beings who keep track of time not merely by habit, as some animals can keep track of the ways of their owners, but by differences—"the year of the big snow," "the day that grandfather died," and so on. Recording time—making history—is, then, a quintessentially human activity.

About 10,000 years ago there appeared permanent settlements with stone buildings, such as the walls of Jericho. It had taken from 500,000 to 30,000 years ago for human beings to move from noticing the passage of time to recording the passage of time. But the change from cave dwellings to stone-walled settlements with separate houses took only about 20,000 years (or perhaps 7000 if we accept the later date of 18,000 for the cave paintings). The rate of development had definitely speeded up.

In a mere 6000 years more, or 5000 ± 300 years ago, there was a knowledge explosion—the invention of writing and numbers—and cities cropped up along major rivers all over the eastern hemisphere—in Africa, the Middle East, the Indian subcontinent, and China. Within 2000 years more, advanced civilization appeared in both western Europe and Central America. Human history appears to be, in this theoretical picture, much more a network or web over the face of the earth than a linear thread tying together single centers that successively occupied the place of primacy.

People lived in caves for a long time before they began to take possession of space in the abstract sense of painting their concerns onto the walls. This slow process parallels that of taking possession of time by making history.

Painting the contents of one's reality onto the walls was even earlier, we think, than was creating built structures of permanent materials.

A long period of experimentation with perishable materials probably led up to more sophisticated concepts of architecture. Scenario 1 (Fig. 1-1a) includes in the Biblical account of early human life the building of the Tower of Babel. This is now thought to have been one of the great ziggurats of Mesopotamia. As we understand them, the ziggurats of Mesopotamia were artificial mountains erected to be meeting places halfway between earth and heaven, where the god and a priest or priestess could meet for the benefit of the people. Beginning in the middle of the fourth millenium B.C., such mountains were formed of millions of sun-dried bricks on the flat plains between the Tigris and Euphrates Rivers. The very quantity of bricks produced a permanent structure from impermanent material.

The next step was to experiment with stone. The effort required to put together structures of found pieces of stone coupled with a growing desire to control the sizes and shapes of stones for specific purposes was overcome no later than the early part of the third millenium B.C., thereby making possible the erection of edifices such as the pyramids, assembled from many pieces of cut stone and given a smooth exterior finish. The dolmens of Brittany and the equally monolithic (made of one stone) circles of stone in England, such as Stonehenge, come at the end of the second or beginning of the first millenium B.C. but they probably represent an earlier stage of experimentation in the use of stone. Stonehenge also represents a sophisticated advance in the technique of keeping track of time (see Figs. 1-2 and 1-3).

At a distance, of 3 to 5 thousand years, how can we expect to understand the erection of Stonehenge—ascertaining the problem for which it was the solution? In the case of Egyptian pyramids, the architecture suggests that there was a link between life and afterlife and the continual caring of the people for their ruler and the ruler for them. (There were other factors at work in Egypt, as we will see in the next chapter.) By linking life and afterlife, the architecture of the pyramids marks the duration and cessation of an event—the life of a ruler—thereby exemplifying one relation between architecture and time. Architecture makes physically present a series of decisions and intentions long after they were determined. In this sense, architecture gives duration to the present.

Another way that architecture is linked to time has to do with its calendric use. Stonehenge is an early edifice that demonstrates this use, but not the only one. The Mayan buildings called observatories are now thought to signify the passage of time rather than to be tools for recording the changes of time. Like the Mayans, the builders of Stonehenge had worked out an intricate system of keeping track of solar and lunar cycles. It is instructive for us to see how well this was done before any of our technical timekeepers were invented and to consider the unforgettable architecture that arose from the desire to keep track of time.

By the time that Julius Caesar came to England, the circle of stones at Stonehenge was already old. At that time, the stones were being used by the Druids, a native priesthood; so a legend persisted that the Druids had built

Figure 1-2   View of Stonehenge. Bluestones and trilithons stand in place, surrounding some that have fallen. (Photo by S. Gorenstein.)

Stonehenge. We now know, however, that the Druids belong to the last century B.C., while the first phase of Stonehenge was perhaps as early as 2500 B.C. and it was finished by about 1700 B.C., at the latest. Many other fanciful theories about the origin and purpose of this great circle of stones have been put forth (see the sketches and discussion in Vatcher and Bergstrom, *Stonehenge*); but not until recently has any theory carried the aura of authenticity. With the publication of R. J. C. Atkinson's *Stonehenge* (1956), followed by the astronomical theories of G. S. Hawkins in *Stonehenge Decoded* (1965) and the scholarly anthropological views of L. E. Stover and B. Kraig in *Stonehenge: The Indo-European Heritage* (1978), we are able to place the monument in a suitable niche in the history of human thought as well as that of architecture. Atkinson gives a straightforward account based on the archeological findings of the site where he was for years the prehistorian in charge of the diggings. Hawkins, an astronomer, "deciphered" Stonehenge as an ancient computer to keep track of solar and lunar cycles. Stover and Kraig are, respectively, an anthropologist and a prehistorian who see the monument as yet another funerary center.

In the 22 years between publications of these books, scholarly thought has reexamined the evidence and connected Stonehenge with other evidence about the cultures that built it. Thus the picture conveyed to us in the Stover and Kraig book is much richer and more complete though perhaps not as exciting as are the theories of Hawkins. Hawkins and many time-obsessed moderns would prefer to see Stonehenge as a sophisticated device for keeping track of time. But even as we examine Stonehenge from this point of view, we must keep in mind Stover and Kraig's admonition: "Men of each age have seen in that monument whatever strength of purpose has animated their own society." For us it is interesting to examine Stonehenge and the question of time. This question is one of the many which can illuminate this or any other great structure. We realize that it is arbitrary to apply one question at a time. But we do so for the insights that may come to us in the process.

Supposing for purposes of argument that Hawkins were correct about the use of the arrangement of Stonehenge as a calendric device, we might then wonder why keeping track of the months was so crucial to early human beings as to justify such a huge expenditure of labor. Living as we do in a society where most of our food comes from the supermarket in roughly the same proportions and quantities every month of the year, it might be hard for the average city dweller to imagine the extreme importance of having exact knowledge of when it is safe to plant so that the danger of late frost is past. The balmy days of April or early May could fool an inexperienced person into

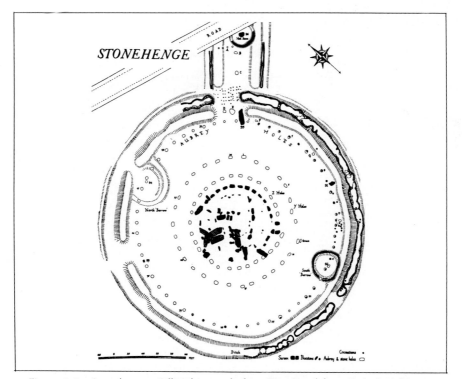

Figure 1-3   Stonehenge. Official ground plan. (Reprinted from R. J. C. Atkinson, *Stonehenge*, 1956, by permission of the Hamish Hamilton Ltd.). All three phases of construction are represented on this plan.

risking an entire store of carefully saved seed in one untimely sowing. A late killing frost could then wipe out any possibility of harvest for that year and leave the planter without seed for the following year. Thus with agriculture came the need for usable knowledge about which moon cycle was which.

We are not arguing here that Hawkins's astronomical theory is necessarily as tenable as he no doubt supposes it is, but rather that he understands that Stonehenge relates to keeping track of the passage of time.

Stonehenge stands in the plain of Salisbury in southwest England. It is the largest and most complete of the megalithic (made of huge stones) complexes found in England. Seen from the air or from a distance, the simplicity of Stonehenge still makes a strong impression. Let us approach it along the causeway from the northeast, as did the ancient users. The earliest version of Stonehenge, already served by this causeway about 4500 years ago, had a circular embankment with a ditch around it (see Fig. 1-4). The circle was about 320 feet in diameter. The material from the ditch once made the embankment about 6 feet high, but now it has been reduced to about 2 feet through attrition.

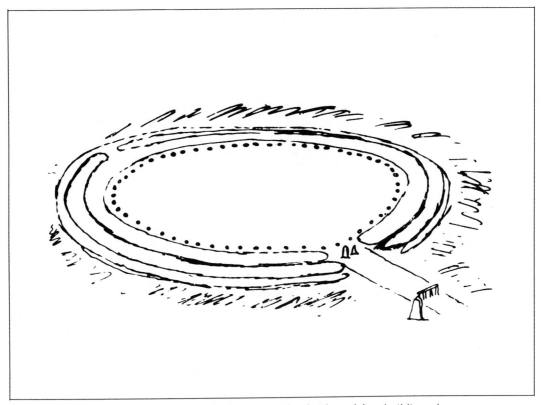

Figure 1-4 Stonehenge, near Salisbury, England. Plan of first building phase, ca. 3000 B.C., with circular embankment and surrounding ditch, 56 Aubrey holes, and Heel Stone on the causeway near the entrance to the circle. (Plan reprinted from Stover and Kraig, *Stonehenge,* by permission of Nelson-Hall, Inc.)

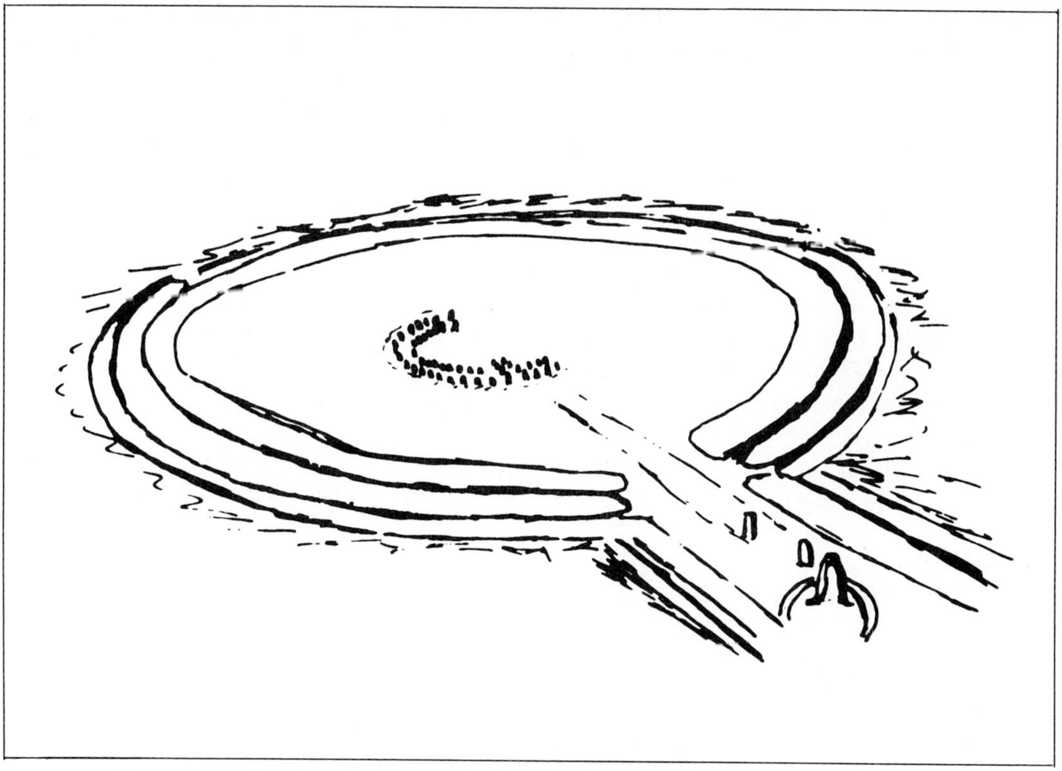

Figure 1-5   Stonehenge, phase 2, ca. 2100 B.C. The causeway has embankments and ditches; and at the center of the area, there is the beginnings of a double circle of large stones (74 and 86 feet). Two more stones are placed on the causeway in line with the Heel Stone. (By permission of Nelson-Hall, Inc.)

Inside the bank are a circle of 56 holes that mark another circle 288 feet in diameter. These Aubrey holes (named after a seventeenth century antiquarian) were 6 feet in diameter and 4 feet deep. After being dug, they were refilled with chalk almost at once. Later 35 of them were reopened to receive cremated human remains. In this, the Aubrey holes are like holes for offerings to the dead found in various neolithic burial mounds, called long barrows, found in Britain.

One feature that still survives from the earliest Stonehenge is the Heel Stone. Placed on the causeway near the entrance to the circle, the Heel Stone is large and irregularly pointed. If one turned and looked at the Heel Stone from the center of the circle on the morning of midsummer, one would see the sun on that day rise exactly over the stone. None of the subsequent rebuildings of the monument has obscured this feature, so that it seems to have remained important to all the later peoples who used it.

The Stonehenge of about 4100 years ago is very different from and much grander than the earliest one (see Fig. 1-5). The causeway, first of all, now has embankments and ditches along its outer edges. This effort has made the 35-foot width of the causeway seem even more impressive. By working on the road over several seasons, the early builders connected it to the River Avon, not far away. Such a relation to the nearest river is common among British henges (stone circles). Only at Stonehenge, however, is the entrance oriented to the rising sun at midsummer. It is also common for henges, such as this one, to be set in cemetery areas, and to have racetracks (here called the Greater Cursus) as an associated feature.

About 2100 B.C., Stonehenge was remodeled and began to look like the monument we visit today. Within the old bank and circle of Aubrey stones, a double circle of great bluestones was planned, the inner 74 and the outer 86 feet in diameter. On the causeway or avenue leading to the circles, two more stones were erected in line, and within the limit of the Heel Stone.

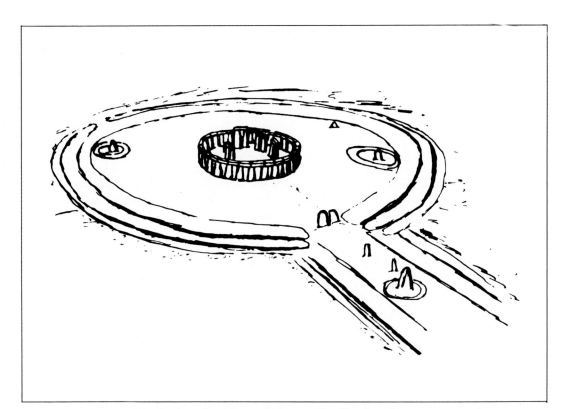

Figure 1-6   Stonehenge, phase 3, ca. 2000 B.C. The Slaughter Stone was set up just inside the entrance. Four Station Stones were set in the outer circle to mark a rectangle (compare with Fig. 1-7). A ring of upright stones made a circle at the center; these enclosed a horseshoe-shaped arrangement of large stones. Finally some of the stones from phase 2 were recut to set up as a smaller circle enclosing a smaller horseshoe group within the circle of large stones. An Altar Stone was placed at the curved end of the horseshoe. (By permission of Nelson-Hall, Inc.)

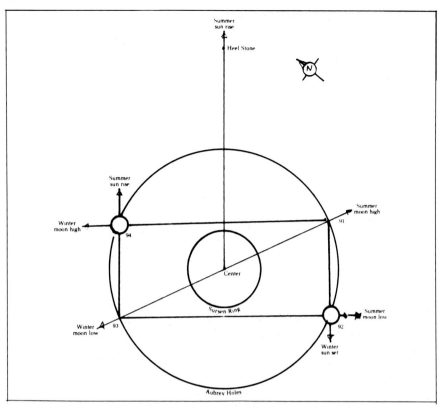

Figure 1-7 Stonehenge, alignments from center and from Station Stones. (Reprinted for S.S. Hawkins, *Stonehenge Decoded,* by permission of the publisher, Doubleday & Co., Inc.).

Apparently Stonehenge II was never finished, because the holes dug to receive the double circle of bluestones (called the Z and Y holes) were never filled. Within a hundred years, a very different pattern using some of the same stones and some different ones was begun. This last building period is divided into three parts. About 2000 B.C. bluestones were removed or set aside (see Fig. 1-6). A Slaughter Stone, possibly part of an unfinished gateway, is just inside the entrance. Four Station Stones are at the edge of the outermost circle; these stones seem by all accounts to have cosmological significance, possibly memorializing the surveyor's marks used to recalculate the axis and center of the sarsen stone structure and by their careful location linking the structure to the cosmos. They do in fact mark the extremes of solar and lunar settings, as sighted along the diagonal through the center of the monument (see Fig. 1-7). Toward the center of the circle, a ring of upright stones, some still capped with their lintels, encloses another group of stones of the same material. Five trilithons (each consisting of two uprights and a lintel) form a horseshoe shape open toward the entrance to the complex and emphasized by having the tallest trilithon opposite the Heel Stone. The five trilithons frame the extreme positions of the sun and moon's rising and setting, as seen from the center of the monument.

A little later, but still during the third building period, a double ring of holes (the Z and Y holes) were dug outside the sarsen circle. Apparently there was a plan to reuse the bluestones from period II. This phase was never completed and the bluestones were never actually inserted into the holes.

Bluestones were finally recut into smooth shapes and set as a circle within the sarsen circle, with others forming a horseshoe within the sarsen horseshoe. Here again we meet possible cosmological significance, according to C. A. Newman (*The Astronomical Significance of Stonehenge*), who points out that the number of bluestones arranged within the sarsens in a horseshoe is 19, which is a close approximation to the 18.61 of the so-called Metronic cycle of the moon's apparent northern and southern extreme positions. Moreover, the sarsen circle consists of $29\frac{1}{2}$ stones, with one stone deliberately half as tall as the others. (The uniform height of the sarsens is 14 feet, achieved by burying them to different depths in the earth.) The number of days in a lunar month is 29.5.

Connected with this last building phase was also placement of the Altar Stone at the curved end of the horseshoe. It has subsequently been overlaid with toppled remains of the largest trilithon. Such ruination probably marks yet another passage of time and change of attitude about the proper use of Stonehenge. Standing at the Altar Stone, with all the circles of stone ringing one in and marking one's place in the cosmos, one can see the full moon nearest the winter solstice rising over the Heel Stone once in 19 years. This is usually the same year that there is an eclipse of the sun, since similar eclipses of the sun recur at intervals of 18 years $11\frac{1}{3}$ days.

Although Hawkins posited that the early users of Stonehenge placed a post in each Aubrey hole in turn and thereby kept track of the sightings made through and along the bluestones of Stonehenge II or the sarsens of Stonehenge III, later consideration of the archeological evidence leads one to question this theory, because some of the later structures are set on top of the circle of Aubrey stones and in fact interrupt the circle. Whatever information about lunar cycles the Aubrey stones embody—and indeed the number 56 can be made to yield correspondence with the cycle of lunar eclipses with a fair degree of accuracy—may have been lost in the transition from the earliest tribal people to later peoples. Or perhaps an early tribal encampment center became elaborated and dignified as a ritual center, as Stover and Kraig postulate, so that no astronomical meaning can be attached to Stonehenge at all.

That Stonehenge was constructed to mark the passage of time may be considered to be indicated by all we know, but not proved from the evidence presented here. All we know with certainty is that archeology has firmly established the passage of time in the different building periods and usage periods at Stonehenge.

BIBLIOGRAPHY

Atkinson, R. J. C., *Stonehenge,* Macmillan, New York, 1956. The first comprehensive account of Stonehenge, based on the author's years of excavations at the site.

Hawkins, G. S., *Stonehenge Decoded,* Doubleday, Garden City, N.Y., 1965. A modern astronomer finds striking parallels between the data of science and the structure of Stonehenge. Not to be read uncritically but to be used as a stimulus for our powers of imagination and empathy as well as a means of engendering respect for the accomplishments of ancient peoples.

Kubler, George, *The Shape of Time,* Yale University Press, New Haven, Conn., 1962. A seminal study of historical knowledge. A book that could possibly change one's ideas about reality.

Marshak, Alex, *The Roots of Civilization,* McGraw-Hill, New York, 1972. The author reexamines the evidence for timekeeping among early Europeans, and in so doing revolutionizes our understanding of history, prehistory, and the knowledge explosion of ca. 5000 years ago.

Stover, L. S., and B. Kraig, *Stonehenge: The Indo-European Heritage,* Nelson-Hall, Chicago, 1978. A thorough and thoughtful study of the monument by an anthropologist and prehistorian utilizing the latest understandings of early people. Copiously illustrated.

Vatcher, L., and P. Bergstrom, *Stonehenge, a Picture Book,* Two Continents, New York, 1977. Fanciful and poetic ideas about Stonehenge as captured in drawing and painting.

2
EGYPTIAN PYRAMIDS
THE USE OF ECONOMIC SURPLUS

The pyramids of Egypt have traditionally been understood as being tombs of the rulers (pharaohs). Since the first Greeks went to Egypt in the sixth century B.C., the pyramids have been one of the greatest tourist attractions of the world. Because of their enormous size and pure geometric shape they stand out not only in their desert site but also in our imaginations. Many fanciful tales have been told about them, but none so strange as the real story of how and why they came to be (see Edwards, *The Pyramids of Egypt*).

The three great pyramids were built during the Fourth Dynasty, (around 2700 B.C.) about 20 miles north of the capital Memphis; today's capital, Cairo, lies across the Nile River from the pyramids and slightly to the north. Of the three, the largest and most imposing is that of Cheops. (So famous were the

Figure 2-1 The three great pyramids of Giza, near Cairo, Egypt. These are from front to back, the pyramids of Cheops, of Chephren, and of Mycerinus. Smaller mastabas and pyramids cluster around these large ones. (Photo courtesy Museum of Fine Arts, Boston.)

pyramids at the time of Herodotus, the Greek historian of the sixth century B.C., that he visited them and gave them the Greek names by which they are still known: Cheops, Chephren, and Mycerinus, for the Egyptian Khufu, Khafre, and Menkaure.) The pyramid of Cheops seems more like a mountain than a building, assembled of more than 6½ million tons of limestone. Its base is 230 meters square and almost perfectly level, and its height is 150 meters. Each triangular face has five acres of surface. The funerary significance of the monument is marked by the evidence of preparation of three tomb chambers: the first was cut in the rock under the pyramid and was reached by a corridor directed toward the polar north. This room, which was not finished off, lies under the apex of the pyramid. A second corridor begins 20 meters in from the entrance and was bored at the same angle through the masonry, leading to a higher tomb chamber also under the apex. This so-called Queen's chamber was not finished either. Finally, the continuing passageway was enlarged to make a gallery of polished stone about 47 meters long and 9 meters high. The walls were corbeled (built in projecting layers that met at the top), and

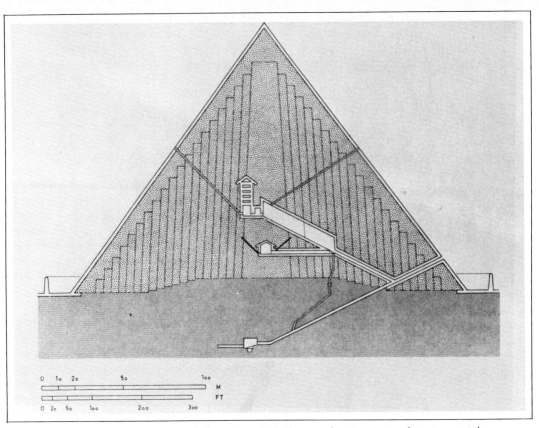

Figure 2-2 Section through the pyramid of Cheops, showing internal passages and tomb chambers. The upper chamber, called by the excavators the king's chamber, had within it a stone coffin that was set in place as the room was built, since it was too big to be carried up the corridor. The middle chamber is called the queen's chamber; it may possibly have been constructed to foil grave robbers. On the exterior, the entrance was masked by the outer layer of casing stones. (Section reprinted from De Cenival, *Living Architecture: Egyptian*, 1964, by permission of the publisher, Jean Hirschen.)

saw-toothed notches in the tops of the walls held the roof slabs. At the top of this passageway was the King's chamber, measuring 10.5 by 5.3 meters and 5.8 meters high, lined with granite. The chamber contained such a huge sarcophagus that it must have been placed there while the tomb was being built, for it could not have been carried in (Fig. 2-2). None of these passageways was visible on the exterior, which was smoothly faced with limestone blocks. In fact, the search for supposed entrances was one of the preoccupations of nineteenth century archeologists.

Austerely simple, the pyramid made its strong impression on the viewer by sheer size and proportion. Even today, with most of the casing stones pilfered for other uses, the pyramids retain their geometric simplicity. The casing stones from these three pyramids were used to build most of the mosques in Cairo and all of the Cairo city wall—without much effect on the size of the donor structures. (Indeed, Napoleon, who conquered Egypt in 1798, once estimated that the stone in the three great pyramids was sufficient to build a wall 10 feet high and 1 foot thick all around France.)

The Cheops pyramid was surrounded by rows of small tombs, called *mastabas*, and three small pyramids, for his courtiers and relatives. Several pits for the ceremonial boats to carry the pharaoh to the sun have also been found. It is appropriate that this pyramid complex should thus preserve representatives of the older tradition of tomb building that resulted in the magnificence of the pyramid age.

Considering briefly the tradition of funerary architecture in Egypt, we may ask if such a tradition is alone enough to explain the origins and function of the great pyramids or if additional factors were at work here.

At the beginning of the third millenium B.C., the modest early tombs marked by a mound of sand possibly held in place by an outer layer of stone gave way to the large and simple geometric forms—the mastabas. (The later Arabs called these artificial mounds after their word for built-up bench.) The ancient Egyptians were actually replicating their house form and material as a marker erected over an underground rock-cut tomb chamber. By the third dynasty, society was sufficiently complex to require large and imposing mastabas for rulers and smaller ones for queens and courtiers.

ZOSER'S PYRAMID

This pattern changed with the tomb built for Zoser (Djoser) at Saqqara, called in English the Stepped Pyramid because of its profile, which seems to be a diminishing series of mastabas piled up one upon the other. Imhotep, Zoser's architect, began conventionally enough in about 2750 B.C. to build a mastaba for Zoser, although this one was to be of stone for greater permanence. The stone mastaba was later enlarged by three upper levels. This second version was in turn enlarged to a final pyramid of six steps containing three times the cubic volume of the second version. In structure, the Stepped Pyramid is a tower with outer buttress walls that slope at 72°, the same slope as the earlier mastabas. It is the largest stone complex in the world. The enormous stepped layers of the tomb rise from a walled-in precinct of 550 by 280 meters that contains ceremonial spaces, shrines, and subsidiary tombs (Fig. 2-3).

THE MEDŪM PYRAMID

During the century that followed, six more large pyramids were constructed—three that we may term experimental and the three great pyramids of Cheops, Chephren, and Mycerinus, which exemplify the full development of the type. Like Zoser's pyramid, another at Medūm was to have been a stepped pyramid.

Figure 2-3   Zoser's stepped pyramid at Saqqara, built for him by Imhotep, the first known architect, around 2750 B.C. Set in a large enclosed area, amid shrines and courtyards, this pyramid is the largest stone structure in existence. Mastabas are seen at left and right. (Photo courtesy of Hirmer Verlag.)

It too was built in stages. From the fact that the innermost portion was carefully surfaced, we can deduce that the Medūm pyramid was enlarged at least twice, as Zoser's had been. The second version was also given a smooth surface. Then a third coating at 52° was added to make a true sloped pyramid finished in turn with a smooth casing of stone. The steps of the first two stages were filled in with stone, but here lay one of the flaws in its construction. The steps were not level but slanted downward and outward. The filling stones were simply laid on top and thus had a tendency to slide off. This tendency was increased by the use of irregularly shaped stones, so that instead of even pressure along the face of the stone, there was great and uneven pressure wherever two stones touched. Under such circumstances, limestone crumbles. When enough weight had accumulated by the placement of a large volume of stone, the whole mass dissolved in a series of slip planes. The structure behaved as a fluid, in a way that we have seen more recently in some accidents involving the debris piled up near the mouths of mines. (Mendelsohn, *The Riddle of the Pyramids*). Visitors to Medūm today find a great ring-shaped mound of debris encircling the towerlike core of the pyramid, 40 meters tall. In other words, today the structure does not look like a pyramid.

THE DAHSHÛR PYRAMID

This experiment in pyramid-building was a failure from which the ancient architects learned immediately. When the Medūm pyramid collapsed, one pyramid was already under construction at the nearby Dahshûr site. Another

Figure 2-4   The collapsed pyramid at Medūm, around 2730 B.C. A ring of debris surrounds the extant towerlike core, some 40 meters tall. Built by encasing the core in a series of outer layers, the pyramid collapsed because the stones composing the outer layers were irregular and were laid sloping outward. Eventually their weight pulled the whole outer mass abruptly downward. (Photo courtesy University Museum, University of Pennsylvania, Philadelphia.)

building plot there had already been prepared for still another. Part of what is now called the Bent Pyramid had already been built at the 52° angle when Medūm collapsed; the angle for the upper portion was then changed to a much lower profile of 43½°, giving the structure its name. The lower profile had two advantages—that of containing less volume of stone and therefore less weight and that of putting less stress on the lower and outer part of what had already been built. Actually, the danger was less at the Bent Pyramid because the packing and outer casing stones were laid perpendicular to the outer sloping face rather than parallel to the ground. In this position they were unlikely to slip.

Perhaps laying the outer stones at an angle proved to be very difficult, for the other pyramid at Dahshûr, the Red Pyramid, has horizontal packing. This pyramid, however, is built entirely at the lower angle of the top of the Bent Pyramid, 43½°. The replication of these features strongly suggests overlapping building periods. While the Red Pyramid (so called because most of its outer casing is gone, revealing inner blocks of local red stone) was being built, the architects had time to consider what had gone wrong at Medūm and what was the best solution for the problem.

THE PYRAMID OF CHEOPS

The builders of the next structure, the great pyramid of Cheops, returned to the 52° slope of the sides but incorporated several devices to make the mass more stable. First they used larger blocks—1 cubic meter—which were well squared. Such blocks greatly reduced the point pressure between blocks by spreading it out evenly over all the surface. Second, they laid each course so that the whole layer of stones curves up slightly at the four corners, being thereby gently dish-shaped. This is the only pyramid with this particular feature.

With the pyramid of Cheops, experimentation with form and construction was complete. The next pyramid, that of Cheops' son Chephren, was nearly as big, measuring 216 meters square and 140 meters tall. Being set on higher ground, however, it appears taller than the Cheops pyramid. The angle is again nearly 52° (52° 20' as compared with 51° 52' for Cheops). The lowest layers of the casing were of granite blocks, but at the top some of the white Tura limestone casing stones of the rest of the surface have survived. As usual, there was an entrance from polar north leading to a chamber at the base and placed under the apex. A second entrance farther north that opened out under the pavement to the north of the pyramid joined the main corridor and led to the tomb chamber in which a granite sarcophagus was found. The roof of this chamber was of gabled limestone blocks like the Queen's chamber and passageway at the Cheops pyramid. The temple and valley temple connected to the Chephren pyramid remain tremendously impressive in the massive simplicity of their pillared design and well-polished pink granite.

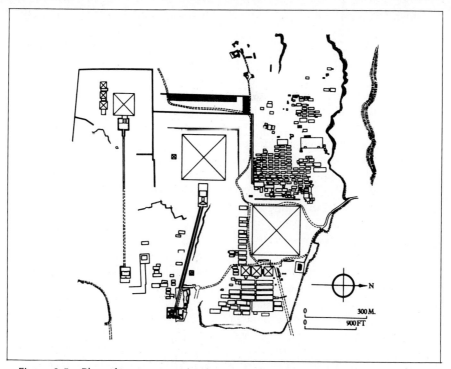

Figure 2-5 Plan of great pyramids of Giza. From north to south, the pyramids of Cheops, Chephren, and Mycerinus, each with associated smaller tombs, causeway to the Nile River, and temples. (Plan from Reisrter, *Giza Necropolis I*, reprinted by permission of Harvard University Press.)

THE PYRAMID OF MYCERINUS

The last of the Great Pyramids was that of Mycerinus, only about one-tenth the bulk of the other two. It is 108 meters square at the base and 70 meters tall, with the usual 52° slant and northern entrance. Like them, it had three tomb chambers, one rock-cut, lying under the apex. From the upper chamber was a blind passageway. The lowest courses of the pink granite of the casing and some of the top of white Tura limestone still survive.

ECONOMICS

From Imhotep and Zoser's Stepped Pyramid, through Sneferu, who built the two pyramids at Dahshûr, to Mycerinus was a brief lapse of time, perhaps as little as 100 years. The curious fact of there being more pyramids than pharaohs added to the certainty of the vast amounts of money spent on these structures makes us wonder whether the simple explanation of pyramids being synonymous with tombs is sufficient to explain what happened. For a hundred years, Egyptians built one pyramid after another; and then abruptly as it had started, the pyramid age was over. Only small replicas of the great structures continued to be built, and even these were of different proportions and significance. Why did this happen?

Living as we do in a post-Marxian age, we cannot resist asking economic questions about all the events of history. To ask economic questions about the building of the pyramids (and by implication, about architecture in general) turns out to be unexpectedly fruitful. Seldom in the history of architecture are economics and architecture as overtly influential upon one another as here in Egypt at the beginning of both as human activities.

Egyptian civilization is based on the productivity of the Nile Valley. Every year for millenniums the Nile has flooded the shelves of land along its banks, renewing the soil by depositing new silt and providing irrigation essential in a land where rain is extremely rare. Since farmers could support themselves and their families on only half the produce of their crops, a division of labor was possible very early in Egyptian history. Priests, rulers, and scribes could live on the farmers' surpluses. During the pyramid age, construction workers could be added to that list without stressing the economy.

As early as 9000 years ago, the domestication of plants and animals began in the Nile Valley. By 5000 years ago, the use of the sail facilitated movement up and down the Nile (where the current runs south to north but the prevailing winds blow north to south). Such an improvement in communication and transportation facilitated unification. At the same time, writing developed—another necessity for governing such an extended territory.

Uniting the thousand-mile stretch of Egypt along the Nile with the settled Delta region was the task of the first dynasties of pharaohs, whose tombs are the mastabas found at Abydos and Saqqara. It was the task of the Third Dynasty pharaoh Zoser and his vizier and architect Imhotep to transform that nascent unit into an economic and political order that would endure with only two interruptions until about 300 B.C. Imhotep is the first architect in history to build large complexes in stone. He was also an astronomer, magician, and medical practitioner, and worshipped later as a demigod. His originality was that of realizing the full implications of what he was doing in building Zoser's Stepped Pyramid. During this process, and directly because Imhotep was able to understand the potential of the arrangements of the personnel and resources that he was manipulating, both architecture and the state underwent permanent changes. Architectural change was made possible by economic and administrative change and in turn made economic and administrative change essential.

Several administrative problems became apparent in an undertaking of such magnitude. How many workers and skilled artisans were needed directly for labor; how many overseers and civil servants to ensure that material and personnel were matched in quantity? Where were the materials to come from; and how were they to be transported and stored until used? How were so many people to be fed? How was such unprecedented activity to be paid for? How

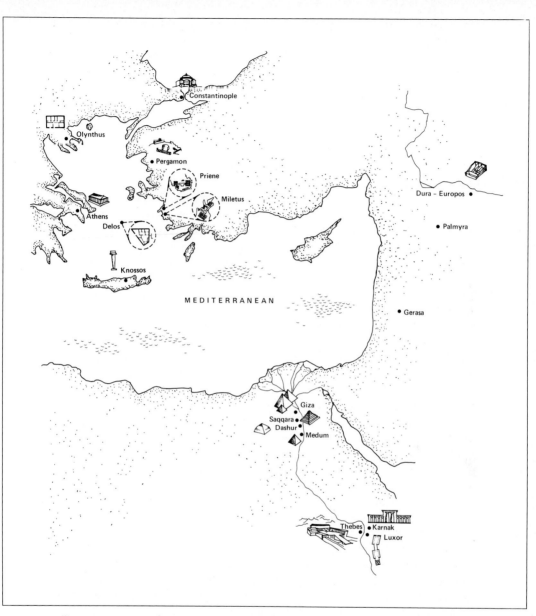

Figure 2-6   Map of Egypt, Greece, and the eastern Mediterranean, showing sites mentioned in the text. (Map by J. Parker.)

EGYPTIAN PYRAMIDS

could large numbers of people be induced to work on the project? How were the wealth and efforts of the society to be concentrated on this one project? When we consider that nothing of such a scale had ever been completed before, except for the mud-brick ziggurats (artificial mountains) of Mesopotamia, we may be all the more impressed with the achievement of Imhotep and Zoser.

Rather that accepting uncritically earlier myths about organization of the labor force in pharaonic Egypt, we should consult the standard work by Edwards, *The Pyramids of Egypt,* and the article by Fitchen, "Building Cheops' Pyramid." Both base their accounts on archeological evidence and on pictures found in tombs.

Workers were needed to quarry the stone and to shape, transport, and haul the blocks from the river bank up to their level in the pyramid and to lay them in place. Large numbers of workers could be employed for placing blocks in the lower courses of the pyramid. Possibly several ramps led to the separate sides of the tomb or else a broad ramp might have encircled the whole building and been raised as the pyramid grew taller. As the structure narrowed toward the top, however, large numbers of workers would have gotten in one another's way. Some means other than brute force and large numbers was thus necessary for raising and inserting the blocks at the upper levels. Fitchen suggests that four-man teams using a simple rocker based on the lever would have been quite sufficient to move even the large blocks of the Cheops pyramid. One man with a lever stood to the right and another with a second lever stood to the left, and two others assisted by handing up and inserting shims to hold the block in place. Layer by layer the workers raised the stone to its destined level and pried it into place. Given the fact that such a technique might have been used for the upper portion of the building, it seems logical to ask if the process may not have also been used for the lower portion, thus drastically reducing the number of workers needed at the site. This reduction would in turn have reduced any drain that the pyramid- building process might have placed on the economy.

Using the same method of lever and shim, the great capstone could have been placed at the center of the lowest level and then jacked up level by level as the courses were added. To ensure the perfect form of the pyramid, the sequence of placement of blocks was crucial. Each face was five acres in area; but despite this great size, the four edges rose straight and true to the capstone. To maintain the true shape, it was necessary to lay the corner blocks first. Then the edges were filled in, except for the center of one side where the ramp abutted against the pyramid. These edge blocks could be placed from inside the perimeter, using the platform of the pyramid itself as a working area. The blocks were then placed concentrically, within the edge, the capstone was rocked up, and the missing block was finally inserted at the edge near the ramp. The process was repeated again at the next level.

Estimates on how many men were needed at the pyramid site vary from 1000 to 100,000. If all work had to be done by muscle alone, then the larger figure might be correct. If such simple devices as a rocker to raise the blocks

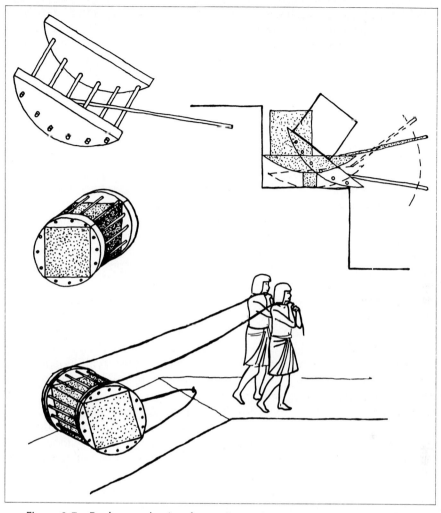

Figure 2-7   Rocker mechanism for use in moving stones into position, when building pyramids and other major structures. Upper left, rocker and lever. Right center, rocker in use, loaded with a block of stone. Left center, block of stone encased in four rockers to make a cylinder. Bottom, cylinder with stone being wheeled up ramp to a pyramid. (Redrawn by L. Dearborn from Mansbridge, *A Graphic History of Architecture*, 1967, by permission of Viking Press; and from *Engineering & Science*, by permission of Calif. Inst. of Technology.)

were used, then the smaller figure would be closer to being accurate. Corroborating evidence for the smaller figure lies in the fact that the workers' villages built near construction sites in Egypt were arranged for a population of four to five thousand, including women and children. In later times for which we have population estimates, such as the Roman Empire, a ratio of one worker on a project to five workers in supporting industries such as food supply is fairly standard. Assumptions for the work force at the pyramids could thus reasonably be that there were 1000 construction workers, 5000 family members, and 30,000 supporting workers and families, adding to a total of 36,000 individuals. The same number again might well have been employed at the quarry sites. If we postulate another 18,000 engaged in or supporting the transportation of stone, food, and other materials, we arrive at a total of 90,000 workers directly involved in pyramid building and not free to produce their own food and clothing. Most of this large number would be living not in agricultural villages but in settlements specifically set up for this purpose; these settlements would have to be erected, maintained, and policed. Pyramid building thus required a quantum leap in population density and in the tight organization of society.

Efficient use of the work force and administrators meant that as one pyramid grew high enough to need fewer and fewer workers (so that they were not getting in one another's way), the crew could be shifted to begin another pyramid. To accomplish these new tasks, Imhotep was able to utilize existing features in the society and combine them in unprecedented ways. He could see that the agricultural surplus, if considered as a national asset, could be used to feed people who did not produce their own food by farming or hunting. Reading and writing were advanced enough to keep track of the enterprise. Transportation up and down the Nile River facilitated movement of people and material. The very pattern of agricultural life, with its periods of several months of idleness at the time of inundation, made additional labor available every year, to assist in any large building project. Beginning with the modest aim of making a tomb for the pharaoh Zoser, Imhotep went on to invent a more lasting memorial—a national state and a bureaucracy. Inventing methods of getting people to cooperate on a large scale without direct one-to-one coercion may indeed be the ultimate achievement of Imhotep and Zoser.

A new organization of society could be and was utilized to create not just one pyramid but six more huge pyramids within the century. The economic organization of Egyptian society had permanently changed from village- to nation-centered. Significantly for the history of architecture, rulers had both decided to build major structures and developed a method of paying for them. When the need for pyramids as catalyst for this new economic and political arrangement had past, the even more permanent concept of the state remained.

One economic question about the building of the pyramids remains. Were they constructed with slave labor? If the direct labor force numbered 100,000 men plus suppliers, transport workers, and quarrymen, a major army would have been required to keep them in bondage. We must remember that there were at the time no super weapons, such as machine guns, which could enable one person to control 20 or 30 others. One could argue that a work force of 1000 per pyramid might have been kept in line by perhaps half as many soldiers, but there is no evidence that there was such a standing army in Egyptian society. What evidence we have suggests rather that willing workers cheerfully competed with one another, as the inscribed names of their groups suggest: "vigorous gang," "enduring gang." There was, moreover, the religious motivation of ensuring the well-being of the society by enabling the great pharaoh to ascend (metaphorically) to the even greater sun god as well as the economic motivation of secure work, with food and housing provided.

Much of our notion about slavery in Egypt comes from Old Testament stories about the Jews' experience there. We must be cautious about extrapolating from the Biblical accounts backward to the pyramid age. The Jews were a foreign people and therefore may have been treated differently from native workers. Moreover, they lived in Egypt during the second intermediate period (1680 to 1580 B.C.) when Egypt was ruled by the Hyksos, invaders from the Near East. These foreign rulers may well have brought with them alien ideas of mass slavery or have felt—as conquerors—entitled to enslave any group of the inhabitants. The Jewish experience was thus not typical of work in Egypt.

When Julius Caesar went to visit the pyramids at Giza and carved his initials on their sentinel, the Sphinx, the pyramids were already very old. More time had elapsed from Cheops to Caesar than has elapsed from Caesar to our own time. With their casings still intact, the pyramids were more beautiful then; but after destruction by time, weather, and human beings, they still remain one of the wonders of the world. And the centralized state, the other invention of the pyramid age, is also still with us. So accustomed to it are we that we rarely stop to think that it had to be invented and developed at some particular point in history.

The great pyramid of Cheops tells us in its simplicity about the earliest state of architecture and in its size about an economy just becoming conscious of its wealth and ability. How architecture is paid for is a constantly fascinating question, whether it be in Egypt, France during the Middle Ages, or today. That the decision to build a tomb could generate an economic system and a government is more unexpected but equally fascinating. The Stepped Pyramid changed not only the appearance of royal tombs but also the economic and political arrangements in Egyptian society.

BIBLIOGRAPHY

Edwards, J., *The Pyramids of Egypt*, Penguin, Baltimore, 1975. The definitive text describing and analyzing the pyramids.

Ceram, C. W., *Gods Graves and Scholars*, Knopf, New York, 1967. *The March of Archaeology*, Knopf, New York, 1970. Both books present glimpses of archeologists' discoveries of the ancient history of human beings.

Fitchen, J., "Building Cheops' Pyramid," *Journal of the Society of Art Historians,* vol. 37, March 1978, pp. 3–12. A careful rethinking of construction methods and organization of the building industry in ancient Egypt.

Mendelssohn, K., *The Riddle of the Pyramids*, Praeger, New York, 1974. A physicist asks why the pyramid at Medūm fell down and comes up with an answer that involves the invention of the nation state and a centralized economy. Well written and well illustrated.

3

EGYPTIAN TEMPLES

TRADITION AS GUIDE OR IMPEDIMENT

From the temples attached to Zoser's pyramid to those built during the Roman period, Egyptian architecture exhibits a remarkable consistency. More than any other architecture, Egyptian religious architecture uses the same kinds of space allocations, materials, decorative features, and principles of siting for the whole duration of Egypt's culture—over 2500 years. Since the solutions remained the same, we can infer that the problems remained the same: if life had changed, architecture would most likely have changed. In fact the archeological evidence we have for what Egyptian life was like during the three millennia B.C. strongly supports this hypothesis that life stayed basically the same.

Life in Egypt was based upon the tension between "the desert and the sown." Every year the Nile River flooded a narrow shelf on either side of the river, both renewing the soil by deposits of silt and providing moisture for the crops. Above and beyond the narrow strip of irrigated agriculture begins abruptly the dry desert region. Within the valley life was safe, abundant, and consistently the same.

THE RIVER, THE MATERIALS, AND DIVISION OF SPACE

One sign of the importance of the river to Egyptian consciousness is the fact that temples were usually oriented toward the Nile (Fig. 3-1). That is, the entrance to the temple lay at the end of a ramp or causeway perpendicular to the river. The river was an inescapable part of all planning and building.

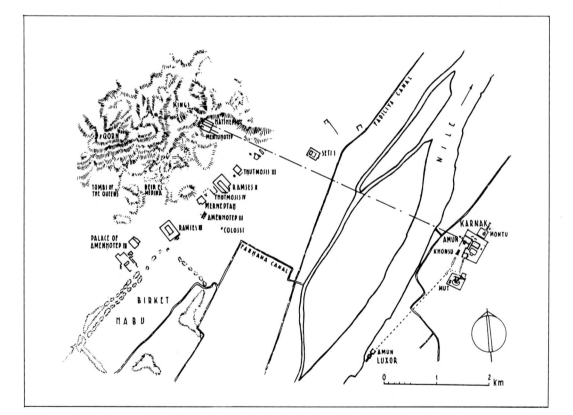

Figure 3-1   Map of Thebes, Egypt. The temples of Amun at Luxor and Karnak are shown on the east bank of the Nile River and the district of funerary monuments is shown on the west bank. The temple of Hatshepsut at Deir el-Bahri is directly oriented to the axis of the Karnak temple, as if to reinforce its dedication to Amun: both are perpendicular to the Nile, whereas Luxor most unusually is not. (Map from Badawy, *A History of Egyptian Architecture,* by permission of the University of California Press.)

Construction materials were transported along the river, and the image of the river as permanent came to imbue all Egyptian art. Thus permanent materials such as granite were preferred for major religious and funerary structures, whereas what we tend to think of as an impermanent material such as mud brick was used for domestic architecture. However, in a dry climate where it rains very seldom, mud brick is quite durable. Some mud-brick warehouses with arched roofs are still in fair condition after about 4000 years. Nonetheless, the superior durability and ornamental possibilities of stone quickly impressed itself on the Egyptians; and experiments led to early mastery of the material and then its consistent use in all major religious buildings, leaving mud brick to be used for the domestic buildings.

Very early in Egyptian history, a three-part division of space was developed (Fig. 3-2). Originating in houses and palaces, this division became basic also for temples and tombs. Houses were divided into three function zones.

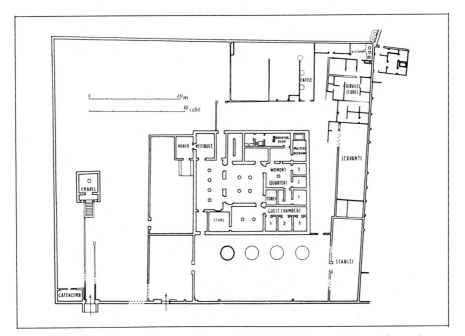

Figure 3-2 House in the north suburb of Tell-al-'Amarna, Egypt, Eighteenth Dynasty. Coming in from the street, one first encounters a small chapel. Turning right, one enters an inner courtyard that leads to a porch and vestibule. Outer and inner living rooms function as the public space of the house. Guests have their own bedrooms and sitting area. The master of the house has his own suite separate from that of his women and children (the latter grouped around another sitting room, labeled women's quarters on the figure). Outside the house are the kitchen and quarters for servants and animals and the garden areas. This house probably belonged to a government official. (Plan by A. Badawy, in *A History of Egyptian Architecture: The Empire or the New Kingdom*, 1968, by permission of University of California Press, publisher.)

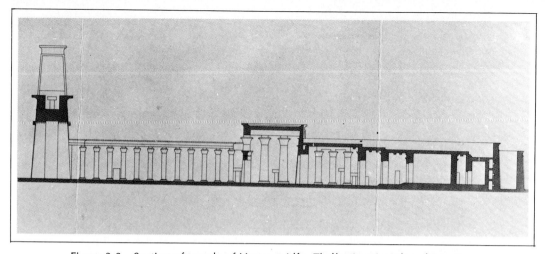

Figure 3-3 Section of temple of Horus at Idfu. The basic principles of Egyptian architecture reveal themselves in this section in which the spatial progression is from large, full of light, and public areas (at left) through enclosed, somewhat darker, and semiprivate areas to small, very dark, and private areas (at right). (Drawing from *Living Architecture: Egyptian*, by permission of J. Hirschen.)

The outermost living room was "public," used for entertaining persons who were not family members. Farther in, a semipublic family room functioned as the focus of domestic life. Beyond that, the bedrooms were entirely private. This formula was flexible and could be expanded or contracted depending upon family status. In a palace, for instance, each wife or concubine would have her own private bedroom and bath as well as a small semi-private reception room. A large public reception room would serve the whole group of private suites. In a small worker's house, the outdoor court would serve as a "public" reception space and the indoor living room as a semi-private room, and there would still be separate bedrooms. Who you were determined where you could go. In houses, for example, guests were put in separate chambers opening off the reception rooms, since they were never expected to penetrate into the private chambers of family members.

The same rules of access governed the numbers and kinds of people who could enter various parts of temples or palaces (Fig. 3-3). The hierarchy of use was directly reflected in the hierarchy of spaces. The outer or first spaces of a temple were large, open, and full of light—and public. The string of spaces gradually became lower, narrower, darker, and more private, until finally the innermost room, where the statue of the god was kept, was the smallest, darkest, and most secret of all.

Function was closely related to the size of the space and to the amount of light. All worshippers were welcome in outer courtyards. Important persons, both courtiers and priests, could go into the halls and middle rooms of the temple. But only the pharaoh and his representative, the chief priest, could go into the innermost sanctuary to perform worship. The privileges of the royal and priestly as well as the traditional stratification of society are exemplified by the plan and section of the temple. If we examine the architecture of another time and place with a different tradition, we can see that different functions and meanings can be attached to similar configurations. In a Romanesque church such as Canterbury Cathedral, it was common to have a crypt (basement) under the altar end, for storing the holiest relics of the saint to whom the church was dedicated. Such a crypt had a low ceiling and was poorly lighted. But instead of being the most secret and private part of the church, it was a section to which individual visitors and great public processions had public access— by means of pairs of stairs flanking the chancel (eastern end of the church). Visiting the relics was a major religious activity in which all the faithful took part. The social meaning of the two spaces was thus determined by the tradition in each case.

To understand the role tradition played in determining the form of Egyptian temples, we will look at three different temples. Two were in Thebes, the major capital city of the New Kingdom, and were dedicated to the sun god Amun. The other was a funerary temple which in later ages took on the functions of the earlier pyramid complexes. It was also in Thebes, but across the Nile River from the first two.

THE TEMPLE OF AMUN IN LUXOR

Probably the easiest of the four to understand is the temple of Amun at Luxor, on the east bank of the Nile, in the southern part of Thebes (Fig. 3-4). In this temple, the gradation from open and public space to entirely enclosed and secret space is quite clear. On the left of the plan is the entrance, an imposing pylon (gateway). Passing through the gateway, the crowds would stay in the outermost courtyard. A second pylon opened into a great hypostyle hall (having a roof that rests on rows of columns) where courtiers and assistant priests were welcome. Only important court officials and priests could pass beyond to the next courtyard, which was somewhat smaller than the first. Beyond this lay another hall placed broadside to the axis and then the sanctuary proper, its small dark rooms set aside for the statue of the god, his official boat, and his treasures, entered only by the high priests and pharaohs.

Both the temple in Luxor and its neighbor in Karnak were rebuilt and added to as was necessary. Bilateral symmetry was customary along the axis that bisected the temple and ran perpendicular to the Nile. Luxor is unusual in being not only placed roughly parallel to the Nile but also not constructed perfectly symmetrically. At Luxor, the first pylon and courtyard are set at an angle to the main axis because the builders respected the small chapel built by Thutmose III that already stood there and was incorporated into this courtyard. When the new courtyard was built, the architect was not allowed to destroy or impinge upon that ancient shrine. Thus, his section had to depart from the customary axiality. A temple was usually begun at the sanctuary, with additional spaces being added like younger new skins around an onion. But at

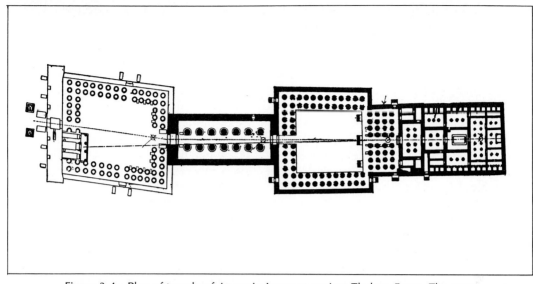

Figure 3-4   Plan of temple of Amun in Luxor at ancient Thebes, Egypt. The court at left is askew because it respected the need for orientation of a small existing temple to Mut. From that court (entered through a huge pylon) one passed into a hall with its roof supported by very large columns. Beyond that lay a second court and then another hall perpendicular to the axis. Beyond was the sanctuary area, with the god's boat in the central room and his statue in the final alcove at the end of the axis. (Plan from G. Jequier, *L'architecture et la decoration dans l'ancienne Egypte*, Vol. I, by permission from Albert Morancé Editions.)

Luxor, when Alexander the Great came to Egypt in the fourth century B.C., the sanctuary of this temple was so old and shabby that Alexander decided to rebuild it. Paradoxically, then, this sanctuary is actually the newest part of the temple, replacing the oldest part.

Plant forms dominate Egyptian decoration. Already at the Stepped Pyramid of Zoser they were used for columns and capitals in the courtyards and temples that clustered around the pyramid's base. At Luxor more than a thousand years later, these stylized plant forms were still being used, lending beauty to the architecture. In the outer court at Luxor, the column shafts and capitals were in the form of budding papyrus plants; in the hypostyle hall, the columns represented two stages of growth: papyrus buds for the shorter columns and open papyrus flowers for the huge columns along the central aisle. The surfaces of these columns were enriched with incised and painted reliefs depicting the pharaoh and the gods enacting the rites performed in each room, and hieroglyphs giving the names and titles of each. Tradition also determined the size and position of these figures, as well as what stories or relationships could be depicted.

More of these painted carvings enriched the flat surface of the outer gateways (pylons) of the Luxor sanctuary. The pharaoh who built the pylon was shown in historical narrative driving his chariot in victorious battle or, in later less warlike times, driving his chariot to the hunt. In all these reliefs, important persons—gods or rulers—were larger (heroic) size and the lesser persons were smaller.

Figures in Egyptian art are depicted conceptually in composite projection —that is, what we actually see is not depicted but rather the parts that we know from analysis and custom are fitted together. Thus, a frontal eye in a profile head is portrayed because a frontal eye was considered more informative. Thus also the shoulders are frontal, whereas the waist, hips, and legs are in profile, with one foot carefully placed in front of the other. Should a pharaoh be driving a four-horse chariot, the outer horse is always carved in outline, and the other three are shown as "echoes," that is, they are repeats of the same shape. Horses are always shown at a flying gallop, for maximum artistic effect. With very little variation, these patterned scenes were repeated again and again on pylons and outer walls for over a thousand years.

The entire form and decoration of a pylon was determined by tradition. A pylon had sloping sides, so that it was noticeably thicker at the bottom than at the top. Into the thickness of the pylon were cut slots for very tall flag poles. The flags and the gaily carved and painted facade made an imposing effect. A recessed doorway, set between the two towers of the pylon, received the processions of rulers, priests, courtiers, and ordinary people who came to Luxor to visit the god on his great feast days. This doorway opened into the outer courtyard, where the procession would pause and fewer people would move forward into the most secret recesses of the temple. Additional pylons separated court from hall and hall from court and inner court from sanctuary, in a pattern repeated in Egyptian temples for thousands of years.

THE TEMPLES IN KARNAK

Farther north in Thebes, and on the same east bank of the Nile, was built Karnak, the grandest Egyptian temple complex (Fig. 3-5). The main temple served for the worship of Amun, and other temples to other gods enriched the complex with their own processional avenues, sets of pylons and courtyards, and sanctuaries at right angles to the main axis. There was also a large Sacred Lake for festival sailings, since water and sun were the twin sources of life and thus were acknowledged in the same sacred precinct.

Like Luxor, the temples in Karnak were a series of open and closed spaces, narrowing progressively down to the smallest and darkest room where the god's statue was kept. Here, however, the sequence was much more complex. Over some 1300 years, pharaoh had competed with pharaoh to add structures that would glorify the great sun god Amun and identify each pharaoh as the beloved of the gods. To walk from the river along the Avenue of Sphinxes and enter the temple complex by passing through one pylon after another, into one courtyard after another, is to penetrate farther and farther backward in time. For 1300 years a living tradition ensured the accumulation of these elements

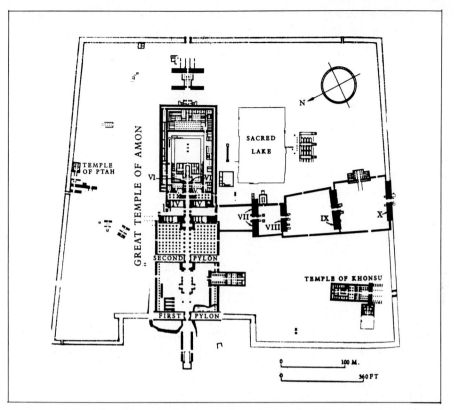

Figure 3-5   Plan of temple of Amun in Karnak at ancient Thebes, Egypt, with Temples of Ptah and Khonsu, and a great processional way to the temple of Mut (pylons VII to X). Built during some 1200 or 1500 years, Karnak began as a simple sanctuary to which rulers added pylons, courts, halls, obelisks, colossal statues, priests' quarters, a palace, and encircling walls. The temple was reached by a processional way lined with sphinxes, stretching westward to the Nile River. The Sacred Lake lay to the south. Note the enormous scale: the temple precinct is about 1500 feet along the west side. (Plan from Chevrier, *Annales*, 36 (1936) p. 86, plate 1, reprinted by permission.)

into the greatest of Egyptian temple complexes. The system of growth by accretion is best expressed in Karnak, where each pylon and court became broader than its predecessor.

Arriving at Karnak by boat like a pharaoh, we disembark at the river's edge (where earlier stood a landing quay and pavilion) and walk toward the outer pylon along the avenue of sphinxes. Long rows of these composite animals (a lion's body with a ram's or man's head) flank the sides of the avenue. At the end of the avenue towers the outer pylon, built during the late Kushite Dynasty (Numidian invaders of the eighth century B.C.) and left incomplete. Within the court and to the right, perpendicular to the main axis, a late palace and temple of a Ramses of the Twentieth Dynasty was inserted through the courtyard wall. Here the pharaoh would reside when he came to visit his father Amun. The traditional three-part division of spaces according to their functions was adhered to in this palace as it was in the temple as a whole.

Once through the gate, we expect, as at Luxor, to be in a great courtyard, but instead, we find a second pylon that looms up. This one, built by Ramses II, is slightly smaller than the outer one. Beyond this smaller pylon, a huge hypostyle hall—nearly 100 meters wide and half as deep—was inserted. To bring light into the center of the room, a portion of the roof was raised about 4 meters higher than the roof over the side sections; the columns supporting the two sections differed, with bundle papyriform columns used at the side and full-blooming open papyriform columns in a larger size standing along the central aisle. So large are these last columns, in fact, that about 100 people can stand on the flat top of one of the capitals. To span the depth from upper roof to lower roof, 4-meter windows of stone repeat in their open work the traditional wooden louvers that were common in Egyptian architecture but here given permanence. Leaving this great hall built by the Ramessides of the Nineteenth Dynasty, we penetrate pylons and cross spaces with statues of various kinds and at one point find ourselves between two obelisks, or tall pointed monoliths set up to honor a pharaoh. One was erected by Hatshepsut—the female pharaoh whose temple we will visit at Deir al-Bahri—but was taken over by her stepson and successor Thutmose III, who obliterated her name in order to claim the obelisk as his own. The tradition of setting up obelisks was enthusiastically adopted by the Romans and was again embraced in the seventeenth and nineteenth centuries.

Beyond the sixth pylon we come to a cluster of treasure rooms that surround the inner sanctuary and finally to the sanctuary itself. The statue of the god is long since gone, as is the boat on which Amun once was carried during festivals to the ceremonial barge for his annual voyages of inspection. But behind the sanctuary area remains still the well-preserved ruins of a festival hall built by Thutmose III of the Eighteenth Dynasty to celebrate his twenty-fifth year of reigning. In its simple geometric forms, this temple deliberately echoes the valley temple of Chephren of more than 1300 years earlier. The roof line with its high center and lower sides was the prototype for the later hypostyle hall of the Nineteenth Dynasty. Many pharaohs built festival halls to celebrate their longevity, but this one secures added prominence by its placement as culmination, perpendicular to the axis through Amun's greatest temple.

Outside the boundary of the Amun Temple proper, several other sacred precincts contribute to the religious preeminence of Karnak. We have mentioned the Sacred Lake where the boat of Amun sailed on certain festivals. There were also separate temples for Khonsu his son, and Mut, his wife, each of which had the traditional succession of pylons and courtyards. The temple of Mut lay to the southeast of Amun's temple and was connected to it by a magnificent avenue with pylons and courts at successive intervals. That of Khonsu lay southwest of Amun and was less elaborate. All shared in the traditional division of space, traditional decoration, and general scheme of public to private and open-light to closed-dark. The whole complex in Karnak extends over 60,000 acres and the Amun temple alone measures about 400 by 100 meters. This temple is bigger than is the combined area of St. Peter's at Rome, the cathedral at Milan, and Notre-Dame de Paris.

THE TEMPLE OF QUEEN HATSHEPSUT

Across the Nile River lies the funerary temple of Queen Hatshepsut (Fig. 3-6). This building incorporates the same principles of design as that of Luxor and Karnak despite its strikingly different appearance. The temple at Deir al-Bahri is oriented to the Nile; that is, is laid out perpendicularly to the Nile and is

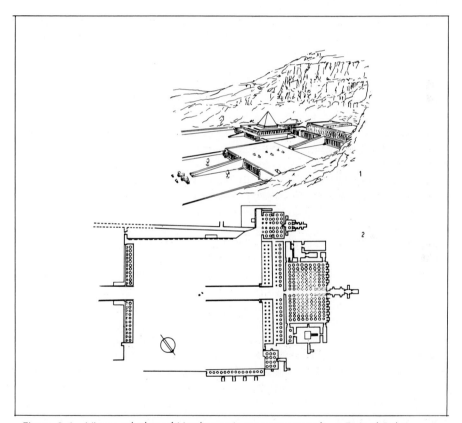

Figure 3-6   View and plan of Hatshepsut's mortuary temple at Deir al-Bahri, near Thebes, Eighteenth Dynasty, Senmut, architect. Like its neighbor, the Twelfth Dynasty temple of Mentuhotep, it is built on a series of terraces. Using the same stone as the cliffs behind it, the temple achieves an unusual unity with its site in both form and material. The lowest terrace was a formal garden with incense trees and other plants. A chapel to Hatshepsut was placed at the end of the axis; other chapels to Amun, to other gods, and to her father Thutmose were placed at either side. (Plan from Badawy, *A History of Egyptian Architecture,* by permission of the University of California Press.)

approached by a direct avenue from the river. Thus it is also oriented to the Amun temple in Karnak. Like its predecessors, this temple includes both open-to-the-public well-lighted spaces and semipublic spaces and small, dark, and private holy spaces. Also like its predecessors, the temple is carved with reliefs that set forth the exploits of the pharaoh queen and show the ruler as being under the special protection of the gods.

There are some features that set this temple apart as being perhaps the most original and beautiful of all Egyptian temples. Foremost among these is the fact that the building is adapted to the site. The rock here occurs in natural terraces with almost vertical faces. Senmut (Senenmut), the architect, utilized these terraces in two ways. First, the temple was built of stone from its own site, so that it blended perfectly with the untouched rock. Second, the profile of the temple repeated the natural terracing but with its scale proportioned to its human users. Since the natural terraces here extend longitudinally, more or less parallel to the river, Senmut organized the outdoor spaces of the temple as a series of broad shelves at three levels. The lowest terrace of the temple was a garden, planted with exotic shrubs such as the incense trees brought back from Punt (Ethiopia or Somalia) by an expedition sent there by Hatshepsut. The processional way from the river into the temple bisected this garden and continued upward by a series of ramps. At the rear of each terrace, a colonnade made a shadow pattern that emphasized the edge of that area and made a distinct transition to the higher shelf. Sheltered behind the upper colonnade at the left was carved a series of historical narrative reliefs telling the story of the expedition to Punt; although the subject matter was unique to this temple, reliefs praising great deeds of the pharaoh were found in other royal buildings. Just as Zoser's acknowledged his own uniqueness and celebrated it on his funerary temple, so did Hatshepsut claim some original status within the tradition of Egyptian monarchy—and rightly so inasmuch as she was the only reigning queen.

Although Hatshepsut's funerary temple emphasized the open and public parts of the shrine more than was usual, it did contain some closed, dark, and private chambers of special religious significance. The most important were the rock-cut chapel dedicated to the monarch's father and the monarch's own false tomb. The latter was also rock-cut. It occupied the most prominent position, as the end of the processional axis through the temple. Major honors were paid here to the dead pharaoh, whose actual tomb was hidden away in the Valley of the Kings behind the ridge to foil possible grave robbers.

One other feature of the temple that must be mentioned is that of having statues of the pharaoh in the guise of Osiris, the god who dies and comes to life again. Here the terrace colonnades were interspersed with large Osiris statues bearing Hatshepsut's features. To contrast with these traditional figures, the architect Senmut experimented with a very simple column type not based on a plant form (Fig. 3-7). The proportions and simplicity of this type have led to its being called proto-Doric by the Egyptologist J. F. Champollion; as such, it was important later for the development of Greek architecture. The abstract quality of the fluted cylindrical shafts is most unusual in Egyptian architecture. These

Figure 3-7 Proto-Doric columns from Hatshepsut's funerary temple at Deir al-Bahri outside the Anubis sanctuary. These columns, striking in their simplicity, seem to have influenced later Greek ideas of construction. (Photo by Harry Burton, reprinted by permission of Metropolitan Museum of Art.)

proto-Doric columns stand before the chapel of Anubis to the right of another series of reliefs recording the queen's birth as daughter of Amun.

In Hatshepsut's funerary temple at Deir al-Bahri, the basic principles of Egyptian architectural tradition dictated the form no less than it did in the earlier temples. Within that tradition, the architect paid attention to what was customary, but he also knew how to utilize variations from the norm that made each of the temples distinctive.

In any architectural tradition, some features are more imperative than are others; in Egyptian architecture, the basic imperatives were permanence and the three- fold classification of space. Even when architects are not conscious of behaving traditionally, they may be doing so, as when twentieth-century architects routinely use planar white surfaces with little or no detailing around doors and windows. Such features are basic to the style begun by Le Corbusier and others in the 1920s, and once carried a strong antitraditional meaning. For comparable examples of intersections of novelty and tradition in painting, see Harold Rosenberg's *The Tradition of the New.*

BIBLIOGRAPHY

Badawy, A., *Architecture in Ancient Egypt and the Near East,* M.I.T. Press, Cambridge, MA, 1965. This book and the author's books on the architecture of the Middle and New Kingdoms provide a clear and concise account of this architecture, having been written by an architect turned Egyptologist.

Iskander, Z., and A. Badawy, *A Brief History of Ancient Egypt,* Cairo, 1954. This may be hard to get, but you could at least read a standard encyclopedia article on Egypt to get some sense of the chronology.

Maspero, G. C. C., *Life in Ancient Egypt and Assyria,* Ungar, New York, 1971. (A reprint of a late nineteenth-century edition.) Such "life in" books can be illuminating, showing us the kind of life that was lived in the buildings we are studying.

Rosenberg, H., *The Tradition of the New,* McGraw-Hill, New York, 1965. An authentic mid-twentieth-century view of tradition, quite different from that of the ancients, but taking the matter with equal seriousness. Rosenberg's rambling is sometimes irritating, but every now and then he has a flash of such insight and wisdom that reading him is worth the effort.

Smith, E. Baldwin, *Egyptian Architecture as Cultural Expression,* Appleton-Century, New York, 1938. A rich and rewarding study of Egyptian architecture. Baldwin Smith has the ability to involve the reader deeply.

Stevenson-Smith, W., *The Art and Architecture of Ancient Egypt,* Penguin, Baltimore, 1958. Copious but not as clearly written as Badawy, this remains a basic source book for beginners, with the usual plans, photos, and useful notes.

4

MINOAN PALACES

SIGNS OF A SOCIAL ORDER

The meaning and function of a particular kind of architecture in our modern world is relatively easy for us to understand because we have knowledge about the social structure for which that architecture is made. For instance, we realize that a certain social context makes possible the dense accumulation of boutiques, galleries, restaurants, and housing that constitutes Greenwich Village in New York City. Similar clusters of types and functions are found in major cities all over the world, especially in highly developed and rich countries.

Another kind of modern architecture results from the way government power is manifested architecturally. "Bureaucratic architecture" is found in developing and poor countries as well as rich ones. A striking example was the

Palace of the Soviets in Moscow, where the idealistic fervor of postrevolutionary Russia was modified by the growing strength of the bureaucracy. The result was a powerful architectural image that both reflected and altered its own social context.

When we turn to ancient times, however, particularly to societies where much of our knowledge comes from archeology, the reverse is true. That is, study of the architecture of ancient times reveals the social structure. To know about the social structure we must study the architecture and the artifacts found in conjunction with architecture. From the types of structures, the arrangements of rooms, and the omissions of elements we might expect, we can learn a great deal about the way in which the society was organized.

MINOAN BUILDINGS AND CULTURE

A good case in point is the Minoan culture of Crete, which flourished during the second millenium B.C. To understand this culture we must turn to the physical evidence of various kinds of buildings and their contents. Although the people had writing (deciphered since World War II, and shown to be an archaic form of Greek), the content of the written record is meager, being mostly inventory lists and orders about stationing garrisons .

We note first of all that the building types found are palaces, houses, and tombs. There are no city walls, which the excavators take to mean that the islanders relied on their isolation, the sea, and their ships as defense. Since we have no evidence of defensive walls around Minoan settlements, it seems reasonable to conclude that warfare between settlements was a minor factor in life in ancient Crete. Naval skill enabled the Minoans to grow rich from commerce. Minoan pottery has been found from the Near East to the western Mediterranean. The pots were found in Egyptian tombs, along with pictures showing Minoans bringing them to their Egyptian customers—Minoans who strongly resemble those painted on the walls of Minoan palaces.

Commerce added to the natural richness of the agriculture base meant that Cretan life during the second millenium B.C. was at a fortunate level of peace and plenty. Some of these riches may have been spent to embellish shrines, but separate temples are unknown here. Much stranger than the lack of ramparts is the total lack of large free-standing temples. What seem to be shrines have indeed been found in palaces and possibly in large houses but not any structures that we can recognize as temples on the older Egyptian or the later Greek models. This startling omission has led one scholar to postulate that the great palace at Knossos is actually a complex shrine and cemetery (see H.G. Wunderlich, *The Secret of Crete*).

Further evidence for Minoan gracious living can be seen in the physical arrangements of dwelling units, and in the scenes painted on their walls. Houses had well-lighted and airy living rooms, separate bedrooms for the family members, ample storage, and bathrooms.

Important houses had pictures of the inhabitants painted in passageways and living rooms. In these scenes, both the men and the women have long black wavy hair, although the women wear theirs in fashionable puffs or bangs. Both sexes are shown as slim and wasp-waisted, with the waist emphasized by a heavy belt. Men are bare-chested and wear a short kilt. Women wear ruffled skirts and very brief jackets that leave their breasts bare. Women outline their eyes with heavy black lines, for emphasis.

Equality between the sexes, suggested by their similar clothing and physique, is demonstrated vividly in the famous mural scene of bull-leaping found on the palace wall at Knossos (Fig. 4-1). Here athletes of both sexes, identically attired in kilts, form a team in which one distracts the bull, a second grasps the long horns of the bull and somersaults onto his back into a standing position, and a third stands ready to catch the second as she jumps down to the ground. Possibly because of lack of direct conventional evidence of Minoan religious customs, archeologists have usually considered this bull-leaping ritual as religious rather than merely athletic.

Figure 4-1   Bull-leaping mural from palace at Knossos, Crete. Many of the entryways and corridors of this palace were enlivened with murals. This one shows the ritual sport (known also from the legend of Theseus and the Minotaur) of youths and maidens leaping over the bull's horns, balancing upright on his back, then leaping off into the arms of a waiting teammate. Equality between the sexes and a vigorous love of life seems to be evident in this painting from late in the second milleneum B.C. (Photo courtesy of A. Kranz, Agora Excavations, Athens.)

Further evidence of equality among persons in this society is seen in the throne room at Knossos (Fig. 4-2). A modest stone throne, rather like a ladder-back chair in its proportions, was found in situ (in its ancient location) in the throne room, apparently for the ruler. Unlike Egypt, where the ruler was so important as to be depicted three to five times bigger than his courtiers, the ruler at Knossos is accompanied by courtiers who equally deserve to sit in dignified comfort. Around the walls of the throne room extends a bench at the same level as the seat of the throne, so that the ruler's councilors could sit and talk with him as equals.

TOMBS AND HOUSES

Compared to the number of houses discovered, the number of Minoan tombs excavated so far is small. All of them, however, are about the same size—about the same size as a medium house (130 square meters). Tombs consist of an entrance, an open court, and the tomb chamber, sometimes cut

Figure 4-2   Throne room of Knossos palace. The throne with its upright back was found in this position. Benches for courtiers and others lined the walls of the room, indicating that the ruler and his followers had a rough equality. The decoration of the room has been restored from extensive fragments; real lilies are combined with imaginary griffins. (Photo by A. D. McKenzie.)

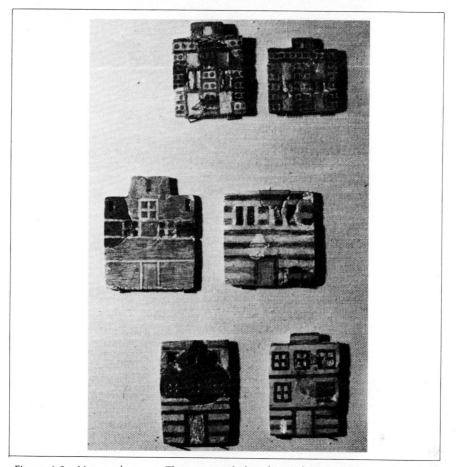

Figure 4-3 House placques. These enameled replicas of Minoan houses are quite small, being about one inch wide, but their bright colors and geometric patterns give us a vivid idea of what a Cretan town of the second milleneum B.C. would have looked like. Roofs were flat and used for outdoor living, some being reached through a small pavilion on top of the house. Some houses have no windows in the ground story, which was probably used for storage. (Photo by A. D. McKenzie.)

from rock into the side of a hill and sometimes underground. So similar are the tomb sizes that one might leap to the conclusion that equality prevailed completely in this society, but a brief look at the houses dispels that notion. These cover the complete range from small, medium, and large, to palatial. Two kinds of archeological evidence bring these houses alive to us: at the site of Gournia, plans for an ensemble of Minoan houses have been laid bare. What these would have looked like in elevation is shown by some small plaques in the form of houses, enameled in bright colors and decorated with stripes and rondels (circular ornaments) (Fig. 4-3). The houses are usually two stories tall, with a pavilion on the roof. Shuttered windows and a door open onto the street. According to the excavations at Gournia, the bottom story was sometimes used for storage and access was through the second story. In size these houses are 80, 130, or 220 square meters, depending on the wealth of the occupants. The plans incorporated features found also in the palaces. Many houses use a central pillar to help support the story above, have stairs that rise to a landing and then double back after a 180° turn, and use light wells to bring both light and ventilation to formal living areas at or below grade. Bathing rooms are often found near the entrances. From the separation of living and sleeping areas, and of both from storage areas even in the smallest houses, we can deduce that Minoans enjoyed a comfortable standard of living not always found in other societies.

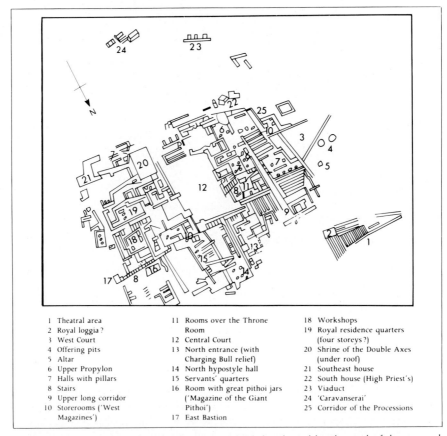

1	Theatral area	11	Rooms over the Throne	18	Workshops
2	Royal loggia?		Room	19	Royal residence quarters
3	West Court	12	Central Court		(four storeys?)
4	Offering pits	13	North entrance (with	20	Shrine of the Double Axes
5	Altar		Charging Bull relief)		(under roof)
6	Upper Propylon	14	North hypostyle hall	21	Southeast house
7	Halls with pillars	15	Servants' quarters	22	South house (High Priest's)
8	Stairs	16	Room with great pithoi jars	23	Viaduct
9	Upper long corridor		('Magazine of the Giant	24	'Caravanserai'
10	Storerooms ('West		Pithoi')	25	Corridor of the Processions
	Magazines')	17	East Bastion		

Figure 4-4 Plan of palace of Knossos as it had developed by the end of the second milleneum B.C. The domestic quarter is at 19, with the grand staircase to the right (in a direct line between numbers 19 and 12). Next to the stairs at 8, facing the court, was a shrine. The throne room is at 11. Ramps and stairs made a grand entrance from 23 up to the area of 6 where loggias (porches) looked out over the valley. (Plan by R. V. Schoder, *Ancient Greece from the Air*, reprinted by his permission.)

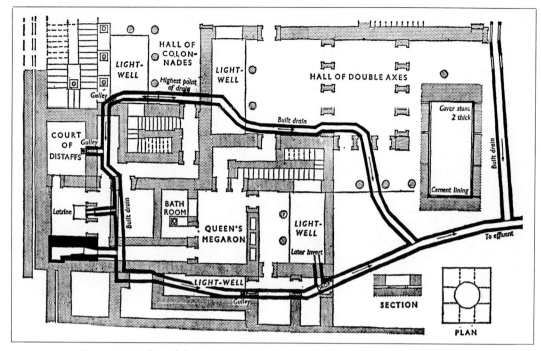

Figure 4-5   Plan of domestic quarter of palace of Knossos. Reception rooms consisting of porch, outer and inner rooms, and light well, were called by the excavators Hall of the Double Axes from the painted decoration found on the walls. A second, smaller suite was termed the Queen's Megaron. The bathroom, semienclosed, had a ceramic bathtub. In the back corner, a latrine was located, which could be flushed into the drain pipes with water from a roof-top reservoir brought to each of the four stories of this part of the palace by pipes embedded in the black thick-walled area at lower left. The grand staircase was found at hall of colonnades, climbing through all four stories of the building up to the level of the central court. (Plan from R. W. Hutchinson, "Prehistoric Town Planning," in *Town Planning Review*, Vol. XXI, 1980, reprinted by permission. Permission also from M. Patterson, holder of the rights to the Knossos Materials.)

PALACES

In the palaces, such as that at Knossos, comfort was carried to the level of luxury (Fig. 4-4). Most striking in this regard was the provision for water supply and drainage. In the domestic quarter of the palace, a roof-top reservoir fed pipes that brought water to all four stories where it was available for bathing and for flushing latrines (Fig. 4-5). The lowest story had its own drain pipes that led the waste water into the nearest river. The room called by the excavators the Queen's Megaron (a ground-floor apartment) included a separate bathroom with a ceramic bathtub, found in the hallway where it had been abandoned by a looter when the palace was no longer inhabited (Fig. 4-6).

Figure 4-6　View of the Queen's Megaron at the Knossos palace (painted by Sylvia Hahn and reproduced courtesy of the Royal Ontario Museum). On the left is a mural of leaping dolphins of the kind of lively naturalism consistently found in Minoan art. The seated women and standing man at center wear typical costume—flounced skirt and bare-bosom bodice for the women and kilt for the man. Both have long hair brushed into ringlets. A small double ax stands on the bench as an object of reverence. Behind the inner set of columns was the bathroom. The bathtub was found in the hall nearby.

This apartment celebrated the joys of water by having a large mural of jumping dolphins on one wall. During at least part of the 1200 years or so that the palace was lived in, pipes brought water in from the exterior, and close study of these arrangements indicates that the ancient hydraulic engineer knew well how to control water and to use its natural behavior to advantage. For instance, one exterior water channel had to bring the water down a rather steep incline, and then turn at about 90° at the bottom. To accomplish this, the water channel consists of steps that are curved rather than angular, which controls the water's velocity and at the same time causes it to make a pleasant gurgle as it flows. At the bottom, the turn is handled by an arc rather than a right-angle joint, so that the water flows smoothly around it without splashing over. This careful attention to water supply reiterates that joyful attention to living in the natural world that is also evident from the naturalistic plant decoration on Minoan walls and pottery.

In addition to the Queen's Megaron, the ground floor of the domestic quarter of the palace at Knossos included a formal reception suite consisting of a porch extending around two sides of a large square outer room or vestibule, which led to an inner room decorated with painted representations of two-headed axes—hence the suite is called the Hall of the Double Axes—and man-sized, figure-8-shaped shields. Separating the porch and vestibule and the vestibule and inner room were sets of double doors that folded back into their deep embrasures. Above the doors, transoms (windows above doors) let in more light and air, even when the doors were closed. At the very back of the inner room, a narrow light well brought light and air in from the hilltop four stories above. An imposing chair or throne was centered in this narrow space, which was separated from the inner room by a low wall. Although this suite is spacious and pleasant, it is by no means grand or magnificent. A very different kind of leadership is made manifest here than the divine kingship of the Egyptian pharoahs. This Minoan mode of leadership is closer to the comraderie of the *Iliad,* though without the war emphasis of the Mycenaean peoples depicted by Homer.

The third major element of the ground floor was also connected to the upper parts of the palace. This was the Grand Staircase. After excavations had been going on at Knossos for awhile (as Sir Arthur Evans reports in *The Palace of Minos*), one day they grew tired of digging down from the top of the ground. Evans ordered the workers to tunnel in from the side of the hill instead. They thereby came upon the Grand Staircase. In ancient times, as the palace had disintegrated, the upper stories of mud brick had melted in the rain and filled in the four flights of stairs, encasing the wooden columns that supported and delimited the stairway. Over time, these columns had deteriorated, leaving their images as voids in the clay. All that was necessary was to replace them with new tree trunks and the stairway stood again with very little need of reconstruction. Because of its completeness, it was one of the most unusual finds in the history of archeology.

What rooms occupied the upper floors of the domestic quarter can only be inferred, as they are completely gone; probably they were bedrooms and sitting rooms. At the top of the Grand Staircase one is at the level of the courtyard that occupied the center of the complex. On the same side of the court as the domestic quarter, but to the north, was the part of the palace where artisans made the luxury items and some necessities for the royal family. Most of this part of the building is gone, having slid off the hill, but the excavators did find here some small statues of women (goddesses? priestesses? worshipers?) in gold and ivory, dressed like the women of the wall paintings. Since no other images have been found that can be interpreted as Minoan deities, we must ask whether this culture believed in so spiritual a god as to be unrepresentable or whether—as is more likely—the god or goddess was represented in human form. Only the fine materials of ivory and gold would distinguish the goddess from her (ceramic) worshipers and priestesses. Such quasi-equality between the human and divine parallels the rough equality we have already noted between ruled and ruler.

Other details of the palace reveal other aspects of daily life among the Minoans. One of the main entrances to the palace led from the north past a lustral area, where travelers could cleanse themselves of the stains of travel, and past a reception hall, into the central court. Proceeding southward, the travelers would see on the west, at about the center of that facade, a shrine next to a broad stairway that led to the throne room and other official chambers. This shrine, though prominently placed, was by no means large or imposing. It consisted of a base ornamented with two large half rosettes, supporting a single Minoan column and capital. Such a column tapered toward the bottom, and was topped by a big cushioned capital. The column seems to have been an abstract symbol for a deity, such as the cross is for Christians. The roof of the one-story shrine was edged with stylized stone replicas of the long horns of bulls. This shrine and the allusions in the old myth of Theseus and the Minotaur are the only clues we have about Minoan religion. (See for instance *Twice-Told Tales* or Mary Renault's *The Bull from the Sea*.)

If travelers from the north had business with the ruler, they would mount the broad stair and go into one of the audience rooms or even into the throne room. There, in addition to the throne and benches already mentioned, they would see on the walls a mural of griffins (mythical beasts) lying watchfully among beds of lilies.

The visitor might be joined there by others who had come from the west across the so-called Theatral Area, a large paved area just outside the west wall of the palace and edged at the north with a low and wide flight of steps once thought to be the distant ancestor of Greek theaters. Some practical difficulties, such as how bulls and acrobats could have been maneuvered on a stone-paved surface, and how the audience could have been arranged on steps too narrow for chairs or stools and too shallow for seeing well while standing, have made us discount the idea that the bull-leaping rituals took place in this space. Unfortunately, no alternate suggestion for its use carries much validity either.

The western entrance to the palace actually led to the basement level. Under the official chambers lay a long series of storerooms called magazines, where grain and oil were stored in great jars about 4 feet tall, called *pithoi*. In the floors, between the rows of jars, were sunk rectangular lead-lined receptacles, some still holding a few odds and ends but most despoiled of their ancient contents before the complex was ruined.

From the basement level, passages led southward to join another en-tranceway coming from the south. The site of the palace sloped steeply to the south, so that from this direction a bridge (called a viaduct), ramps, and stairs were necessary to reach even the basement level. Along the south side of the structure, long verandahs stretched at two levels. From these, a fine view of the valley could be obtained. Entering the palace from the porches, one wound around to the major steps that led up to the level of the throne room. Some of these passages were also decorated with murals, such as the large picture of a "prince" among lilies, and another of a servant carrying a rhyton (a wine vessel, in this case V-shaped, and footless, which therefore had to be emptied before it could be put down). The bull-leaping mural was found in the passages along the west side of the palace.

Covering the walls with murals to improve their appearance seemed like a good idea, because the construction methods and materials used were not inherently beautiful. The Minoans made walls of irregular stones (rubble) held together usually with mud mortar and sometimes braced with wooden uprights, crossbars, and diagonals. Walls were then finished with stucco, painted or not, or sometimes with thin revetments (facing slabs) of gypsum (very soft stone of the marble and limestone family). The same gypsum was used also for floors. The floors were renovated periodically by having new layers placed over the old, much as we might cover an old kitchen floor with a new one. Like ourselves, then, the Minoans practiced "quick and dirty" architecture. That so many of their structures have lasted until now indicates that they built well enough for their purposes, and then some.

During the long period that the Knossos palace was in use, it went through several rebuildings. In the earliest period, it may have been several separate structures grouped around a central open plaza, rather like the little town of Gournia. Gradually connections were added from one building to the next, so that in time the complex enclosed the plaza, and the plaza became a central court. The rounded corners of the earlier buildings were replaced later with right-angled corners. We have mentioned already that gypsum floors were renewed by being paved over with another layer of gypsum.

Best estimates of the building periods and their duration are as follows: Prepalace to 2000 B.C.; old palace to 1700 (destroyed by earthquake); new palace to 1380 (with a catastrophe about 1550); and postpalace to 1150.

THE DEATH OF MINOAN CULTURE

Not forever could this graceful and happy life persist. Minoan culture failed in the last century or so of the second millenium B.C. for two main reasons. For several centuries, a vigorous new wave of Greek-speaking tribes had been coming down into Greece from the north. Settling into the inhospitable valleys of mainland Greece, they needed to support themselves by commerce or by piracy, and thus they entered into competition with the Minoans. Their pottery, though not so fine as Minoan ware, is found in most of the same places around the Mediterranean.

If the Minoans had once been able to protect themselves from this competition, they could not do so after the second disaster that befell them, which was a volcanic eruption of the island of Thera, one of the most stupendous ever recorded. Apparently the earthquake, tidal waves, and fallout of ash from this explosion so devastated Crete that the Minoan civilization never recovered. Instead, the Mycenaeans took over both the commercial shipping and the once-rich farmland of the Minoans, possibly even living in their palaces and governing the territory that had formerly been Minoan. This conquering race was not immune to the pleasures of domestic comfort, however, for we find bathrooms surprisingly similar to Minoan ones in the palaces of the Mycenaeans on mainland Greece.

According to Aldous Huxley's essay "Comfort," each society gets the degree of comfort, not that it devises technically but that it believes it deserves.

He cites, for instance, the Roman use of central heating in Britain before the year 300, contrasting it with the English avoidance of central heating as late as 1950. Technically, the English could have been at least as comfortable as the Romans, but ideologically they didn't approve. It is interesting to detect in the distant social environment of ancient Crete an attention to comfort, and especially plumbing, that modern Americans can relate to and approve of.

BIBLIOGRAPHY

Evans, A., *The Palace of Minos,* Biblio & Tannen, New York, 1921. Gives a fabulous account of early excavations on Crete; known for what it reveals of the excavator's *hubris* as much as what it tells us about the Minoans. Remains indispensable to an understanding of Minoan culture.

Graham, I. W., *The Palaces of Crete,* Princeton University Press, Princeton, N.J., 1962. A handy guidebook to the major sites.

Mirinatos, S., *Crete and Mycenae,* Abrams, New York, 1960. Gorgeous pictures and informative text, by the discoverer of Thera, who first postulated the volcanic theory of the end of Minoan civilization.

Prezzos, D., *Minoan Architectural Design,* Mouton, W. De Gruyter, Hawthorne, N.Y., 1983. The author presents compelling arguments for considering the Knossos palace a civic center.

Renault, M., *The Bull from the Sea,* Pantheon, New York, 1962. Compelling novel set in ancient Crete.

Robertson, D. H., *A Handbook of Greek and Roman Architecture,* Cambridge University Press, New York, 1964. Only a few pages on Knossos, but those few are as crammed with information as is humanly possible. Available in paperback, this is a useful addition to the library of any serious student of architecture.

Wunderlich, H. G., *The Secret of Crete,* Macmillan, New York, 1974. Written by a geologist with some inventive notions about what might have happened at Knossos.

5
GREEK TEMPLES
MATERIALS AS DETERMINANTS

From the coasts of Turkey to North Africa, Sicily and southern Italy and the Greek mainland itself stand the ruins of Greek temples. Ranging in their completeness from a few shapeless lumps of weathered limestone to the impressive array of temples along the ridge at Agrigento, Sicily, and varying in both size and decoration, they all have the distinguishing characteristic of being made of stone. In this chapter we will examine the ramification of having stone as the material—what possibilities use of it opened and what liabilities use of it incurred.

Architects have employed many materials in their structures, at different times and places. In ancient Greece their concentration on the use of stone furnishes a strong case for the importance of material and makes it simpler for us to realize what differences can be attributed to the material employed.

THE INFLUENCE OF EGYPT ON GREEK ARCHITECTURE

During the first three or four centuries of the second millenium, many invaders moved into the peninsulas now called Greece and Turkey. The older cultures of Crete and Mycenae became so disrupted that the period has been called a Dark Ages. In the seventh century B.C., the invaders—Dorians and Ionians—had become settled enough that cultural life began to revive. The development process was stimulated by contact with foreign peoples. Greek soldiers served as mercenaries in Egypt, and Greek scholars went there to study. During the seventh century B.C., these people, and the traders who followed them, seem to have carried home to Greece some information about Egyptian buildings, such as the use of colonnades, the techniques of using large stones, and the idea of permanence as particularly appropriate for religious buildings. Stimulated by this flow of information, and enabled by their new wealth to afford real architecture, the Greeks began in the seventh century to build monumental (that is, large and permanent) architecture. According to the archeological evidence, until this time the Dorian and Ionian invaders had been building only in wood, mud brick, and thatch, materials with a long history of use for domestic architecture. They turned to stone when improved economic conditions in seventh century Greece created a surplus of wealth available for permanent building. The Greeks reinforced the Egyptian idea of permanence with their own quest for ideal beauty and perfection of form. Greek architecture may be seen as a series of experiments in the embodiment of ideal form in stone.

By this time, there had been architects in Egypt for almost 2000 years. For Greece, however, architecture was a new profession. In *The Ancient Greek Architects at Work,* J. J. Coulton discusses the beginnings of the design process in a country, geared to a particular clientele and undertaken by a professional group, all of whom were new at the enterprise. The very fact that monumental building was an unusual activity at first forced both architects and patrons to be uniquely conscious of what they were doing.

At first few buildings could afford the services of the professional architect and only a handful were deemed worthy of so much thought. Only temples in the seventh century were made of stone. Drawing upon their recently acquired knowledge of Egyptian models such as the temple at Deir al-Bahri, the Greeks made a series of experiments that within a century matured into the classical form of the temple. There may also have been some influence from Minoan and Mycenaean architecture, especially with respect to column forms, but what may have been visible from those older cultures 400 or 500 years after their collapse is not known to us.

THE QUESTION OF WOOD VERSUS STONE

Only at one site has any physical evidence of the wooden phase of Greek temple building come down to us. At the Temple of Hera at Olympia, one wooden column survived to Roman times. We are told by the Roman traveler Pausanius that the temple was at first made of wood and over the centuries the wooden columns were replaced by columns of stone of various diameters, as current taste dictated; but one of the original wooden shafts was left, witness to the great age of the temple (seventh century B.C.). By finding evidence of columns of many diameters here, archeologists have confirmed this ancient account.

Architectural historians and classicists formerly made a big issue of the question of the timber derivation of Greek stone temples. Some claimed that every detail of the appearance of a temple was a direct translation into stone of forms that had been logically worked out in wood. This is still a moderately interesting question. Figure 5-1 shows the standard diagram for this derivation. If we compare it with Fig. 5-2, we can see that indeed some of the forms, such as the solid triglyphs equaling the ends of the beams that support the roofs, or the resulting spaces between them—"voids" to be covered by carved slabs called metopes—do seem to carry over from one material to the other. However, other details such as the peglike forms (mutules) can be given functions in the wooden originals only by pushing the evidence very hard. So what can then be the explanation if that of direct translation from wood to stone is too simple?

The best answer to the question so far seems to be that details of the stone forms are a kind of stylization of details of wooden forms. Just as a pair of heraldic lions on a Mesopotamian seal may not be taken as literally describing the behavior of lions but represent some observations of the characteristics of these animals, so too the peglike mutules represent rather than replicate the process of fastening a building together. They are an image of rather than a description of the details of fastening. Such details, then, are stylized allusions to older methods and materials. We can term them architectural abstractions.

In literature we say that authors who control words precisely to get the effects they want are articulate. In architecture the precise control of the areas

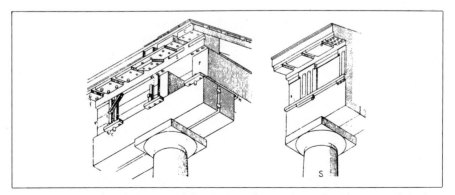

Figure 5-1 Timber derivation of the Doric order (as drawn by Choisy). At left, the upper part of a colonnade of wood; at right, the same in stone. Compare with Fig. 5-2. Parts that were functional in wood become decorative in stone.

Figure 5-2   Another version of the wooden prototype for the upper part of the Doric order (as drawn by Kawerau).

of transition is similarly called articulation. These transition areas are the joints between floor and wall, wall and ceiling, and wall and window or door. The joints are articulated as baseboards, mouldings, jambs—an elaboration intended to draw our attention to the joint and to the architect's thought about it. In this way, mutules in Greek architecture might be saying to us, "Someone considered both the joint and the process of joining. These little pegs signify that thought." Thus we are justified in speaking of them as architectural abstractions. They look like they are joining pegs but they actually have no such function.

In the seventh and sixth centuries, when stone architecture was developing, wood and the stone that followed it were used in a simple post and lintel fashion. Stone is stronger as a post or column than as a lintel or beam—that is, it is stronger in compression than in tension. Thus, when a weight is placed above a stone column, pressing vertically down on it, the stone is intrinsically suited to bear this pressure. However, if the upper weight presses down at an angle or if the stone that carries the weight is stretched horizontally (as a lintel is), then the stone is not nearly as well-suited to the task. To support the same weight, a horizontal stone must be bigger (and hence stronger) than a vertical one. At each site, the local stone was pressed into service, with its character thereby determining the form and appearance of the temples. If a particular quarry yielded soft stone that crumbled easily, then decorative details and sculpture had to be generalized rather than finely detailed. If a variety of limestone was stronger, then beams could be longer and columns spaced farther apart. These differences in strength affect the size and shape of stones used in different positions. The trial and error process of building with different kinds of stone during the seventh and sixth centuries B.C. soon showed the Greek architects how close together the columns had to stand and how thick the beams had to be to handle not only their own weight but also that of the rafters and of the roof. This strength would vary from stone to stone, on a local basis, which accounts for some of the variation we see in the proportions of temples during the early period.

TERRACOTTA

It was during this same early experimental period that roof tiles of terracotta (baked clay) were invented in Greece. Being more fire-proof than are wooden roofs, they contributed to the permanence, which was a goal of these architects. The whole culture was concerned with eternal forms, whether of human beauty (in statues) or of political arrangements (in laws). Public buildings were also expected to be permanent, and thus were made of stone. Tile roofs also contributed directly to the evolving form of public buildings, because their weight was greater than that of the previous wood or thatch, which in turn necessitated spacing colonnades more closely together and limiting the width of the building. Clay models of early temples (found in tombs) show them with high pointed roofs; the use of terracotta tiles changed the profile after the seventh century to a wide, gently sloping roof. The weight of the tiles thereby contributed to the stability of the structure, setting up compressive forces that the stone columns were ideally suited to handle. Late in the Hellenistic period, the stronger and therefore more economical use of wooden trusses to support roofs changed the forms and proportions of buildings again, since columns could then be spaced more widely apart. Wooden beams are made from trees that are able to bend and twist without distorting their shape; wood can therefore take distortion much better than can stone. A light-weight and relatively thin framework of wood can thus do the same work as a heavy one of stone. Wooden roof structures can be both more economical and more varied in form.

Beginning in the seventh century when the Greeks first began to build monumentally, continuing in the fifth when their skill reached classical perfection and balance, and the third when new kinds of experiments with proportion and detail changed the appearance of Greek temples, three kinds of architectural vocabularies, called "orders" were developed. At every point in a building where blocks of stone came together to form edges, characteristic details were worked out for articulating that edge. Such clusters of details were different along the Ionic coast of Asia Minor from those in mainland or western Greece. From the steps to the peak of the roof, every element of the building

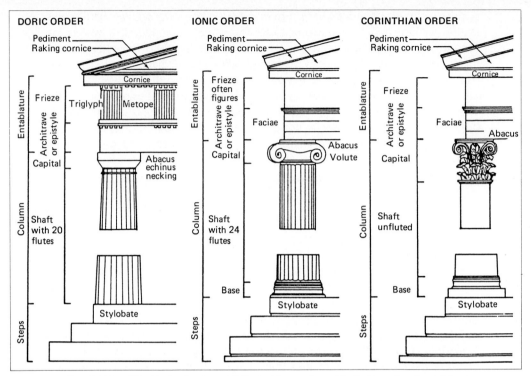

DORIC ORDER

Pediment
Raking cornice
Cornice
Entablature
Frieze
Triglyph   Metope
Architrave or epistyle
Capital
Abacus echinus necking
Column
Shaft with 20 flutes
Stylobate
Steps

IONIC ORDER

Pediment
Raking cornice
Cornice
Entablature
Frieze often figures
Architrave or epistyle
Faciae
Capital
Abacus Volute
Column
Shaft with 24 flutes
Base
Stylobate
Steps

CORINTHIAN ORDER

Pediment
Raking cornice
Cornice
Entablature
Frieze
Architrave or epistyle
Faciae
Abacus
Capital
Column
Shaft unfluted
Base
Stylobate
Steps

Figure 5-3   The Doric, Ionic, and Corinthian orders. Corinthian developed from Ionic in the late fifth century B.C. and was used extensively by the Romans because of its versatility. Ionic and Doric were developed in the seventh to fifth centuries, with Ionic being possibly earlier than Doric. (Drawing by L. Dearborn.)

had its characteristic form and was assigned specific carved and painted decoration. Such a cluster of details is called an order. The three classical orders are Ionic, Doric, and Corinthian (see Fig. 5-3).

Experiments in early forms of the Ionic order were made along the Aegean coast of Asia Minor (Turkey), while the western Greeks as far away as southern Italy and Sicily were trying out the first versions of Doric. Much later, the versatile Corinthian order, which changed only the capital of the Ionic, was used throughout the Greco-Roman world. The orders have been both a blessing and a curse for architecture. Every time they have been rediscovered (for instance, in France in the eighteenth century), they have captured so much attention that architecture itself has seemed to consist of the manipulation, variation, and utilization of Doric, Ionic, and Corinthian; or, by contrast, any architecture that eschewed them was by so doing considered virtuous and hence satisfying.

Even today, these orders raise more questions than can be answered here. Such as, how can one create an architecture that the passage of time and accumulation of dirt actually improve? When dirt collects in the flutes and volutes of the Ionic order, for example, its form is emphasized (and hence improved) by this natural shadowing. How can an architecture become a shared vocabulary between users and designers? Which questions about architecture are worth generations of concentrated professional effort?

Architecture might be defined as creation of a structure that is rigorously and profoundly thought about before it is built. The result goes beyond the utilitarian and into the realm of art. Since perfection of form, idealized beauty, was valued highly in ancient Greek culture, the Greeks had no doubt that achieving perfection was an effort well worth not merely generations but centuries of concentrated effort from both the professional architects and the skilled artisans who cooperated to build the classical stone temples we are studying here. How to use stone in the best scale and proportion was the formal question that occupied sculptors as well as architects, thereby giving them common goals and methods. They worked first on temples, during the seventh and sixth centuries. By the late fifth century other public buildings were given the same careful treatment.

Careful treatment could raise even a utilitarian building to the level of architecture. For instance, the arsenal at Piraeus was not only very large but the finest of its kind. By the excellence of its plan and execution, the arsenal went beyond the merely utilitarian. So also, temples, theaters, government buildings (stoas), when subject to the detail-conscious Greek architect, went beyond functionalism. Not until the twentieth century did an architect (Mies van der Rohe) say, "God is in the details," something which the ancient Greek architects knew and practiced long ago.

Materials for this long period of experimentation in stone architecture were close at hand and of excellent quality. The Mediterranean basin may be thought of as a great pool of water lying among various stones which have here and there a sparse covering of topsoil and vegetation. These heaps of stone were early turned to good use as building materials by the Greeks, though it is interesting to note that they were not inclined to use richly veined and colored marbles but rather white and grey-blue marbles and the various local limestones. (See Wycherly, *The Stones of Athens*.) Stones were quarried and used as close to the source as possible, because of the prohibitive cost of transportation. For example, the builder of a temple in southern Sicily had at hand a coarse limestone that was fairly easy to cut but weathered with equal ease. Sicilian temples were surfaced with a stucco made of marble dust, some of which still adheres in places (see Fig. 5-4), both to protect the surface from weathering and to make this stone look more like the beautiful Pentelic marble of Athens. Where it has adhered, it still protects; where it is gone, the surface is pitted and rough.

In places such as Athens, where marble of two neutral colors was available, the Greeks allowed themselves subtle coloristic effects. A little blue-grey Elusinian marble was used in two buildings on the Acropolis at Athens, for instance, as a foil to the white Pentelic marble. On the Erechtheum, the frieze was of the darker stone, however, with white bas-relief figures

Figure 5-4   Detail of Doric temple at Selinus, Sicily. The coarse limestone was protected from weathering by a coating of stucco made of marble dust; where it clings, it still protects. Use of the marble dust also made the Sicilian temples more like their models on the Greek mainland. (Photo, author.)

pegged into this blue-grey background. In the Propylaea, there are several steps and sills emphasized by use of the blue-grey stone. Most subtle and effective is the substitution of dark marble as a bottom step for the wings flanking the processional way. All the columns of the west side of the Propylaea have bases at the same level, but the columns to left and right are smaller than those in the center, and should by the rules have a smaller base of steps. Because the bottom step has dark marble there, the eye sees the top three white side steps only as pertaining to the shorter columns above, while all four steps of the base at the center remain white and are therefore seen as deeper, properly proportionate to the larger columns above.

The Acropolis was the highest place in any Greek city. On it were sited the most important temples of the community. The Acropolis at Athens is frequently cited as the most perfect example of an ensemble of temples and auxiliary structures of the classical period (Fig. 5-5). The unification of the ensemble is largely effected through the use of material. Here 200 years of experimentation came to fruition. Within the constraints of one material and one simple structural system the Greek architects were able to achieve maximum and elegant variation. One need consider only the group of buildings that survive on the Acropolis at Athens to be impressed with the versatility of the system: One structure was large and symmetrical and decorated with sculpture and Doric (the Parthenon); one was medium-sized, asymmetrical, and decorated and Ionic (the Erechtheum); one was medium-sized, asymmetrical, and undecorated and Doric (the Propylaea); and one was tiny, symmetrical, and decorated and Ionic (the Nike temple). Part of the richness of the ensemble is the variation within the simple post and lintel structure and in the use of basically one material, Pentelic marble. Apparently

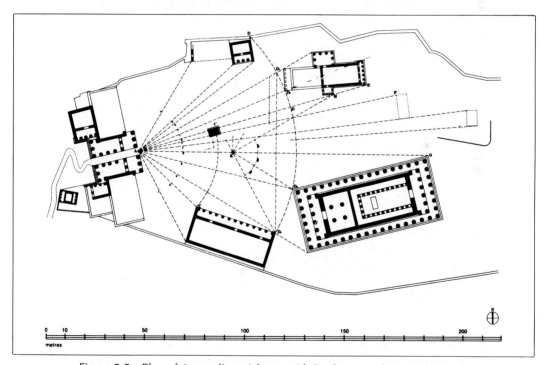

Figure 5-5   Plan of Acropolis at Athens, with Parthenon at lower right. Each building was placed to be seen at an angle, as a three-dimensional mass, from the entrance. (Plan by C. Doxiados, *Architectural Space in Ancient Greece*, by permission of M.I.T. Press.)

Figure 5-6   The Parthenon, Athens, 437 to 432 B.C. Ictinus and Callicrates, architects; Phidias, sculptor and supervisor of construction. Made completely of marble, the Parthenon is Doric but includes some Ionic details such as the tall columns in the room at the western end. The building was heavily damaged by an explosion in the seventeenth century, again to some extent by restoration ca. 1900, and most recently is being eroded by smog. (Photo, author.)

giving up structural experimentation "freed" the minds of the architects to consider increasingly sophisticated detailing.

MARBLE

Let us look more closely at one of these buildings, the Parthenon, to see how one material—marble—was exploited to the fullest in its construction (see Fig. 5-6). First a rectangular platform was built at the edge of the Acropolis, to provide a firm base for the temple. The exterior surfaces of this platform are of Pentelic marble. On this base the columns that surround the inner building (*cella*) were set up, eight across each short end, and seventeen along each side (counting the corner columns twice). Like the walls of the cella, these outer columns were of Pentelic marble. Above the columns and below the roof, on the exterior, ran a frieze of alternate square slabs with relief sculptures (*metopes*) and striated slabs (*triglyphs*): above the inner porch columns and continuing around the top of the cella wall ran a frieze depicting the great procession in honor of Athena. These friezes were also of marble, with the addition of paint and some few bronze fittings. Into the wide angle of the gabled roof were fitted sculptured groups of the gods, likewise in painted marble. The cella was divided into a small and a large room. In the large room, Doric columns were stacked in two tiers to support the roof and to form a backdrop for the great statue of Athena. In the smaller room, a single tier of tall thin Ionic columns supported the roof.

When we look at photographs of the Parthenon (see, for instance, Hege and Rodenwalt's *The Acropolis*) or even when we go to visit it, we are tempted to interpolate from its present golden-white state backward to an as-new state of shiny white. It is hard for us to remember that the completed Parthenon not only appeared dazzling because of the wax coating that protected its surfaces, but also might have seemed (to us) garish. All the sculptures were painted, and most of the architectural features were picked out in primary colors. Our eyes are more accustomed to neoclassical "purity" so it is hard for us to approve of such excesses. But the large, simple form of the Parthenon could absorb the red and blue of the triglyphs, the green and yellow of the recessed ceiling panels, and the variegated dapplings of the long frieze. Even the cult statue of Athena would have had painted blushes on her ivory cheeks.

Perhaps the fact that the sculptor Phidias supervised the erection of the Parthenon is related to the special qualities of the temple in more than an incidental way. A sculptor would tend to exploit the nature of the material in this fastidious way, seeing to it that the columns swelled subtly to give a sense of life to their support of the entablature and roof and to counteract the optical illusion of convergence of parallel lines. A sculptor would no doubt see to it that sculptural decoration included all the known possibilities: square metopes with stiffly old-fashioned half-round reliefs; an illusionistic frieze running around the top of the cella, in low relief; and rich three-dimensional figures in the pediment. These figures were all carved of the same marble as that used for the steps and columns. Only the huge statue of Athena inside broke away from the use of this one material. It was of gold and ivory (on a hidden armature of wood and iron) and stood in the large inner room, lit by a combination of direct light from the open doors to the use of east, indirect light bouncing up from the reflecting pool at its feet, and filtered light coming through the thin marble roof tiles. Even this exception to the prevailing material was subtly enhanced by the behavior of the marble surrounding it (see Fig. P-2).

The Parthenon incorporated, then, variation by color from what one expected Pentelic marble to be. It also incorporated subtle changes from the standard form of Doric temples, such as the inclusion of Ionic details and the unprecedented width of the eight-column facade. (Six columns were the norm.) Numerous variations from the common way of doing things were combined in this building to make it surpass the standard expression of its kind of architecture. For once, enough money, talent, time, resources, and thought came together in one building project. You may read about these variations, technically called refinements, in *The Parthenon*, but let us note a few here:

1 Floors swell up slightly, not only to shed rainwater but also to push back against the weight of the superstructure.

2 Columns lean in slightly.

3 Walls lean inward, but the frieze leans outward.

4 Corner columns that would otherwise seem naked and lonely stand a little closer to their neighbors.

5 Columns do not taper smoothly toward the top, but swell slightly in the middle so that they seem to have parallel sides (*entaisis*) (Figs. 5-7 and 5-8).

Entasis is so subtle in the Parthenon that the naked eye can hardly pick it out. However, at some Sicilian temples that survive from the experimental phase of Doric development, the entaisis is grossly obvious.

The Parthenon is a tour de force with respect to use of marble. Not only were the columns and the sculptures—that is, the parts that required the highest quality material in order to make a satisfactory aesthetic statement—made of marble, but so was every visible feature of the building. The steps and floor, the columns and walls, the entablature and cornices, the pediments and even the roof tiles were marble. Try to imagine a modern office building including the decoration made entirely of one material . An all-steel skyscraper, for instance, with steel louvered windows instead of glass, with steel floors, with steel partitions and stairs, with steel desks and toilets, with steel sculptures and wall hangings. Impossible to imagine, and yet, Ictinus and Callicrates, the architects who designed the Parthenon, restrained their palette in this way. By concentrating on one material and by thinking deeply about its possibilities as well as recognizing its limitations, they achieved a rare perfection in this building.

Figure 5-7   A view of the base of three steps supporting the Doric columns of the north side of the Parthenon. The perceptible curvature is the result of careful thought about both shedding rainwater and giving a sense of life to the buildings. Compare with Fig. 5-8. (Photo by D. Gardner.)

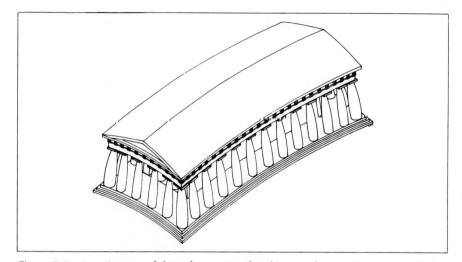

Figure 5-8   A caricature of the refinements of architectural proportions as applied to the Parthenon. The steps curve up in the middle of all four sides, and the entablature follows. Columns swell slightly as they taper upward; they also lean inward, which means that the corner columns lean in toward the corners of the cella. The walls of the cella also lean inward slightly, but the frieze at the top of the wall leans outward. (Drawing from J. J. Coulton, *Ancient Greek Architects at Work*, copyright 1977. Used by permission of the publisher, Cornell University Press.)

During the process of building, architects took careful thought about the many details, striving for beauty of form. They were responsible for planning the building, ordering the materials, determining nuances such as scale and proportion and use of color, designing the decorative program which usually meant choosing also the sculptor(s) and artisans to carry it out, and finally supervising the work force. For the Parthenon, every aspect was thought out as fully as was possible with this method of construction and with this kind of stone. The result was a temple that even in its present ruined condition captures the imagination and causes aesthetic rapture of many.

THE PARTHENON AND THE HEPHAISTIEON

One has only to compare the Parthenon with its much-more-complete rival, the Hephaistieon at the edge of the agora, to see what a difference small details make in creating life and grace. Without such graceful refinements, the Hephaistieon is sturdy but lifeless. The Hephaistieon was perhaps built in 450 B.C., the Parthenon in 437–432 B.C., so the difference cannot be accounted for by date. The Hephaistieon was a competent building, but the Parthenon an extraordinary one. Apparently both the program and the budget of the Parthenon were more ample than those for the Hephaistieon. Both buildings used the same material and the same simple structural system. They did not

Figure 5-9   Parthenon columns and entablature at southeast corner, showing triglyph-metope frieze and the peglike forms that refer to the process of putting the temple together. (Photo by A. Dean McKenzie.)

have the flexibility of wood or steel; they did not utilize the arch which was to open up so many possibilities for their successors, the Romans. Producing a perfect Greek temple is rather like writing a perfect sonnet—harder to do than a free-form effort but more of an accomplishment when the artist brings it off.

In the case of the Parthenon, because of the exquisite material of which it was made, the passage of time and the accumulation of dirt and oxidation have increased its poignancy. It seems to be one of those rare buildings that is irresistible. Whatever the season, the weather, the time of day, its Pentelic marble responds to light like a finely tuned instrument to a fine musician. Stones not battered or chipped by various remodelings or by the explosion of 1687 during the war between the Turks and the Venetians retain their crisp detailing and their warm smoothness. Though most of the painted color is gone, time has added the new golden hue of traces of oxidized iron in the stone. Perhaps the builders of churches of Gothic Europe equal those of the Parthenon in their elegant understanding of the nature of stone; they do not surpass it (Fig. 5-9).

BIBLIOGRAPHY

Bruno, V. J., *The Parthenon,* W. W. Norton, New York, 1974. A collection of essays about the Parthenon. Included are discussions of its refinements and its sculptural decoration.

Coulton, J. J., *The Ancient Greek Architects at Work,* Cornell University Press, Ithaca, N.Y., 1977. Detailed discussion of what Greek architects did, how they did it, and how they had to think to do it. Very interesting. Recommended highly.

Doxiades, K. A., *Architectural Space in Ancient Greece,* M.I.T. Press, Cambridge, Mass., 1972. To be read for its concepts rather than details, because 60 years of excavations have revised some details. Read especially the Introduction and the part on the siting of the buildings on the Athenian Acropolis.

Hedge, W. and G. Rodenwalt, *The Acropolis,* Weyhe, New York, 1930. A symphony of excellent photographs of all the buildings on the Acropolis, with many details of the stonework.

Travlos, John, *Pictorial Dictionary of Ancient Athens,* Praeger, New York, 1971. A basic source with photographs and plans of individual monuments, each with bibliography.

Wycherly, R. E., *The Stones of Athens,* Princeton University Press, Princeton, N.J., 1978. Fascinating discussion of use of materials at one site, and of what excavation has revealed about the physical fabric of Athens, building by building. Read especially the part on the Parthenon.

6

GREEK HOUSES AND CITIES

THE UBIQUITOUS PROTOTYPE

The house was the first human structure, once human beings left the caves and the trees. For how many thousands of years did necessity result in patterned building, in habitual response to standard problems of climate and safety and materials, before someone made the leap to conscious *design* of the shelter? No sooner had architectural history as a discipline begun in the seventeenth century than speculation about the origins of the house became a major topic. Some early—perhaps outrageous—theories on this matter are set forth in Rykwert's *On Adam's House in Paradise*. We now have too much information from prehistoric archeology to be comfortable with these purely speculative early theories. Yet we do not have enough information to retire the question permanently.

THE EGYPTIANS

Archeologists tell us that no later than 18,000 years ago a period of trial and error in house building began. By about 3000 B.C., house types in ancient centers such as the Nile Valley would have been well-established. During the second millenium, spatial differentiation within the house began to follow differences in function. The Egyptian house type had three kinds of space: the quasi public, where visitors were entertained; the semiprivate living rooms of the family; and the private chambers. The same spatial divisions were adapted to the whole range of Egyptian domestic architecture—one-story single-family dwellings, multistory houses both small and large, and palaces. The same tripartite division extended to other building types such as temples, becoming a basic principle of Egyptian architecture.

The conceptual leap from house to city was more difficult for the Egyptians. The evidence for complex urban living in Egypt is meager at the supposed major centers of the culture. A few worker's villages are known, with a shrine set next to an open space, an overseer's house, and a barrackslike repetition of standard housing units. Only once, at Tell al-Amarna, which was a preplanned new town, was there a complex relation of major monuments to open space, to the river, and to dwelling units.

THE GREEKS

We have seen that the Greek temple, while using only one material (stone), exhibited a range of subtle variation within the type that far surpassed Egyptian temples in expressiveness. Similarly, the Greek house and the Greek city exhibited a range of solutions clustered around basic prototypical concepts. These solutions were more subtle and sophisticated than either Egyptian or Minoan ones had been.

Reasoning always from the human perceiver outward to the world, the Greeks habitually made explicit, specific, and physical any ideas they had. Their thought grew from the physical concreteness of house to somewhat more abstract city. By inspecting what they made and how they made it, we can learn what these concepts consisted of and, in their major public buildings, what architecture meant to them.

To see how the Greeks managed the conceptual leap from house to city, we will turn first to their treatment of the house, basic constituent of the city. Since Greek culture spread over nearly the whole Mediterranean area, and lasted more than half a millenium, we expect to find variation in the house form depending on location and date. By comparing houses found at Athens, Olynthus, Priene, and Delos, we get a sense of the variety found within the developing Greek tradition.

ATHENS

Already at Athens in the fifth century B.C., the basic prototype of the Greek urban house was found (Fig. 6-1a). Most houses were small and modestly furnished, because much of daily life for the men took place in public spaces and buildings; and men and women did not have a joint social life. From the irregular street, a narrow passage led to the central courtyard of the house. Rooms of different sizes opened onto the court. Inasmuch as exterior walls had no windows, doors and windows onto the court were the major source of light to the rooms. If the house were the residence of an artisan, one room was used as a shop to sell whatever was made on the premises. The manufacturing might spill over into the courtyard, which was also used for household tasks and for children's play. In structure, the house had stone foundations and walls of mud brick. Rooms were irregular in size, limited by the size of the wooden beams to support the flat roofs which could be used as additional living space. Should a family need a larger house, they might purchase the one next door and open a door through the party wall. Even in the fifth century B.C. it was apparent to the Greeks that urban living required special provision for water supply and drainage. Excavators have found wells, cisterns, and aqueducts, as well as

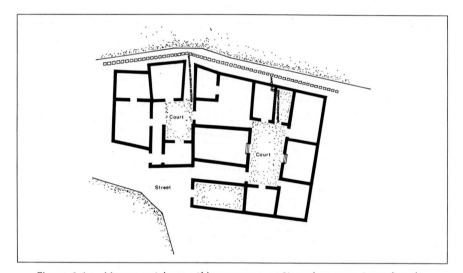

Figure 6-1a House at Athens, fifth century B.C. Since lots were irregular, the outlines of houses were also irregular. Each house reached to the perimeter of its lot, leaving an open court at the center as outdoor space, quite the opposite of the common American pattern of having the solid house of block surrounded by an irregular doughnut of space. Rooms were set around the court, taking their light and air from it. The court was an all-purpose space. (R. Martin, *L'Urbanisme dans la Grece antique*, 1956, reprinted by permission of the publisher, A. & J. Picard.)

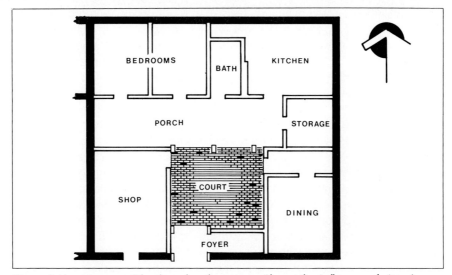

Figure 6-1*b*   House at Olynthus, fourth century. Shows the influence of city plan on house form, as the orthogonal grid produced houses of great regularity. The courtyard continued as center of the house. Bedrooms were placed on the north side of the house, opening to the south. Houses at Olynthus routinely had bathrooms, placed next to the kitchen for access to warm water and for shared access to the drains. Space was provided also for storage, for a stable, for the owner's office, and for formal dining. (R. Martin, *L'Urbanisme dans la Grece antique*, 1956, reprinted by permission of the publisher, A. & J. Picard.)

drainpipes to carry waste water out of the house to the sewer that ran under the street or alley. The prototype, then, included enclosed space both roofed and open to the sky; workrooms, quiet rooms, storage space; capacity for expansion; provision for eating, sleeping, bathing, and excreting. These features were organized around the courtyard, which remained the invariable focus of the Greek house in all its variations, and was to remain as prototype for the Mediterranean house of later centuries.

OLYNTHUS

At our second site, excavations at Olynthus in northern Greece have revealed not only large and comfortable country houses but also a level of urban living that surpassed that of the Athenians of a century earlier (Fig. 6-1*b*). The new part of Olynthus was built and destroyed within the fourth century B.C. Houses here were regularly laid out within a rectilinear street grid; they were about the size of a small American tract house (10 by 30 feet or 20 by 30 feet). Farther north than Athens, possibly feeling the demands of the climate more severely, Olynthus showed an early and sophisticated appreciation of solar heating, inasmuch as the bedroom part of every house faced south with a porch in front that shielded the chambers from the summer sun but admitted the winter sun. Houses regularly had bathrooms with built-in bathtubs. Many bathrooms had washstands as well, and at least one very modern-looking toilet has been found. From the bathrooms, drains ran to the sewers under the alleys or streets. Source of water for the house was either the public aqueduct or individual wells. These houses were much more regular than the earlier ones at Athens. They included a formal dining room as well as an office and/or storeroom and a kitchen and bathroom suite as well as one or more bedrooms on the main floor, all opening onto the courtyard. Uniting the kitchen and bathroom shows careful consideration of conservation of effort and resources. Two-story houses had additional bedrooms on the north side of the house, above the downstairs bedrooms and facing southward for warmth. As in Athens, the only openings from the rooms were onto the court, so that the outer wall of the house was blank. Materials of construction were the same, with the addition of mosaic floors in the dining room and its vestibule. Unlike Athens, shops were not usually built as part of the house.

PRIENE

At Priene in the third century B.C. we find further variation on the urban courtyard house (Fig. 6-1c). Some of the differences may be accounted for by date and some by location, inasmuch as Priene was on the western coast of what is now Turkey and was then Ionian Greece. The city was located on a south-facing hillside, so again the main rooms were on the north side of each house, facing south for the winter sun. Here, however, the main room was a proportionally very large and tall reception room for entertaining; cooking was done on its porch. At least one inner chamber could be entered only from the reception room (for privacy perhaps), but the other small rooms opened as usual onto the court. At one corner of the street wall, a recessed door was set, which opened onto a narrow passage that ran into the house along the side of the courtyard and ended in a narrow room probably used as a stable for one donkey or horse. As one stood in the street and looked along the exterior walls, panels of shadow made by the recessed doorways created a strong contrast to the white stucco of the blank walls; an architectural imagination had been at work here. Interestingly enough none of the houses had bathrooms. Bathroom functions no doubt took place elsewhere or were handled very informally. Apparently the house was still undergoing experimentation. Bathrooms were not an invariable part of the concept. At Priene, public fountains were located at the corners of residential blocks, and the gymnasium included a room with many washbasins. Thus, the city made public provisions for needs not satisfied by the private houses.

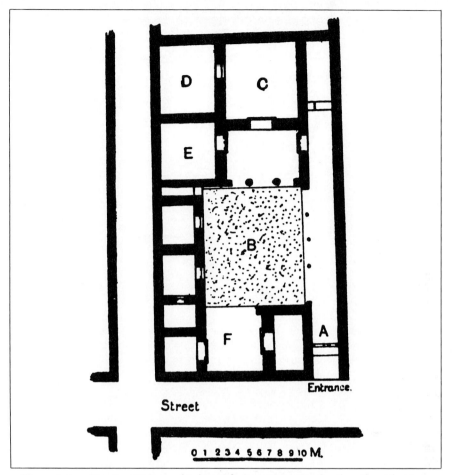

Figure 6-1c House at Priene, third century B.C. More regular than the Athenian houses but less opulent than those at Olynthus, the Ionian houses at Priene were centered on a large reception suite (resembling the ancient megaron) facing the courtyard. Smaller rooms opened onto the court or into the reception room. The stall for one donkey, located next to the main door at Olynthus, was at Priene placed at the far end of the entrance corridor. The door was the only opening onto the street; it was recessed far enough to make a dramatic shadow pattern in the long block of otherwise featureless facades. Houses at Priene do not seem to have had bathrooms. (Reprinted from B. C. Rider, *The Greek House*, 1916, 1965, by permission of the publisher, Cambridge University Press.)

DELOS

In the second century, in Delos, a difficult site was managed with elegance (Fig. 6-1d). First, Delos was very hilly, so much ingenuity was required to adapt houses to the steep terrain. The houses were more regular than those in

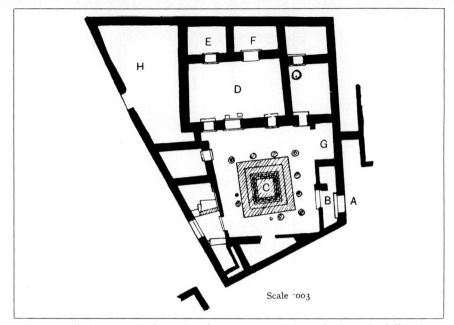

Scale ·003

Figure 6-1*d*   House at Delos, second century B.C. Despite the irregular hilly site, houses were made to seem as regular as was possible. This type incorporated the best features of the Greek houses shown in Figs. 6-1*a* to 6-1*c*, such as mosaic floors and bathrooms. They also made provision for saving water in cisterns under each courtyard. Because of the hilly sites, houses might have entrances on more than one level; three- or four-story houses often had exterior windows in the top story or two. (Reprinted from B. C. Rider, *The Greek House*, 1916, 1965, Cambridge University Press, by permission of the publisher.)

fifth century Athens but less regular than those in Priene or Olynthus. Entries on more than one level were common; and many houses incorporated interior balconies above their courtyards. There is some evidence that suggests that there were exterior windows above the ground story.

A second problem was water supply, since Delos has no rivers. To be able to live there at all, people had to find a way to save rainwater. Therefore each house was built around the traditional courtyard, but here the court paving was the lid of a cistern. Water that fell on the roofs in winter was carefully led into the cistern to be saved for the rainless months of summer. (By August the rainwater saved from April must have tasted unpleasant enough to spur the Greeks to mix wine with the water for drinking, as they still do.) Many of the houses, if not most, incorporated bathrooms that were located on the ground floor and drained into sewer pipes under the streets. Through these prudent arrangements and with the wealth engendered by their success in commercial shipping, the Delians were able to afford to pave the floors of their houses with mosaics and decorate their walls with painted geometric patterns. Their houses were both comfortable and attractive.

THE GREEK CITY—MILETUS

The urban house in the Greek world thus changed over time, and so did the form of the Greek city. During the archaic period, before 500 B.C., one main street divided colonial cities and long narrow blocks of houses ran perpendicular to it, as at Paestum in southern Italy (Fig. 6-2). Planning during the classical

Figure 6-2   Plan of Paestum, as revealed in an aerial photograph. The major east-west street was the main thoroughfare of the Greek city founded in the sixth century B.C. From it, long narrow blocks were laid out perpendicular to the first street. At the center, temples and the agora occupied an open area where three temples still stand. The Greek wall surrounded the city where the modern road is outlined in white. In Roman times, a second major street ran perpendicular to the first; this north-south street is marked in white here. (Photo reprinted from J. Bradford, *Ancient Landscapes*, 1957. Crown Copyright, by permission from Her Britannic Majesty's Stationery Office.)

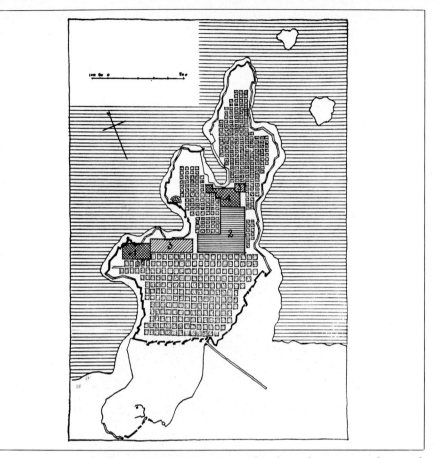

Figure 6-3 Plan of Miletus, western Asia Minor. After the earlier city was destroyed by Persians, a regular fifth century B.C. city was laid out next to the ruins, to occupy a three-part peninsula. At the north lay small blocks containing large houses; at the south, large blocks with small houses. The residential areas were in the pattern of a regular grid. Between the sets of houses lay the public areas (1, 2, 3, 4 and 5). A wall surrounded the city loosely, leaving room for a permanent green area between wall and houses. The first city planner, Hippodamus of Miletus, grew up here and spread this practical way of laying out cities all over the Greek world. (Plan from R. Martin, *L'Urbanisme dans la Grece antique,* 1956, by permission of A. & J. Picard & Co., publishers.)

period of the fifth and fourth century B.C. was exemplified by Miletus, whose checkerboard pattern with large blocks of small houses grouped together and small blocks of large houses was relieved by spacious open areas ringed by stoas and other public buildings (Fig. 6-3). This prototypical grid plan is associated with Hippodamus of Miletus, the first city planner whose name has come down to us. He seems to have been able to persuade other city governments to adopt the plan of his native city, for Aristotle tells us that Hippodamus "discovered the method of dividing cities" (*Politics,* ii; 5), and adds, "The difficulty with such things is not so much the matter of theory but that of practice." (vii; 10.11)

PERGAMUM

A more dramatic urban effect was seen in the plan of Hellenistic Pergamum (Gk. Pergamon), adjusted to the hilly terrain in a striking arrangement of fanned terraces (Fig. 6-4). Rather than a geometric regularity like Miletus, Pergamum's plan regularized the steep terrain with elegant attention to the ensemble of buildings and spaces. Vistas from different locations on the hilltop were carefully considered, as were views from the lower city to the skyline above. The needs of individuals for variety and recognizability were reconciled with

Figure 6-4   Pergamum, western Asia Minor, as it appeared in the second century. The dramatic skyline was formed by pulling buildings toward the edge of the citadel. From left to right along the skyline we see the temple dedicated to the emperor Trajan with its surrounding porticoes, the library and temple of Athena, and the Great Altar. In the foreground are a series of buttressing stoas leading to the small temple later dedicated to Caracalla, and at center is the theater. (Drawing from J. B. Ward-Perkins, *Cities of Ancient Greece & Italy,* 1974, by permission of George Braziller, Inc., publisher.)

the demands of geography in a sophisticated manner rarely equaled in urban history.

As a prototype for Greek urban development, however, Miletus and not Pegamum was the norm. All over the Greek world, cities of checkerboard pattern were common after the middle of the fifth century. Within that regular envelope, a standard package of urban buildings and spaces could be found, filling the needs of a society that highly prized clarity.

THE BASIC PLAN OF THE CITY

The center of the city was left open, to be used for many different activities. Here the market was held and when needed the troops would assemble. Here was the focus of city government. In time, specific buildings were provided for the council to meet in, the executive to administer in, and the laws to be recorded in. A separate building might hold the city archives. Fountains marked the corners where major streets entered the open space; and stoas (long porches with offices and shops) lined the edges. In stoas, the enclosed rooms or porch spaces could be rented from the city by bankers, lawyers, and persons who traded in valuable commodities of small bulk, such as jewelry (Fig. 6-5). Near the edges of the open space (agora), commemorative sculptures were set up to honor heroes and gods.

The rest of the built-up area of the city was a mixture of houses with and without shops. Usually the item sold was manufactured on the premises. Large temples and small shrines could be located among the houses, as could street fountains. In some cities, such as Corinth, Athens, and Pergamum, there was more than one major group of big public buildings—temples with porticoes and with open spaces for festivals and markets.

The wide variety of building types within the city contributed to the meaning as well as functioning of the city. Public life took on increased richness from the buildings and spaces provided for it. Different kinds of structures were made for different activities, such as the theaters for play cycles during the festival of Dionysius. For public use, baths were provided at the gymnasiums, where schools, exercise rooms, and gardens were also located. By making these experiences public, a Greek city deliberately inculcated a particular concept of community life and mutual responsibility. Political activity at Athens had a formal site, the Pnyx, and the many informal corners of the agora. Religious processions crossed the agora on the Panathenaic Way, with all the people part of the parade or of the audience. For the women, confined mostly to the home, there were the street fountains where they went to get water and to gossip with their neighbors; they also went to the temple and the theater. For the men, the whole array of public spaces and buildings enabled them to carry out their obligations and receive their rewards as citizens. This variety of building types in the Greek city articulated what the

Figure 6-5   Stoa of Attalos, Athens, second century B.C. Donated to Athens by the king of Pergamum, this structure stretched along the east side of the agora. On a basement podium rose two stories of shops with covered porches and a wider terrace. The whole structure was of marble. It has been reconstructed and is now the Agora Museum. Bankers, lawyers, and merchants rented the spaces from the city of Athens. Philosophers—Stoics and others—paced the open spaces of the stoas. (Photo by Agora Excavations, by permission of the American School of Classical Studies at Athens.)

Greeks meant by city—a place of complex social interaction and multiplicity of function, balanced between private houses and public gathering places.

Contrast this with the fewer building types known from Mesopotamia. There, as late as the Persian era of the sixth and fifth centuries B.C., a city consisted only of houses (some with shops), temples, palace, and an open, all-purpose space commonly used as a marketplace. The social system in Persia was monarchial, with little or no expectation of citizen participation, and the paucity of building types reflected this reality. Residents of classical Athens (fifth and fourth century B.C.) set out deliberately to achieve a city form suited to the sophistication of their political concepts. They boasted that they preferred to live richly rather than to be rich. What a contrast with modern America, where public poverty amid personal wealth is the normal state of things!

These examples of house and city show us the Greeks defining the problem of architecture more widely than the Egyptians, with more refinement than the Minoans and more sophistication than the Persians. In struggling with the development of the house and the question of what a city should consist of, the Greeks created prototypes that moulded Mediterranean life for over 2500 years and that still affect us. Our ideas of what is possible in that climate and in a democratic society seem permanently affected by their prototypical experience.

There is no need to think that Greek definitions are the only ones possible, even though the urban house of the Greek type still dominates the Mediterranean area. The excellence of the Greek prototypes, however, does challenge us to find our own—one that will perhaps be wider, and more sophisticated and necessarily as adequate for us as theirs were for them.

BIBLIOGRAPHY

Badawy, A., *Architecture in Ancient Egypt and the Near East,* Massachusetts Institute of Technology, Cambridge, Mass., 1966. Brief accounts and excellent diagrams of architecture (including houses) and urban design in these two cultures.

Lawrence, A. W., *Greek Architecture,* Penguin Books, Baltimore, 1957. This book is not only informative but also beautifully written. As usual with this Pelican series, this volume provides much help to the beginner, with plans, sections, and photographs, and with copious notes that constitute a bibliography for the monuments cited.

Martin, R., *L'Urbanisme dans la Grece antique,* Picard, Paris, 1956. Even if you don't read French, look at the excellent plans and pictures in this thoughtful study.

Rykwert, J., *On Adam's House in Paradise,* Museum of Modern Art, New York, 1972. Wonderful study of all the wrong-headed early notions about the origins of architecture.

Wycherly, R. E., *How the Greeks Built Cities,* Macmillan, London, 1967. Now also in paperback. Basic study of all the building types that made up a Greek city.

INTERLUDE A

The interludes discuss the questions and examples which have been raised. Each interlude includes a review of the questions and a summary description of one major monument from each chapter. The questions and monuments will then be compared in a different order, to show how the cumulative interplay of examples and questions enriches our understanding of architecture. Illustrations will be chosen to bring out features of the monuments not considered during the initial exposition in earlier chapters.

In Chaps. 1 through 6 we considered the questions of time, economics, tradition, social context, material, and prototype. The monuments emphasized were Stonehenge, the great pyramids at Giza, the temple at Deir al-Bahri, the palace at Knossos, the Parthenon, and the city of Pergamum.

1   The question of time in relation to architecture may be overt, as an obelisk acting as a giant sundial in a city plaza, or implicit. At Stonehenge, for instance, if the complex really does keep track of astronomical time as has been suggested, that is one mode of implicit relations with time. Even if it does not, time is implicit in our understanding of the monument, since we know that it had at least three building periods, separated by centuries.

2   Economics in relation to architecture may be an active or a passive interaction. In Egypt during the pyramid age, the architecture played an active role in bringing a new economic system into being. The economic system is more often the actor and the individual building is the receiver of the action; this was certainly the case with respect to the temple at Deir al-Bahri.

3   The question of tradition in relation to architecture varies from the extreme, where every detail of form and organization and function is preset, to the opposite, where the entire aim of the architect is to escape from traditional expectations and produce something completely original. The funerary temple at Deir al-Bahri is in the second mode rather than the first and yet incorporates many traditional elements.

4   The question of social context in relation to architecture is best encapsulated by Winston Churchill's famous remark, "We make our houses and then our houses make us"—a reciprocity of action. So too we understand architecture reciprocally from the context, as in the case of using what we know of Stone Age tribal life to understand Stonehenge as a functioning structure in its original context. On the other hand, we learned most of what we know about Bronze Age life in Crete by the study of Knossos and other palace and town sites with their associated ruins of buildings, remnants of pictorial murals, and small objects such as pottery sherds. That is, we have learned the context from the architecture.

5   The question of material in relation to architecture can be a straightforward one, as among the Greeks, who systematically explored the capabilities of marble and limestone for the erection of buildings that were structurally simple (post and lintel) but aesthetically sophisticated. Or the question can be more elusive, as with the Minoans who used materials (rubble and mortar) that were not attractive, covering them up with murals or with thin slabs of gypsum; they also used bright colors as if to distract the viewer from the innate qualities of the materials. In thus using subterfuge to extend the range of architectural effects, the Minoans were beginning an architectural exploration that would come to magnificent fruition with the Romans.

6   The question of prototype in relation to architecture is bound up with the questions of tradition and originality (see Kubler, *The Shape of Time*). A long period of experimentation in the Greek world flowered in the fifth century B.C. in the prototypical forms for house and city in the Mediterranean world. Though original in their own way, pyramids never had the same influence as prototypes, perhaps because they were not adaptable to any other use.

Out of all the possible architectural examples from each period and place, we are for simplicity's sake concentrating on only one at a time. The brief description of each monument repeats for the reader the most necessary information.

1   The first monument is Stonehenge, an arrangement of two kinds of stones set in circular patterns with additional stones marking a rectangle outside the circle and some huge stones within the circle set in a horseshoe configuration that opens toward the solitary heel stone at the entrance. All this was encircled by a ditch and circular mound, and probably related to other moundlike constructions in the same area. The function of Stonehenge is so far from being obvious that many fanciful notions have been put forth about it, among the most engaging of which is Hawkins' theory that Stonehenge is a huge calendrical device. Stonehenge was built during the third millenium B.C.

2   The second monument is the set of three great pyramids at Giza in Egypt. Two of these are enormous and the third is very large. They are constructed of solid stone. Usually described as tombs for pharaohs, and in fact containing tomb chambers, the pyramids are perhaps less directly functional than the title of tomb would indicate, because there were seven large pyramids in all but fewer than seven pharaohs during this period (ca. 2700 to 2600 B.C.); one pharaoh is known to have had three pyramids. Each pyramid was part of a complex that included a temple at its base, a causeway to the Nile, a temple at the edge of the Nile, and auxiliary tombs sometimes in the form of smaller pyramids or mastabas.

3   The third monument is the funerary temple of Queen Hatshepsut at Deir al-Bahri. Built by her chief architect and vizier, Senmut, this temple both honored the god Amon and served as a permanent memorial to the only reigning queen of Egypt, in somewhat the same way that pyramids had been memorials 1200 years earlier. The form of the temple was one of great originality in its architectural replication of the physical form of its setting as a series of terraces and colonnades made of the stone of the site, and in its incorporation of an exotic garden as a major feature of the ensemble.

4   The fourth monument is the palace at Knossos, built in Minoan Crete during the second millenium B.C. Around a large courtyard were grouped domestic quarters, artisans' workshops, reception and audience rooms, a throne room, and subsidiary rooms grouped over a long series of storage rooms and, at the south, loggias looking out over the valley to the south. At the edge of the courtyard but within the body of the palace stood a shrine, one of the few discovered for this culture. Outside the palace to the west lay a paved area edged to the north with gently rising stairs that may have served as the earliest theater.

5   The fifth monument is the Parthenon, a temple to Athena located on the Acropolis at Athens, and built in the fifth century B.C. With eight columns along each short side (east and west) and seventeen on the long sides, the Parthenon was unusually wide for a Doric temple; it also incorporated Ionic decorative details and even a set of four Ionic columns in the treasure room at the west end. The entire building was of Pentelic marble, but selected parts were painted decoratively. It was richly enhanced also with sculpture.

6   The sixth monument is the city of Pergamum, which flourished during the third and second centuries B.C. It may have been the first city consciously developed as a work of art. Set on a high hill, the upper city occupied a series of descending terraces. On these terraces, the major buildings were pulled forward as close to the edge of the hill as was possible, to form a skyline. Although these buildings included the usual elements of a

Greek urban "package," they were not set in the grid pattern that had been common for Greek cities since the early fifth century. Pergamum thus carried the development of urban form forward innovatively.

Having reviewed the questions and the monuments separately, we can now experiment with cross comparisons that combine the two in different patterns than before. As we do this in each Interlude, we will be developing a extended repertoire of questions that are to be applied to every monument. Our understanding of architecture will be deepened not arithmetically but geometrically, just as two people have only one possible relation but seven people have 35,000 possible relations.

The relation between time and architecture was examined at Stonehenge, where the whole structure has been considered a time-keeping device. Less directly, we have noted time as marking and being marked by evolutionary development of the Doric order, in examples from Sicily and from mainland Greece. The so-called timelessness of Egyptian architecture was noted in passing, and was validated to the extent that the same concerns and same solutions and even same decorative details persisted in Egyptian architecture over much longer periods of time than in, say, Greek architecture. Even at Karnak, however, the passing of time may be noted from our own perspective if we merely compare modern photographs of the ruins with a modern archeologist's reconstruction of the temple in its prime.

Some different concepts of time and different values placed on permanence must surely have influenced the architects of the pyramids as compared with those at Knossos. At Giza, the builders went to a great deal of trouble and expense to use permanent material—stone—and to assemble the pyramids in the most stable way that they could. That is quite different from what happened at Knossos, where irregular boulders were used without much shaping, and were piled up into walls for which mud was frequently used as mortar. In the climate of Crete, mud mortar is far from being permanent. The structural and maintenance problems caused by this material contributed to frequent rebuilding of the palace. The pyramids were essentially maintenance-free. It is thought-provoking to realize that a civilization as relatively permanent as that of the Egyptians (over 3000 years) should plan for its monuments to last long after anyone from that culture remained to care for them, while the much more ephemeral Minoans built in such a way as to require repairs that were unlikely to be carried out over long periods of time. Each culture was nonetheless consistent in its behavior.

From learning about the economic effects of constructing the pyramids, we can guess something about their social context. The student's collateral reading in such books as *Life in Ancient Egypt and Assyria* will tell more about daily life and the way society was organized. A society where life was good, even for commoners, with abundant food assured by the annual flooding of the Nile, is bound to be less fragile than one in northern regions such as England where the climate is much less friendly.

Other economic and social questions are raised by the very existence of Stonehenge. We know so little about the social organization of the tribes that built Stonehenge and rebuilt it over the centuries that we cannot even imagine how their wealth could be manipulated to pay for the erection of such a huge monument. In contrast, for the Parthenon at Athens we have some of the most explicit data about the details of construction, including costs, that have come down to us for any historic structure. The Athenians were following one of their venerable traditions when they had inscribed on marble slabs the cost and duration of finishing the Parthenon. We know, for instance, that it took a team of five or six men about 6 months to flute one of the columns after it was set up. We learn how much each of them was paid; and we know that the team consisted of both slaves and free men, both citizens and foreigners, all paid at the same wage—though presumably the owners of the slaves collected their wages.

A further economic fact about the Parthenon is that it was built with the surplus from the Persian War. Athens had acted as coordinator for that all-Greek effort. The other cities had sent either men or ships or money or some of each. At the end of the war, not all the money had been used up. Some Athenians argued that the surplus should be returned to the other cities, but others claimed that Athens had been paid to win the war and had done so, and that the extra was rightfully hers. About 30 years after the war, Pericles led the movement to spend the money in beautifying Athens, rebuilding the Parthenon and so on. How does this kind of information affect our ideas about the ideal beauty of the Parthenon; or our sense of that process of experimentation that resulted in the harmony of forms in classical Greek temples? Perhaps the Greeks invented not only the prototypical Mediterranean house but also the prototypical rationalization for keeping something that did not belong to them.

The Greeks were inventive in their combination of using a traditional methodology of building, using traditional materials, and having an unusual degree of forethought and refinement when they built the Parthenon. Whereas the Parthenon may be considered the culmination of a tradition, the house and city patterns of the Greeks started a tradition that would dominate the Mediterranean world and have even wider influence when carried by the Spaniards to the New World. These domestic and urban traditions were dynamic, unlike the self-contained traditions of Egyptian architecture. For a culture that valued permanence, the Egyptians built ephemeral cities. Those of the period of Karnak have left relatively little mark not only on the Mediterranean world but even on Egypt itself. Only the formal qualities such as stylized plant forms of the stone columns have survived and were copied again in the unlikely social context of the new American society of the 1830s, for the Egyptian revival style, and again in what might be called Egyptian revival revival during the 1930s. On American soil, however, these forms were innovative and not traditional. (See Chap. 21.)

Some of the decorative details of Egyptian architecture can be understood more completely if the social context as well as the physical context is considered. They used, for instance, a capital in the form of the head of the goddess Hathor who was shown as a woman with cow's ears. A cow goddess seems to be a fairly good symbol of the fertility principle, since both the Nile River and cows themselves periodically renewed their abundance with minimal assistance from humans. Also, Egyptian society emphasized and honored human fertility, so much so that descent and property were matrilineal. Knowing these social factors, we realize that the Hathor capitals are highly meaningful rather than merely strange.

Among the Greeks, slight differences in social context were manifest in definite formal differences in architecture. The Ionian Greeks of the west coast of Asia Minor and the Dorian Greeks of the mainland were alike in their culture, social organization, and speech (in which there was as much difference as there is between British and American English). Yet their long residence in separated geographical areas and long experimentation with plan, scale, proportion, and detail led to quite different effects within the constraints of the same structure and material. As early as the eighth century B.C., the Ionians began the experiments that led to the classical Ionic order of the fifth century B.C., whereas the Dorians began their experiments with Doric in the seventh century B.C. In general, the Ionians were much more interested in making enormous temples, a tradition that culminated in the Temple of Apollo at Didyma. As Doxiados has shown (*Architectural Space in Ancient Greece*), the political experiences and philosophical outlook of these two branches of the Greek people are reflected in the different arrangements of their sacred precincts and even in the degree of closure of public open spaces such as the agora. The Dorians tended to organize their precincts around a shaft of open space, whereas the Ionians preferred closed compositions (see Fig. 5-9).

It was the same Greeks who had developed the use of marble and limestone to the furthest expression of what those materials were capable of who demonstrated in their domestic architecture that the material used was less important than what was done with it. The marvelous adaption of the Greek urban house to its setting and its society could not have been improved even if each house were made of solid marble. The humble materials of field stone, mud brick, tile, and paint were sufficient, when combined with a plan that took full advantage of the site and the climate.

During this early period in the history of architecture, many prototypical forms were developed that have remained dominant to a greater or lesser degree during the whole sweep of western architecture. Some features, or perhaps we should say some effects, of the temples at Karnak and Athens have persisted in religious architecture. Even a church of the 1980s, though not using any historical allusions in its detailing, will incorporate light in a way that increases the religious symbolism of the edifice. In the same way, the concept of the construction of the theater today stems from the first timid experiment at Knossos and incorporates the more successful solution at Pergamum, not directly but indirectly by utilizing what was learned there about the relations of the seats to the stage building and the degree of arc of the semicircular seat arrangement. So too, the imagination of several succeeding ages was captured by the imagery of Egyptian pyramids. Changes in the pyramid form were as great as were adherence to it: pyramids at Meroë in southern Egypt (of the first millenium B.C.) are tall and thin, and the famous pyramid at Rome (now built into the third century A.D. wall of the city) was both tall and thin and made of shiny white marble. In twentieth century cemeteries, the pyramid in many shapes and materials continues to be used as a decorative and symbolic motif.

The reader is encouraged to continue this process of examining each monument in terms of all the questions. In some cases, the reader will not know enough to develop these comparisons to any great depth, but the exercise of attempting to do so will in itself enrich the understanding of the complexity of architecture.

BIBLIOGRAPHY

Kubler, G. *The Shape of Time,* Yale University Press, New Haven, Conn., 1962. Tradition, originality, and other basic art history concepts organized in a little book that tells us more about how we think than most tomes of philosophy do. A must.

7

SECULAR ROMAN BUILDINGS

THE INVENTION OF INTERIOR SPACE

Certainly there had already been spatial differences in Egyptian architecture. In that culture, space could be defined on the basis of who was excluded from it: the sanctuary of a temple and the private bedrooms of a house or palace were limited strictly to the very few who had the right to be there.

GREEK ARCHITECTS AND SPACE

Greek architects seem to have been the first to manipulate the experience of space in such a way that all comers got the same experience. At the Acropolis in Athens, for instance, all the people in procession at the official Panathenaic festival as well as the individual devotee at any time walked up the same ramp or stairs, passed through the propylaeum (gateway), walked along the north flank of the Parthenon, and came at last to the east end of the building where the altar stood. All might mount the steps and pass through the porches into the cella to view the great gold and ivory statue of Athena. This series of experiences involved both closed and open areas, and a short part of the path bisected the propylaeua so that the visitor had an experience of axiality.

In the classical Greek world, however, the dominant spatial experience was polar not axial (see Doxiados, *Architectural Space in Ancient Greece*). That is, the space was organized to refer back to the person viewing the space, so that the viewer became the pole around which the space was organized. In this system, the angular view is emphasized, so that the building is seen as a three-dimensional object, almost as a sculpture. The building is set so that viewers perceive it in a series of shifting but always angular relations to themselves. The architectural experience consists of the interaction between the buildings in their settings and the observer. Architectural effect depends upon personal response. There is no effect if there is no viewer (Fig. 7-1).

Later in the Hellenistic period, the Greeks experimented with more complicated space. At the Temple of Apollo at Didyma, for instance, inside

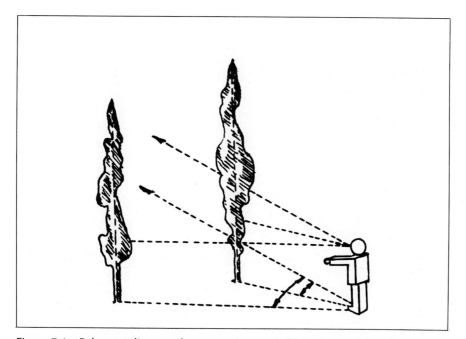

Figure 7-1   Polar coordinates—the measurement of objects in space by reference to distance and angle from the observer rather than by placement in a three-dimensional grid. The ancient Greeks composed their groups of buildings according to the principle of polar coordinates, whereby the viewer is the pole around which the space is organized, according to C. Doxiados. (Diagram reprinted from his *Architectural Space in Ancient Greece,* by permission of M.I.T. Press. Cf. Fig. 5.6.)

and outside were deliberately conflated to produce an experience of great sophistication. Visitors arrived at Didyma, a suburb of Miletus, to find a very large Ionic temple (about 350 feet long). Climbing to the porch, they found their way into the cella barred by a door sill 6 feet high. On either side of it, however, there were barrel-vaulted passageways leading down and inward. When visitors emerged from one of these, they stood—surprisingly—in a vast outdoor space surrounded by the podium and cella walls of the temple and open to the sky. Ahead of them, at the back of this open-air cella, stood a small Ionic temple which marked the sanctuary and the sacred spring. Here one of the famous sybils (prophetesses) of the ancient world would utter cryptic admonitions. Priests of the Apollo cult, standing by to receive the utterances, would then climb to the top of the great inner staircase at the opposite end of the open-air cella and mount to the top of that gigantic outer sill where they stood to repeat the oracle to the crowd gathered on the outer porch (Fig. 7-2).

ROMAN USE OF OUTDOOR SPACE

We will consider briefly several of the varieties of Roman outdoor space: theater, amphitheater, circus, colonnaded street, forum. Then we will discuss

Figure 7-2 Temple of Apollo at Didyma, in western Asia Minor near Miletus, ca. 300 B.C. to the second century. Inside and outside are here mixed. Inside the double colonnade some 350 feet long is placed not a conventional temple but a sunken court open to the sky. At the back of the court stood a small temple only the foundations of which are visible here. This inner sanctuary marked the spot of the sacred spring where the oracles were delivered. (Photo by A. Dean McKenzie.)

indoor roofed spaces. The outdoor spaces could be of many shapes, but all were designed to enhance and glorify the communal life.

As early as the fifth century B.C., the Greeks had built theaters with stone seats set into the slope of a hill and arranged in an arc that abutted the paved floor of the circular orchestra. A separate stage building was placed opposite the seats, tangent to the circle. During the Hellenistic time period, the orchestra was no longer circular because part of the circle was sliced off so that seats and stage building were closer together. Not until the Romans began erecting permanent theaters of stone in the late first century B.C. did the stage and seats unite to form an enclosure shaped like the letter D. The earliest Roman theaters were temporary wooden structures, but in the first century Marcellus (a grandson of Augustus) built one of stone that still stands in downtown Rome and still bears his name. A further difference from Greek practice was Roman use of arched substructures to support the seats of the theater. No longer were theaters confined to hillside sites; using arched supports meant that the Roman theater could become an important architectural statement wherever it was needed in the urban design. Seated on their hillside, a Greek audience had looked over the top of the stage building to the world beyond, but in a Roman theater, spectators and actors were enclosed within a controlled space, deliberately cut off from vistas of the outer world and concentrating on the performance at hand.

A second type of outdoor entertainment space in the Roman world was the amphitheater, of which the most noted example was the Colosseum, or Flavian Amphitheater, in Rome (Fig. 7-3). (It was called the Colosseum because a 100-foot-tall statue, the Colossus, stood near it. We call it the Flavian Amphitheater because the Flavian emperors who ruled after Nero built it.) Large crowds could gather in this elliptical structure to witness the gladitorial combats that were the Romans' favorite violent sport. Sometimes the arena was flooded and mock naval battles were staged, or the less warlike water ballet was performed. We know from wall paintings that an amphitheater existed in the southern Italian town of Pompeii as early as the first century B.C. Apparently the old custom of holding such combats in the forum, as Vitruvius records, was abandoned by the early first century. The elliptical shape was designed to increase the number of spectators and the visibility of the event. Like the theaters, amphitheaters were set up on supporting arches, and could be placed wherever they were needed.

All major cities of the Roman Empire had a circus as well as an amphitheater and a theater or two. Roman stadiums seem to have developed from the Greek: both were shaped like a long narrow U and both were used for racing. An example in Rome is the Circus Maximus, where horse and chariot races were held. Races were easily as popular as the gladitorial games and were the delight of all levels of society. In fact, the Circus Maximus is just below the windows of the palace on the Palatine Hill, so that to watch the races the emperors need only go out on a balcony and look down.

Theaters, amphitheaters, and circuses were extremely important in the daily life of ancient Rome because the problem of how the conquerors of

Figure 7-3 Colosseum (Flavian Amphitheater), Rome, Italy, last third of first century, as shown on a coin minted from 238 to 244. A lion and an elephant battle inside the arena, watched by a crowd whose heads are shown as dots except for one larger figure, possibly the emperor. Outside stands the enormous statue (colossus) that gave the amphitheater its popular name. (Photo reprinted by permission of Fototeca Unione, Italy.)

the world were to keep themselves occupied was an acute one. About half the population of Rome lived on the dole, an ancient welfare system that provided their food; many others were rich and did not have to work for a living. As nearly as we can understand, people lived crowded into apartment houses. They spent most of their time outdoors in the mild Mediterranean climate, going home only to sleep. Bread and circuses were then necessities of daily life, circuses being all the available entertainment that filled up the time of the half that never worked and the other half that had 180 official holidays a year.

Other outdoor spaces were arranged for general rather than specific use. Beginning in the late first century B.C., cities had also the luxury of colonnades built along their main streets, separating the sidewalks from the paved street and providing shade from the blazing sun and shelter from occasional torrential rain. This custom seems to have begun simultaneously in Syria and in Rome itself, from whence it spread throughout the Empire. (See Fig. 7-4, a colonnaded street in ancient Gerasa, now in Jordan.) The colonnade served to emphasize by its presence the open space of the streets and to differentiate major public streets from the modest streets of residential areas. Often the colonnaded streets were punctuated with triumphal arches (particularly in the western part of the empire) or tetrapylons (four-sided gateways) in the east. Fountains as well as honorific statues were frequently inserted into the colonnades.

The two main streets of a Roman town—the *cardo* and the *decumanus*—led from the main gates to the center of the town and intersected there at right angles. As with many subtle Greek ideas, the idea of axiality became in Roman hands a strong declarative statement that was relatively culture-free. That is, no one needed to explain to a stranger that a straight street led from the gate to the central business district and then on to the gate on the far side of town; a glance was enough to make this plain. The same linear form being repeated at right angles to the first in town after town of the Roman world left no doubt that interlocking axes were the basis of Roman town planning.

Every Roman city had a major public area at the center, placed usually to one side of that major intersection. The forum was used like the Greek agora for a multitude of purposes. By the second half of the first century B.C., the lessons of Hellenistic urban development were assimilated to Roman practice, and the forum was treated as a great outdoor room, completely enclosed by porticoes (roofed colonnades) standing in front of walls or buildings. At one end of the rectangular space stood a temple to the chief gods of the Roman state, Jupiter, Juno, and Minerva. Civic office buildings and the law court (basilica) were placed along the sides or at the other end; colonnades unified

Figure 7-4 Colonnaded plaza and streets in Gerasa (Jerash, in present-day Jordan). The unusual oval shape of the forum alerts the visitor to the high quality of urban design at this site. The main street runs northward from the plaza and is intersected twice by lesser colonnaded streets (one visible here at left center). Above that side street are the columns of the sanctuary of Artemis:—the short ones lined her courtyard and the tall ones ringed the temple itself. (Photo, author.)

the great courtyard. Statues were placed between the columns or just in front of them or (in the east) on pedestals jutting from the columns. The space itself was thus available for many different functions—civic, religious, and commercial.

The pressure of population and activity on the forum in the city of Rome led, by the middle of the first century B.C., to the decision to provide separate *fora* (forums)in more convenient locations for the activities that consumed the most space and caused the most disruption. Separate fora were thus built near the Tiber River—one for selling produce and one for selling animals for meat. The old forum was left for political use and sale of less bulky items. This solution was not sufficient, however, so that one after another of the rulers of Rome added more fora to serve as the headquarters of the government of a world empire.

The first of the new fora was that built by Julius Caesar at the edge of the old Roman forum (called the Forum Romanum). Caesar set the basic pattern that was to be followed in all later fora: an open rectangular court completely surrounded by colonnades, accessible through a monumental gateway opposite a great temple. He also set the pattern of payment for the forum by buying the land and materials and paying the laborers from the spoils of the campaign in Gaul. A Roman ruler did not have the right to seize land for the good of the state. If he wanted some land for civic purposes, he had to persuade the owner to sell or donate; some emperors did not scruple to apply force to landowners in order to carry out their building schemes (see Fig. 7-5a and b).

Figure 7-5a   The imperial forums, Rome. From left to right: the temple, basilica, forum, and markets of Trajan; the forum and temple of Augustus, with the forum of Caesar visible below it; the long narrow forum of Nerva (Forum Transitorium); and finally the square forum of Peace, built by Vespasian. Just beyond the forums are the bulk of the basilica of Constantine and the temple of Venus and Rome, with the Colosseum at the top of the photo. The dates of the forums range from 50 B.C. to 125 A.D. (Photo by W. Connor of the model of Rome in the Museo della Civilita Romana.)

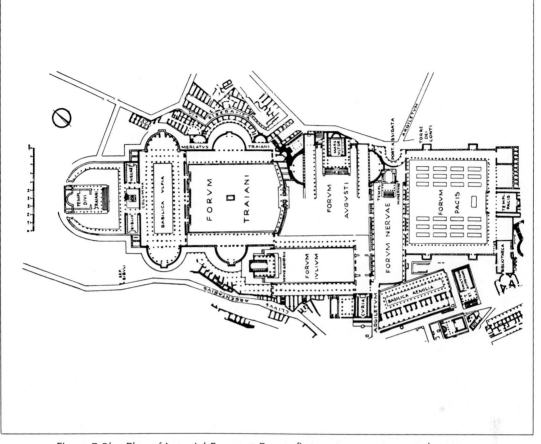

Figure 7-5*b*   Plan of Imperial Forum at Rome, first century B.C. to second century A.D. All the fora have an open court surrounded by colonnades and an entrance at one end opposite a temple at the other end. All are rectangular in general configuration, although their edges are enriched by exedra both rounded and squared. From left to right: the Forum of Trajan includes the temple dedicated to him by his successor Hadrian, the Greek and Latin libraries flanking the column of Trajan, the basilica that carries Trajan's family name, the forum proper with the markets and probable administrative offices organized around the Via Biberatica; the Forum of Augustus with its temple to Mars; below it the first imperial forum, that of Julius Caesar with its temple to the goddess Venus who was considered the ancestress of his family; the narrow Forum of Nerva, mostly a monumentalized segment of the street called Argiletum, but also containing a temple of Minerva; and at right the Forum of Peace built by Vespasian and Titus, with a small temple to Peace, flanked by another pair of Greek and Latin libraries and reached through a formal garden with long, narrow beds of flowers and trees. At the bottom of the plan, the Curia and Basilica Aemilia form the upper edge of the Roman Forum, which goes back to the sixth century B.C. and was much more irregular. (Plan courtesy Fototeca Unione.)

After the first addition under Caesar, one forum after another was added to the complex: Augustus's, at right angles to Caesar's; the Forum of Peace built by Vespasian and Titus at the close of the Jewish War, on the other side of Augustus's from Caesar; that of Nerva, called the Forum Transitorium because it occupied a narrow passage from the old Roman forum parallel to Augustus's Forum; and finally that of Trajan (finished by Hadrian), parallel to the older one of Julius Caesar's. The axes of these great open spaces interlocked tightly (as one can see in the beautiful diagrams of Bacon's *Design of Cities*). The richness of the spatial experience within the group of fora was intense. Axiality within each forum, however, was not repeated outside it in any adjacent or preparatory spaces, as it would have been in a city of the seventeenth century, for instance. Close inspection shows, in fact, that there were no great axial boulevards leading to any of the fora. Indeed, these great public spaces were not even separated or joined by the sorts of narrow winding streets that served as connectors elsewhere in Rome. Instead, one forum opened directly into another, and all of them together formed an interlocking border for the original Forum Romanum.

Within these adjacent courtyards were inserted roofed spaces, not only obligatory temples but also in several cases libraries or basilicas. The basilicas of the fora were an old-fashioned type with wooden truss roofs, which we will discuss when we look at early Christian architecture. At other places in Roman cities, however, experimentation was going on in the use of vaulting to cover large interior spaces. Thanks to their easy access to both money and talent, the emperors were first to make experiments with vaulting, particularly in their palaces. These experiments with interior space may be seen most clearly in palaces and other imperial constructions.

Only fragments of the Golden House (palace) of Nero have come down to us, since his successors built over its site in a conscious attempt to obliterate his impact on the city and thus win favor with the people. What remains however shows that Nero and his architect Severus were both innovative and daring. Using the technology of concrete construction which the Romans had been experimenting with for about 150 years and incorporating the spatial elaborations of the late Hellenistic period, they produced a large and complex structure. Its octagonal dining room, for instance, was domed and from its hidden windows indirect light flowed down upon those gathered below. Subsidiary rooms, also lighted from above, added an envelope of multifaced space around the central octagon. One of the rooms had a stair-shaped fountain down which water gurgled to humidify the air and to add its pleasant chatter to the festivities.

Experiments with complicated indoor spaces were carried further at the Emperor Hadrian's villa at Tivoli in the hills outside Rome, in the second and third decade of the second century. Hadrian seems to have been his own architect, one of the few architects in history with resources that matched his imagination. His palace, which sprawled for acres over the hillside, was composed, like the forum complex in Rome, of a series of interlocking axes. There were both indoor and outdoor spaces as well as roofed outdoor spaces that provided transitions from the one to the other. The plan of any one structure was dominated by bilateral symmetry, but the group of spaces was very free in its composition of large and small, open and closed, dark and light spaces. This palace further resembles the fora at Rome in having spaces that locked into one another rather than processional ways.

Experiments in spatial complexity bore fruit in the public bath buildings that Hadrian and other emperors built all over the empire. Baths were particularly rich in their spatial forms and relations and seem to have carried rich symbolic meanings, which made them particularly suitable for donations by public benefactors. In the Greco-Roman world, it was considered essential for rich persons to appear generous. They were expected to endow their cities with structures necessary for the common life. By endowing baths in so many Roman cities, emperors were acquiring local importance and relevance and receiving local glory.

We will look only at the Baths of Caracalla in Rome, as an impressive member of this class of buildings (Fig. 7-6). Caracalla, who was emperor in the third century, understood well the propaganda value of erecting a magnificent public bath building in Rome as well as creating an endowment for its maintenance. The bath occupied a very large area, being surrounded by its own wall and supplied by its own aqueduct. Within the wall were ample

Figure 7-6   Baths of Caracalla, early third century, Rome. Mosaic and marble revetments and pavings are mostly gone, but the concrete and brick structure endures in large part. Only the central vault has fallen in. Note the two human figures standing in the far archway to get an idea of the scale of this interior space. (Photo by J. Null.)

gardens where one could stroll with books from the two libraries, one for Greek and one for Latin manuscripts. On the back wall was a half stadium, built over the reservoirs of the baths. At the center of the complex stood the elaborate bath buildings, with separate spaces for hot, cold, and tepid bathing, as well as steam baths and hot dry baths. Rooms for massage, dressing, and only lounging about were provided along with interior courtyards for exercise and latrines with marble seats. People went to the baths to spend a half day or full day, to fill up numerous holidays. They strolled on pavements of inlaid marble or mosaic and looked at walls and vaults richly decorated with mosaics or slabs of decorative marble (revetments). No expense was spared to make the decoration equal in splendor to the vastness of the vaulted spaces. Each of the hot, cold, and tepid baths was vaulted in a different shape.

These vast interior spaces were made possible by use of concrete construction in combination with stone and brick to form vaults and domes (MacDonald, *The Architecture of the Roman Empire*). By the early years of the second century, Roman architects knew how to build a free-standing domed structure such as the Pantheon. Hadrian may also have been the architect for this structure, although he enjoyed the conceit of labeling the building "M. Agrippa made me" after Augustus's son-in-law of 150 years earlier. Unlike the domed interiors of baths, which always had auxiliary structures to buttress their spreading thrusts, the Pantheon is completely self-supporting. The Pantheon remains one of the outstanding buildings of the world, despite centuries of low maintenance. No one who visits it can fail to be impressed by the contrast between the sculptural mass of its temple portico (porch) facade and the vast volume of its interior space. The contrast would have been even more acute in ancient times when a traditional temple courtyard with colonnades would have obscured one's view of the great cylinder and one would have seen only the traditional temple porch. Like the baths, the interior of the Pantheon was enriched by mosaics (now gone), marble revetment, and inlaid floors. But its greatest glory was the occulus, or opening at the top, some 38 feet wide, which was the sole source of light for the interior, except for what filtered in through the doorway. Roman architecture manipulated light with as much enthusiasm as it did space, and in this interior the two are welded in an impressive manner. Since the intellectual concept of the Pantheon's interior is so very simple—a cylinder topped by a half sphere of the same radius—the visitor is unprepared for the staggering impact of the space. Standing at the center, one is barely aware of the alternately rectangular and semicircular niches behind pairs of columns that enliven the lower walls. One is more conscious of the coffering (recessed square paneling) of the ceiling, leading up to the open "eye" at the top of the dome. Indeed, some observers have reported a most dynamic effect of this coffering, which seems to converge evermore rapidly on the occulus. In certain lights and from certain positions, the dome is perceived as a cylinder opening out into and including the vastness of outer space (Fig. 7-7).

Roman organization of space was not the same as was Greek organization of polar space. An observer of Greek architecture was required to comprehend

Figure 7-7   Pantheon, Rome, 125. Built and possibly designed by the Emperor
Hadrian. Better than a camera, this painting catches the vastness of the interior,
nearly 140 feet in diameter. (A painting done in the eighteenth century by G. P.
Panini, reproduced courtesy of Samuel H. Kress Collection, National Gallery of Art,
Washington, D.C.)

the space from a fixed entry point; the visitor observing Roman space was expected to experience it by moving through it. One was expected to walk directly through the center of the space so that the same features were set at the same distances to left and right, in bilateral symmetry. The Egyptian idea of axial progression seems to have been combined with the Greek idea of public architecture. Grandeur, especially grandeur of scale, was always the goal of the Roman architect. Roman space was more overt and less subtle than was Greek space. Although angles in Roman architecture are present and are used for dramatic effect, they are present through the interlocking of axes rather than through scenographic arrangement of panoramas. Roman space has proved astonishingly transcultural. It has been rediscovered and reused at many times and places in the west after the fall of Rome. Designed to serve a multicultural empire, this space has been easily understood not only by expert archeologists and architects but also by many educated persons some 2000 years later.

A great deal of the poetry of architecture seems to be tied up with the idea of space. Architects, architectural critics, and architectural historians seem to use the word in a variety of allusive ways in an attempt to find verbal equivalents for some of the aesthetic and psychological effects of architecture. The problem of how to verbalize architecture may go back as far as the Romans, who invented, or discovered, space in their built environment.

Is the space endless and amorphous, like that of the galaxies, or defined, separated, enclosed, and molded? Both kinds are a locus around which things and events occur and have relative position and direction, but the architectural space is more akin to mass, the measured amount of material contained, or to volume, measured occupied space. The Romans quickly saw that such space can be open or closed as well as public or private. The architectural manipulation of space became a major theme in their architecture.

BIBLIOGRAPHY

Bacon, E., *Design of Cities,* Viking, New York, 1967. Many beautiful diagrams of ancient, medieval, and later plans for cities.

Boethius, A., *The Golden House of Nero,* University of Michigan Press, Ann Arbor, Mich., 1960. A study of the great palace, and of ordinary urban housing that influenced European housing for many hundreds of years.

Doxiadis, C., *Architectural Space in Ancient Greece,* M.I.T., Cambridge, Mass., 1972. A translation of his doctoral dissertation from the 1930's, this book is inaccurate in some details but stimulating in its treatment of the way buildings were grouped.

MacDonald, W., *The Architecture of the Roman Empire,* Yale University Press, New Haven, Conn., 1965. Illustrated copiously with both photographs and drawings (the latter by B. M. Boyle). Excellent study of the Markets and Forum of Trajan.

MacDonald, W., *The Pantheon,* Harvard University Press, Cambridge, Mass., 1976. The definitive work on the Pantheon to date.

Zevi, B., *Architecture as Space,* Horizon, New York, 1979. Stimulating, with many good plans.

8

ROMAN ENGINEERING

THE BUILDING INDUSTRY

In considering Roman treatment of space, we encountered important building types such as the great vaulted spaces of the baths and of imperial palaces, or the older tradition of post and lintel structures as seen in the temples and basilicas. Besides these, the Romans were builders of large numbers of structures that today we would classify as civil engineering projects. These included roads, aqueducts and sewers, bridges, harbors, and city ramparts. So firmly built were these structures, so abundantly spread throughout the empire, that even today one finds many examples surviving, from the harbor at Leptis Magna in North Africa to Hadrian's Wall in northern England and as far east as the fortress city of Dura-Europos on the Euphrates River in present-day Syria.

While examining typical examples of these engineering works, we will also cover such questions as how the building industry was organized in Roman times, and what difference that made in what could be built. By implication, the wider questions of the limitations and possibilities inherent in any approach to organizing the building industry will become apparent.

HISTORICAL EVIDENCE ABOUT ANCIENT BUILDING PRACTICES

How do we know about Roman building practices? In Chap. 7 we discussed the Colosseum depicted on a coin and the Circus Maximus on a bas-relief, so we know that those two sorts of evidence are available. We can conclude that the Romans made frequent use of plans, because permanent plans survive in the form of mosaics, marble reliefs, and wall or manuscript paintings. Most famous of these carved plans is the marble plan of Rome, placed in the third century on the outer wall of the Forum of Peace (Fig. 8-1). In this plan, every street and even every building was represented in plan, each type of edifice shown by a different conventional symbol. About half this plan has been recovered and set up on a wall in the Vatican gardens. A mosaic plan with the measurements of rooms has been published by MacDonald in *The Architecture of the Roman Empire*.

More general information has been preserved in manuscripts, such as the map of the late Roman road system of Italy.* Other information comes from tomb paintings that depict architects and builders at their work.

At least two major architectural engineering manuscripts from the turn of the millenium have come down to us. The architect Vitruvius dedicated his books to the Emperor Augustus, in the last years of the first century. His work drew heavily on architectural treatises from the classical and Hellenistic periods, mostly lost to us, and also on his own practical experience in building. His comments on the education of architects are both revealing and amusing, because he apparently expected the architect to be a multifaceted genius skilled in mathematics, drawing, history, philosophy, music, medicine, law, astronomy, and cosmology.

The other treatise is by Frontinus, who was supervisor of the aqueducts of the city of Rome at about the same time. His is a matter-of-fact approach to technical problems of the system. He simply describes the municipal water system and prescribes ways for his successors to keep it functioning.

Finally, ruins and buildings still in good condition are an important source of information about Roman building practice. From both Rome itself and its provincial cities there still exist a great many examples. Now ruined are the

*As shown in *Die Peutinger Tafel*, K. Miller, ed., republished in Stuttgart by F. A. Brockhaus, Abt. Antiquarian, 1962, after an early Christian manuscript.

Figure 8-1 Detail of the Marble Plan of Rome, third century. Colonnaded streets and buildings with porticoes are represented by rows of dots, some enclosed in squares to indicate elaborate bases, and others shown as single or double lines to represent walls. Documents and mosaic plans are our other evidence for the sophistication of the architectural profession in the Roman Empire. (Plan courtesy Fototeca Unione.)

Roman port in Ostia (visible only in aerial photographs) and the harbor at Leptis Magna, now silted up. In good condition are the aqueduct in Segovia and the ramparts of Rome.

THE ROMAN ROAD SYSTEM

The Roman road system is a good starting place for an understanding of how the building industry was organized. An excellent transportation and communication system essential for the maintenance of the empire was made difficult by the fact that at the center of the empire lay the Mediterranean Sea, which could be traversed only by boat and then only at certain times of the year. Such circumstances made land transport more crucial. The Romans consequently developed the first interstate highway system, used by commerce, private individuals, and government couriers as well as marching armies.

Roads were built and maintained by the imperial government. To build the roads, an engineer-architect (the two professions were not really distinct) who was likely to have been trained in the army was assigned a particular sector. He was also assigned a sufficient number of soldiers to do the actual construction. Materials were purchased in large amounts and in standardized measures, so that economies of scale were realized. After the engineer had surveyed the path of the road, his troops began work. In the mountains it was necessary to carve out the path through solid rock; in low-lying areas, a roadbed deep as 12 feet might be needed. Large boulders were placed at the bottom of the trench for the road and smaller stones were laid on top of them until ground level was reached. In the western part of the empire, the standard paving stone was basalt; in the east and in North Africa a shiny white limestone was used. So well built were these roads that they remained the major European communication system until the eighteenth century. The ancient Via Appia outside Rome, lined with Roman tombs and evergreen trees, is still impressive. Such roads conquered the endless deserts until the shifting sand reclaimed the ways. Traces of the old roads can still be made out in the Syrian desert at sunset in the raking light, or after a rain when tiny plants spring up among the rows of pebbles that mark the edges of the road.

CITY RAMPARTS

Architect-engineers trained in the army would also have been involved in the erection of city ramparts. During the long Pax Romana, city walls were largely symbolic. When the barbarian invasions of the third century occurred, however, walls were built or rebuilt around all the major cities of the empire. In 270, for instance, a complete new circuit of walls was put up around Rome in about 6 months, under the general supervision of the soldier Emperor Aurelian (Fig. 8-2). Aurelian's wall measures nearly 19 kilometers around. It includes 381 towers spaced about 100 Roman feet (29.6 meters) apart. There are eight major gates plus several posterns (small gates). The major gates are usually faced with marble to increase their beauty and their imposing effect. The posterns, now mostly bricked up, were simple arched openings in the wall. The wall is of brick and concrete. Some buildings were incorporated into the wall; others were torn down for materials to use between the faces of the wall. Originally 7 1/2 to 8 meters tall, the wall is now 10 meters tall in some places because of subsequent rebuildings, in 403 and later. To facilitate movement of soldiers from place to place, rampart walks were built into the inside of the wall. Some seem to be carved out of the solid wall, whereas

Figure 8-2   Porta Appia, Rome, 270 and later, built by Emperor Aurelian and made taller in the early fifth century. The towers flanking the gateway are faced with marble which contrasts strongly with the utilitarian brick and concrete structure of the wall. Aurelian's wall was built in 6 months by gangs of city workers under the supervision of military engineers. It was intended to deter roving bands of Germanic invaders. (Photo from Fototeca Unione.)

others appear like ledges supported by arches. Most stretches of the wall have one rampart walk, but in places where the wall was made taller in the fifth century, there is a second walk at the higher level. Here and there on the outer surface of the wall, latrines still survive; the waste material would have fallen into a ditch below the outer face of the wall.

BUILDING WORK CREW

The emergency of 270—invasion by Germanic tribes—made it necessary to use amateur labor in building this set of walls. Each section of the walls was built by a neighborhood gang, under the direction of experienced military engineers. Under ordinary circumstances, construction was the carefully subdivided business of the various trades: demolition experts, unskilled and skilled workers such as the hod carriers or the carpenters who made the wooden forms for concrete wall and vaults, producers of the large amounts of standardized building materials (stone, brick, wood for framing, marble for veneers, mosaics, concrete which involved lime, sand, and aggregate), painters, and the supervising architect-engineers who were also responsible for surveying and for laying the building out on the ground.

In addition to the military training and experience mentioned already, there was a second method of developing the necessary professionals. Greek practice had called for the sons and nephews of architects to enter the family business and be trained by their older relative. Among the Romans this method was supplemented by liberal arts schooling that drew upon an accumulated library of architectural texts. These men were then attached to a professional architect to learn the practical rudiments of the trade by doing tasks with and for him in his office and in the field.

GREEK AND ROMAN BUILDING PRACTICE COMPARED

The Greek system of building could be characterized as custom-made, and that of the Roman's as mass-produced. With the Greeks, the building industry was organized so that the edifice was the cooperative product of many skilled artisans working together. The Greek architect made some planning decisions and some decisions about details, but his creativity was sharply limited by tradition. Organization of the Greek building industry depended upon fine tuning of the relation between quality of local stone, local craft traditions, budget and local patriotism, and the amount of architectural attention that could be afforded. In Greek architecture, knowledge of how to erect a major building and finish its details belonged as much to the individual artisan as to the architect. The architect, in fact, relied on this knowledge to fill out the scanty indications of the process and the intended result.

Among the Romans, on the other hand, a structure was the result of combining many preformed standard items like ingredients in a recipe. Each worker, in this case, was a cog in the assembly line. The architect, neither hampered nor helped by a strong craft tradition, was much freer to make decisions about the form of the building. The Roman architectural imagination was limited only by the ability of carpenters to construct form work—and that ability was developed to a highly sophisticated degree. The architect became a form giver whose grand concepts were realized by an army of unskilled and a smaller number of skilled workers. There was a great gulf between the common worker and the highly educated architect. Many of the workers were slaves who shared neither language nor customs with the professionals who were their overseers. Other members of the building industry seem to have continued in the older tradition of apprenticeship to learn the skills necessary to their craft or trade.

Roman building called for the piling up of great quantities—even millions —of separate pieces of aggregate (stone or tile used as filler in concrete) and other types of materials, which had to be shipped to the site in the proper order and amount. At the site, the architect and his assistants had to supervise the placement of the materials by hundreds of workers, while the workers made none of the design decisions. Coordinating the work of so many types of workers was difficult. Many more aspects of the design and of the building process had to be spelled out in plans. Roman architects usually coped with the variables in this task by overbuilding, making the structure more massive than we would now consider strictly necessary, so that any oversights or inadequacies would be compensated for. Structural systems as well as the way the work of construction was organized had to allow for realities.

BUILDING MATERIALS

That innovation was possible within the traditional trades is well illustrated by the developing use of concrete as a major building material. For many centuries mortar had been used in construction, but the Romans seem to have been the first to recognize its potential as a building material in its own right. By the end of the second century B.C., experimentation with arched forms and cements had progressed to such an extent that arched forms were no longer being hidden within passages (as in the temple of Apollo at Didyma) but were brought forward to appear in the facades of such buildings as the Sanctuary of Fortuna at ancient Praeneste. Even the most daring architect could not design with these possibilities in mind without an existing body of knowledge that had been accumulated by masons, carpenter-form makers, and contractors. It is significant that the knowledge explosion about how to build in concrete came in Italy where volcanic ash (*pozzalana*) was readily available for use with sand, lime, and water to make a concrete distinctive in its properties: not only did it dry quickly and consistently, but it was also extremely hard, durable, and waterproof. The vaulted style of building that developed in Italy in the first centuries B.C. and A.D. spread then throughout the Roman world, but always with local variation depending on local materials and the experience of local workers with those materials.

It was imperial patronage that made possible the early and continued experiments with vaulting. Typical in its imperial patronage and variety though unusual in its quality and geographic distribution was the work of Apollodorus of Damascus. Under the Emperor Trajan he built a famous bridge over the Danube River so that Roman conquests could be further extended into barbarian territory. He is also thought to have built the forum and markets of Trajan in Rome, and to have been influential on Hadrian's design for the Pantheon.

The results of these experiments were applied to production of public and imperial buildings at first in Rome, capital of the empire. The continuing determination of the emperors was to build public works all over the empire, as physical manifestation of the fatherly care of the emperor for his people. For the first mass society, these emperors utilized the services of both civilian and military architects and engineers. By the time of the late empire (fourth century), the emperors were quite conscious of the need for trained architects. They set up architectural schools not only in the capital cities but also in major provincial cities.

The Roman Empire may be described as a network of cities connected by roads and sea routes. The urban life of the empire was impossible without experts to design and maintain aqueducts and sewers (Fig. 8-3). Every city had officials who were charged with the building and upkeep of aqueducts and sewers; these were assisted by workers, often gangs of slaves that belonged to the municipality and whose sole function was to keep the system of water supply and drainage operating well. From the Etruscans (an Italian people who

Figure 8-3 Aqua Claudia, outside Rome. (As painted by Thomas Cole and reprinted by permission of the Wadsworth Atheneum, Hartford, Conn.) Built by the Emperor Claudius in the first century, to add to the water supply of Rome. The water was collected from mountain springs and brought across the valley on stilted arches so that it could be delivered to the hilltops within the city of Rome and hence flow by gravity to fountains and baths. This aqueduct was broken by invading Goths in the early fifth century.

Figure 8-4   The mouth of the main sewer, Cloaca Maxima, of the city of Rome used to be visible where it emptied into the Tiber River. The Romans learned about drainage from the Etruscans; under its Etruscan kings, the forum area of Rome was first drained during the sixth century B.C. This sewer seems to have been rebuilt under Augustus at the beginning of our era. Late nineteenth and early twentieth century rebuilding of the banks of the Tiber has concealed the Cloaca Maxima. (Photo from Fototeca Unione.)

preceded them), the Romans learned to carry water over considerable distances, running in channels underground or along the sides of hills or carried on the high stilts of visible aqueducts. In the city, water was distributed not only to baths but also to public fountains in every quarter.

Also from the Etruscans came the engineering knowledge of how to drain away waste water and storm runoff. Waste water and storm drainage were led to sewers running under the streets and thence out to the nearest river—in the most "modern" fashion. Until the banks of the Tiber River in Rome were rebuilt in the late nineteenth century, it was possible to see where the ancient Cloaca Maxima (great sewer) emptied out into the river (Fig. 8-4). This was the sewer that was begun under the Etruscans in a project set up to drain the valley between the central hills of Rome so that the valley could be used for a market area common to all the tribes who lived on the various hills. Over time, the sewer was extended in several branches, but all emptied out into the Tiber. Down in the subbasement of San Clemente Church in Rome, one can hear the loud roaring of the sewer on the other side of the wall, functioning as it has for about 2500 years. Such engineering works may be invisible, but their importance to an urban society can scarcely be overestimated.

BRIDGES

Another necessity of life in a river town such as Rome was bridges. Over the centuries, many were built and then again swept away by the rampaging river during a flood. However, the Pons Milvia, or Milvian Bridge, still survives from Roman times (Fig. 8-5). To build this bridge the engineer studied carefully the behavior of the water under normal and flood conditions. The roadbed of the bridge was carried on round-headed arches high enough to be above normal flooding. Each pier was wedge-shaped in plan, pointing into the current to deflect debris that the river might be carrying while in flood. The piers were built in an early form of caisson, a kind of waterproof wooden chamber sunk in the bed of the river to provide space for the workers who were placing the stones and concrete of the bridge supports. Knowledge of how each river behaved, as well as how local materials would behave under various stresses, was essential for successful bridge building. Successful building thus depended on cooperation between the various members of the building industry.

Figure 8-5   The Pons Milvia (Milvian Bridge) at Rome, oldest of the surviving Tiber bridges at this city, dates from 109 B.C. Tufa and travertine, laid up without mortar, were used to construct its semicircular arches and the pointed bulwarks which point upstream and deflect large debris from piling up against the bridge and temporarily damming the river. (Photo from Fototeca Unione.)

If an emperor wanted to build a new harbor, for instance, he would need not only his chosen architect-engineer but also local support of trained workers, material, and of course money. Emperor Claudius in the first century provided the impetus for finishing the new harbor (called Porto) near Ostia, when the mouth of the Tiber River was in danger of silting up and thus interfering with shipment of food and building supplies to Rome. This harbor was hexagonal in shape, with wharfs and warehouses surrounding the sheltered harbor. A special canal connected the harbor with the river, so that the building materials, food, and incoming passengers could be transshipped to Rome on smaller boats or barges. Later, Emperor Septimius Severus in the third century rebuilt the harbor of his native town, Leptis Magna in North Africa (in what is today Libya). Unfortunately, that harbor silted up soon afterward, so that its grand facilities were scarcely worn before being abandoned to the invading Vandals.

An increasing sophistication of building design thus went hand in hand with increasing complications with respect to the organization of the building industry. The careful work of Greek artisans who participated in the design as well as the erection of a building was superceded by limited responsibility for elements of an edifice, such as the beauty of the mosaics or the strength of the piers—all under the overall direction of the architect and often with the demanding patronage of an emperor or other powerful client. Groups of workers, such as the carpenter-form makers, still affected the results of the building process at least as profoundly as did the nature of the materials and the vision of the architect.

BIBLIOGRAPHY

Ashby, T., *The Aqueducts of Ancient Rome,* Clarendon, Oxford, 1935. The basic work on the water supply of the city of Rome. Illustrated.

Brown, F., *Roman Architecture,* Braziller, New York, 1967. Succinct and well-illustrated handbook with the basic structures presented in interesting fashion.

Macaulay, D., *City,* Houghton Mifflin, Boston, 1974. A picture book about the construction of a Roman colonial city, including the sewer system and everything above it.

Richmond, Ian A., *The City Wall of Imperial Rome,* McGraw-Hill, New York, 1971. Comparable to Ashby's book on the aqueducts. Enough illustrations to make one yearn for more.

Von Hagen, V. W., *The Roads That Led to Rome,* World, Cleveland, 1967. A travelogue, well-illustrated and well-written, about the roads that knit the Roman Empire together.

9
EARLY CHRISTIAN ARCHITECTURE

ADAPTIVE REUSE

Reuse is a word often heard in architecture today. Cities have always been rebuilt: it is their nature to change. In the past 200 years the pace of such change has been accelerated. In previous periods change was slower since new ways had to be found to use what was there before. Starting with a city from the late Roman period, we can see how buildings were adapted over time to suit new uses, and the fabric of the city was subtly changed. Some of the major early Christian buildings are other examples of reuse as a result of adaptation to different needs.

DURA-EUROPOS

Dura-Europos, an ancient town of Mesopotamia, was located on the right bank of the Euphrates River in what is today Iraq (see Fig. 9-1). When the soldiers of

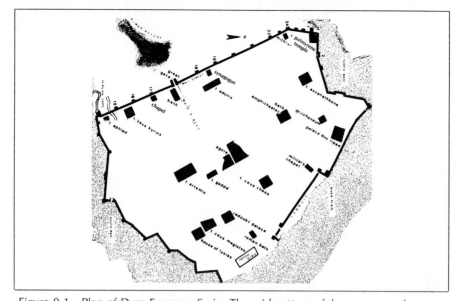

Figure 9-1 Plan of Dura-Europos, Syria. The grid pattern of the streets can be seen from the way the buildings are aligned with the straight wall at top. More irregular walls follow the contours, except at bottom, where one section has crumbled away. The agora is at center, just off the main street. The most noteworthy buildings are located along the straight wall: at upper right, the Temple of the Palmyrene Gods, remodeled from a tower of the wall; in the middle, the synagogue; and the Christian building, labeled chapel. Both synagogue and chapel were originally houses. (Plan from C. Hopkins, *The Discovery of Dura-Europos,* by permission of the publisher Yale University Press.)

Alexander the Great settled down to rule what had been the Persian Empire, they founded cities like this one all across the Middle East and gave them European names—hence Dura (the old Semitic name) plus Europos (the Greek name). The town is an example of gradual renewal of a settlement by an evolving culture.

As can be expected in a Greek town, there was an agora at the center surrounded on three sides of the rectangle by stoa-like buildings. Through intermarriage the population became less and less Greek and more and more Mesopotamian, and the open space filled up with irregular structures; thus by 100 A.D. the open market resembled an oriental bazaar. The new population used the space in ways that matched the developing orientalism of the society.

In the original plan, the Greek grid was surrounded by a wall rather loosely flung around the city on the hilly sides, advantage being taken of the terrain for defense, but with an almost straight wall along the flat desert side. There were changes through time in how this wall and its towers were used. For over 200 years, until the third quarter of the second century, when peace prevailed, there was little need for a defensive wall. The flat-roofed tower at the north extremity of the wall became a sanctuary. A major reason for this reuse of the tower had to do with the local tradition of worshiping on a high place. The gods honored in the northern tower were Palmyrene gods from the nearby capital Palmyra. (Palmyrenes frequently hired themselves out as mercenaries; while garrisoning Dura-Europos, they set up this temple to their own gods.)

The wall of Dura-Europos is important for us today because it has preserved two additional sanctuaries of major importance. During the third century, the Persians invaded this area several times. Their favorite types of warfare were raids, or sieges, in which they undermined the walls of the city they were attacking. To prevent the Persians from marching in through the holes created in their desert wall, the people of Dura-Europos reinforced the wall with a huge earthen embankment that was fairly shallow on the desert side but 35 meters deep on the inside. If the Persians tried to dig a tunnel under so much dirt, there was no collapse. The houses of the blocks nearest the wall were filled up with dirt and became part of the embankment.

It is fortunate for our study that Dura-Europos was threatened in this way, because two of the houses immured had already been reused for religious buildings. Both were small Mediterranean courtyard houses built probably in the first century. About the middle of the second century, perhaps in 165, one was turned into a Christian church (see Fig. 9-2). The house was changed very little, except for wall decorations, which are in the museum at Yale University. Though modest, this house church at Dura-Europos is one of the very earliest churches that has come down to us.

More unusual is the other house at Dura-Europos that was made into a religious building—a synagogue. The main meeting room of the Dura-Europos synagogue was painted in bands of pictures of Old Testament stories. Until this synagogue was found, it was not known that Jews of the ancient world used visual representations of human figures in their synagogues. Here in this provincial town, then, significant artifacts have been preserved through having been accidentally covered up in the embankment.

ADAPTIVE REUSE OF OLDER STRUCTURES: ADDITIONAL EXAMPLES

In Rome, some early structures have survived by being incorporated in later buildings. For instance, under the church of Saints Giovanni and Paolo lie the remains of an early apartment building. Originally it had shops along the sloping street and apartments above, in the usual pattern. Within that pattern, a Christian church was built, one which became later the titular church of a bishop. Inserted as it was within the crowded residential framework, Saints Giovanni and Paolo resembled the house church at Dura-Europos.

Early Christian building types grew out of the adaptive reuse of older structures for reasons having to do with the general history of the period. In the late Roman era, a variety of cultural strains made up the society of the empire, many of which contributed to the development of Christianity. For instance,

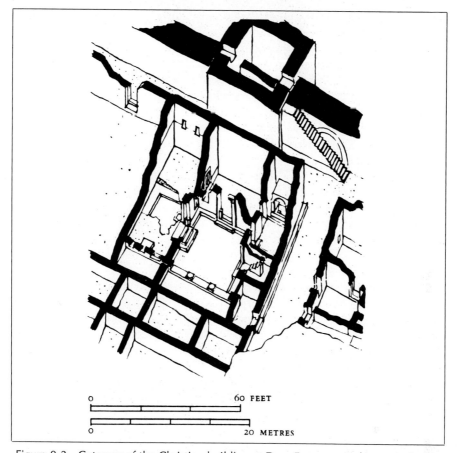

o   60 FEET

o   20 METRES

Figure 9-2 Cutaway of the Christian building at Dura-Europos. At the center is the courtyard open to the sky. The rooms surrounding the court were used for congregational services, with the baptistry located at upper right. This room, with its wall paintings of Biblical scenes, is now set up at the Yale University Art Gallery. At the upper edge of the diagram runs the city wall with a tower reached by a flight of stairs. In the third century, to strengthen this wall, a great embankment of earth was added to the inside, burying the chapel and synagogue and thus preserving them. (Drawing by Lampl for Krautheimer, *Early Christian and Byzantine Architecture,* based on J. W. Crowfoot, *Early Churches in Palestine,* Fig. 1, reprinted by permission of Oxford University Press.)

Jewish and Persian forms of worship were adopted, and Christian theological ideas were represented with both Old Testament and Mithraic symbols. Because Jews and half-assimilated pagans—potential converts to Christianity —lived in cities, the major cities of the imperial network became in turn important centers for the church's expanding network. Church organization was patterned after imperial government, with both titles and costumes being carried over into the new community. As the population became Christian, the old pagan buildings no longer had a religious use. They became houses, stores, and other public structures, as excavation has shown. Parts of the old buildings were used again to decorate new ones.

In the first, second, and third centuries, the Christian religion was officially outlawed. At that time, worship of the emperor as a god was a unifying political and religious concept. Christians who would not worship the emperor were considered traitors and were therefore persecuted.

In the early fourth century, Emperor Constantine the Great had a vision which changed the status of Christianity. As he was sleeping before an important battle for control of the empire, he saw a cross in the sky. Next morning he ordered his soldiers to put a cross on their shields. When Constantine's forces won the battle, he decided to stop the official persecution of Christians. Meetings of the sect for worship were made legal. After a while Constantine and his family became Christians. They are responsible for some important Christian buildings of the second quarter of the fourth century. The early Christian period begins with this legalization and extends until the beginning of the Dark Ages in the second half of the sixth century, overlapping somewhat with the Byzantine era.

In the fourth century, it was not clear in people's minds what a church should look like. Until the time of Constantine, Christian worship had taken place in borrowed structures. Traditional religious buildings had a negative association with pagan worship that prevented their adoption for Christian use. It took a while to work through this question of what images or forms would be proper for a religious building in the new Christian sense of religion. Both in building types and in decoration, it was well into the fourth century before the iconography (meaning of forms) and the content of the religion were compatible. (See *The Age of Spirituality,* and Panofsky's *Renaissance and Renascences.*)

TOMBS AND CATACOMBS

One possible alternative was to use an imperial tomb as a church building—a satisfactory combination of iconography and building, stating the Christian message of resurrection after death. The church of St. George at Salonika in Greece was originally an imperial tomb. It is a massive round building, rather like a coarse version of the Pantheon. The church of Santa Costanza in Rome is of the same type. Following the imperial tradition going back through Hadrian and Augustus to the Etruscans, Costanza, the daughter of Constantine, built a fine circular tomb for herself. Santa Costanza also adopted the plan and section of the Pantheon, with a lower space that introduces one to the high central domed space. This tomb was also later used as a church.

Another tomb type associated with the death and hence the resurrection of Christ, is the catacomb, which was not a new concept. Even in pagan times, it had been prudent to excavate underground corridors in stone to inter people in slits in the walls rather than use up precious agricultural land around a city. Mixed Christian and pagan catacombs, purely pagan ones, and even Jewish ones, are known to have existed in several cities of the empire, such as Syracuse, Antioch, and Alexandria. The Christians made something more meaningful of their catacombs than did others who used them.

Among the Romans it was customary to form burial societies, in which members could count on the group burying them and caring for their widows and orphans. At the same time, it was illegal to have political meetings or to belong to religions that the state proscribed. The Christians therefore called themselves a burial society. Among the burial corridors were occasional rooms where an important person could be honored by a free-standing coffin at one end or in the center. The Christians gathered in such a room around the remains of one of their martyrs, using the coffin as the table for their sacrificial meal.

When Christianity became legal, among the very first churches that were built out in the open air were shrines to favorite martyrs buried in the catacomb areas. The combined function of tomb and place of celebration of the martyr became the theme for a special type of shrine. Here the people came to honor not only the martyr but also the dead from their own families who were buried in the catacombs and to have memorial services for them. The building was then a special-event church, where people went at stated intervals after a death. A typical church of this kind was St. Agnese in Rome, a simple truss-roofed basilica with an apse at one end. It was built after 330, of brick-faced concrete, a favorite Roman combination that persisted in Italy into the early sixth century. Looking at the interior, we can see that the altar table in the shape of a tomb has become universal. The columns are of different materials, because they have been reused from different earlier buildings.

Reuse of buildings and their elements was common among the Romans. Most famous is the case of a public latrine at Ostia, where the seats are of marble slabs that had previously been gravestones. The sides carved with names, dates, and so on, were placed downward for their new use as seats. This reuse took place during the second century.

Not merely gravestones but a whole cemetery site could be reused—and was in the two famous examples we will now discuss. The Church of the Holy Sepulcher in Jerusalem (345) and the basilica in Rome dedicated to St. Peter (about a decade earlier) (see Figs. 9-3 to 9-5).

CHURCH OF THE HOLY SEPULCHER

Constantine and his family were patrons of the two structures. Helena, mother of Constantine, became a Christian long before her son. She made a pious journey to Jerusalem, hoping to find the True Cross on which Jesus had been crucified. (You can read an interesting account of this in Evelyn Waugh's novel *Helena*.) The Christian community in Jerusalem preserved knowledge of where the events of Good Friday and Easter had taken place and were able to guide her to that area. She arranged to build a church at the site of these events,

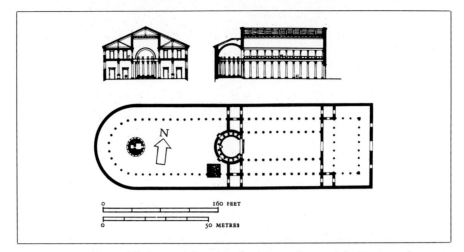

Figure 9-3   Plan and sections of the Church of the Holy Sepulcher in Jerusalem, as built in the second quarter of the fourth century under the patronage of the imperial family, especially the Dowager Empress Helena. The church consisted of an atrium for catachumens, the church proper made of a high nave flanked on each side by a pair of side aisles, a rotundalike apse, the square Rock of Calvary, and a small rotunda enshrining the Holy Sepulcher. Processions could leave the church through the doors at the end of one aisle, circle the Holy Sepulcher and the Rock, and return to the church by doors in the opposite aisle. (Drawing by Lampl for Krautheimer, *Early Christian and Byzantine Architecture,* 1985, based on E. K. H. Wistraud, *Konstantins Kirche am Heiligen Grab,* Fig. 1 by permission of Wettergren & Kerber, publishers.)

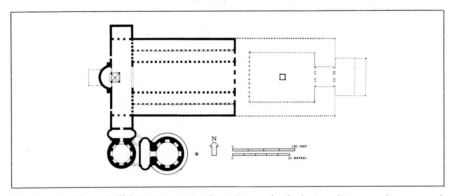

Figure 9-4   Plan of Old St. Peter's Basilica, Rome, built during the second quarter of the fourth century under the patronage of Emperor Constantine. Like the Church of the Holy Sepulcher, St. Peter's had a tall nave and lower side aisles. The atrium, or gathering place out in front, may never have been completely enclosed. The apse is separated from the nave by the bema (later called a transept), an oblong space as tall as the nave. The main altar, designated here by a square enclosing an X, stood over a second-century shrine to St. Peter. Outside at the south end of the bema stood two Pantheon-like rotundas built as imperial tombs and later reused as chapels. Between

Figure 9-5   Courtyard of Old St. Peter's Basilica during the construction of the new (Renaissance) structure. In the foreground is the shrine that enclosed the ancient pinecone. Behind it (shaded) is a wing of the papal palace. Across the center of the picture stretches the portico through which one entered the church. Rising above that, one sees the gabled nave and the sloping roofs of the lower side aisles. On a much vaster scale, Michelangelo's drum and south transept apse indicate how the new church gradually encroached upon the old one. (Drawing by G. A. Dosio, reprinted by permission of Staatliche Museen Preussicher Kulturbesitz Kupferstichkabinett, Berlin.) Compare with Fig. 17-3.

the right one and the north arrow is a small square with a dot, the location of the obelisk that stood on the spine of the circus of Nero where St. Peter was crucified. (Plan by Lampl for Krautheimer, *Early Christian and Byzantine Architecture*, based on A. Fraser, *A Graphic Reconstruction of Old St. Peter's*, M. A. Thesis, N.Y.U., 1957 reprinted by permission.)

which had happened very close together. The cross had been set up on a hill, and Jesus's body was then taken down across a small valley and placed in a new tomb of a row cut in the rock opposite.

When Helena and her architects attempted to build the new church, it became apparent that the ancient geography was a problem They therefore cut out the hill site where the cross was supposed to have stood, leaving an outcropping of stone but otherwise leveling off the hill, as was the Roman practice. They thus obtained a level site that extended over the small valley to the tomb, whereon they put up a compound structure that ultimately had several uses. This particular church had to cope with three problems: a meetingplace for the congregation, preserving the Rock of Calvary and access to it, and preserving the tomb and access to it. A separate solution was found for each problem.

Like Roman houses, and the earlier Pantheon, the Church of the Holy Sepulcher had an atrium in front where people who perhaps did not belong to the faith could gather because they were curious and interested. The congregation assembled for the eucharistic service was accommodated in an interior space. At the far end of that space were doors leading to the courtyards in back. Individuals or processions could go to the Rock of Calvary and to the tomb and then back into the church. Later than the fourth century, a rotunda was built over the tomb area. Many churches throughout the next 1200 years copied the style of this rotunda—that is, some of the features, such as the use of twelve columns were the same. Medieval churches reused some but not all of the architectural ideas of the Church of the Holy Sepulcher.

As a solution for a congregational meeting place, early Christian architects adopted the Roman basilica, a law-court building—a type that was appealing because it could handle large numbers of people and had some relation to the law, for Christians considered themselves to be living under the new law given by Christ.

Among the Romans, the basilica was actually a function rather than a type of building. In theory it could be round or elliptical, but it was generally a narrow rectangle with either a wooden truss roof or vaulting. The Christians opted for the wooden roofs, perhaps because of poverty. However, the social and architectural organization that had made great vaulted structures possible no longer existed in the west, where the truss-roofed basilica became dominant. Adapted from Roman models was division of space into a high central nave with lower side aisles. Galleries were frequently placed over the side aisles. At least one short end was an apse, a curved space where the image was set up that legalized the proceeding in the building. In the Roman basilica, it was an image of the emperor, without which nothing that took place in the court was valid. In the Christian basilica, the image was of Christ. Christ was then thought of as judge and ruler.

The other basilica associated with Constantine is St. Peter's in Rome. To make clear the connection between this structure and his sovereignty, Constantine directed that it be built (after 330) with a ground plan in the form of a cross, the sign under which he had conquered. Like St. Agnese, this basilica was built in a cemetery area—in fact, over the cemetery in which St. Peter was buried.

In the first century, Nero built a circus in this area outside the built-up city. The area was used for a long time as the site of horse races and chariot races. To add a little zest to the chariot racing, the Romans would sometimes crucify criminals or rebellious slaves along the spine of the circus. St. Peter was crucified here and then buried in the adjacent cemetery. The cemetery continued to be used for another 250 years, until Constantine decided to build his great memorial church there in honor of Peter.

Already in the second century (ca. 160) a shrine had been built over Peter's grave. Excavations under the present building began in 1965 and physical evidence has confirmed many of the traditional explanations of the location and form of the church. Some fragments such as columns match early depictions of Peter's shrine. The bones of a man of about 65, found just where Peter's bones ought to have been, are at least suggestive. Thus, a strong tradition and physical evidence connect Peter with this particular site. The evidence helps to explain the compelling religious reasons for building old St. Peter's here, even though the area was not physically satisfactory as a site for a very large church. The slope of the land down to the river and the interfering preexistence of the cemetery that had to be preserved meant that site was difficult and troublesome to prepare. Tons of fill dirt were needed, for instance, to make a level platform for the church. The cracking and sagging that finally caused old Saint Peter's to be torn down and replaced was probably caused by the church's having been built on filled land.

Like the Church of the Holy Sepulcher in Jerusalem, the basilica of St. Peter's was planned to include the spot of the martyr's death, on the spine of the circus, as well as the site of his tomb. The final form is what we think of as the traditional early Christian basilica form: an atrium out in front; a big porch, called a narthex, with three sets of doors; the church, which was limited to the baptized Christians; and the ceremonial area across the back, called a bema, or (later) transept. Old St. Peter's incorporated both an association with the legal structure of Rome and the moral authority of the martyr.

The obelisk of the circus went on standing at the side of the new church. Today it stands in the great ceremonial plaza of St. Peter's, reused for the fourth time: once to proclaim an Egyptian pharaoh, once to mark the spine of a Roman circus, once to commemorate the death of a martyr, and now as a focus for crowds that gather in the plaza for ceremonial occasions. (See also Figs. 17-1 and 17-3.)

The form that reached its epitome at St. Peter's was seldom copied in its own time. St. Paul's outside the walls at Rome, built during the same decade by the same patron, was of the same pattern. But already in the fifth century in Santa Sabina a simplified form without a bema and with single instead of double side aisles was used. Even with imperial patronage, the church of Sant'Apollinaire in Classe in Ravenna—built in the second quarter of the sixth century—retained the simpler fifth-century form. It was not until Charlemagne in the eighth century attempted to revive the Christian days of Rome that more basilicas of the Constantinian type were built. (See W. Sanderson, "The Sources and Significance of the Ottonian Church of St. Pantaleon at Cologne.") Charlemagne's needs to legitimize his regime with imperial Roman associations were so similar to Constantine's that the imperial basilica was suitable to both.

In the early Christian period, shrinking imperial resources made the need to conserve a factor in architectural design. At the same time, the forms of new buildings reused associations which gave authority to innovative building types designed for the new social order. This set of circumstances would again give special energy to the adaptation of traditional structures and designs in the period of Charlemagne and after the French Revolution, just as they did in the early Christian era.

BIBLIOGRAPHY

Kraeling, C. H., *The Christian Building,* J. J. Augustin, Locust Valley, N.Y., 1967. An account of the discovery and significance of this early house-church, which you may visit at the Yale University Art Gallery.

Krautheimer, R., *Early Christian and Byzantine Architecture,* Penguin, Baltimore, 1965. The first half of this book deals with the origin and development of architectural forms to serve the newly Christian society of Europe.

Krautheimer, R., "Introduction to an Iconography of Medieval Architecture," *Journal of the Warburg & Courtauld Institute,* vol. 5 (1942) pp. 1–33. What copying meant and other questions of meaning in early medieval architecture.

Lewis, S., "Function and Symbolic Form in the Basilica Apostolorum at Milan," *Journal of the Society of Art Historians,* vol. XXVIII –2 (May 1969) pp. 83–98. Together with the same author's, "San Lorenzo Revisited: A Theodorian Palace Church at Milan," *Journal of the Society of Art Historians,* vol. XXXII –3 (Oct. 1973) pp. 197–222, an important study in the adaptation of imperial architectural forms to new Christian meanings.

Panofsky, E. *Renaissance and Renascences,* Harper & Row, New York, 1972. This and other writings by Panofsky on iconography make us aware of the many layers of meaning a work of art can have.

Van der Meer, F., and C. Mohrmann, *Atlas of the Early Christian World,* translated by M. F. Hedlund and H. H. Rowley. Nelson, London, 1958. Not only maps, but photographs of monuments and important persons as well as interpretive essays.

Ward-Perkins, J. B., "Constantine and the Origins of the Christian Basilica," *Papers of the British School at Rome,* vol. 22 (1954) pp. 68–89. Should be read together with the next two articles: G. T. Armstrong, "Constantine's Churches: Symbol and Structure," *Journal of the Society of Architectural Historians,* vol. XXXIII –1 (March 1974) pp. 5–16 and T. C. Bannister, "The Constantinian Basilica of St. Peter at Rome," *Journal of the Society of Architectural Historians,* vol. XXVII –1 (March 1968) pp. 3–32.

Weitzmann, K. (ed.), *Age of Spirituality,* Metropolitan Museum and Princeton University Press, 1979. Scholarly articles of the highest caliber, copious illustrations—a fine record of the definitive exhibition about the transition from the ancient to the medieval world.

10

BYZANTINE ARCHITECTURE

MONUMENTS AS VISIBLE MEMORY

Almost a thousand years after Pericles, Ictinos and Callicrates had worked together to build the Parthenon, another threesome created the church of Saint Sophia in Constantinople (today called Istanbul) (see Figs. 10-1 to 10-4). The church is also called Hagia Sophia, a name meaning holy wisdom. The patron was the Emperor Justinian and his architects were Anthemius of Tralles, a mathematician, and Isidorus of Miletus, an engineer. Together they produced a building that has dominated not only the skyline of Constantinople but also the building traditions of the orthodox world ever since.

Originally there would have been an atrium out in front, like that of old St. Peter's. In Christian churches the atriums were places where visitors and those not initiated into the religion could gather. An important functional aspect of

Figure 10-1 Saint Sophia, Istanbul, built between 527 and 532 by Anthemius of Tralles and Isidorus of Miletus. The huge central dome is supported by pier buttresses on the sides and by smaller half domes on the ends. A ring of windows is set between smaller buttresses at the base of the dome. Minarets were added at the corners in the fifteenth century. (Photo by R. Hummel.)

the atrium remained in that it acted as a transition space from the secular world to the sacred realm. During the Constantinian era, the inner and outer narthexes (porches) had been reserved for catechumens (those studying the religion who are not yet full members); later in Justinian's time, the narthexes were useful transition zones and gathering places for processions. By the sixth century, nearly everyone in the city was Christian, so the atrium remained to commemorate an earlier state in church development. After coming together in the atrium and passing through the narthex, the procession would extend the full length of the church, terminating at the main altar in the apse (a semicircular area at the east end of a church) opposite the main door. The liturgy called for many processions, making a longitudinal church very useful. At the same time, the principles of philosophy and theology demanded a centralized church, one whose round or polygonal shape symbolized the unity and perfection of God. A circular church would be best of all, theologically, because the circle is considered the most perfect of all geometric forms. In a centralized building with altar at the very center, the congregation is led to focus on God as the center of all things.

In Saint Sophia, both ideas are combined in a form of great beauty and high intellectual interest. From the doors across the huge central space to the altar at the opposite end was a longitudinal processional way, and yet the center of that space is under a great dome which gives the whole building a central focus. The space under the dome reconciles in a creative way this constant problem connected with planning churches. The central space is extended along the main axis by large semidomes over the apse and near the main door; these in turn are each encircled by three smaller half domes that are closer to the ground. Because of all of these curves, the extension of the central space seems to reecho the central focus rather than disturb it. Parallel to the main axis, there are large aisles separated from the main space by a screen of columns on each side. The building is thus nearly square, space being wrapped in an envelope of space.

The interior is further complicated by galleries over the side aisles and over the narthex. All these upper spaces were reserved for the women, similar to the galleries in Jewish synagogues. Men stood below in the aisles (ambulatory), with the great central space reserved for the drama of the liturgy.

Today the atrium is gone and the building sits in an amorphous outdoor space that is used as a museum for pieces of architecture and small auxiliary

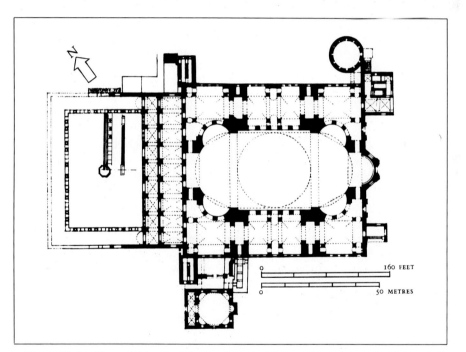

Figure 10-2   Plan of Saint Sophia, Istanbul. At left was the atrium, of which only traces remain today. Doors through the outer and inner narthex led to the vast interior (a circle elongated with half circles) flanked by an aisle on each side. An apse stood opposite the central doors. Galleries on the upper level repeated the dimensions of the aisles and inner narthex. (Plan reprinted from E. Swift, *Hagia Sophia*, 1940, by permission of Columbia University Press.)

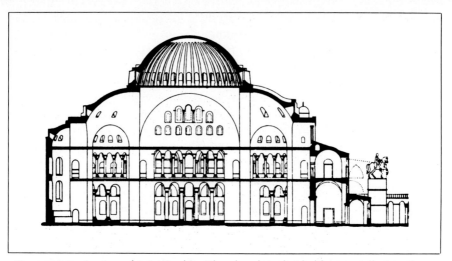

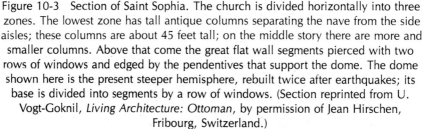

Figure 10-3 Section of Saint Sophia. The church is divided horizontally into three zones. The lowest zone has tall antique columns separating the nave from the side aisles; these columns are about 45 feet tall; on the middle story there are more and smaller columns. Above that come the great flat wall segments pierced with two rows of windows and edged by the pendentives that support the dome. The dome shown here is the present steeper hemisphere, rebuilt twice after earthquakes; its base is divided into segments by a row of windows. (Section reprinted from U. Vogt-Goknil, *Living Architecture: Ottoman*, by permission of Jean Hirschen, Fribourg, Switzerland.)

structures, such as tombs. From this space and from the streets one can see the piling up of complicated parts of the building near the ground that become larger and simpler as they get higher, culminating in the great curve of the dome. When first built, the dome's curve echoed the curve of the hill on which it stood, reiterating the geographical shape architecturally; but now the minarets added by the Turks a thousand years later punctuate the sky at the four corners of the dome and give a dramatic rather than serene impression. The dome we see today is also steeper in profile than was the original, which has partially collapsed in an earthquake more than once since 537 and had to be rebuilt. Both the large external buttresses and the steeper pitch of the dome are thought to be later attempts to stabilize the outward thrust of the weight of so large a span. The original architects suspected there might be problems and made some interesting attempts to alleviate them in advance. For instance, as the walls grew higher, their material changed, with denser stone used at the bottom and lightweight pumice in the dome.

At the base of the dome is a ring of windows (40 of them) that bring light evenly into the interior. The light dramatizes the spiritual aspect of the interior. In describing the dome, Justinian's historian Procopius said that it appeared to be suspended from heaven on a silver chain rather than supported by the piers below.

Such an apparent dematerialization of the structure was highly valued in Byzantine architecture. It grew out of the Roman tradition of covering up concrete with elegant surface finishes, so that a Roman building could appear to be marble even though it had only a quarter or half of an inch of the costly stone rather than the solid marble of Greek construction. By Byzantine times, the architects were able to use this construction technique to add spiritual meaning to their buildings. At Saint Sophia, the walls are enriched with revetments (veneers) of marble and porphyry, mostly in colors of greys and creams and some dark red, so that the whole surface looks like a venerable piece of elaborate embroidery. It later became common in Byzantine churches to cover the interior surface with gold mosaic. Light striking this surface would shimmer and the whole wall would seem to dematerialize. An architectural experience was thereby a natural equivalent of the spiritual experience it induced. Such a building could serve as a model for Christians who were admonished to strive for the decorporealized life. To bring Saint Sophia up to date by incorporating these discoveries, during the eleventh and twelfth centuries, figured mosaics with gold backgrounds were added at the gallery level, but the church was originally aniconic (without pictures). The church's abstract dedication to holy wisdom is unlike the usual dedications of churches to persons (St. Peter) or things (Holy Sepulcher). Details of the building

Figure 10-4   Saint Sophia, Istanbul; view of upper walls and dome. The hemispherical dome is set on spherical triangles called pendentives. These span between the arched walls (lower left and upper right) and the attached half domes (lower right and upper left). Both domes and walls are pierced with windows. (Photo, R. Hummel.)

emphasize its close connection with the patron inasmuch as the capitals of columns include the linked initials of Justinian and Queen Theodora among the abstract leaf forms (Fig. 10-5).

In the account of the festivities of the opening day of the church, Procopius tells us that the procession formed at the Golden Gate, across the city to the west, and that everyone including the emperor walked in solemn order to the front of the church. By walking, the emperor was stressing his humility before God. However, he was not above a certain human boasting, for when the procession reached Saint Sophia, it paused and Justinian went in alone. He looked around at what he had caused to be created and declared, "Solomon, I have outdone you!" Preparation for this glorious day had taken years, and since then the building has already endured longer than Solomon's Temple.

Justinian ruled during the first half of the sixth century. He was a fortunate man in many ways. For one thing, he found the woman he loved, Theodora, married her, raised her to be queen and co-ruler with him, and discovered that she was as bright as he and possibly even more forceful, despite her humble origin as the daughter of a bear keeper. For another, his predecessor as emperor had possessed financial genius, leaving such a large treasury that Justinian could easily build in all the lands of the Roman Empire. Justinian obtained all the propaganda benefits of stimulating the economy through an intensive building program, without the negative reactions caused by having to extract the money from an unwilling populace.

Figure 10-5   Capital from Saint Sophia, showing intertwined initials of Justinian and Empress Theodora. Derived from Roman composite capitals (with both volutes and leaves), this one shows a new aesthetic sensibility in that its richness is achieved by shadow and line rather than by modeling. Since Saint Sophia originally had no figure decoration, these initials must have seemed all the more prominent. (Photo by R. Hummel.)

Figure 10-6   Interior view of SS. Sergius and Bacchus, Istanbul, early sixth century, built by Justinian before he became emperor. Like many subsequent churches, this one has a high central space enveloped in a lower undulating ring of space. This ring is here seen at both ground and gallery level. Present decoration of the interior dates from its use as a mosque; note the capitals and compare with Fig. 10-5. (Photo by R. Hummel.)

While still prince, before becoming emperor, Justinian had built the church (527) of Saints Sergius and Bacchus near the imperial palace in Constantinople (see Fig. 10-6). Although much smaller than Saint Sophia and less carefully built, this church seems to have served as a means for trying out some new ideas. The exterior is a series of volumes that culminate in the shallow dome at the top. This arrangement emphasizes that the dome at the center is the highest point, and the outer space is the lower aisle (called an ambulatory). A narthex led from the original atrium (now gone) into the interior. The plan of the church and one's experience of it confirm the fact that the inner volume is set askew in the outer shell of the church. Why this is so has not been determined. The inner space is fairly complex—a kind of space that probably draws upon first- and second-century Roman experiments in convoluted space. The dome over the central space is supported by piers. Between the piers, columns are set to form exedrae (niches) that are alternately rectangular and curved. We can look through the screen of columns to see the ambulatory space beyond, which undulates because of the different protrusions into it. The central space might be said to pulsate. It is further enriched by the galleries placed above the ambulatory.

It is possible that the architects of Saint Sophia, Anthemius and Isidorus, were also the architects of Saints Sergius and Bacchus. Certainly they learned a great deal from it, with its centralized space given longitudinal emphasis by placement of the altar opposite the main door, a large inner volume interlaced with a narrower outer volume by means of billows of space that bulge outward from between the strong piers that support the dome, a nearly square plan with the circular central space nestled within it, and a clear light that bathes all the interior forms.

In 532 Anthemius and Isidorus were given the task of designing a new church to replace Constantine's Saint Sophia, which had burned down in a fire. They must have already studied the design problems of this kind of domed structure with space wrapped in space. Once Justinian decided to rebuild the church, his architects turned out the design for it in a mere 6 weeks, which would have been nearly impossible if they had not already been thinking about the problems. Justinian seems to have been in a great hurry, for the church was built in only 5 years, a feat that would be difficult even today. There was a plague raging in the city during 532, which struck the emperor himself. Justinian may possibly have vowed to build a great church if he recovered. This church would be dedicated to the holy wisdom of God, and would stand near the palace. Such a theory would explain the haste in building and the close connection of the church with Justinian.

Saint Sophia remains an important monument in all the meanings of the word. As a commemoration of the Emperor Justinian and possibly of a particular event during his reign, the plague of 532, it bespeaks both a person and an event. Visitors to it who have never heard of the Justinianic recodification of all the laws of the empire will no doubt remember and honor him for this building. A monument enkindles remembrance, especially of an historical fact, event, or person. Moreover, the monument honors the person or event by provoking remembrance. Some examples may make this clear. Obelisks have been favorite monuments ever since the time of the early Egyptians. They were set up to honor particular rulers and were inscribed with their names and titles. The Romans were fascinated with these old monuments, transporting many of them to the city of Rome, where one, for instance, was set up in Nero's circus next to the cemetery that was later to be the site of Old St. Peter's Church. A smaller Egyptian obelisk was transformed in the seventeenth century into a baroque monument by Bernini when he remodeled the small plaza in front of the Pantheon; this obelisk, which now sits in a fountain, has a sculptured elephant as its base.

Whole buildings can be monuments in this sense. The Parthenon was built with money left over from the Persian War: it commemorates the victory of the Greeks as well as Athenian dominance among the victors. Even utilitarian structures can also have a monumental function; one such is the Aqua Claudia, finished by Claudius in 52 and bearing his name, which was also his family name; the aqueduct thus commemorates the entire Claudian family.

The Roman world had many monuments which were useful only in the sense of being propaganda statements, such as the Arch of Titus at the Roman Forum. Titus and his son Vespasian built not only the Forum of Peace but also this arch to commemorate their victory in the Jewish war. On the arch are depicted scenes of this victory, such as the soldiers carrying off the great candlesticks from the temple at Jerusalem. The memorial thus depicts the event that the builders want remembered. Whereas the Jews looked on their defeat as a terrible tragedy, to the Romans it was a triumph of law and order over a group that was trying to destabilize the state by revolution. The emperors were not being hypocritical for praising themselves for thus restoring peace; they sincerely thought they had done well.

The other two meanings of the concept of "monumental" are somewhat interconnected. They are also particular to art historians' uses of the word. The second meaning is "large and simple" and the third is "scaleless." The pyramids are monumental not only because they are related to particular pharaohs but also because they are so large as to be unforgettable. Large churches, large palaces, large freeway interchanges have this quality of monumentality, by virtue of their size. The pyramids and freeway interchanges share also the quality of simplicity, achieving their effect by means of proportion and size and not by piling up of details.

The simplicity of such large objects carries us into the third meaning of monumental—scaleless. The only way to ascertain the size of an obelisk is by measuring it against the building it stands near. The obelisk does not contain within itself any designation of its own scale. By extension, when an object of art gives up or forsakes an idea of scale, it can be called monumental even when it is small. Although this sounds paradoxical, some objects seem to have so much strength within themselves that the question of scale becomes more or less irrelevant to the memorable effect they make. There is a famous statue of Charlemagne, for instance, which is only about 12 inches tall, but it has so much presence, that it is always described as monumental.

With these additional meanings, we might reexamine St. Peter's and discover that it has many levels of monumentality. Not only are St. Peter and his martyrdom commemorated here, but also Constantine the builder and his conversion. The legalization of Christianity was, as it were, embodied in the fabric of this church.

In the same way, Saint Sophia, the major monument discussed in this chapter, has several aspects that suggest monumentality. We can also say that it has several symbolic functions as well as its intended liturgical function: it is a place of assembly, a royal chapel, the site of an aesthetic experience that aspires to the sublime. Saint Sophia is very large, with a simple grandeur that is unforgettable. Since this church was deliberately built at a dramatic and monumental scale, we cannot speak of it as being scaleless. Nonetheless, it is interesting to note that churches that derive from Saint Sophia's spatial complexity have subsequently been built at every scale from the petite to the gigantic. One can cite examples in this tradition from the Church of the Holy Apostles, built in the sixth century in Constantinople, to the Church of the Archangel Michael, built in the seventeenth century in Archangel, Russia. All have central domed spaces enveloped by supplementary spaces that can be glimpsed from the main space and combine with it to form a rich spatial experience that folds in upon itself. All have domes or semidomes over subsidiary spaces. Even Frank Lloyd Wright in the twentieth century could not do better for an orthodox church (the Church of the Annunciation in Milwaukee, Wisconsin), than base his design on the tradition of Saint Sophia.

During the same years that Saint Sophia was being built, Justinian engaged another architect to put up another monument to him in Ravenna, Italy, then the capital of the Western Roman Empire. This is the church of San Vitale, the builder of which was Julianus Argentarius (see Fig. 10-7). It was built between 526 and 547. Like Saint Sophia it has a high central space, although here there is a conical roof. Again like Saint Sophia, this central space is enclosed in surrounding ambulatory and galleries, set off by a screen of columns that undulate outward into the passage. Hexagonal in plan, San Vitale is more thoroughly centralized. It has overt imagery, not only that of Bible stories shown in mosaics on the walls near the altar but also mosaic portraits of Justinian and Theodora with their courtiers and the bishop that flank the altar. In the old Roman tradition, these royal images validated the actions taking place at the altar. San Vitale is an early example of the use of gold-background mosaics, which makes the light shimmer and the walls seem to dissolve. Close inspection of the column capitals, however, brings us back to the corporeal world, for just as at Saint Sophia they carry the intertwined initials of Theodora and Justinian. Both in the east and in the west of his empire, Justinian was determined to be remembered.

After the conquest of Constantinople by the Turks in the fifteenth century, Saint Sophia became a mosque. It also became the model for a magnificent series of domed mosques in the newly named city of Istanbul and throughout the Ottoman Empire. This further development of the image of Saint Sophia is best exemplified in the work of Sinan in the sixteenth century, or the seventeenth century Mosque of Sultan Ahmed I by his pupil Mehmet Aga. This structure is more perfect than is Saint Sophia, and equally grand; but it is perhaps a shade less interesting because it is completely symmetrical around both axes (see Fig. 25-6).

Figure 10-7   Mosaic of the Emperor Justinian, from San Vitale, Ravenna, Italy,
526–547. Julianus Argentarius patron. This mosaic was placed near the altar to
validate the ritual. Justinian wears a crown. He stares out at us with big eyes that
denote spirituality. His halo was an imperial emblem later taken over by Christian
figures. (Photo from A. Busignani *I mosaici Ravennati* by permission
of Sadea Editore, publisher.)

Saint Sophia may thus be said to have two sets of offspring. More than
almost any other structure, it succeeds in memorializing its patron. In addition,
few designs have ever been so widely accepted and copied. Saint Sophia is a
monument in all senses of the word: it stimulates remembrance and induces
one to honor those memoralized; it is large and simple—so much so as to seem
to be scaleless.

BIBLIOGRAPHY

Cutler, A., "The Tyranny of Hagia Sophia," *Journal of the Society of Art Historians,* vol.
   31, no. 1, March, 1972, pp. 38–50.
Downey, G., "Byzantine Architects, Their Training and Methods," *Byzantion,* vol. 18,
   1946–1948, pp. 99–118. Compare this account with MacDonald's description of
   the situation of Roman architects.
Krautheimer, R., *Early Christian and Byzantine Architecture,* Penguin, Baltimore, 1965.
   The second part of the book is invaluable for its survey of the range and depth of
   the Byzantine tradition, especially in Turkey, Greece, and Russia.

Van Nice, R. L., *Saint Sophia in Istanbul, an Architectural Survey,* Dumbarton Oaks, Washington, D.C., 1965. Despite the modesty of its title, this well-illustrated book is the definitive study of the church; it is a work on which Van Nice spent his life.

Ward-Perkins, J. B., "Notes on the Structure and the Building Methods of Early Byzantine Architecture," in D. T. Rice (ed.) *The Great Palace of the Byzantine Emperors,* second report, Edinburgh, 1958, pp. 52–102. This essay, carefully read and compared with Downey's essay and with pp. 137-160 of MacDonald, *The Architecture of the Roman Empire* (cited in the bibliography for Chap. 8, page 113), will help the student develop a sense of historiography. Each scholar has his own views and methods, and thus his selection from the scanty facts is different.

11
ARCHITECTURE OF THE DARK AGES
IN THE SERVICE OF POWER

During the years from 400 to 800, a new European economic and social system came into being. The great human effort that had been the Roman Empire crumbled slowly away in the east but fell with a crash in the west. Because of invasions from the north and east in province after province of Gaul, Spain, Britain, the western part of North Africa, and even Italy, barbarians came to outnumber native Romans (see Fig. 11-1). The barbarians had moved in to participate in Roman life, but their very presence changed it to something quite different. Not only invasions but several other factors combined to cause the end of the antique world and a need for its replacement. Prominent among the factors were war, plague, famine, and the concomitant changes in the economic system. Whole classes of productive workers were wiped out, and those who were left were too few

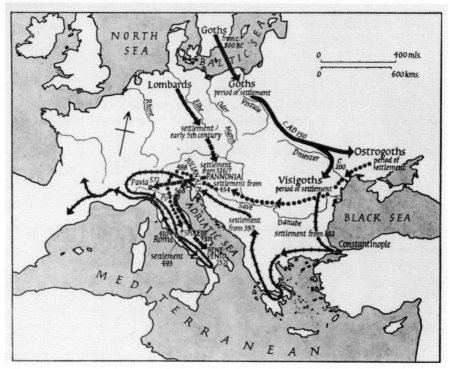

Figure 11-1   Map of one wave of migrations in Europe, ca. 150 to the end of sixth century, showing especially the movements of the Goths and Lombards. Additional groups of nomads attacked Europe and North Africa (e.g., the Huns, Vandals, Northmen, etc.) for another 700 or 800 years. The chaos caused by these invasions and resettlements disrupted law and culture severely enough that we call the period of the fifth to the eleventh centuries the Dark Ages. (Map reprinted from D. Talbot Rice, *Dawn of European Civilization*, 1965, by permission of Thames & Hudson Ltd., publishers.)

to carry out all the functions of a society as sophisticated as Rome had been. (See Boak, *Manpower Shortage and the Fall of the Roman Empire*.) To cope with the interacting effects of these factors, a new world outlook motivated by new factors was essential.

Christianity gradually became the activating principle of the new order of society, so that after several centuries of relative lawlessness, a new political order came into being. Power was, as always, based on strength, but authority was thought to come from God. For the first time, order in society was understood to come from agreement with moral order as set forth in divine commandments. It is significant that this new order was based in the northern European home of the Franco-Germanic tribes that had developed from intermarriage between the invading Teutonic peoples and the resident romanized Celts, since Christianity and the new Franco-Germanic tribes developed in western Europe at about the same time.

The invading tribes brought into this new geographical context some new aesthetic ideas. They were nomads, so their art was of necessity portable. Even as they moved to western Europe, were converted to Christianity, and began to settle down, their favorite art objects were small but richly decorated items such as gospel books, jewelry, cups, portable altars, and reliquaries. The objects were decorated with animal motifs, but not natural looking animals of a realistic tradition but highly abstracted, convoluted, and intertwining forms. The new aesthetic patterns brought by the barbarians may be taken to stand for a whole new outlook on human relations and on the organization of society. Already in the fourth century within the Roman world there had been a movement away from naturalism. Classical beauty and the idealized human form were discarded. Instead, human figures with short stocky bodies and proportionally larger heads were used for their expressive strength. (See L'Orange, *Art Forms and Civic Life in the Late Roman Empire*.) A good example is the contrast between the classical reliefs that were reused on the Arch of Constantine in Rome and the reliefs newly carved for the same arch.

We know from the writings of St. Augustine of Hippo and others that Romans living at the beginning of the fifth century felt themselves to be living at the end of the world. Disintegration was in the air, and division was being exacerbated by the barbarian invasions. For instance, in the early fifth century, Rome was sacked for the first time in its history. Some people responded to these shifts by withdrawing completely from the world as hermits. Others formed small communities of persons with the religious motivation to live peacefully together worshipping God. In the early years of the fifth century St. Benedict founded western monasticism at Monte Cassino, a mountaintop in Italy, where a community of monks agreed to live under the rules he set down. (Nearby, his sister St. Scholastica founded a convent for religious women.) The monastery seems to have been much like a large Roman country house or villa. To be suitable for monastic groups in northern Europe, however, various adaptations had to be made to the plan. We can examine these adaptations by looking at the plan for the monastery at Saint Gall, Switzerland (see Fig. 11-2).

SAINT GALL ABBEY

The plan for Saint Gall was rediscovered at the beginning of the twentieth century (and discussed extensively by Walter Horn and Ernst Born; see Bibliography). At first, it was thought that the plan described precisely what the monastery in Saint Gall looked like, but further study has shown that it was rather an ideal plan, to which the actual monastery was more or less to conform. Apparently Louis the Pious had commissioned Haito, bishop of Basel, to draw up such an ideal plan for him to use as a pattern for other monasteries. The biggest building would be the church. In plan it was similar to Trajan's basilica, except that towers were added at the four places where the curves of the semicircular apses met the straight walls of the nave. Next to the church was a sheltered place (the cloister) for the monks to walk as they said

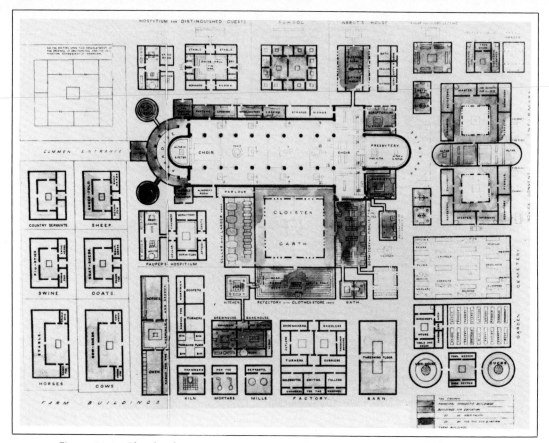

Figure 11-2 Plan for the monastery in Saint Gall, Switzerland. This monastery was founded in the late eighth century by Irish monks sent to convert the pagans. By 806, the emperor Louis the Pious, successor of Charlemagne, commissioned Haito, bishop of Basel, to make an ideal monastery plan which could be followed by Saint Gall and other monasteries. The largest building was to be the church with an apse at each end and the enclosed cloister at one side. Living quarters and such auxiliary structures as hen house and bakery were placed at appropriate distances from the church. All necessary activities for self-sufficiency were provided. (Plan translated into English for I. Richards, *Abbeys of Europe,* 1968, and reprinted by courtesy of the Hamylyn Group Picture Library.)

their prayers. There had to be a dining room (refectory) for the monks, and this one had toilets below it; and there had to be places for the monks to sleep (dormitories) and a bath for them to keep clean. The abbot had a separate house, as did the novices. There was also a house for visitors to stay, since there were no inns at this time. There was a school, a cemetery, and a hospital. Additional buildings and enclosures were necessary to allow the monastery to be self-sustaining—stables and a barn, blacksmith's quarters, an orchard and a garden, a dairy and a brewery, a hen yard and pig sty, and so on. Every function was laid out on the plan in the functionally appropriate degree of proximity to the church.

One of the most interesting features of this monastery is the combination of Roman and northern European (non-Roman) architectural forms. Whereas the church and cloister with attached living quarters for the monks mimic the patterns of the imperial basilica and the Roman villa, the other buildings incorporate northern types that were known in the area for the previous 2000 years. Not only the shepherd's hut but also the hostel for visitors and the abbot's house were squarish and built of timber with high pitched roofs of thatch, with the primitive device of a smoke hole above the hearth (no chimney) and the simplest of interior partition walls. Such details of the plan have been clarified for us by excavation at the site and leave no doubt that in Saint Gall the architecture was a mixture of Roman, early Christian, and northern European forms.

The invading Teutonic peoples, being nomads, did not have an architectural tradition of their own. At first they seem to have utilized whatever buildings still existed from the Roman era but later drew equally upon whatever indigenous non-Roman forms were available, particularly for domestic rather than monumental architecture. In that respect they were like the Greco-Mesopotamian people of Dura-Europos who drew upon both Greek and Middle Eastern architectural traditions.

The process of adaptation of old forms to new purposes is even more apparent at the palace and chapel which Charlemagne built in Aachen (also called Aix-la-Chapelle). The site has two names because it lies on what became later the border between France and Germany but was then the very center of his kingdom.

CHARLEMAGNE

Charlemagne and the rulers who succeeded him for the next 400 or 500 years moved around from place to place. The ruler went to one place where he had a household or palace and lived for a while, judging the local people, eating what was available locally, hunting in nearby forests—living, that is, solely on the local economy. When all resources were spent, the court rode off to the next place and repeated the process. Consequently, a ruler did not connect himself with a specific city the way that Constantine had connected himself with Rome and later Constantinople. Nonetheless, of all the residences where Charlemagne paused, the one most connected with his name is this one in Aachen, possibly because of the palace (now existing only as foundations) and the chapel he built here between 781 and 800. The existence of this palace and chapel, his permanent residence, serves to distinguish Aachen from his other residences and Charlemagne from other nomad rulers. All that we have of the palace are the support structures for what was probably the audience hall (Aula Regia), connected by a long covered two-storied cloister to the palace chapel. Even this fragment of the palace carries still the message that Charlemagne intended:

I am a Roman emperor. Roman emperors have palaces. Even if I am basically a Germanic nomad, I have to have a palace if I am to function as a Roman emperor. This building places me in the tradition of the good Roman emperors. In the throne room my people can come to seek audience, and have their wrongs righted in the ancient tradition of classical rulers.

It is worth noting that Charlemagne's new political order had the name of the Holy Roman Empire.

The Roman emperors had always been heavily involved with construction. Hadrian, for example, had a life-long passion for architecture that resulted not only in creation of the Pantheon but also in construction of Hadrian's Wall in England (built at the northern edge of Roman-occupied territory, to keep the barbarians out), Hadrian's baths in Leptis Magna (in present-day Libya), and Hadrian's aqueduct in Athens, to mention only four of hundreds of structures he was responsible for all over the empire. He had the resources of the empire at his disposal, which he used to build widely and well.

We have seen the same process operating with Constantine and with Justinian I. Not only did Justinian build magnificently in Constantinople and in Ravenna but also he used the large amount of money left by his predecessor for building all over the empire. His court historian, Procopius, writes that by law, nothing was built in the Byzantine Empire without the emperor's permission and knowledge. Even if we discount that claim somewhat, given the still-active principles of municipal patriotism in the Eastern Roman Empire, which would have induced many local dignitaries to build for their cities, the claim gives us some idea of the importance of the political context for architecture at that time.

The Dark Ages that intervened between Justinian I and Charlemagne are characterized by a drastic reduction in literacy, an increase of violence and lawlessness, and an almost total dearth of new architecture. In the western half of the Roman Empire, the authority of the Roman emperor was no longer honored. Trade had broken down and cities had become depopulated as people withdrew for safety and nourishment to their farms.

In his temporarily effective revival of Romanism, Charlemagne tried to bring back to life the idea of the Roman Empire. Since he and his people were Christians, he took as his model the Christian emperor Constantine. The amount of Europe under his control gradually expanded until it included most of France and Germany, as well as what are today the Low Countries and Switzerland and the upper half or more of Italy. Charlemagne deliberately revived Roman law in the lands under his control, since tribal law was not suited to the sedentary and more sophisticated society of his multicultural Empire. As a Christian and as a patron of learning and the arts, Charlemagne enhanced the role of religion by building both churches and monasteries. In the monasteries, making new books and copying and saving old books were important activities, all tending to nurture the revival of Roman culture. Because of the nature of politics and the state of the economy of the time, Charlemagne by himself was not able to overcome the tendency toward disintegration and local self-sufficiency. His monastic foundations, however, became places where the ideas of the unity of Christianity were nourished, and to some extent they fostered the ideas of cultural unity that persisted despite provincialism.

In *Renaissance and Renascences,* Erwin Panofsky provides a wonderful description of Charlemagne's efforts. Suppose that your car has broken down (Panofsky writes) and that you need transportation desperately. You can't get a new car, but remembering your grandfather's old Stanley Steamer out in the barn, you appropriate it. You kick the tires and they fall apart, but after checking out the whole car you realize that for the price of a set of new tires and a new battery, you can have the thing running again and thus solve your transportation problem. Your new tires and battery may not match, but they and the old car provide a temporary solution. In the same way, the Roman Empire was dead, but since it hadn't been for very long, Charlemagne was able to revive it with his transformations. Of course it was old, and the worry of whether or not it would last very long persisted.

Charlemagne thought that the Christian Roman emperors had set models for him that he could copy unquestioningly. He did not allow for the fact that the Romans had never solved the problem of legitimate accession to power. When an emperor died, there was a scramble for power. In the context of the Franco-Germanic world of around 800, this problem could be solved by leaving the kingdom equally to all Charlemagne's sons, but at the cost of dismembering the kingdom so laboriously put together. The effect upon art and architecture was to place them in a fragmentary political context which effectively plunged them again into an obscurity that lasted almost another 200 years.

CHARLEMAGNE'S INFLUENCE

The idea of the Holy Roman Empire, however, did not die. About the year 1000, the Ottonian princes of Germany succeeded to the title of Holy Roman emperor and made another conscious effort to revive the past. This time, however, they were just that much farther away from the ancient Roman past. They therefore turned to Charlemagne for a model, and their art and architecture were based on that of 200 years earlier rather than that of 400 or 600 years past. In fact, their art reflects both Charlemagne's art and through him the Carolingian ideas of Christian Roman art. The concept of Holy Roman Empire was destined to have a very long life. After the Ottonian emperors, there was a long period of relative unimportance followed by one of major importance under the Hapsburg emperors beginning in the sixteenth century. The entity called the Holy Roman Empire did not finally disappear from the political scene until the dissolution of the Austrian-Hungarian monarchy after World War I.

In the palace chapel in Aachen, Charlemagne's ideas of using the past were most fully worked out by his architect Odo of Metz (see Figure 11-3). The plan was based on that of San Vitale, which Charlemagne had seen on a trip to Italy. San Vitale was built by Emperor Justinian I in the city which had a century earlier been the capital of the barbarian rulers of Italy, so it was architecturally attractive to a "barbarian" emperor. In Aachen the idea of a tall central space with surrounding ambulatory was repeated. Both churches had galleries above the ambulatories and a rectangular apse opposite the entry. The columns at the gallery level in Aachen were reused from imperial buildings in Ravenna or Rome. Most materials used in Aachen were local, however. Originally there

Figure 11-3 Interior of Charlemagne's palace chapel in Aachen; Odo of Metz, architect. The angular piers support round-headed arches that are decorated with two colors of stone, set in stripes. At the gallery level and above it, columns are placed between the piers to form a screen; these columns were brought to Aachen from Ravenna. The different amounts of light allowed to enter through the slit windows of the original building period of the first decade of the ninth century and the much later Gothic expanses of stained glass are apparent at the sides and center of the picture. (Photo reprinted by permission from Bildarchiv Foto, Marburg, Germany.) Compare with Figures B-1 and 2.

Figure 11-4   Gatehouse at Lorsch, Germany, begun 767, once the entrance to a monastery. This gateway presents a fascinating mixture of Roman and Germanic elements: the triple entry, attached columns, round-headed arches, and Ionic capitals are ancient Roman, while the colorful stone pattern, stumpy proportions of the upper order, tall pointed roof, and chevron or zigzag pattern are Germanic. (Photo by A. D. McKenzie.)

were mosaics in the vaults, but none such as San Vitale had. Arches were alternately two colors of stone, a northern idea of decoration.

Rather than a mosaic portrait of the emperor, as is seen in the chapel in Ravenna, the chapel in Aachen used a throne to symbolize the emperor. Originally the western entrance of the chapel was flanked by circular stair towers. Over the door was a large window. In front of this window the throne was placed in the gallery, where the emperor could sit high above all others at the religious services, looking diagonally down across the church to where the mass was being said at the altar in front of the apse. (A recent dendrochronological study suggests that the throne was installed around 1000.)

It is worth discussing one change in plan and therefore in effect. At San Vitale there were columns placed in pairs between the piers that marked the octagonal edges of the central space. These columns were set back from the straight lines that connected the faces of the piers, in such a way as to delimit semicircles that billowed into the surrounding ambulatory—a subtle space of interpenetrating parts. By contrast, in Aachen, the forms were simplified. Omitting the small columns at ambulatory level produced a space that was perhaps more segregated into distinct bays and stronger and certainly simpler.

An example of the kind of metamorphosis that went on to change the Roman world to the medieval world is that of the gateway from the monastery in Lorsch (see Fig. 11-4). It has elements of the old Roman architecture and elements of the new Germanic manner. In plan, this gatehouse is very similar to the old Roman gateways at major entrances to cities. Beginning at least by the first century, a three-part formula was followed. Between each of the three openings there would be a column attached to the wall as there is here. The column is topped by a composite capital, often used by the Romans, with the acanthus leaves of Corinthian and the volutes of Ionic style. These attached columns support a kind of reduced or simplified entablature. Above that are pilasters, again a common feature of Roman archways. Here, these are rather distorted versions of Ionic with a redoubling of the capital. Between them are tall round-headed windows, again a Roman feature. There are also, however, some features that no amount of explaining can classify as Roman. No Roman would ever have used this kind of piebald, diamond pattern in the stone of the upper part of the gatehouse. This tells us immediately that non-Roman ideas have affected this gate. Second, note that the pilasters in the upper story support not the round arches or the entablature we might expect but rather a sort of zig-zag motif. Such a motif was common in Teutonic decoration, persisting as chevrons in the architectural decoration of the Normans (in England) as late as 1100. As a final non-Romanism, there is a pitchfork motif at the top that is unthinkable except from a barbarian context. The gatehouse in Lorsch thus displays a combination of features from the two cultures that came together here.

All three structures—the gatehouse in Lorsch, the monastery in Saint Gall, and the palace and chapel in Aachen—were strongly affected by the society for which they were built. This is most strikingly obvious in the combination within each of Roman and non-Roman forms, appropriate to the mixed culture for which they were built. In turn, each furthered the political arrangements desired by their builders and especially by their ultimate patron Charlemagne. That is, each structure proclaimed specific features of the Holy Roman Empire, hoping to manifest that idea as a physical reality.

BIBLIOGRAPHY

Boak, A. E., *Manpower Shortage and the Fall of the Roman Empire,* Greenwood, Westport, Conn., 1974. A short but highly interesting account of the series of catastrophes that beset Rome in the second half of the third century, decimating the population and weakening the Empire, thereby setting the stage for the next era in European history.

Gall, E., *Cathedrals and Abbey Churches of the Rhine,* Abrams, New York, 1963. This book has some good photographs of the palace chapel in Aachen and later German churches.

Hinks, R., *Carolingian Art,* University of Michigan Press, Ann Arbor, 1962. This book relates the small and portable arts to their social and architectural contexts.

Horn, W., and E. Born, *The Plan of St. Gall,* University of California Press, Berkeley, 1979, 3 vols. A superb book, and a detailed study of all the kinds of buildings shown on the eighth-century plan, newly discovered in the twentieth century.

Krautheimer, R., "The Carolingian Revival of Early Christian Architecture," in W. E. Kleinbauer, (ed.) *Modern Perspectives in Western Art History,* Holt, New York, 1971. A standard explanation of reuse of Christian Roman architectural forms in the new political context of the Holy Roman Empire.

L'Orange, H. P., *Art Forms and Civic Life in the Late Roman Empire,* Princeton University Press, Princeton, New Jersey, 1965. Because life was different after 300, the state and art both had to change. L'Orange examines the nature and meanings of those changes and shows their interdependency.

Panofsky, E., *Renaissance and Renascences,* Harper & Row, New York, 1972. For this chapter and the chapters on Renaissance and revival architecture, Panofsky's book is essential background. Not easy reading, but well worth the trouble. Panofsky was one of the great art historians of the twentieth century.

Sanderson, W., "The Sources of the Ottonian Church of St. Pantaleon in Cologne," *Journal of the Society of Art Historians,* vol. 29, no. 2, May 1970, pp. 83–96. This article discusses how the Constantinian basilica form was used and reused in Charlemagne's time and later.

Talbot Rice, D., (ed.), *Dawn of European Civilization,* McGraw-Hill, New York, 1965. Superbly illustrated and well-written, this book has essays by authorities on many aspects of the history of the Dark Ages.

INTERLUDE B

Since Interlude A, we have considered the questions of space, the organization of the building industry, adaptive reuse, monumentality, and the political context of architecture. In doing so, we emphasized the following structures: the Pantheon, the Pons Milvia, Old Saint Peter's, Saint Sophia, and the palace chapel in Aachen. To enrich our repertoire, we will pause now and discuss each of these buildings in terms of a different question. First, here is a brief description of each building:

7 The Pantheon is a free-standing, cylindrical, domed structure in the city of Rome. It was built in 125 by the Emperor Hadrian. Set originally in the traditional porticoed courtyard and entered through a pedimented portico that looked like a traditional

temple facade, the Pantheon is surprising for such a context because of its large and simple interior volume, a cylinder topped by a hemisphere. The interior is lit only by the doorway and the large occulus in the dome.

8   The Pons Milvia is a bridge connecting the two banks of the Tiber River at Rome. Built in 109 B.C., it has survived numerous floods of the Tiber because of its strong construction and a plan well-adapted to the terrain. Piers set on the banks and in the riverbed carry round-headed arches which support the road. The piers in the river have pointed deflectors extending upstream so that flood debris cannot easily lodge against the bridge.

9   Old Saint Peter's is the only building of this set that no longer exists, having been torn down in the early sixteenth century to build the present church on the site. Dating from about 330, Old Saint Peter's was built by the Emperor Constantine. It had a courtyard in front, like the Pantheon, and an inner and outer entrance porch system called a narthex. The building had a wooden truss roof and light walls pierced by windows along the upper nave walls and along the outer aisles. In plan it was T-shaped with an apse at the east end opposite the doorway. In section it had a high nave and progressively lower side aisles (two on each side); the cross shape of the T, as tall as the nave, was called the bema. At the crossing there was a baldachino (permanent canopy) over the shrine of Saint Peter, placed above the first-century cemetery that Saint Peter's Church covers.

10   Saint Sophia, built about 200 years later, was both more splendid and more complex. It was built in Constantinople by the Emperor Justinian and was designed by Anthemius and Isidorus. The church successfully resolves the problem of longitudinality versus centrality in Christian churches, by combining the two ideas in one plan. A centralized, domed space is extended and bolstered by semidomes and smaller semidomes to east and west. This great volume is wrapped in the shorter and thinner outer layers of aisles, galleries, and narthex.

11   The palace chapel of the Emperor Charlemagne was built in Aachen in Northern Europe just before the year 800. It was a centralized space, again wrapped in aisles (called here "ambulatories") and galleries, and focused on the altar set in a rectangular niche opposite the door. Over the entrance, Charlemagne's throne was placed in the upper gallery. The building had a conical roof, and stair towers flanked the entrance.

An equally brief review of each question follows:
7   *Space* has long been considered a major question in architecture, both with respect to the interior space enclosed by the building as well as the outer space moulded by the shape of the building and by the way it interrelates with both natural environment and the surrounding buildings. As early as the pyramid age, Egyptians were interested in organizing exterior space, but it was the Romans who most fully developed interior space. The emotional potential of great vaulted spaces was exploited for both public structures like the Baths of Caracalla and private rooms such as the dining space in the

Golden House of Nero. For instance, the expected spatial experience of the forecourt of the Pantheon and the surprising spatial experience of its interior were juxtaposed in a most sophisticated manner.

8 The great vaulted spaces of Roman architecture depended on a particular organization of the building industry, one that could readily supply the millions of standardized parts and the cheap labor to erect structures. Some of this labor was highly skilled, such as that of the carpenters who did the form work, but much of it was unskilled or semiskilled, such as that of the hod carriers and mixers of mortar. All had to be fed and housed. All had to be directed by architects who took on themselves more responsibility for the finished building than their earlier colleagues, who had been able to rely on master artisans working in a quite differently organized building industry.

9 Many of the ideas of Roman architecture and some of the actual physical components were reused during the early Christian period. Rebuilding, remodeling, adaptive reuse, and preservation turn out, in fact, to be typical architectural concerns of the past as well as of today. We saw how a whole concept of a building type, the basilica, was transformed because of a need to house a new function: indoor congregational worship. The change of content actually changed the form.

10 Some of the new Christian basilicas which reused Roman architectural ideas incorporated earlier Roman ideas about the importance of monuments. Old Saint Peter's, for example, was a monument to both St. Peter and its builder, Constantine. We saw that Santa Sophia, which was otherwise quite without representational decoration, carefully included the intertwined initials of the rulers Justinian and Theodora, so that the church serves most definitely as a monument to them.

11 The close association of both these churches with emperors reminds us that architecture must frequently be viewed in its *political context*. This was most clearly manifested in the palace chapel in Aachen, which exemplified Charlemagne's efforts in the political realm to recreate the world of late antique Christian Rome. That he was trying to do this among semibarbarian people in northern Europe created both a problem and a potential; his chapel, as we might expect, shows a mixture of influences.

We could begin our cross comparisons of questions and examples by considering the palace chapel in Aachen in terms of its space. The differences between this chapel and the church of San Vitale after which it was modeled are subtle but significant (see Figs. B-1 to B-3). Very little architectural change can have widely different effects. Consider, for example, the difference in a large lecture hall if it had murals or mosaics on the walls. What if the seats were covered in apricot velvet rather than yellow plastic and the floors in patterned carpet rather than vinyl. Wouldn't the experience of the space be quite diffferent even though the walls, floor, and ceiling remained unchanged structurally? On the other hand, if an architect is allowed to make more than cosmetic changes, the new building may strongly remind us of the original and yet be different enough to make its own statement, as in the one in Aachen.

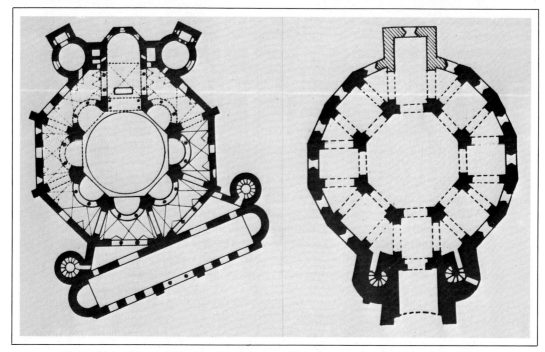

Figure B-1   Plans of Charlemagne's Palace Chapel in Aachen (right) and San Vitale in Ravenna (left), built in 806 and from 546 to 548, respectively. Both centralized churches are based on octagons and both have the main altar in a niche opposite the entrance, an arrangement whose directional pull contradicts the centrality. Small columns are placed between the piers of San Vitale, but behind the circumference defined by the piers so that the space billows out into the ambulatory. No such columns are found at Aachen. The outer wall of San Vitale is strictly octagonal, whereas at Aachen the exterior is sixteen-sided. Stair towers are located in similar places, flanking the entry, but the effect is dispersed at San Vitale and strongly concentrated at Aachen: that is, the effect is subtle at San Vitale and frank at Aachen. (Plans from Beckwith, *Early Medieval Art,* 1964, by permission of Thames and Hudson, publishers.)

If we consider the plans of Aachen and San Vitale, we see that the piers of both define the periphery of the central space. The way in which this is done changes from the church of San Vitale to that in Aachen. In the San Vitale church the space between the piers is complicated by having a pair of columns set there to divide each segment of the periphery. The columns are also set back from the straight line between the piers, marking out curved segments that protrude into the ambulatory. The central space may be said to billow out into the corridor and the space of the corridor to undulate. In the church in Aachen there are no such columns. Rather, the central space is marked out strongly by the piers alone. In this way, the space at Aachen is simplified, more clearly paralleling the character of the tribal Germanic people who replaced the Romans.

Figure B-2   Sections of San Vitale, Ravenna, and the Palace Chapel at Aachen. In both churches, ambulatories with galleries above surround a high rounded central space, and round-headed windows admit indirect light through these auxiliary spaces, except at the top. The scale of the openings and spaces is larger in the older building, by about 25 percent. The emperor and empress are symbolically present at San Vitale in their mosaic portraits placed in the apse opposite the entrance (but not visible in this sketch); at Aachen the emperor's throne was placed at left on the gallery level so that he could observe the ritual at the altar in the opposite niche (note sight lines). (Sections from Giedion, *Architecture and the Phenomena of Transition,* 1971, by permission of Harvard University Press.)

There is also a spatial difference created by the way in which the ruler had himself depicted in relation to the altar. For San Vitale, Justinian had himself and Theodora portrayed in mosaics flanking the altar. The portraits are rich in color and design but have little impact on the space. By contrast, Charlemagne's emblem being his throne, a rather crude stone seat was placed on the gallery level, over the entrance doors, where he could sit and observe the ceremonies at the altar in the niche opposite the door. Charlemagne's symbol thus occupied actual space whereas the Byzantine mosaics did not. Between the throne and the altar a dynamic tension is set up along the diagonal axis through space. By intruding three-dimensionally and symbolically, the Carolingian created his own way to reconcile centrality and longitudinality. The placement of Charlemagne's throne, suggesting as it does the often bitter dialogue between church and state during the Middle Ages, adds political significance to the space.

The organization of the building industry changed radically from the Roman to the early Christian and Carolingian periods. Try to imagine yourself in Old Saint Peter's. If you lift your head to look up through the trusses of the roof to the rafters and the underside of the roof covering, you will see the more easily handled and obtainable building materials of the later period, suggesting a different building industry. Before the fourth century, typical Roman construction for major buildings involved masonry vaulting, such as that used for the Pantheon. Even in the first years of the fourth century, Constantine could complete the great vaulted basilica begun by his predecessor Maximinius, also in Rome. But by 330, this was not possible. From that time in the west, vaulted buildings were not erected. One likely explanation is that there was a shift in the way the building industry operated. If we ask why, we can receive no universally accepted answer; but one possible one is that the tremendous plague that occurred in the 260s caused so much dislocation that the building industry could not recover. We know that 40 percent of the urban population of the empire died in this plague, decimating a population greatly reduced by the wars and invasions of the rest of the century. If large numbers of workers were wiped out, the sophisticated arrangements for the delivery of personnel and material to a construction site would have had to be simplified. Technology and forms from an earlier stage of development would be used again, such as the truss-roofed basilicas of the first century. This change in the numbers and kinds of artisans available may have been accompanied by a modification in

Figure B-3   Interior of San Vitale, Ravenna. Even in a black-and-white photograph, the way in which the surface of gold-background mosaics serve to scatter and reflect the light is apparent. The result of this reflection is that the surface seems to shimmer and the wall behind the surface to "dissolve" somewhat. These effects were deliberately developed to make an interior space which would enhance the spiritual experience of the visitor. Appropriately, the mosaic decoration is concentrated in and near the apse area, where the main altar stands. (Photo by G. Hall.)

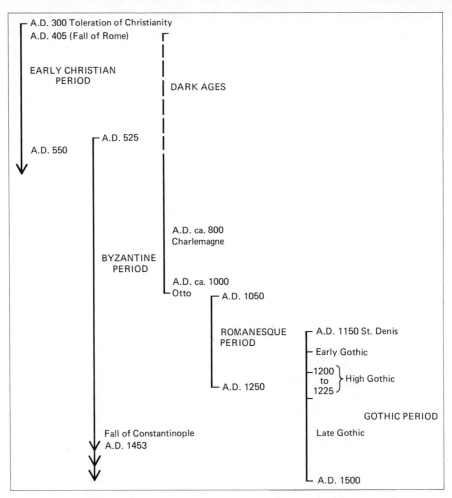

Figure B-4   Medieval time line showing overlapping building periods.

available materials. In late antiquity, deforestation led to difficulty in finding enough wood for fires to bake brick; builders had to shift to the use of stone. Even in the fifth century, beautiful brickwork was still possible, but only for special buildings put up under imperial patronage, not every public and private building.

We have almost no written records that pertain to the organization of the building industry during the Carolingian times. Charlemagne's trip to Ravenna to inspect the monuments there shows that study of old structures was combined with oral tradition among the remnants of the older Romans and the earlier conquers of Italy such as the Visigoths and Lombards. The Franks could utilize this knowledge of construction for their own purposes.

A clear example of reuse can be seen in the columns of Santa Sophia, according to Banister Fletcher. He relates that the dark-red porphyry columns that stand in the exedras of the four corners of the central space were taken by Justinian's crews from the temple of Jupiter at Baalbek. In the same way, the dark green columns that separate the central space from the side aisles are said to be from the temple of Diana at Ephesus. All these columns were reused not so much for the common reason of saving the trouble of cutting new ones—inasmuch as the trouble of transporting them would have been considerable—but rather for that of making a propagandistic statement. Justinian wished to assert by means of the fabric of his building that the new religion, Christianity, had so completely conquered the old paganism that the Christians could steal the columns from the old gods. The old gods could not do anything about it, because they were no longer potent forces. (It had always been a Roman custom to seize the statue of the chief god when they conquered a people to show that that god with his domain now belonged to the Romans.) Since the red porphyry slabs on the walls exactly match the columns, it seems that additional columns may have been sawed up to make the revetments. Throughout Saint Sophia, older ideas and methods were also reused, such as the domes and the atrium and the gradation of materials from heaviest at the bottom to lightest at the top.

When we considered the Aqua Claudia as an example of Roman engineering, it was important to note that there was a practical reason for its tall stilted arches: in order to disperse the water within the city by gravity flow, the water had to enter the city from as high a position as was possible. Besides the practical, there were aspects of this aqueduct that indicate directly the Roman desire for monumentality. According to Von Hagen (*The Roads That Led to Rome*), the Romans felt that things of utility could also be things of beauty. Since it was essential to have aqueducts, they decided to make them as beautiful as possible, through the use of good materials and excellent crafting. An impression of vigor was created by the rough surface of unadorned stone. This aqueduct begun by Caligula and finished by Claudius always carried their family name. Roman society did not have a public works budget similar to the kinds that exist today. Instead, pressure was put on rich families and individuals to provide funds for such structures for the community, not only for aqueducts but also for markets and theaters. Skillful municipal governments would induce competition among rich people as to who could be the most generous to their city. Thus simple utilitarian structures became monuments.

Such considerations lend automatically to questions about the political context of architecture. Claudius was able to have his aqueduct finished more easily because he was emperor, because the government monies were under his personal control. In building the Pantheon, Hadrian was influenced by the existing political situation at the time. He reused an inscription from a structure built by the popular hero Agrippa, in order to create goodwill among the people. Even a bad emperor such as Caracalla realized that erecting useful buildings such as baths carrying his name would help erase from people's minds some of his bad deeds.

The very name of the Pantheon, which literally means "all the gods," tells us something about the political situation in which it was built. The empire at the time consisted of Rome and the other cities of Italy that it had either federated with or conquered. In addition, various peoples throughout the Mediterranean basin were connected to Rome in different ways, but each retained their local law and customs and gods. One of the problems of the empire was a diversity of languages, cultures, outlook, and religion. Beginning in the second century and continuing until the empire became Christian, in the early fourth century, a constant preoccupation of the emperors was to find a religion to unify the empire. It is possible that the Pantheon is the earliest archeological document we have that is evidence of this imperial concern. Christianity finally became the solution of the political problem, but not without a severe struggle during the third century against the religion of Mithra.

BIBLIOGRAPHY

Fletcher, Sir Banister, *A History of Architecture,* 18th ed., Scribners, New York, 1975. An old war horse first published in 1896. It gives a paragraph plus (usually) some graphics to every major building in the western tradition.

12

CASTLES AND FORTIFIED TOWNS

BUILDING FOR PROTECTION

To live safely, people come together to live in cities, according to Aristotle. A preoccupation with safety is reiterated in a different way by Vitruvius, who characterizes architecture as having firmness—by which he means the ability to stand up under use—as its primary trait. Whatever society the architects and clients live in, they must think of safety, either by making sure the building will not fall down or by safeguarding its users from outer dangers. Today we do not live in a society where the inhabitants of St. Paul go in daily fear of invasion from Minneapolis, but we are preoccupied in other ways about safety.

The great question of defense and safety has a variety of architectural answers, once we get past the cave. The Minoans relied on their fleet and on the island location of their civilization. Many peoples have built walls around settlements. Some countries, such as Egypt, have been able to rely on deserts or other natural barriers, which might well be further enhanced by human beings. Some frontiers have been so long that they were very difficult to defend. We have seen that the very length of the Roman frontier contributed to the ease with which barbarians could invade the empire and increased the difficulty of defending it. The Roman frontier stretched from England diagonally across Europe along the Rhine River, through the Balkans, along the eastern border of Asia Minor, through the Middle East about halfway through what is now Iraq, and around the desert edges of the settlements of North Africa. A major task of emperors was to inspect the frontier and build whatever fortresses were necessary, such as Hadrian's Wall in England.

With the disintegration of the Western Roman empire, a period of danger and legal chaos ensued. At first there were numerous invasions from the east and north, with nomadic tribes coming as far west as England, Spain, and North Africa, and seizing movable property such as cattle, women, and children, and then displacing the settled inhabitants as time went on and taking over the agricultural land. In turn, the conquerors had to defend their territory from neighbors and from marauders, as was the case during the earlier Dark Ages in Mycenaean Greece. An individual farm was fortified by a stockade fence around the farm buildings that enclosed enough outdoor space for animals and retainers. In the north, a fortified farmstead was likely to have a watchtower, with the other buildings arranged within the fence or wall to form an open space at the center, like a courtyard. Towers of this sort survive in England as entrances to Saxon churches. Inasmuch as the church might be the only nearby stone building, parishioners could take refuge there, where they would be safer from an assault than they would be in their own cottages.

Charlemagne attempted to bring order to this unsettled period by reestablishing the Holy Roman Empire; but his temporary solution was followed by another two centuries of disorder. After about 1000, relative stability was achieved by a system based on land holding and mutual obligation. The castles and the fortified towns of the Middle Ages stand as emblems of a continuing concern for safety in building and in life. The castle and later the fortified town were the local solution to the local need to live safely.

In this chapter we will examine a Norman castle in England, a castle in northern France, and a fortified town in southern France and discuss how each provided safety for residents. When the Normans invaded England in 1066, they conquered the Angles and the Saxons, who had been the earlier wave of conquerors some 600 years before. To impose their rule and military presence, the Normans, like the Saxons before them, built many castles. At first, they reinforced a hill by digging a ditch around it, using the material from the ditch to enlarge the hill. Then they built a stockade around the top to make the area harder to attack; so the Normans with their horses and heavy armor were safe inside unless they wanted to venture out to oversee the serfs working in the fields or raid their neighbors.

Their next step was to build a massive tower or keep out of stone. The English word "keep" is equivalent to the French *donjon,* from which comes our word "dungeon," meaning now an underground prison. A keep then was tall and round or rectangular. It was placed at one corner of the stone wall that had replaced the stockade. The space enclosed by the wall was ample enough to hold the lord's retainers and their cattle, in case of enemy action. Should the invaders manage to get through the wall or over it, the lord and his soldiers could retreat into the keep and hold off the enemy as long as possible. Warfare at this point in the eleventh or twelfth century was largely a matter of siege. Invaders camped in front of a castle and tried to starve out the defenders. The defenders in turn hoped that they had enough stores in the cellars to outlast the invaders, who were dependent on what they could find in the countryside. Warfare was a matter of nerves and endurance; not too many people got killed, but property changed hands often enough to make things interesting.

THE TOWER OF LONDON

The Norman conquest of England is a good case in point. There was some question about succession to the throne of England, so William I, Duke of Normandy, took advantage of the confusion, conquering England by invasion and swift action. Coming to London in the winter of 1066–1067, he dug in at the southeast corner of the city in the angle between the old Roman wall and the river. His first fortress was an arc of earthworks, possibly topped with a palisade, called the Conqueror's Ditch. As soon as his rule was established, he proceeded to build a proper donjon, now known as the White Tower of the Tower of London (see Figs. 12-1 and 12-2). Between 1078 and 1087, a Norman bishop, Gundulf, worked as builder of the new castle, the oldest Norman castle in England. In form it probably echoes the late Carolingian palaces of the tenth century in northern France, and it may replicate the Norman ducal palace at Rouen. Originally one entered the keep at the west end of the south front and climbed a wooden stair to the middle story. (The basement was used for storage.) By the twelfth century a covered stair with a tower replaced the early wooden one. Covered entries were common in the twelfth century. The entrance faced the river. This one was destroyed only in the 1680s.

Stone walls 12 to 15 feet thick formed the great keep, which was a rectangle 107 by 118 feet and 90 feet high. The keep was placed in a stone-walled court (a bailey) that replaced the old ditch and bank. The keep was divided north and south by a cross wall and the eastern side was half-divided again to make the chapel and its crypt. The chapel's rounded apse protruded at the southeast corner, and there was a round stair turret at the northeast corner. This turret was also used as an astronomical observatory until Greenwich was built. The interior of the keep was divided horizontally into a basement and originally two upper stories, the top one being two stories tall;

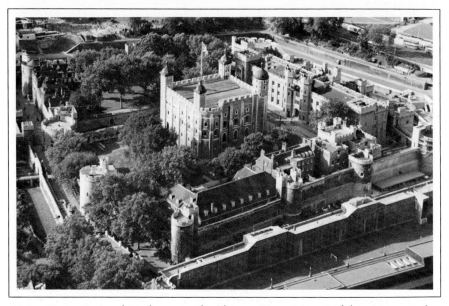

Figure 12-1   Tower of London, near the Thames River (just out of the picture; to the left, but originally flowing under the bridge at left center) at the corner of the Roman wall which then stood between the tower and the line of buildings perpendicular to the river. The White Tower, built by Bishop Gundulf for William the Conqueror in 1078–1087, got its name in the thirteenth century when it was whitewashed. The small old windows of the upper story contrast with the enlarged windows of the lowest and middle stories. The semicircular protrusion reveals on the exterior the location of the Chapel of St. John (see Fig. 12-3). Later kings added additional towers, walls, and other buildings. (Photo courtesy of the British Tourist Authority.)

an additional floor was later inserted so that there are now three stories above the basement. The double-height area was the king's quarters, serving as a royal residence from the time of William I to that of Charles II, about 600 years. For comfort, every story had fireplaces and at least two privies set into the walls. The original small windows can be seen in the top story, but the middle story now has larger windows from about 200 years later. The most beautiful feature of the tower is the Chapel of St. John, which has an ambulatory that goes around the sides and apse and is separated from the nave by piers that are widely spaced along the sides but closely spaced to emphasize the apse (see Fig. 12-3). A castle would normally have a resident chaplain, who would not only perform the religious rituals but also write the lord's letters, keep track of business records such as taxes, teach the heir to read and write, and go on diplomatic missions.

Around the White Tower, the usual concentric castle of the Middle Ages grew up as king after king added to the castle's defenses. From 1200, the Tower of London was a storehouse for arms and armor; and after 1248, housed the government mint, which was active in the Tower until 1812. The original keep, whitewashed in 1240, as was then customary, still carries the name White Tower even though the whitewash has long since washed away. In 1240, the tower was provided with leaden drain pipes from the roof so that water would not stain the new white walls. Also at this time, defenses along the western outer walls between the White Tower and the city were strengthened with many arrow slits and battlements, an impressive concentration of fire power. Earlier in the thirteenth century a moat had been built around the castle, but it was dry; the great moat full of water was completed in 1285 even along the

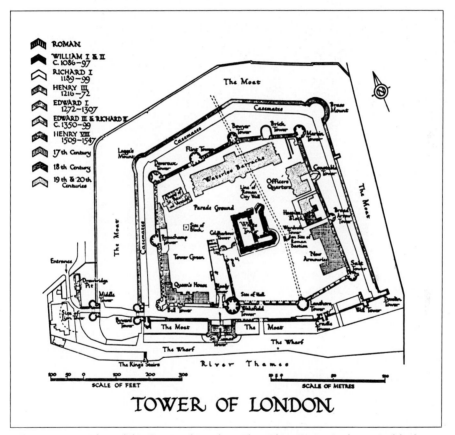

Figure 12-2   Plan of the Tower of London. The White Tower is shown in black at the center, and the line of the Roman wall is shown by a double line of dashes. Like the castle at Carcassonne (see Figs. 12-5 and 12-6), the Tower of London was well fortified against inhabitants of its urban area and invaders from elsewhere. (British Crown copyright—reproduced with permission of the Controller of Her Majesty's Stationery Office.)

Figure 12-3 Chapel of St. John, White Tower, Tower of London; a view of the interior. Built in the late eleventh century, this royal chapel is sturdy and simple. The columns that separate nave from aisle are more closely spaced to emphasize the apse where the altar stands. The chapel nave is two stories tall, as was all of the upper section of the White Tower before an additional floor was installed in the thirteenth century to subdivide it into more useful rooms. (Photo by B. Sarnacki.)

river side, requiring extensive cutting and filling. The moat was finally drained in 1843.

Like most castles, the White Tower was as hard to get out of as to get into, and thus made a satisfactory prison. Its first recorded use as a prison was for the detention of Jews in 1290 during their expulsion from England; and its last state prisoner was Rudolf Hess after World War II. Many English monarchs used it as a personal prison, such as Henry VIII for some of his wives. Shakespeare was one of many noted writers to spin romantic tales about the prisoners.

At the Tower of London site, additional towers were built and enlarged to hold the activities that in smaller castles would take place within the keep itself. Stores and provisions for the expected sieges would be placed in the underground levels of the keep. It was important to have a well within the castle also, so that the defenders would not die of thirst. The well water was often contaminated by water from the moat seeping through the ground table, since the moat was usually used for waste disposal as well as defense. The ground floor of the keep was the guard room, where the soldiers stacked their arms and sat around waiting for action. From this room, the drawbridge spanned the moat. In large castles, there was a separate guard house at the gateway, and the keep was on the opposite side of the internal courtyard.

In the larger castles, the ground floor of the keep, the great hall, was the general social gathering place for the lord and his retainers. Its fireplace served not only for heating but also for cooking. People sat around the trestle tables at mealtime and at idle moments, but at night the tables were stacked against the wall to provide room for the people to sleep on the floor. The Greeks and Romans had valued privacy—an unobtainable luxury during most of the Middle Ages for most of the people. As time went on, the great hall was often enhanced by a gallery at one end; the lady of the castle and her women would sit there, away from the noise and confusion below. By the thirteenth century, part of the gallery was enclosed to provide a private bedroom for the lord and lady; or another whole floor of the keep above the great hall was oftentimes set aside for their use.

Norman England was not the only country that provided opportunities for men of valor and daring. In the twelfth century, a series of religious and military adventures called the Crusades began. Large armies of knights and their men, following the dukes, earls, and kings of Europe, traveled to the Holy Land to try to win it back from Muslim rule. For nearly 150 years, large parts of the eastern coast of the Mediterranean Sea were in European control, as were parts of what are today Jordan and Syria. Landless younger sons carved out for themselves dukedoms and kingdoms. Being numerically a minority, it behooved them to build castles here to better dominate the natives. They studied the castle forms used by the various Muslim kingdoms, which had been based on Byzantine and late Roman forms but had changed in response to changing patterns of warfare after the Muslim conquest of the area in the seventh century.

CASTLE OF COUCY

Castles in France incorporated concepts of defensive safety from the Crusades, from the Norman conquest of England, and even older ones from the Carolingian period. Only a generation after the death of Richard the Lion-Hearted in 1199, the Lord of Coucy built a stronghold in Picardy, north of

Paris, during the years 1223 to 1230 (see Fig. 12-4). This castle had four corner towers grouped around a huge donjon that was twice as tall as the towers. This donjon was the largest in Europe, being 90 feet in diameter and 180 feet tall and able to house 1000 men during a siege. The corner towers linked by curtain walls which enclosed an area of two acres, were 90 feet tall and 65 feet in diameter. Three of the curtains were flush with the steep sides of the hill; on the fourth was a fortified inner gateway next to the donjon. This side was further protected by a moat, guard towers, and the portcullis of the outer gate. Between the outer and inner gateways was the "place d'armes," a walled space of 6 acres with stables and room for training combats as well as camping areas for additional retainers if need be. A separate church stood in one corner of this outer area.

Coucy was built by Enguerrand de Coucy III, member of a family important in this part of France for 400 years. Members of the family married into royal houses and exerted both power and influence in the affairs of Europe. (See Barbara Tuchman's *A Distant Mirror.*) Something of the self-image of this family can be seen in the gigantic scale of architectural elements of the

Figure 12-4 Castle of Coucy, France; view of encircling walls, all that still stands. Towers of such a wall were placed two bowshots apart. Their shape was based on Roman and Islamic military experience and was brought to France by returning Crusaders. Coucy was built in the thirteenth century by Enguerrand de Coucy, weakened by an earthquake in the seventeenth century, restored in the nineteenth century by Viollet-le-Duc, and destroyed during World War I. (Photo J. Feuille, Caisse Nationale des Monuments Historiques et des Sites, Paris.)

castle stairs, with risers of 15 or 16 inches, window seats 3½ feet from the floor, and so on, and in the imposing effect of the castle on its hill. The walls of the donjon were 18 to 30 feet thick; built into the walls was a spiral staircase that reached all three floors. The structure had an open hole, or "eye," in the roof that was repeated in the vault of each ceiling below, making it easier to hoist arms and provisions, to give orders simultaneously from the middle level to all the assembled men at arms, and to light the interior. The donjon was equipped with kitchens, ovens, cellars, and other storerooms. A rainwater fishpond on the roof and a well in the deepest basement helped to ensure self-sufficiency. On each floor, huge fireplaces with chimneys sent out warmth in winter. Latrines were strategically placed for use by the large garrison. Privies, set in bays of the exterior walls, had a hole in the bottom so that the waste material could be deposited into a ditch below. In the donjon there was one privy per story, with drains leading to vaulted stone ditches with vent holes that could be opened for cleaning. The garrison had also a separate latrine building. Sanitation at Coucy was probably better than was that at the palace of Versailles, where 500 years later human waste was collected in portable toilets.

Under the castle, vaulted passages led to storerooms and secret exits through which the castle could be provisioned during sieges. From the top of the tower, visibility extended for 30 miles, so that no invader could arrive unnoticed. The need to see an approaching potential threat was another reason for placing the castle on a hilltop.

Coucy was sited in a rich agricultural area, and its lands also included 7000 acres of forest land. From the land, the Lord of Coucy received taxes, land rents, dues, tolls, milling fees, and so on, enough not only to build the castle at Coucy but also to build or reconstruct castles and ramparts on six other fiefs. Enguerrand III felt himself in direct competition with the king of France, building Coucy to rival the king's castle in Paris, the Louvre. Enguerrand employed 800 stonemasons on Coucy, and 800 other artisans such as carpenters, roofers, iron and lead workers, painters, and wood carvers. The chapel that he built next to the donjon was larger than was the king's chapel, Saint Chapelle; it was vaulted, carved, gilded, and painted. It had very beautiful stained glass, but this was destroyed less than 100 years later.

Beginning in 1386, a later Lord of Coucy remodeled the castle, making it more like what we imagine a palace to be. A banquet hall 50 by 200 feet and another hall 30 by 60 feet were added in a new wing. Between the donjon and the new wing, a lady's boudoir was added. Indoor tennis courts, new stables, terraces with parapets, additional storage areas especially for wood to use as fuel, a kennel, latrines, and a water tank with four pipes to supply the kitchens were also added.

Though the largest and in many ways the most important castle of the Middle Ages, Coucy was not strong enough to withstand the forces of time and nature. In 1692 an earthquake shattered much of it, cracking the donjon from top to bottom. During the nineteenth century, there was some sentiment in favor of restoring the castle, and the French architect Viollet-le-Duc restored its roof and stabilized the fabric. However, the castle was blown up by the Germans during World War I.

Like many if not most castles of the Middle Ages, Coucy showed the pattern of a central donjon to which were added auxiliary towers and walls and other buildings. It was unusual in acquiring these structures in only two building periods. It shared the common experience of having a town grow up next to it. Where the hill widened out, a town of 100 houses and a church grew up in the late thirteenth and fourteenth centuries. The townspeople made their living by supplying to the castle those items that could not be produced within it or on the estate, such as imported cloth and spices. The people relied on the Lord of Coucy for protection, and would retreat into the castle in case of danger.

CARCASSONNE

Other towns of the late Middle Ages were like fortresses themselves. Inhabitants of such a town thought of themselves as having community solidarity against invaders in the same way as a castle did. A good example is the town of Carcassonne in southern France (see Figs. 12-5 and 12-6). Like a castle, Carcassonne had both an outer and an inner rampart. Some of the buildings inside backed up against the wall, and others were distributed along winding streets. One of the buildings next to the wall was the citadel of the local lord. This location enabled the lord to defend himself not only against invaders but also against the townspeople. The medieval social system was conceived as one of mutual obligation and care, but actually operated to the greater

Figure 12-5　View of Carcassonne, in southern France. This late medieval walled city was restored in the nineteenth century by Viollet-le-Duc. For defensive purposes it was placed on a hilltop, and had an outer and an inner circuit of walls (both visible here) as well as numerous towers. (Photo by S. Blatz.)

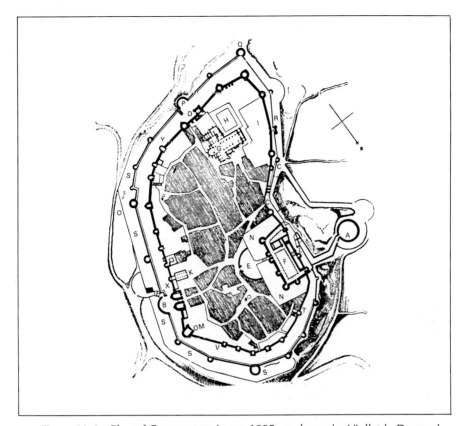

Figure 12-6   Plan of Carcassonne in ca. 1285, as drawn by Viollet-le-Duc and published in his "Essay on the Military Architecture of the Middle Ages." At A is a defensive outwork called a barbican. Other barbicans are at E and P. Gates are at B and C, with postern at D. Towers are marked M, O, Q, and T. At F is the castle, surrounded on three sides by its moat N. The moat of the town lies to the north and east, at S. A second node for the pattern of the town was the church and cloister at G and H. Note the irregular street pattern, familiar enough to the residents but confusing for outsiders.

advantage of the people at the top of the social scale. Every now and then the people at the bottom would become so dissatisfied with their lot that they would incite dangerous riots, creating danger for the lord within the city.

Other towns were completely independent. (See Rorig's *The Medieval Town* for an account of German mercantile towns of the late Middle Ages.) The laws in those days were extremely local. If you lived in the countryside you were subject to the lord and whatever he said was the law. Towns had their own laws. If you could run away from the estate into a town and live there for a year without being caught, then you were free and your children could have a much better chance in life. The saying was, "City air breathes freedom." To protect this freedom, the city needed walls and the citizens were the garrison.

Sometimes a town would grow up in an existing structure or at an existing site. The Roman amphitheater at Arles in southern France, for instance, became a town during the medieval period. The arches that had ringed the amphitheater for easy access were filled in with stone walls for safety and privacy, and the arched supports of the seats became walls, floors, and ceilings of the tiny town. The arena was used as the town plaza. These were dangerous times, and people needed any safe refuge they could find.

Some medieval towns, such as Venice, were surviving commercial centers, but such was rarely the case, because for so many centuries trade had withered away. Some survived as the seats or "capitals" of bishops. Most new towns were those that grew up outside a castle or a monastery. Later, as trade began to revive, new towns developed at crossroads and at river crossings. These new commercial cities helped to "contaminate" the feudal system, with their new ideas about independence rather than dependence, about freedom rather than obligation, and about money rather than barter.

Fortresses and fortified towns were the standard answer to questions of defense in Europe until gunpowder made them gradually obsolete after the fifteenth century. The problem of safety has changed, not disappeared. The United States, without walls but with gunpowder and later developments such as nuclear weapons, spends nearly one-third of its national budget on defense. To that should be added the amounts spent on building inspections and other aspects of building code enforcement, mostly enacted to ensure safety. Safety continues to be an important question for society as a whole, and for architects in a particular way.

BIBLIOGRAPHY

Charlton, J., (ed.), *The Tower of London: Its Building and Institutions,* Department of the Environment, Her Majesty's Stationery Office, London, 1978. Plans, photographs, history, and fascinating trivia about the greatest castle in England.

Grimal, F., and L. Toubert, *Cite' de Carcassonne,* Caisse Nationale des Monuments Historiques, Paris, 1966. The walled city in southern France, restored accurately in the nineteenth century by Viollet-le-Duc. Many pictures.

Rorig, F., *The Medieval Town,* University of California Press, Berkeley, 1967. Despite of its general title, a specific study of late medieval German commercial cities. Very well done; brief.

Russell, J. C., *Medieval Regions and Their Cities,* Indiana University Press, Bloomington, 1972. Cities in their economic and geographic setting.

Tuchman, B., *A Distant Mirror,* Knopf, New York, 1978. All you could want to know and more about the lords of Coucy and their castle.

13

ROMANESQUE MONASTERIES

MANIFEST PURPOSE

From 400 to 1000, a new social order developed in western Europe. It was based on fragments of Roman urban life, on newly important rural self-sufficiency in the form of great landed estates, on the new religion of Christianity, and on the crude vigor of the invading Teutonic peoples. An uneasy mixture, this new European population was unstable at any scale above the local unit. The local units, either reduced cities or newly important farming estates, became perforce even more self-sufficient after the conquest of the Near East and North Africa by Islam in the seventh century. As trade across the Mediterranean was curtailed, that sea became a barrier rather than a conduit. The conditions of life in Europe became progressively narrower and more rigid. Not until after the Ottonian revival of about 1000 did insularity develop into regionalism.

MONASTERIES

During the long medieval period of 500 to 1500, much economic and cultural, as well as religious activity, was centered around the monasteries. We have seen that castles and fortified towns provided safety *in* the world; monasteries and churches provided safety *from* this world. But they also showered many economic and social blessings on their local areas.

Religion was responsible for the basic pattern of medieval life, whether it was lived in a castle, town, or monastery. The faithful were held in common bonds based on religious guarantees and rewards. Religious obligations linked individuals together and religious sanctions strengthened the tie. Husbands and wives; parents and children; great lords, knights, peasants, and slaves; abbesses and nuns; lay and religious persons each had mutual duties to which God was the witness and Heaven the reward. Perhaps one reason for recurring intolerance of Jews and Muslims and heretics lay in the fact that such persons did not participate in the same system of obligations and rewards, so that Christians could never be sure how these non-Christians would behave.

As nearly as we can ascertain, the network of religious mutuality functioned then as does economic motivation now. The kind of religious behavior that dedicated all activity "to the honor and glory of God" was found in secular life, although modified by circumstances. In the monastery the behavior was at its strongest, affecting both the community and the building form.

To enter a monastery or convent was preeminently to withdraw from the world. One might wish to withdraw from the immorality of the world to the purity of the religious life. Or one might flee from the dangers, both physical and moral, of the world to the literal and metaphorical safety of the cloister. Medieval life might be caricatured as divided between predator and prey—and if you had no wish to be either, you withdrew completely, giving up personal possessions, sexual activity, and your own will. Because of laws of primogeniture, many younger sons and daughters were placed in convents during the later Middle Ages regardless of their personal preference. This custom continued until late in the eighteenth century, causing recurring crises, as can easily be imagined. A religious community of serious and enthusiastic volunteers still has many problems relating to living together peacefully and happily and in keeping with professed religious goals. If the group consists largely of persons who are there against their will or even ones who are there without strong religious convictions, the common life may continue but the religious goals will surely be neglected. Beginning in the eleventh century and continuing on through the eighteenth, there was frequent need to reform such monastic communities.

In its earlier and more authentic form, however, the religious life was one that was freely chosen. By praising God and petitioning for the needs of human beings, religious individuals performed a socially valuable task. This was the chief but not the only means by which monks and nuns made their energies available for service to the world, by giving up the world. The services could be social, cultural, political, and/or directly economic. Whatever the services, the motivation was religious, and the structures used to house the activities were religious buildings.

That persons of all classes had to work and had a vested interest in work being done well and quickly was a profound revolution of attitude. Often a monastery—especially a Cistercian monastery—was deliberately located in an inaccessible area. To provide for their own needs and those of their dependent peasants, the monks out of necessity and choice went to work clearing forests, building roads and bridges, and introducing advanced farming methods and labor-saving devices. It was in monasteries, for instance, that water power and wind power were first developed. Since the monastic community as a whole was responsible for both work and prayer, these labor-saving arrangements were essential to enable them to carry out their religious vocation. Because the work of the monks was not only seasonal as farm work had always been but also daily and hourly, punctuality was also important with respect to the physical labor of the community.

Foremost was the service of prayer. The monks prayed for all who did not or could not pray. They prayed at set times of the day, called the hours, and during the Mass. To pray properly, they kept close track of time, thereby developing a concept of punctuality. For the first time, work was the occupation of intellectuals, and efficiency at work became a great preoccupation of the monks. Embodied in the physical arrangements of the monastery we can perceive new attitudes toward work and punctuality. Indeed, as Tawny writes in *Religion and the Rise of Capitalism,* our modern world was incubated in the monasteries of the Middle Ages.

A community of monks or nuns could consist of as few as 12 (replicating the number of the apostles) or as many as 100 monks and two or three times as many serfs and peasants. Sometimes all were of the same status; but more often than not, the hierarchical nature of late medieval life was reflected in a division between those who did the physical work of the convent and those who handled the required liturgy and ritual prayer.

Obeying St. Benedict, founder of western monasticism, the monks also prayed while they worked. Some cooked and scrubbed, some copied books or wrote new ones in the scriptorium, some ran the infirmary. Sometimes medical services were a kind of alms offered to the people of the region.

Some social services had to do with the virtual monopoly on literacy enjoyed by the monasteries. During the early Middle Ages, only monks, nuns, and priests were literate, but under Charlemagne's orders, monastic education was made available to some of the sons of the aristocracy. This was a natural extension of the book-copying activities of the scriptoriums of monasteries and convents and of the scholarly and literary activities of the religious community. In addition, being educated and presumably individuals of good will and discretion because of their religious calling, the monks were naturally called upon to carry out diplomatic missions. They served both the hierarchy of the church and the secular rulers as ambassadors and negotiators.

The worldly impact of monastic activity was an active sign of the religious motivation that brought about the founding and maintenance of these communities.

Each social service activity required physical space within the monastery complex. Already in the ideal plan for St. Gall, only 300 years into the monastic millenium, provision was made for all activities the community needed in order to be self- sufficient (chicken coop, well house, blacksmith's shop) as well as activities undertaken in service to those outside the community, such as visitors or sick people. The plan for St. Gall (see Fig. 11-2) details the mill and hen houses as clearly as the novices' dormitories and the church.

MONT-SAINT-MICHEL

We may gain a clearer understanding of the architectural consequences of this phenomenon of religious motivation by examining in some detail the monastery of Mont-Saint-Michel (see Figs. 13-1 to 13-3). Located on an island off the coast of France, at the juncture of Normandy and Brittany, the Mont-Saint-Michel we now visit was begun in the eleventh century. Hence it stands close to the middle of the 1000-year span during which monasticism was a major shaper of culture and erector of buildings.

Mont-Saint-Michel has been evocatively described by Henry Adams in his *Mont-Saint-Michel and Chartres*. Much is made in this essay of the symbolic link and severance with mainland society that is provided by the causeway to the island. This road disappears under high tides, isolating the religious community from the rest of Normandy and so from the tumult of the times.

Even before the eighth century, the island had appealed to hermits for its qualities of inaccessibility and inhospitality. The hermitage was succeeded in 708 by the first monastery, built on the lower slopes of the hill but well above the reach of even the worst storms. From the Carolingian era (ca. 800) are the crypts under the present terrace in front of the western facade. These may once have been the monastery and church. During the late Middle Ages and after, these subbasement areas were used as burial sites for the monks, the bodies having been interred with quicklime to speed decomposition. Some late tenth-century structures may survive in the other crypt area now called Notre Dame sous Terre. The early buildings were probably used and then remodeled by the Benedictines to whom the island was entrusted in 966 by Duke Richard the Fearless of Normandy. (From being the feared invaders of the ninth century, the Normans had become in the early tenth century the rulers who gave their name to the peninsula.) From Richard's time onward, though not without several periods of reform, Mont-Saint-Michel remained in Benedictine hands until the time of the French Revolution.

Thriving in their new home, the Benedictines planned and in 1017 began to build the great Romanesque church that crowns the hill. Such a location was compatible with the old tradition of locating shrines to St. Michael on tops of mountains. Only the south wall of the nave still exists from that early eleventh-century building period. The church seems to have been completed about 1084. A sketch in the *Bayeux tapestry* (ca. 1066) shows the new church balanced on the hilltop and propped up at each end by massive substructures.

Figure 13-1   Mont-Saint-Michel, off the coast of France where Normandy and Brittany come together. It is on an island isolated at high tide but connected to the mainland by a causeway at low tide (as here). Within the encircling wall, the village huddles at the bottom of the hill. The monastery buildings climb the hill, and the church with its spire crowns the hill. Construction spanned the seventh to fifteenth centuries, with most of what is visible here dating from the eleventh to the thirteenth centuries. (Photo by R. Hummel.)

These were apparently not strong enough, because in 1103 the north wall of the nave collapsed and had to be rebuilt, being finished in 1117.

Attached to the church were a number of chapels, both honoring special saints and providing numerous altars so that many priests could say Mass every day. Later in the gothic period each chapel provided an opportunity for different donors to gain merit by furnishing altars, windows, and so on.

For the daily life of the monastic community, various buildings and outdoor spaces were provided. Separate quarters for the novices and for the professed monks, refectories (dining rooms), a chapter house for community meetings, a cloister where the monks could walk and pray outdoors but under shelter, an infirmary, and a special house for the abbot were all built and rebuilt as the community grew and changed. The abbot (who usually came

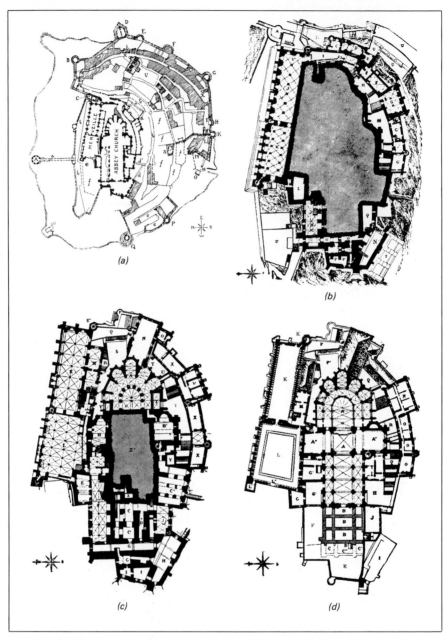

(a)

(b)

(c)

(d)

Figure 13-2a   General plan of the island of Mont-Saint-Michel, with the abbey
church at center, the Merveille as the tall thirteenth-century monastery building, and
the town occupying the southern half of the island. At A is St. Aubert's fountain. B
to Q are bastions of the wall rebuilt during the Hundred Years War. St. Pierre is the
parish church for the village. (Plans from H. Masse, *Mont S. Michel*, 1902.)
Figure 13-2b   Lowest level of the monastery of Mont-Saint-Michel. The grey at
center is the rock of the hill at the center of the island. At P, P1, Q, and Q are some

from a noble family) might have spacious quarters, while the rest of the monks lived very simply. Such differences based on rank were taken for granted in medieval society (and are not unknown even today). But we must remember that by the standards of the time, to have a bed (even if hard) and regular food (even if meager) and to live peacefully as well as usefully was to be truly blessed.

Just as the church needed rebuilding from time to time, so did the monks' quarters. At first these were at what is now the crypt level, and included a refectory, kitchen, and closed-in cloister as well as dormitory, infirmary, and workrooms which were at the church level. Although these are the earliest monastery buildings which have survived, there must have been earlier ones of the periods, ca. 800 and 1000, that were probably considered not worth saving when the earliest church became the crypt.

In the early twelfth century, Mont-Saint-Michel came under the influence of Cluny, the greatest Romanesque monastery, and began to expand. Between 1156 and 1188, more monastic buildings were added, to be found now under the later monastic buildings. This twelfth-century expansion also included towers, but they have not survived their precarious perch on this hill.

In the early thirteenth century, Mont-Saint-Michel was the headquarters of a royal French military order. As such, it received the attention and funds necessary to build new monastic buildings. Because space was restricted, the new towerlike monastery was based on the earlier conventual structures, which therefore became the cellars. In 1203, the great hall capable of seating 200, was built; in 1220, the magnificent knights' hall, some 90 feet long; and from 1225 to 1228, the cloister and refectory (originally a dormitory) were added as the top story, making the Merveille a rare perfect example of early thirteenth-century residential architecture.

Inasmuch as the Middle Ages was a period of frequent warfare, defense of the island required physical barriers as well as prayers. The causeway and tides

---

of the earliest substructures—crypts that probably date from the eighth-century hermitage. At K and J are the lowest levels of the Merveille.

Figure 13-2c   Intermediate level of the monastery of Mont-Saint-Michel. At C, C', and C" are early vaulted spaces from the ninth century, used for a long time as funerary chapels and burial sites; C" is called Notre Dame sous Terre (our lady under the earth). At L and K are the middle level of the Merveille, and at A the crypt area under the apse of the church. Both the apse and its crypt were rebuilt in the fifteenth century after the twelfth-century apse collapsed. The abbot's quarters are at X, X, and X, and the hostel and infirmary for pilgrims is at H.

Figure 13-2d   Highest level of the monastery and church of Mont-Saint-Michel. In the eleventh century the church extended over the crypts at B, but three bays later collapsed and a facade wall was erected closer to the transept. The late apse is shown at A'. At K is the top story of the Merveille, used at different periods as a library and as a refectory. At L is the cloister, with the doorway at L' that once led to the chapter house (now gone). The street of stairways is shown at Q, and the upper parts of the abbot's house at N and O.

Figure 13-3   Interior of the abbey church at Mont-Saint-Michel. The nave in the foreground was built in the eleventh century and has the round arches of the Romanesque period. Beyond the crossing, the late gothic apse can be seen, flooded with light from its prominent windows. In the apse area all arches are pointed, yet the fifteenth-century gothic echoes the sober simplicity of the early nave. (Photo by W. Connor.)

were the first line of defense; the walls of the island were a second barrier. Within the walls, the oblique and curvilinear streets and passageways presented no problem to local residents but baffled invaders. Founded on a rock, Mont-Saint-Michel was proof against even the strongest storms. The fortress aspects of it were strengthened in the fourteenth century by towers and garrison headquarters erected as late as 1393. The island was part of the line of defense during the Hundred Years War between France and England (1337–1453).

Additional building was necessary in the fifteenth century because both the Romanesque choir and crypt under it collapsed in 1421. These were replaced from 1446 to 1521 in a soberly beautiful version of late French gothic architecture. A wooden tower over the crossing burned in 1564 and was replaced in 1900 by the rather spindly present one.

In addition to the church and monastery proper northwest of the church, separate quarters for the abbot were built along the south side, beginning in 1260. The abbot's role as garrison commander, responsible for defense of a sector of the coast, which might seem to us an unlikely combination because of his role as spiritual leader of the monks, was common at the time. In fact, there were separate orders of military religious persons, such as the Knights' Templar, whose duty it was to defend the site of the temple at Jerusalem and the routes leading to it from Europe. The knights had to defend a number of castles and fortified towns, especially ones located in the eastern Mediterranean. The knights were prepared to fight for Christianity against both infidel and heretic.

At Mont-Saint-Michel, the abbot used his separate quarters to entertain kings, nobles, prelates and important visitors and to carry out his tasks as military commander. Hospitality was an important aspect of monasteries in an era that was very poorly provided with public accommodations. Regular inhabitants of a monastery could be joined from time to time by both religious and lay visitors. Whether lords or pilgrims, provision for all was made. Some monasteries had separate accommodations for women visitors; at others, women were not permitted. If commoners arrived at the mount on a pilgrimage to honor St. Michael, they could be accommodated in the church itself. Parish priests traveling with a group of commoners would say Mass at one of the many side altars in the church that otherwise accommodated the many priests among the monks.

Even in the rather cramped quarters of this monastery—piled up rather than spread out—many of the social services customarily performed during the Middle Ages by monastic groups were nonetheless offered.

Visiting the island today almost inverts the history of the site. One first arrives at the late town and passes through the fifteenth century defenses and next visits the quarters of the abbot-commander before proceeding to the church. At the church one sees a mixture of fifteenth century and earlier materials, back to the eleventh century. Then one visits La Merveille, proceeding from the top—latest—down to the cellars and sub-cellars—earliest. One finally visits the crypts, which remain from the earliest surviving religious buildings here, possibly tenth century.

In the small town that circles the base of Mont-Saint-Michel, one can perceive evidence of the relation of monasteries to their context. The early Middle Ages were a time of dispersed settlement, when urban life was greatly curtailed. At that time, there was only a hermitage on this island. The next phase generally involved a group of monks going to an isolated place and living apart from the world, supporting themselves by the work of their hands. We may see this phase in the Carolingian and early Norman phases of the mount.

THE TOWN

As pilgrims began to visit St. Michael's shrine in increasing numbers and as royal and aristocratic interactions with the monastery increased, a group of buildings came to cluster outside the monastery gate. Fishermen and others who helped to provide food for the monks and their guests lived here; the merchants who brought liturgical incense and furs and special cloth for vestments, as well as other items of value, stayed here. The town was similar to many that grew up after 1100 at the gates of monasteries.

Other towns had a different religious origin. Some urban settlements from Roman times, for instance, managed to survive through the Dark Ages by being the seat of a bishop. After the collapse of Roman government and during the long lapse of secular authority, the bishop was the only legal authority. All kinds of cases were tried, in his courts; and whatever trade there was focused on his needs and wants. His retainers and visitors thus provided the reason for existence of the town.

In most towns, whether surviving Roman ones or those of new growth, many of the social services mentioned here as being performed by the monastery came to be offered by the cathedral or parish church. Notable were services to the sick, hungry, homeless, aged, widows and orphans. The social welfare work done during the Middle Ages was done by individuals or groups for religious reasons that involved hopes of a heavenly reward. The cathedrals of the gothic period, located as the central focus of a town, are the climax of a process and a world view that was dominant for a thousand years.

BIBLIOGRAPHY

Adams, H., *Mont-Saint-Michel and Chartres,* numerous editions available. A loving meditation on two buildings that lifted Henry Adams out of himself and permanently altered his view of the world.

Braunfels, W., *Monasteries of Western Europe: The Architecture of the Orders,* Princeton University Press, Princeton, N.J., 1980. The best book now available on monasteries.

Conant, K. J., *Carolingian and Romanesque Architecture 800 to 1200,* Penguin, Baltimore, 1959. The plans and other text drawings are supplemented by good photographs. In the notes are copious bibliographic references. All in all, a basic reference as well as a pioneering history of the period.

Conant, K. J., *Cluny: les e'glises et la maison du chef d'ordre,* Impr. Protat Frertes, Macon, 1968. Conant spent many years of his life studying Cluny. See also Joan Evans, *Monastic Architecture in France,* Cambridge, New York, 1964.

Fry, T., et al., (eds.), *Nineteen Eighty: The Rule of Saint Benedict,* Liturgical, Collegeville, Minn., 1980. A new printing and commentary on the basic rule of western monasticism.

Horn, W., and E. Born, *The Plan of St. Gall,* University of California Press, Berkeley, 1979. A magnificent, thorough and beautiful study of an early ideal plan for a monastery. Architectural history at its best. A summary of this large work has more recently been published: Lorna Price, *The Plan of St. Gall in Brief,* University of California Press, Berkeley, 1982.

McEvedy, C., *Penguin Atlas of Medieval History,* Penguin, Baltimore, 1961. Note especially the maps on pp. 17, 25, 47, 53, and 85 for significant changes in the political geography of Europe during our thousand years.

Scott, Sir Walter, *Ivanhoe,* numerous editions available. The villain is a Knights'

Templar. Recommended for a romantic nineteenth century view of the Middle Ages; not to be taken seriously as factual history.

Swarzenski, H., *Monuments of Romanesque Art,* University of Chicago Press, Chicago, 1974. All Swarzenski's monuments are in the range of 12 inches tall.

Tawny, R. H., *Religion and the Rise of Capitalism,* Harcourt, Brace, New York, 1926. An early study of the difference in mind-set between the medieval world and our own.

14

GOTHIC CATHEDRALS

NEW STRUCTURAL POSSIBILITIES

To the question of what causes structural innovation, we are accustomed to receiving answers that base it on technology; structural innovation is largely or exclusively considered a result of new resolutions of outstanding technical problems. Problems from the Romanesque era had to do with the need for fireproofing and the aesthetic limitations caused by the structural behavior of round-headed arches and vaults. To understand gothic architecture in its structural aspects, however, it is necessary to go beyond such technical problems. At the beginning of the gothic era, there were other factors which had at least as much impact on structural development as did technology. A relative widening of educational opportunities and an economic change and increase of wealth together nurtured an intellectual climate that fostered innovation. Society could afford the luxury of changing tastes, and artists of all kinds felt a corresponding sense of freedom. The clergy who were prominent in the patronage of architecture were impelled by the new insights they gained from Neoplatonism to commission churches with new aesthetic form. Gothic architecture may be thought of as the physical manifestation of the intersection of all of these factors.

Gothic may also be seen as the culmination and transformation of earlier experiments. Stained glass had been used from at least the early Middle Ages. In the twelfth century, however, the writing of Dionysius the Areopagite set out a new image of God as "dark light"—an image ideally suited for expression in stained glass windows of dark red, dark blue, and dark green, with touches of yellow and white. This glass was one element of the new gothic synthesis.

A second element was pointed arches. Common in the architecture of Burgundy during the Romanesque period, pointed vaults with ribs became widespread in Norman architecture in England about 1100 and in Normandy a little later. From simple to increasingly complicated vaulting, gothic architecture has sometimes been seen entirely as a series of experimentations in the forms of arches and in their decorative possibilities. The exterior counterparts of arches are buttresses. Romanesque architecture had also used buttresses in various ways, mostly as reinforcing piers on the exteriors of buildings. But in the Norman architecture of England, as early as the last quarter of the eleventh century, the flying buttress was used to carry the weight of the vaults down to the outer walls. These angled buttresses were enclosed, however, within the aisle roofs and therefore were not visible. They were structurally but not aesthetically useful. Gothic architecture has been studied (for instance by Robert Mark et al.; see bibliography for this chapter) as a series of experiments in the placement and design of flying and pier buttresses.

The development of gothic architecture as a process of experimentation can be thought of as a family tree, which includes not only French gothic but also English and German cousins. Let us examine very briefly the development from Autun and Durham to Saint Denis, Sens, Laon, and Notre Dame in Paris. Then we will linger at Chartres, seeing in the fullness of this high gothic example what the structure and style were capable of. Further developments in Bourges and in Kings College Chapel, Cambridge, St. Elizabeth in Marburg, and St. Maclou in Rouen will complete our survey of this kind of structure. The examples cited are arranged in chronological order as well as in an order based on development of the concepts of gothic architecture.

ROMANESQUE ARCHITECTURE AND EXPERIMENTATION

From 1000 or 1050 until about 1200 or 1250, European architecture consisted of regional styles that in one way or another emulated the surviving Roman structures of the separate regions; the architecture is thus called Romanesque. In Autun, Burgundy, somewhat to the south of Paris, characteristic elements were Corinthian capitals that could appear quite "classical," combined with tall, pointed arches and bas-relief sculpture of astonishing originality. The interior elevation of this church, along the nave walls, imitates the arrangement and proportions of the openings of the Roman gates of Autun, which still survive today. However, the round-headed Roman arches of the gate are at the lower level transformed into pointed arches, between the piers of the nave. Since the Order of Cluny had its headquarters in Burgundy, pointed arches like these were spread by the Cluniac monks all over France as they built churches to accommodate the pilgrims of the eleventh, twelfth, and thirteenth centuries; thus the pointed arch became widely known. Its properties were tested in a wide variety of materials and for varying plans. The pointed arch had at least two important advantages. Pointed arches of differing widths or heights could easily be combined in one vaulted bay, something that was awkward and difficult when round-headed arches were used. Second, the pointed arch compared with a round arch of the same height is relatively narrow for its height. The forces set up by the weights of vault and roof (the thrust) could more easily be controlled by using a pointed arch, because more of such thrusts came down within the supporting pier. The thrusts tend to push more downward rather than outward, as they do in round arches or vaults. For the architect, this means easier control, greater freedom, and less need for massive masonry walls. For the first time, large expanses of window were possible.

Further experiments had to do with vaulted roofs for churches. Some new ideas about roofs were tried by the Normans when they were building a series of great churches after their conquest of England. In these churches, begun between 1066 and 1100, we see direct expressions of the Romanesque, such as round-headed arches, big heavy piers, and in Durham (see Fig. 14-1) use of chevron (zigzag) ornament. At the turn of the century, however, the first large-scale experiment with stone vaulting using both ribs and pointed profiles in arches and vaults was made in Durham. The architects of these Norman churches were the first to grasp the idea that part of the problem in earlier Romanesque architecture had been the use of simple vault forms of semicircular profile, because such forms put a tremendous burden on the columns or walls below, inasmuch as the weight of the upper part of the structure pushes outward rather than downward. A new discovery was that by using pointed arches and vaults, the whole structure became more stable. We now know that this is because the thrusts are directed more nearly vertically. The new structural stability meant that the architects could experiment with lighter walls and more as well as bigger openings in the walls. Being less constrained by the structure, they could try out wider varieties in elevations, sections, and plans. Together with the new freedom went release from an old problem—the danger of fire, which was much less the case with stone vaults than with wooden truss roofs. The only source of artificial light in these buildings was candles or torches, so that there was a constant albeit small danger of fire. Moreover there was always the possibility of the church's being struck by lightning. Stone vaults did not make churches completely fireproof, but they did improve the odds.

To support the thrust of the vaults and to brace the upper part of the church against wind, the architect of Durham Cathedral used both angled and

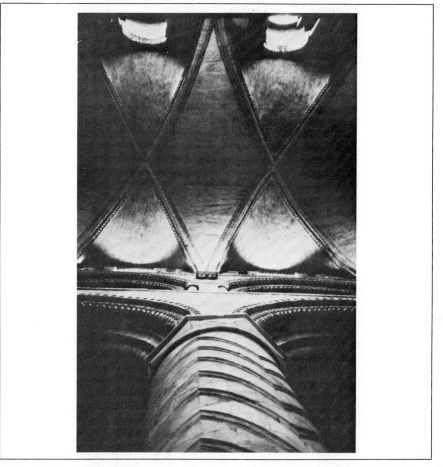

Figure 14-1   Durham Cathedral, England, Vaults and pier, ca. 1100. Pointed ribbed vaults were extensively used in Norman churches first in England and then in Normandy, from whence they spread to the Ile de France region and made possible the development of gothic architecture. Here a heavy round pier with chevron decoration supports an intermediate story with smaller columns and arches and then the four-part vaults of the ceiling. Arches of different widths but the same height could easily be combined to make a roof of great strength and flexibility. (Photo by R. W. Hummel.)

pier buttresses. Most of the weight of roof and vaults was supported by short heavy piers inside the cathedral.

TWO INNOVATIVE CHURCHES IN CAEN

Being satisfied with the results of these experiments on the frontiers of England, the Normans carried the ideas of pointed arches and vaulted roofs home again to Normandy in the early years of the twelfth century. In Caen, their capital, two important churches were built just as England was being conquered. William the Conqueror built the Abbey of Men (St. Etienne) and his wife the Countess Matilda built the Abbey of Women (La Trinité), to expiate the "sin" of marrying without special permission, since they were cousins (too close to be legally married). Both churches originally had wooden truss roofs. Early in the twelfth century, these roofs were removed and replaced by stone vaulting. Since the piers and walls were not originally designed to support stone vaults, the present connections are rather awkward. The new vaults sit lower than did the wooden roof, giving the interior a heavy feeling. The Normans apparently thought that the improved fireproof quality, the change in acoustics, and the appearance of strength were preferable to the old arrangements.

THE ABBEY OF SAINT-DENIS

Remodeling was completed by 1125. Word of these new arrangements must have traveled around France and reactions were apparently favorable, because we find them incorporated into newer buildings and even expanded upon. Most striking developments are still to be seen at the church of Saint-Denis, located today in a suburb to the north of Paris, but then an abbey out in the countryside. This was a major church in two ways: it was the royal church of the French kings, where their coronation regalia was kept, and it was thought to have been designed by Christ himself, who had appeared in a vision to the abbot during Carolingian times and drawn the outlines of the building.

By the 1150s however the old church was in very bad condition, its walls leaning and bending. The abbot at that time, a brilliant, upwardly mobile commoner named Suger, having reformed the monastery and reorganized its finances, turned to the problem of repairing the church. He decided that the central part was the most venerable, so he would not touch it; rather, he would support it by bracketing the old center between new east and west ends. For the west end he copied the two-tower facade that the Normans had developed, and for the east end he decided upon a bold experiment with the new pointed arches and ribbed vaults. He tore down the old east end of the church, and using the old walls of the crypt as foundations for new walls, built a new ambulatory around the east end. Instead of heavy walls that completely enclosed the space, Suger turned his wall sections perpendicular to the line of enclosure, making them into buttresses. Between the buttresses he filled in the spaces with stained glass. The roof of the ambulatory was made of pointed, ribbed vaults, supported on the inside by slender columns and braced on the outside by buttresses. Suger's ambulatory in Saint-Denis is considered the first gothic structure because here for the first time we have all the elements that characterize gothic brought together in one structure—pointed rib vaults, flying buttresses, and stained glass (see Fig. 14-2).

We are fortunate to have remaining to us (translated and annotated in 1946 by Erwin Panofsky) the book that Suger wrote about his architectural work in Saint-Denis. It is interesting to note that he writes at length about the

Figure 14-2   Ambulatory of Saint-Denis, near Paris, France. Called the first gothic structure, this ambulatory was built by the Abbot Suger in 1140–1144. It combined pointed ribbed vaults, stained glass windows, and buttresses (not visible here) in a way that made possible an interior flooded with colored light. (Photo J. Feuille, Caisse Nationale de Monuments Historiques et des Sites, Paris.)

theological significance of the stained glass and the dark light that it brings to the interior, as well as about the magnificent materials that were used in decoration, especially those that catch and reflect light such as gold and jewels, but not at all about the structural experimentation. As builder and patron, Suger knew quite well what effects he was after, but he was not a master mason to whom the physical fabric of the building was the most important object of his consciousness.

Suger's idea was that of all entities in the universe (he called it created nature), the one that is the best image of God is light. Light, he wrote, we cannot live without. It comes to all of us, whether we are bad or good, just or unjust, master or slave. The light from the sun grows our food and fuel; it is pervasive and essential. He pointed out that one can neither touch it or package it—confine it as human beings like to do. Light illuminates everything for us, so that we can understand the world in which we live. Thus Suger thought that a church which made light more apparent to us would be one that by its very nature would instruct people, even without sculptures or paintings that tell stories. If people could be made to notice the light in a church, they would begin to know about God without even realizing they were being taught.

By adopting and expanding the new structural ideas that the Normans and others had experimented with, Suger was able to make a theological point that was very important to him. The light inside a gothic church is not the everyday light of the outdoors, because the colors of glass used were almost entirely dark, with some golds and a very little white to separate them. On the brightest day, the sun pours through the windows, making spots of color on the walls—one way that forces us to notice the light. On a dark day (overcast or rainy), it is very dark inside the church, despite all the windows. We are thereby conscious of the absence of light. If we study the church over time, we experience how the interior of the church behaves in different lights. That architectural experience is carefully controlled here to give people a religious experience.

CHURCHES IN SENS, LE MANS, AND LAON

Probably next in point of development was the church in Sens, which was begun in 1142 (before Suger's project) but not completed until well after the ambulatory in Saint-Denis was built. The problem was to apply the new gothic ideas to a whole church, and the result here is still a little awkward. Sens uses all three elements—stained glass, flying buttresses, and pointed ribbed vaults. The elevation of the wall of the nave is divided into three parts: the arched openings between nave and side aisles: the smaller arches above, called the triforium, and the high windows called the clerestory. The proportions of these parts to each other and to the whole are crude. The vaults above were divided into six parts by the crossing ribs.

After Sens, and still in the twelfth century, was built the nave of Le Mans. Here there still exists a very early gothic part and a later part in which the elements are handled more freely and exuberantly. In section, the nave of Le Mans is more complicated than is that of Sens, with pairs of side aisles flanking the nave; the outer ones are lower, the inner ones higher, and the nave, the highest of all. There is a complicated system of buttressing in the thirteenth century choir to carry the weight of the heavy outer roofs as well as the stone vaulting over the two flanking aisles on each side. Because the mortar used to join the stones of a gothic vault was not waterproof, the stone vaults had to be covered with an outer roof, which was made of a wooden truss system supporting a roof surface of either slate or lead. Such a roof was made as tall and pointed as was possible, both to increase the effect of height for aesthetic purposes and to bring the weight of the roof more nearly to the vertical.

The next set of experiments had to do with the divisions of the nave wall. Gothic structure made taller buildings possible, but it was not initially obvious whether a three- or a four-part division of the wall would be the most pleasing. At Laon, designed in the 1170s and finished before 1230, a four-part division was used, with a gallery opening to the nave through arches that were inserted between the nave arcade and the triforium. Having built Laon this way and studied the effect, French gothic builders seem to have decided that the four-part elevation introduced too many horizontals into an interior that they wanted to appear as vertical as possible. They went back to a three-part elevation, but each part was elongated (see Fig. 14-3).

But the builders decided to retain the effect achieved at Laon of the laciness of the interior. The walls could be more ethereal because of the structural advantage of having buttresses on the exterior. Unlike the rational acceptance of stone as material in a Greek temple, or the denial of the material, by the Romans, who covered their structures with marble revetments and mosaics, gothic builders transcended the innate qualities of stone.

Figure 14-3 Interior elevation of Laon Cathedral, France, showing the nave from the north side of the choir. An early gothic experiment (begun around 1165) to achieve height by piling up four stories—the nave arcade, gallery, triforium, and clerestory. (Photo J. Feuille, Caisse Nationale des Monuments Historiques et des Sites, Paris.)

Paradoxically, they used the solidity of stone to fill the interiors with light and its thickness and heaviness to build lacy structures highly economical of material.

NOTRE-DAME DE PARIS

By about 1200, the elements of gothic were well understood and could be assembled into masterly buildings, even though the architectural theory of the time was based on philosophic ideas rather than engineering possibilities. The mathematics of the buildings was geometry rather than calculus (which had not been discovered yet). Buildings were laid out on the ground with pegs and string, according to a pattern worked out beforehand on paper with compass and ruler. The facade followed the same geometric pattern. We can see this beautifully expressed in the facade of Notre-Dame de Paris. At Notre-Dame, the facade is composed of nine more or less equal squares (three cubed, which is very appropriate for a trinitarian religion). The three portals at the bottom, with their rich relief sculpture, are topped by a band of sculptured figures and again by the two towers flanking a space of the same size. The band of figures across the middle of the facade ties the large rose window to the rest of the facade (see Fig. 14-4).

The importance of geometry may be seen most vividly at Milan Cathedral in Italy, where for almost 200 years there was a vicious battle over whether the scheme should be based on an equilateral or isosceles triangle or a square. People were close to killing one another over this question; their vehemence was partly owing to the fact that they were ignorant about what was actually structurally required to keep the building standing. They worked from empirical evidence only: if a building stood, keep the method by which it was constructed; if it fell down, discard the method. Considering themselves responsible builders, they hesitated to risk using a system they were not personally acquainted with. (See J. Ackerman, "The Gothic Theory of Architecture at the Cathedral of Milan.")

THE CATHEDRAL IN CHARTRES

Although Notre-Dame de Paris and the cathedral at Chartres were built during the same decades, the facade of Notre-Dame is more perfect in its geometry because it was built at the end and not the beginning of the process. Parts of these two cathedrals, along with the entire buildings at Reims and Amiens, are the prime examples of high gothic, of the first quarter of the thirteenth century. During this period, transepts did not extend beyond the outer wall of the side aisles. Spatially, transepts are differentiated from the aisles by being as tall as the nave and often having their own side aisles with auxiliary chapels. The

Figure 14-4 Facade of Notre-Dame de Paris, built 1200–1250. Four or five master builders served as architects of the facade. Notable for its geometric regularity, 3 × 3 units, and integration of sculpture with architecture, Notre-Dame was the model for the spread of this royal style into areas dominated or influenced by the kings of France. The massive west wall was essential structurally to support the towers and their projected spires, which were never built. Three doorways pierce this wall; and sculptures of saints line the piers and make a frieze between the arches of the doorways and the rose window above. (Photo by W. Connor.)

crossing is the place where the main longitudinal axis of the nave and choir is intersected by the perpendicular axis of the transepts. Frequently there was a tower over the crossing. Both the transepts and the nave were divided into a series of compartments, called bays, defined by the piers and by the ribs that separate one section of vault from another. In a gothic church, the piers were closely similar, except for the four piers at the crossing; in a Romanesque church it was common for the piers to alternate in form, ABAB or ABBA. The compartments of the aisles were also bays, usually square or rectangular like the nave bays, and usually proportionally related to the nave bays (one-half or one-quarter size). (See Figs. 14-5 and 14-7.)

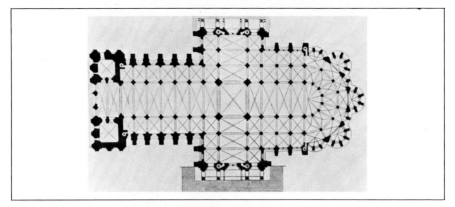

Figure 14-5   Plan of Chartres Cathedral, France. The western facade and towers date from the middle of the twelfth century; all the rest is gothic of 1193–1225; the facade sculptures of the north and south porches were set in place during the next fifty years. Heavy buttresses set perpendicular to the line of wall support the vaults and roof. The walls are thus mere screens into which large stained-glass windows are inserted. The ribs of the vaulting are shown as X's in the rectangular bays, elongated where they span the nave and choir and nearly square in the aisles and ambulatory. Each of the five radiating chapels is roofed with ribbed vaults arranged in a wedge pattern. The transept, as tall as the nave, is centered between apse and west front; it extends only one bay's width beyond the side walls of the choir. (Plan reprinted from R. Branner, *Chartres Cathedral*, 1969 by permission of W. W. Norton & Co., Inc.)

From Chartres we can gain more information about how the structural system made certain aesthetic effects possible and even necessary. Experience had shown gothic architects that the point where the flying buttress meets the pier was a point of weakness and potential damage to the structure; today we would say that the forces are not in equilibrium here. By experience they had learned that the problem could be solved by adding more weight right there at the corner, above the intersection. This weight could be a plain block of stone—but how much better for the aesthetic effect of the whole building if it were handled decoratively. Thus we sometimes see the block in the shape of a cone with curls, rather like a stylized tree, and sometimes made into a niche with a statue in it. The statue added to the intellectual content of the cathedral and its weight lent stability to the structure, but the curled cone was the more common form.

Let us now look at Fig. 14-7, the interior of Chartres, paying special attention to the form of the piers. We can see that one is octagonal, with attached colonnettes of circular form, and the next is round, with octagonal colonnettes. This kind of variation is not structurally necessary, but it gives the interior an effect of variety within unity. This was done partly in acknowledgment of the character of the local stone, which is strong but does not accept fine detailing and elaboration. Careful thought and excellent crafting are essential to achieve maximum effect with this rather coarse stone. Careful masonry is evident throughout the building. For example, the kind of webbing that makes up the stone vaults here requires individual decisions about every single stone. Each stone curves both horizontally and vertically, and has to be carved to fit exactly in one place. Gothic architecture is economical of material but extravagant of labor.

This process of cautious experimentation sometimes resulted in perfection from a structural point of view—perfection that might not even have been realized at the time. Beauvais Cathedral's daring vaults collapsed soon after they were finished and had to be rebuilt more sturdily. Until Mark and Wolfe did their study in the twentieth century on gothic structure, however, there was little awareness that the opposite situation was the case at the cathedral in

Figure 14-6   Section of a Chartres Cathedral model showing the photoelastic interference pattern in simulated wind loadings. (This photo supplied by Robert Mark was produced during his experiments on gothic wind loading.) The way the pointed arches and flying and pier buttresses act to resist wind loading and similar stresses can be "frozen" into the plastic model and photographed for further analysis. Use of the pointed arch allowed maximum flexibility and strength with minimum material, but demanded highly skilled labor. Gothic architects, lacking modern mathematics, worked experimentally rather than theoretically.

Figure 14-7   Interior of Chartres Cathedral, from aisle across nave to triforium and clerestory on opposite side. The pointed arches, ribbed vaults, and stained glass of the gothic style are all visible here. In the foreground, one pier has an octagonal core with round colonettes attached, and the next has a round core with octagonal colonnettes—a pattern repeated all along the nave. The stone of the structural elements is too coarse to show exquisite detailing, but it could be employed in such simple but effective variation as this A B A B pattern. (Photo by G. Hall.)

Bourges, where height and proportions and structure were perfectly adapted to one another. The study has shown that the profile and placement of the flying buttresses here were perfectly designed to control the forces set up by the weight of the vaults and the outer roof, and by the forces of the occasional winds from either direction. Bourges was built between 1192 and 1275, with the erection of the flying buttresses of the nave coming toward the end of that period and the choir completed by 1214. In Bourges, the flying buttresses do exactly what they must do by way of support; and they do thus with both economy and elegance. The buttresses were slightly steeper in their angle than were those in Chartres, which made them work better. By the time Bourges was finished in 1274, however, it was slightly old-fashioned, so it was not copied. The structural solution could not be utilized again, because the appearance was not forward looking.

What happened to gothic structure after this quarter century of full realization of its possibilities, after this period of equilibrium? The natural human tendency seems to have been to experiment even further, to see what else can be done with the vocabulary at hand.

THE CHURCH OF SAINT ELIZABETH IN GERMANY

One new idea can be seen at the church of St. Elizabeth in Marburg, Germany, built in the thirteenth century. At this time there was a revival of popular religion through the preaching of the new orders of Franciscans and Dominicans. They needed large structures in which many people could gather to hear sermons, not music. The hall church was a direct response to this need, because the side aisles were as tall as the nave, which meant that the congregation perceived of themselves as part of one group, or community; and the acoustics were better here for the spoken word.

KING'S COLLEGE CHAPEL IN ENGLAND

In England, other kinds of variations on gothic went on being built for a long time. In both England and Germany, in fact, the gothic period persisted until the beginning of the sixteenth century, long after the Renaissance had begun in Italy. English gothic is beautiful and well worth detailed study. We have ignored it in this chapter because until the fifteenth century it was much less innovative structurally. While the French were trying to make taller and taller buildings, the English stretched theirs out along the ground and put their energy rather into the decoration of the space. We'll look at only one, King's College Chapel, Cambridge, which was built between 1446 and 1515 (see Fig. 14-8). It was basically a long rectangular box, fairly flat along the walls and with huge windows separated by the pier buttresses that support the roof. The style is called English Perpendicular, because the elements are flat, with intersecting right angles, especially in the large windows. At the roof, however, exuberance breaks loose. Instead of being simple four- or six-part vaults, with pointed profile, these vaults are inverted cones in shape and their surfaces are patterned with a multiplicity of larger and smaller ribs, so that they are called fan vaults. The network of ribbing is mainly decorative, which is the traditional approach of English gothic. Lierne vaulting, fan vaulting's cousin, became popular in Germany, where its delicacy was particularly appreciated. This kind of gothic helped to prepare the way for German rococo, also an architecture of grace and delicacy.

THE CHURCH OF SAINT MACLOU IN FRANCE

The last French example we will look at is also very late—from 1500 to 1514, the same years that Old St. Peter's was being torn down and the new

Figure 14-8 King's College Chapel, Cambridge, England, built 1446–1515, interior. Late English gothic architects made extensive use of fan vaulting, where the ceiling was formed by conoids intersecting or tangential to one another, their surfaces enriched by ribs that converged toward the wall shafts. Windows were treated as flat surfaces also subdivided into many tall narrow panels. This chapel is noted for its unity and fine acoustics. (Photo by R. Hummel.)

Renaissance structure was begun in Rome. The latest French gothic seems to have been influenced by both the structural experiments of French gothic and the decorative patterns of English gothic. The style is called Flamboyant. We now use the word to describe people who use showy gestures, even though the root meaning in French is "flamelike." One could possibly say that Flamboyant gothic uses flame motifs so exuberantly as to create a showy effect. The example we'll look at is St. Maclou in Rouen. Here gothic reaches its ultimate experimental form: the facade is bowed out rather than straight; the apse has the usual collection of small chapels but they are arranged symmetrically instead of axially; the vaults are as complicated as is any English fan vault; and the gable over the main portal has become a false front that is very lacy and transparent. Even here the same structure with buttresses and flying buttresses and pointed vaults is used along with stained glass.

The effects at St. Maclou as well as those at each of the other churches we have mentioned depend upon glass for noticeable light and upon a minimum of stone used to maximum effect. The structure used here gives the architect both a series of opportunities and a set of constraints. Some effects but not others could be achieved. For instance, in order to get a large interior space, the architect had to use columns and piers as supports. Today we could use reinforced concrete or steel trusses to easily get a 100-foot-clear-span interior; the Romans could use concrete vaults with massive supporting piers to get the same size interiors. The round-headed arches and vaults of the Romans did not allow them to open up the walls to light, however.

A thousand years after Roman architecture, gothic became an international style. It flourished for nearly 400 years, until the Renaissance revival of classical antiquity. Even then, its structural lessons were often incorporated into architecture that was given a classical appearance, such as the Pantheon in Paris and St. Paul's in London, where gothic structural ideas of economy of material and control of thrust are incorporated behind Roman columns, pediments, and domes.

BIBLIOGRAPHY

Ackerman, J., "The Gothic Theory of Architecture at the Cathedral of Milan," *Art Bulletin*, vol. 31, June 1949, pp. 84–111. What gothic architects thought of structure and form.

Branner, R., (ed.), *Chartres Cathedral*, Norton, New York, 1969. Includes old documents and a collection of critical and analytical essays from the nineteenth and twentieth centuries.

Fitchen, J., *The Construction of Gothic Cathedrals*, Clarendon Press, Oxford, 1961. A detailed study of construction methods and results.

Mark, Robert, et al., *Experiments in Gothic Structure*, M.I.T., Cambridge, MA, 1982. A collection of revised essays about gothic structure, from civil engineering research done over fifteen years or so by Mark and a series of collaborators.

Von Simson, O., *The Gothic Cathedral*, Harper, New York, 1964. Beautifully written, well illustrated, and interesting. After tracking the history of gothic architecture, the author concentrates on its culmination at Chartres.

15
RENAISSANCE ORIGINS

THE INDIVIDUAL ARCHITECT

BRUNELLESCHI

In the city of Florence, Italy, between 1419 and 1450, an architect, Brunelleschi transformed the architecture of his native city. Medieval building practices and methods of architectural design were replaced by new concepts and procedures derived largely from study of ancient Roman examples. In architecture as well as in the wider culture of the time, the movement was called the Renaissance (a rebirth of the old ideas in new form). The impact of a solitary architect is rarely so dramatic as was

Brunelleschi's. His achievement raises questions about how a single individual can make a significant difference in a chosen field.

Part of Brunelleschi's success was a result of the fact that he was a Florentine. You may read about the unique role of Florence in the rather chaotic political situation of Italy during the fifteenth century in Louis Martines, *Power and Imagination*. Each of the Italian city states by a series of historical accidents came to have its own particular form of government and social organization. In Florence, the ruling families were wealthy and well-established, but aristocrats shared power with the merchant class. As compared with other Italian cities of the same era, economic well-being was widely distributed in Florentine society. In the early years of the fifteenth century, wealth allowed for a fair amount of leisure time, but the sons of merchants did not on the whole turn to idle amusements. Rather, for most of them the sport was learning and the discussion of ideas. One idea that fascinated them was how to represent three-dimensional forms on a two-dimensional surface—a problem discussed by the ancient geographer Ptolemy in a manuscript brought to Florence about 1410. The flow of ideas in Florence is demonstrated by the rapidity with which the new idea of one-point perspective turned up in the painting of Masaccio, who used the new science in his fresco of the Holy Trinity (before 1428) and in the sculpture of Donatello (from 1416). Painters, sculptors, and architects had been exchanging ideas on perspective with each other and with mathematicians. It was Brunelleschi who did the first experiments with one-point perspective, and who wrote about it in a treatise circulated after 1420.

Brunelleschi had been trained as a sculptor. In 1401, he entered a competition for new bronze doors for the baptistry of Florence Cathedral, but lost out to his rival Ghiberti. Brunelleschi and his friend Donatello went to Rome, where they stayed for several years, studying the ancient monuments. Brunelleschi examined the ruined and still standing Roman buildings and made measured drawings of them. This experience turned him permanently away from sculpture and toward architecture. Even in a dilapidated condition, ancient buildings showed a breadth of conception that was impressive, and their construction methods were distinctively nonmedieval. The two aspects of Roman construction that seem to have impressed Brunelleschi the most, judging from his later use of them, were the decorative use of columns, capitals, and so on, and the construction of domes of brick held together with mortar. After his study in Rome, Brunelleschi was ready to take on the greatest architectural challenge of the fifteenth century.

About one hundred years before Brunelleschi's trip to Rome, construction of a new cathedral had been started in Florence. By the end of the second decade of the fifteenth century, it was time to build the dome over the crossing of nave and transept. An octagonal drum was in place to receive the drum, but existing architectural technology offered no suggestions for covering the 138 feet 6 inches of the span. The Florentines seemed to think that when they got to that point in the building, God would send someone to vault it for them. Brunelleschi—who had been particularly interested in the dome of the

Pantheon in Rome—was ready to be that someone. After some political manuevering, (which Manetti covers in his fascinating biography of Brunelleschi, his teacher and friend) Brunelleschi got the job, which he worked on from 1420 to his death in 1446 (Fig. 15-1).

What Brunelleschi "inherited" was first a church complete except for dome and facade. The piers that supported the drum and were to support the dome were designed and built earlier and could not be strengthened without destruction of the proportions of the interior of the church. Moreover, the workers were trained in medieval building methods, so their limited skills were what Brunelleschi had to work with. Finally, one of the commission's requirements was that no ugly scaffolding was to mar the skyline of Florence while the dome was being erected. As if these were not enough constraints,

Figure 15-1 Santa Maria della Fiore cathedral, Florence, thirteenth to nineteenth centuries, dome by Brunelleschi, 1420 on. In the foreground is the separate baptistry (mostly thirteenth century) and at right the bell tower. (Photo by A. Dean McKenzie.)

Brunelleschi was forced to accept his old rival Ghiberti as his partner for the project.

From his study of the way the dome of the Pantheon was built, Brunelleschi realized that by laying the brickwork of his dome in a circular pattern within the octagon of the exterior shape, a very strong circular arch could be created. Each layer of the horizontal arch would be complete and self-strengthening as soon the last bricks of that layer were in place. By building in layers, the need for scaffolding was minimized; and whatever was needed could be placed within the dome as it went up.

Brunelleschi's position at that point in time where medieval and Renaissance ideas met is nowhere made more clear than by study of the structural features of the dome. In profile, one can see that the dome is pointed, so that gothic ideas of directing the weight of the dome downward rather than outward as much as possible were followed and moreover, traditional building practices like the use of ribs and webbing could thereby be employed. At the same time, the idea of the circular arch of bricks was Roman. The idea of placing each brick so that it slanted from up at the outer edge to down at the inner edge seems to have also been Roman. Each circular arch then is not truly horizontal; it is in the form of a slice of an inverted cone. The whole circular ring behaves rather like an inverted umbrella, as recent computer analysis of the dome has shown. The weight of the dome pushes outward but the conelike rings pull inward, thereby setting up equilibrium. The living medieval tradition and the newly rediscovered Roman past were combined by Brunelleschi in a creative manner that permanently altered the course of architecture. So impressive was this solution to the problem of the dome that a hundred years later, when Michelangelo was working on the dome of the new St. Peter's in Rome, he sent to Florence for detailed information about the Florence dome. Michelangelo claimed that he could build a bigger dome but not a better one. (St. Peter's dome is in fact smaller, being only 137 feet in diameter, inside.)

Although Brunelleschi's major work, the dome was not his first architectural commission in Florence. In 1419 he was asked to remodel the facade and courtyard of the Foundling Hospital, a commission which also shows a combination of medieval and classical elements in his early work (see Fig. 15-2). Such details as the Ionic capitals show Brunelleschi's careful study of ancient Roman prototypes, as do his use of round-headed arches. Arches supported on columns can be traced back to late Roman and early Christian buildings such as St. Agnes.

Still medieval, however, is the way that he used building materials. Stone elements were placed in deliberate contrast with smooth stucco wall surfaces. His attenuation of forms is also late medieval, suggesting a spiritualization of forms. In his idiosyncratic combination of forms, Brunelleschi betrays his position of being at the hinge between the Middle Ages and the Renaissance. These awkward passages in Brunelleschi's early buildings show that he was not working in a fully developed tradition but was rather creating a new vocabulary. For instance, at the the Foundling Hospital, the columns and their arches

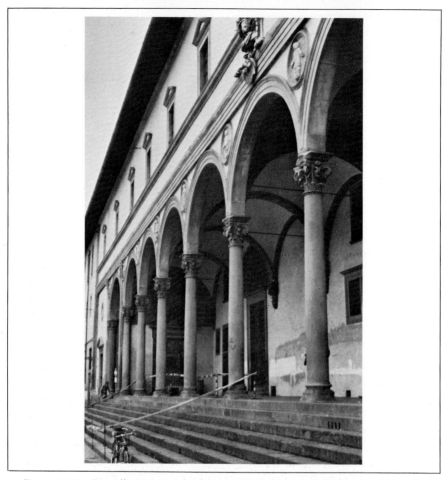

Figure 15-2 Foundling Hospital, Florence. Facade remodeling by Brunelleschi, 1419, with decorative plaques of babies in swaddling clothes by the della Robbia studio. Clearly visible in this picture are the brackets on the walls that terminate the transverse arches, an awkward solution derived from medieval precedents and not unexpected in this transitional building. (Photo by W. Connor.)

support an entablature divided horizontally by three bands. When this banded layer reaches the extremes of the facade, it bends at right angles and becomes the edge of the wall; it is like a classical fluted pilaster on the wall, but does not have the base or capital of a pilaster. The arches of the portico are repeated on the inner wall of the porch, but here they are actually supported by the wall and not by columns. A console that seems to hover incongruously in the "space" of the wall serves as a column capital.

Brunelleschi had a chance to try out his ideas in a complete building when the Medici family commissioned him to begin expanding and renovating the church of San Lorenzo (see Fig. 15-3). Work on this church began in 1421 and continued in stages until 1460, even after Brunelleschi's death. (Its facade, in fact, was never finished.) In the articulation of the parts in relation to the whole and in the control of space, Brunelleschi incorporated ideas which seem to have been developed from the geographical studies of Florentine scholars who had been studying Ptolemy's works during the previous decade. Tested in San Lorenzo was Brunelleschi's own study of perspective, as well as his understanding of the kind of objective space suggested by Ptolemy but forgotten during the Middle Ages. Elements of the interior—the even spacing of uniformly dimensioned supports (the columns along the nave) and the geometric division of wall and ceiling by entablature, windows, cornice, and paneling—all depict and indeed insist upon an explicit new delineation of space. Brunelleschi made physically present a space that seems to be objectively organized, independent of our perception of it—quite the opposite of Greek space organized by polar coordinates.

Figure 15-3   San Lorenzo, Florence. Brunelleschi, 1421 on. Although this was a remodeling, Brunelleschi was able to incorporate his new understanding of space and of perspective, using columns, architraves, pilasters, and other linear elements to delimit the edges of a consistent and objective three-dimensional interior. (Photo from Alinari, courtesy Editorial Photocolor Archives.)

No matter how innovative San Lorenzo was, it still shows traces of the kinds of awkwardness we noted with respect to the Foundling Hospital. The problems may have resulted from the architect's having to incorporate elements of the older existing church. In the final work of his life, Brunelleschi created a smooth and elegant synthesis of all that he had learned and practiced—the church of Santo Spirito begun in 1445 but not completed until 1482, long after his death (see Fig. 15-4). At first glance Santo Spirito resembles San Lorenzo, but distracting inconsistencies between new and old have been eliminated. Division of space by repetition of elements is used again, indicating thereby the architect's control of interior space. A regular square bay becomes the module, repeated once in each arm of the transept, twice in the nave, and once for the crossing. As before, the soft grey stone local to Florence has been beautifully cut to form the window frames, columns, and other articulating elements, set against the creamy plaster of the walls. All is clarity, order, and reason, with each part's role in the ensemble plainly visible in the ample light from the many windows of the upper wall of the nave.

Brunelleschi thus brought to perfection in Santo Spirito the architectural vocabulary he had been developing. At the same time, Santo Spirito embodies some of Brunelleschi's most original ideas. One innovation was the treatment

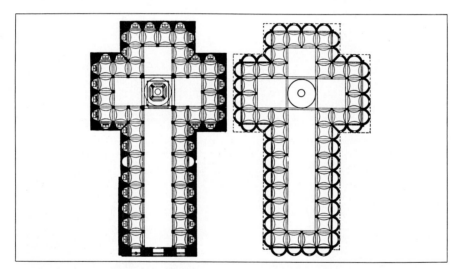

Figure 15-4 Santo Spirito, Florence. Begun by Brunelleschi in 1445. On the right, as planned, and on the left, as built. The regularity of San Lorenzo is further refined here. A band of square modular units forms an ambulatory which completely surrounds the interior. Each bay serves also as a chapel, with the altar placed in its own small apse. The apses were to have protruded on the exterior, giving it an undulating appearance, but as finished after Brunelleschi's death, they were incorporated within the thickness of the wall, and the two modules just inside the main entrance were omitted. (Plans from B. Levi, *Architecture as Space*, copyright 1957, 1974, reprinted by permission of the publisher, Horizon Press, New York.)

of the side aisles, which were made to extend in exactly the same manner around the nave, transepts, and apse. The unity of the whole was achieved by enclosing the equal dimensions of nave, transepts, and crossing in a narrower and shorter envelope of space that was the same on all sides. Unity was highly valued in Renaissance architecture, but here Brunelleschi expresses individuality as well. To alleviate all this rectangularity, he opened the outer walls in a series of curves. Each small square module of the aisles was conceived as a chapel with a curved apse. Brunelleschi originally planned to have the curve of the apses show as an undulating exterior wall, but as actually constructed, the curves were hidden within the thickness of the wall and visible only on the interior. Even so, they impart a liveliness to the design. Regularity and geometry were kept from mastering the composition. A further innovation was the placement of the main altar at the center of the crossing rather than in the apse. The effect of this location, with the altar truly the focus of the entire experience of the building, suggests later High Renaissance and baroque fascination with centralized churches.

Later individual architects affected the development of Renaissance architecture almost as much as did Brunelleschi. Even though the most important ones, Alberti and Michelangelo, were also Florentines it is indicative of the changing circumstances of the second half of the fifteenth and beginning of the sixteenth centuries that these men both did their most important works in other places.

ALBERTI

Unlike Brunelleschi and Michelangelo, who began as sculptors, Alberti began as a churchman and diplomat, common careers for intellectuals at that time. His first major work of architecture was the book *De re aedificatoria* ("about architectural matters"), written about 1450 and inspired by the manuscript of Vitruvius that had been rediscovered earlier in the fifteenth century. Alberti was deeply interested in the theoretical aspects of the arts; he had written a treatise on painting in 1436 and later wrote one on sculpture.

In the 1440s, Alberti was asked by aristocratic patrons to remodel the exterior of the church of San Francesco in Rimini and the facade of Santa Maria Novella in Florence. The constraints involved with the latter task were tight because at least the lower part of the facade already existed. Alberti thus had to utilize what was there and make his upper part agree with the lower part with respect to colors and materials and still produce in the whole facade a statement that was considered modern—that is, Renaissance—as well as thoughtful. He managed to do this by subtle adjustments of the geometry of the encrustation and by use of the stunning new device of the huge scroll form that masks and emphasizes the transition from higher nave to lower side aisles. In fact, this motif was to become a great favorite all through the baroque period. Antique features of the facade, for which Alberti is credited, are the outlined pediment at the top, the inscription, the facade division by column, and entablature, and the treatment of the doorway as a triumphal arch.

At San Francesco, Alberti was free to follow his own judgment. The interior was left substantially as the gothic church that it was, but the exterior was transformed by the ideas that Alberti had garnered from his study of ancient Roman architecture. The doorway to the church and the walls that flank it were treated as a Roman triumphal arch, with paired niches for coffins of the patron and his wife. The motif of niches for sarcophoguses (coffins) between simple strips of wall was continued all around the building. Articulation of door jambs, windows, etc., was in a vocabulary derived from Roman examples. The plan for the pediment area, which was never finished, was to have it terminate in a large arch.

The architecture of Alberti thus used the bold sturdy forms recommended by Vitruvius rather than the late Roman and early Christian details that Brunelleschi preferred. Renaissance architecture can thus be said to have filled out as it advanced from adolescence to maturity.

Alberti's architecture later in his career seems to demonstrate a working out of ideas about proper architectural expression of the concept of support. In his middle works, Alberti preferred solid walls, especially as support for arches, and not a row of columns such as Brunelleschi had used—which is particularly evident in his design for San Sebastiano, which you can read about in Wittkower's *Architectural Principles in the Age of Humanism*. Alberti's experiments with the wall as a basic constituent of architecture directly prepared the way for the work of Michelangelo.

The culmination of Alberti's work can be seen in the church of Sant' Andrea in Mantua, where for the first time in Renaissance architecture the facade and the interior elevation of a building repeated the same motifs (see Figs. 15-5 and 15-6). This repetition produces a complete clarity and an unprecedented unity in the building. The repeated motif is again a Roman triumphal arch, but this time worked out more three-dimensionally (or "plastically," as art historians say). The doorway is set in a tall recess that rises to the bottom of the attic story and is articulated by pilasters. This recess causes a deep shadow that emphasizes the vertical division of the facade into the contrasting areas. Intellectually and visually, the facade is knit together by the repetition of the same elements at different scales. Giant pilasters frame the outer edges of the facade and the edges of the central recess. Smaller pilasters, fluted like the giant ones, frame the door itself. Between the pilasters on the facade are sets of three superimposed niches—another repetition. The recessed doorway is as tall as the highest niche on each side. The total effect is both rational and complex.

The interior of the church is integrated in a manner not seen heretofore. The same elements as the facade are repeated along the nave, as a series of interlocking triumphal arch motifs. The aisle spaces behind these arches interlock three-dimensionally in a way that suggests the baroque complexity of a hundred or two hundred years later. Alberti sets out in this church the motifs

Figure 15-5 Sant'Andrea, Mantua. Built by Alberti in 1470. Illustrates a very early use of the Roman triumphal arch motif to organize the facade and also one of the first attempts to integrate interior and exterior by repetition of the same units. Pairs of large pilasters set up on tall bases support the architrave and pediment. (The arched "cap" above the pediment was added later by another architect.) Between the pilasters the wall is divided into three zones by doors at the bottom, then curved niches, and then windows. Between the niches and the windows runs a secondary architrave supported by smaller fluted pilasters and bent back to edge the tall niche for the main door. This niche is flanked by arches that reach nearly to the architrave and are related to the large central arch as the small pilasters are to the larger ones. (Photo by W. Connor.)

and combinations that would continue until 1945 to be important formal elements.

MICHELANGELO

Michelangelo Buonaroti carried these concepts even further, during the first half of the sixteenth century. He too was a Florentine but was called to Rome

Figure 15-6   Sant'Andrea, interior elevation. The motifs repeated from the exterior include pairs of pilasters flanking a wall segment divided into three zones by door and panels, the upper one round like the two central circles on the facade. Between the pairs of pilasters are large arches leading to side chapels. The surface treatment of the barrel vaulted roof is represented by the square pattern at the top of the drawing. (Drawing from R. Wittkower, *Architectural Principles in the Age of Humanism*, 1971, by permission of Academy Editions, London, publishers.)

during the papacy of Julius II for whom he painted the ceiling of the Sistine Chapel. Michelangelo worked in Rome under the Medici Pope Leo X and later chiefly on St. Peter's. (See Chap. 17.) Famous as a sculptor, Michelangelo had done other architectural work for the Medici family in Florence: a mortuary chapel for them in San Lorenzo (see Fig. 15-7), and the library and its vestibule that they donated to the monastery of the same church.

In San Lorenzo there already existed an old sacristy (a room in which sacred vessels, vestments, etc., are kept), designed by Brunelleschi a hundred years earlier (see Fig. 15-8a). The new Medici chapel, being placed symmetrically opposite the old sacristy across the apse of the church, came to be called the new sacristy (see Fig. 15-8b). For this family monument, Michelangelo utilized both the same materials and a similar vocabulary of architectural details, so that the clarity and unity of the whole church was enhanced by this addition. The same beautifully cut gray stone articulates all the points of transition, door jambs, window frames, and edges of floor and of ceiling. The same creamy plaster covers the walls. Like the older sacristy, the newer one is covered with a dome, but this one is set higher, subtly but definitely changing the proportions of the space and setting up a tension in the viewer. Even more than the older chapel, this one is enhanced by superb sculptures, all by Michelangelo: a Madonna and Child before the wall opposite the altar, and portraits of Guiliano and Lorenzo Medici on the sides, each turned toward the Madonna and Child, and each set in a niche above a cenotaph (a tomb erected in memory of someone who is buried elsewhere) on which recline the allegorical nudes of Dawn, Evening, Night, and Day. The tension dimly perceived in the proportions of the room is reiterated in the poses of these strong muscular figures.

Like Brunelleschi and Alberti before him, Michelangelo utilized the architectural ideas handed on to him by tradition but was innovative in ways that changed the course of architectural development after him. Since Michelangelo thought of himself primarily as a sculptor, his architectural ideas were "anthropomorphic" in ways not seen since perhaps the time of Phidias. The

Figure 15-7   Medici Chapel, San Lorenzo, Florence. Built by Michelangelo in 1520–1534. Using a vocabulary of dark stone trim against light-colored walls, Michelangelo repeated Brunelleschi's treatment in the old sacristy, which is bilaterally symmetrical to this new sacristy on the church plan. However, Michelangelo's chapel is four zones tall and Brunelleschi's is only three. Here the wall surfaces are enriched by articulation as niches, and the whole chapel achieves unity by being ornamented also with sculpture also from Michelangelo's hand: a memorial figure in a niche above a cenotaph with allegorial figures on the visible wall is replicated with variations on the opposite wall. Both memorial figures look toward the statue of Virgin and Child flanked by angels, placed on the wall opposite the altar. (Photo Alinari, courtesy Editorial Photocolor Archives.)

Figure 15-8a   Section through Brunelleschi's old sacristy in San Lorenzo, Florence, built 1419–1428. The cube of the base is crowned by a dome with lantern, over an intermediate story of arches and pendentives. A ring of round windows pierces the base of the dome. Lines of articulation are expressed in dark stone against the light plaster walls. (Section reprinted from P. Murray, *The Architecture of the Italian Renaissance*, 1963, 1972, reprinted by permission of B. T. Batsford, Ltd., publisher.)

Figure 5-8b   Section through Michelangelo's new sacristy (Medici Chapel) in San Lorenzo, Florence, built 1520–1534. Though using the same elements of dark stone and pale plaster and the same shape of cube crowned by dome, Michelangelo also injected some original elements that change the chapel significantly. First, there is a four-part instead of a three-part elevation; the intermediate story tends to pull our attention upward, a pull intensified by the coffering of the dome. Second, within the articulation of the dark stone, a second skin of architectural elements in light stone makes a strong setting for the sculptures and cenotaphs. (Section also from Murray.)

integration of forms found in Alberti's work becomes with Michelangelo almost organic in its unity. This is a marked feature of his work as he matures, with each architectural member being made to do as much work as possible and to carry its load with dignity and vigor, much as the limbs of an athlete's body.

Michelangelo's work on the Laurentian Library exhibits his keen architectural wit. In the 1520s, he added a reading room to the monastery, setting it over an existing refectory, on the restricted urban site. Like the Medici Chapel (new sacristy) of the same decade, the library's vocabulary is essentially early

Renaissance in its simplicity, clarity, restraint, and human scale, but somewhat more muscular. Michelangelo even seems to have repeated the grid pattern of Brunelleschi's interior of San Lorenzo. A generation later, he completed the work by building a vestibule for the library. The main purpose of this vestibule was to house the tall stairway necessary to climb up to the library. Into an upright rectangle of space, of rather modest dimensions, Michelangelo inserted an enormous flight of stairs that nearly fill the floor area. They curl at the edges and have their railings set in about a quarter of the way from each outer edge of the stair—an unexpected placement that charges the stairway with tension. The walls of the space are articulated with the traditional gray stone but are carved into some very untraditional shapes. For instance, the blind niches that take the place of windows are framed by pilasterlike strips that taper downward, not upward as we expect. There are pairs of columns that seem to support the architecture above, which is a common enough feature, but the columns have two features that are most uncommon. First, they are themselves supported on giant consoles, or brackets, not on the customary pedestals or plinths. Second, they are recessed into the wall instead of standing in front of it. Having been one of the masters who determined the classical style of the High Renaissance (1500–1523), Michelangelo now was the first to break from that pattern into a freer style. In doing so he helped to originate the mode called Mannerism, and pointed to the incipient baroque. He experimented directly with the emotional effect of architecture on the viewer, an issue which became central to the baroque period.

The role of the individual architect in the Renaissance period was very like that of the individual in any Renaissance field: new emphasis was placed on individual experience and on individual credit for originality. In the life and work of each of these three men we can see that the architectural decisions each was able to make were influenced by the situation of their lives, and even by the particular city in which they worked. However, each had an individual view that went beyond these limitations. Consequently, the work of each led to problems that others worked on during the next 400 years. Many of the projects were never built as the architect had imagined them to be, but even their fragments and concepts were so rich in meaning that they have had powerful influence.

BIBLIOGRAPHY

Ackerman, J. S., "Architectural Practice in the Italian Renaissance," *Journal of the Society of Architectural Historians,* vol. 3, no. 3, October 1950, pp. 3–11. A general account which may usefully be compared with MacDonald's description of Roman architectural practice.

————, *The Architecture of Michelangelo,* Penguin, Baltimore, 1971. Noted for its insights, this book is also highly informative.

Edgerton, S., Jr., "Florentine Interest in Ptolemaic Cartography as Background for Renaissance Paintings, Architecture, and the Discovery of America," *Journal of the Society of Architectural Historians,* vol. 37, no. 4, December 1974, pp. 279–292. A fascinating account of the intellectual ferment in Florence during the first two decades of the fifteenth century.

Gadol, J., *Leon Baptista Alberti, Universal Man of the Early Renaissance,* University of Chicago Press, Chicago, IL, 1969.

Hyman, I. (ed.), *Brunelleschi in Perspective,* Prentice-Hall, Englewood Cliffs, N.J., 1974. A collection of documents related to Brunelleschi.

Mainstone, R., "Brunelleschi's Dome," *Architectural Review,* September 1977, pp. 157–166. A thought-provoking analysis of the engineering of the Florence cathedral dome.

Manetti, *Life of Brunelleschi,* Pennsylvania State University Press, 1970. Manetti was a disciple of Brunelleschi, and his biography has the authenticity of a personal witness.

Millon, H. A., "Rudolph Wittkower, *Architectural Principles in the Age of Humanism:* Its Influence on the Development and Interpretation of Modern Architecture," *Journal of the Society of Architectural Historians,* vol. 31, no. 2, May 1972, pp. 83–91. An intelligent comment on the effect of Wittkower's book on twentieth century architectural thought.

Prager, F. D., and G. Scaglia, *Brunelleschi: Studies of His Technology & Inventions,* M.I.T., Cambridge, MA, 1970. Chapters 2 and 3 deal with the dome; note especially pp. 53–54 on "Confluence of Classic and Gothic."

Rowe, Colin, and Robert Slutzky, "Transparency: Literal and Phenomenal . . . Part II." *Perspecta,* no. 13–14, 1971, pp. 293–296. A study, with many diagrams, of Michelangelo's design for the facade of San Lorenzo, Florence.

Wackernagel, M., *The World of the Florentine Renaissance Artist,* Princeton University Press, Princeton, N.J., 1981, A. Luchs (trans.). Note especially pp. 19–37 about the Florence cathedral project.

Wittkower, R., *Architectural Principles in the Age of Humanism,* Tiranti, London, 1952. Basic to understanding the thinking of Renaissance architects. Read especially the section on Alberti.

16
RENAISSANCE PALACES

FORMAL PATTERNS

The word "formal" as used in architectural history means "concerned with the outward form of something as distinguished from its content." Already we have noted that the Greeks used the well-developed forms of the Doric, Ionic, and Corinthian orders for their temples and other public buildings. The Romans changed the Greek orders, adding, for instance, a base to the Doric order and usually leaving off the fluting. In many Roman buildings, the Greek orders were used as decoration and not as a structure. In other words, the Greek orders were used for their formal characteristics. Later, Romanesque monasteries and churches again transformed the visual elements they inherited from the Romans.

In this chapter we will immerse ourselves in a sensual and intellectual experience of noticing what things look like and what meaning is attached to that appearance. By analyzing buildings according to their formal qualities, we will learn something about architecture and something about the methodology of architecture history.

Renaissance palaces are convenient for such study, because they offer distinct visual patterns. One can argue that study of appearance is particularly appropriate to Italian Renaissance palaces, since the patrons and architects vied with one another, especially with respect to the look of the public facades and that of the interior courtyards, rather than, say, the adequacy of the plumbing system or the beneficial effect of the building on small children. Since they concentrated more on the facade of the building than on any other aspect of it, we can in fairness take the facade as standing for the entire building. In a profound sense, Renaissance society was one in which the appearance of power was a form of power, and thus in a public sense, the facade *was* the building. (See Lauro Martines, *Power and Imagination*.)

We will inspect three groups of palaces, in Florence, in Rome, and in Venice, but confine ourselves to only a few examples.

Each of the cities had its own political, economic, and geographic character. Therefore, the facade in each city displayed a different combination of elements found in ancient Roman architecture and reused during the Renaissance. These elements included attached half columns and pilasters, large windows, rhythmic grouping of bay elements, cornices, repetition, and ornamentation based on Roman prototypes. Note that neither the materials nor the structural systems of Roman architecture were of importance. It was an erudite and visual allusion to antiquity that mattered and that contributed to the desired appearance.

To get a quick understanding of the possible richness of the manipulation of architectural elements, you may want to read Colin Rowe's piece on the facade that Michelangelo designed (but never built) for the church of San Lorenzo in Florence. (See bibliography, Chap. 15.) With the help of Rowe's diagrams, you can see all the various ways the eye and the mind can divide, group, and regroup the elements into triangles and H's, P's and T's—all of which possibilities are latent within the design. As one's attention flickers from one pattern to the other, whether one consciously realizes it or not, one's interest in the building increases. The viewer is never bored, because there is something new to be discovered at each glance. Churches and palaces were two building types whose facades were most highly developed in this way.

Palaces were as widely distributed in Renaissance Italy as are supermarkets in modern American towns. New commercial wealth created by merchant families during the early Renaissance enabled them to vie with the old aristocratic families in building palaces. By using the building for both business and residence, and by sharing with several generations of the same family, a merchant family could afford a palace. As we know from *Romeo and Juliet,* competition between families during the later Middle Ages oftentimes led to fights and even killings. Now it manifested itself in the distinct visual patterns of the palace facades. The differences were only marginal, because the function and basic message were the same, but there had to be enough differences so that others were impressed with a new solution to a common problem.

In dealing with the palaces, we will limit our study to matters of open and closed patterns, balance, and the amount and kind of decoration resulting in effects of simplicity or richness. Other aspects of the formal qualities of these buildings, such as proportions and number theory, are discussed in detail in the Rowe article and in Wittkower's *Architectural Principles in the Age of Humanism*.

When Wittkower's book was first published in 1952, formal qualities were the principal subject matter of architectural history, whereas now they take their place among a long list of equally important aspects of architecture that must be studied concurrently—tradition, economics, structure, and so on, as the titles of the chapters of this book suggest. The older way of writing architectural history was logical for two major reasons. First, most architectural historians were originally art historians. They brought to the study of architecture the tools that had proved so successful in the study of painting and sculpture. The main question in those fields is, "What does it look like and why does it look like that?" Since, for instance, not even such a huge and important painting as that on the ceiling of the Sistine Chapel could possibly have the economic effect as did pyramids or the Great Wall of China, it was possible to consider economic and other social questions as belonging to the social history of art, and as not being vital to the study of art itself. Second, the study of art and architecture by period and style proved to be immensely fruitful with respect to enhancing knowledge and understanding of the objects. One would not lightly abandon a method that worked so well. Without relinquishing interest in style and period, architectural history has since expanded to reflect the utilitarian aspects of the built environment. Hence, the long list of questions this book is concerned with.

For this chapter only, we will not discuss most aspects of the following: data about how the building was used, either in its entirety or in its parts; questions of new versus reused buildings; economics; structure; and the emotional effect of the building on either its inhabitants or its observers, except insofar as any of these are related to the visual appearance of the building. For these other questions about Florentine palaces see R. Goldthwaite, *The Building of Renaissance Florence: An Economic and Social History*. It must be admitted that even a study that tries to confine itself to the formal qualities of Renaissance palaces must sometimes invoke their sociopolitical context to a limited extent in order to reveal the meaning of the formal qualities.

RUCELLAI PALACE

We will see such a necessity in our discussion of the Rucellai Palace in Florence, built primarily between 1446 and 1451 and continued in the late 1450s. There had been substantial houses in Florence built during the late Middle Ages, but this palace is the first of the new group that were ornamented with forms taken from ancient Roman and not medieval prototypes. The Rucellai Palace was actually a remodeling of existing houses, brought together visually by a new facade and supplied with a new interior courtyard that also unified them. This palace is usually attributed to Alberti, but new research has suggested that the actual supervisor and contractor was likely to have been Bernardo Rossellino. Just as in the case of his churches, Alberti may have been responsible for the original concept of the building and then entrusted its erection to another: or the second architect may have been completely responsible for the palace, as he was for a very similar palace in Pienza. (See Mack, "The Rucellai Palace: Some New Proposals.")

The design of the Rucellai facade is based upon study of the Colosseum in Rome (see Figs. 16-1 and 16-2). The Colosseum pattern of a first story in Doric,

Figure 16-1   Facade of Rucellai Palace, Florence, Italy, built between 1446 and 1451 and later, by Alberti or Rossellino. The three-part elevation uses ancient forms derived from the elevation of the Colosseum in Rome but flattened here into linear patterns. Pilasters in the Doric, Ionic, and Corinthian orders divide the facade into bays, each containing a door or window. The stories are separated horizontally by entablatures that serve as string courses, and a large heavy cornice tops the whole facade. Plans to continue the facade toward the right were never carried out. (Photo by J. Null.)

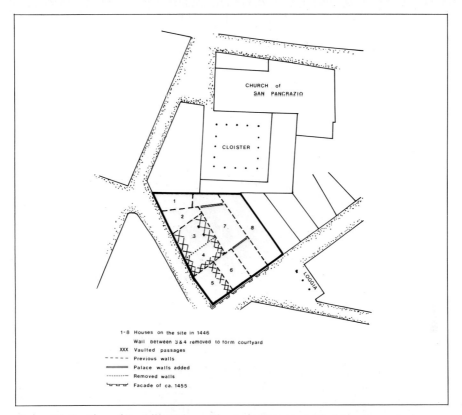

CHURCH of
SAN PANCRAZIO

· CLOISTER ·

LOGGIA

1-8 Houses on the site in 1446
Wall between 3 & 4 removed to form courtyard
XXX Vaulted passages
----- Previous walls
Palace walls added
.... Removed walls
Facade of ca. 1455

Figure 16-2   Plan of Rucellai Palace. The property on which this palace stands was gradually assembled by the Rucellai family and the buildings were remodeled into a palace for the extended family. (Plan redrawn from C. R. Mack, "The Rucellai Palace: Some New Proposals", *Art Bulletin*.)

a second in Ionic, and a third in Corinthian has been adapted here, with arched openings between the orders. In keeping with mid- fifteenth-century interest in wall surfaces, however, the attached half columns of the Colosseum are in the Rucellai Palace flattened into pilasters: as such, they echo the fourth story of the Colosseum, which has pilasters and not columns. Instead of the open arches of the Colosseum, which would hardly be suitable for a house, the openings are glassed. Within the large round-headed arch, each window has two elongated openings which are also round-headed; this whole ensemble is reminiscent of medieval compositions with double windows. Both the voussoirs of the windows and all the other blocks of the wall surface are outlined by the shadows that lie in the curved indentations between blocks. By adding texture to the wall, this device makes us much more conscious of the wall surface and hence its flatness than we would be if the wall were left unadorned and therefore unnoticed. A small variation in the appearance of the wall become a self-referential message about the wall.

STROZZI PALACE

For contrast, we will look at another Florentine palace to see what a different architect could do with some of the same elements. The Strozzi Palace was built by Giuliano da Sangallo and Cronaca between 1489 and 1507 (see Fig. 16-3). The form of the stone blocks that make the surface of the wall has been manipulated here in a more assertive way. Each palace was not only the headquarters for the family business but also the fortress within which the extended family was safe from its rivals. So this palace was made to appear strong, so that the family strength was truly thereby increased. Whereas the Rucellai Palace had repeated vertical emphasis in its pilasters, the Strozzi Palace is basically horizontal with emphasizing rows of stone, called "string courses," that separate the stories visually. The lowest story has blocks of stone rusticated (finished with a protruding rough surface and deep joints) as if they were bulging under the weight of the upper floors. The middle story has less protrusion and the top floor is fairly smooth. The impression of strength at the lowest level is emphasized also by the few openings—only doors and some high windows. In the middle and upper stories, arcades of round-headed windows bring a great deal of light into the interior. The whole facade is topped off with a heavy cornice, which the viewer reads as pertaining to the whole composition.

Figure 16-3 Strozzi Palace, built by Giuliano da Sangallo and Cronaca between 1489 and 1507. New emphasis on a central doorway; same emphasis on heavy cornice and arched windows as that of the Rucellai Palace. The wall surface flows between and around the windows, uninterrupted by pilasters; the surface becomes smoother and flatter as the wall rises, story by story, in a way that formally indicates the nature of masonry structure. (Photo by Alinari, from Editorial Photocolor Archives.)

The other thoughtfully composed element of these palaces was the inner courtyard. Either rectangular or square, the courts were provided with colonnades, usually on all four sides, which served as outdoor hallways (feasible in the Mediterranean climate). Like the Greek house earlier, the Renaissance palace depended on its court to bring light and air to many rooms of the house. The court was also used as private outdoor space. Most important to the builders and to our discussion is the fact that architects and patrons competed to have the most elegant courtyard. The columns customarily supported arches which in turn supported either the upper wall or possibly an upper porch, called a loggia. One formal problem that occupied architects for at least 75 years was the question of the corner support. At first, as at the Rucellai and Strozzi Palaces, the corner column was the same size as all the others and spaced at the same distance. Not liking this attenuated effect, architects later tried designing thicker columns or using an L-shaped pier in the corner or a smaller pier with a column in front of it—various attempts to indicate that the corner support seemed to be doing more work than the other supports and should thus appear stronger.

CANCELLERIA PALACE

The Rucellai and Strozzi Palaces by no means exhaust the interesting features of Florentine palaces, but we will jump now to the Rome of the end of the fifteenth century to look at the Cancelleria, a very early Renaissance palace built there between 1468 and possibly 1498. Power and wealth were shifting to Rome during the last half of the century, so the rich began to build palaces like the new type in Florence, since that architecture was perfect for displaying taste and power and money. For a long time the Cancelleria was attributed to Bramante, but we now have good reason to doubt that he went to Rome so early. It is still possible that he might have been connected with the palace at a distance, like Alberti with some of his projects, but we have no evidence of this.

The palace is so long that it needs several doorways, but for the first time the central one is emphasized with bigger door jambs and with relief carving set above it. (Emphasizing the central door would become a major feature of Baroque architecture a hundred years later.) The whole facade is given unified treatment in the depth of carving around the individual stones. The windows are further articulated by being set between pairs of pilasters. The same kind of detailing is carried through into the courtyard, where the rectangles enclosing the windows utilize proportions called the golden rectangle, which is a rectangle of such proportions that if you subtract from it a rectangle of the same proportions, what is left is a perfect square. The golden rectangle, with almost the ratio of 5 to 8, has fascinated architects and others over the centuries, being both stimulating and satisfying, even to people who do not know that is what they are looking at. Its use in the Cancelleria is another indication of

Renaissance preoccupation with mathematical proportions as formal elements.

The courtyard of the Cancelleria has a different solution to the problem of the corner column—an L-shaped pillar. If the single column at the Strozzi Palace was too skimpy, this L-shaped pillar may be too robust, so difficult is it to arrive at the proper formal solution.

MASSIMO PALACE

Quite a different approach to the formalities of architecture may be seen in the Massimo Palace of 1532. This was built in Rome by Peruzzi, in a style called Mannerism. Just as the perfect moment of classicism in ancient Greece had lasted only about 25 years, so also did high gothic and the high Renaissance each last about 25 years (1200 to 1225 and 1500 to 1525, respectively). High Renaissance came to an abrupt end partly because of the political disruptions embodied in the Sack of Rome in 1527 by imperial troops. After that, adherence to perfection as embodied in architectural rules seemed pointless. The mood in architecture, as in the other arts, was rather one of irony, of emphasis through distortion and deflection of expectations. In keeping with such a mood, architects were no longer interested in perfection, restraint, balance or wholeness. The Sack of Rome seemed to be such an aberration

Figure 16-4   Facade of Massimo Palace, Rome; built by Peruzzi in 1532. Paired pilasters flanking windows, a heavy cornice, and emphasis on the individual stone blocks of the wall unite this palace with the Florentine formal traditions for palace facades. The screen of columns before the dark recess of the opening, the curved facade, and the horizontal windows treated like picture frames are new. (Photo by Alinari, from Editorial Photocolor Archives.)

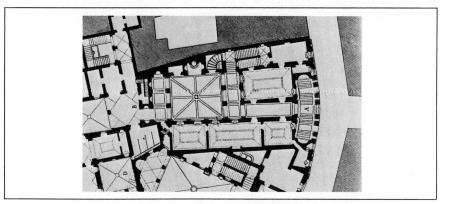

Figure 16-5   Plan of Massimo Palace. At A is the dark entranceway behind its screen of columns. A corridor leads past reception rooms on either side to the courtyard and portico at B. (Florentine and Venetian palaces used their ground floors for storage and business.) At D is the courtyard of Massimo's brother's palace, also built by Peruzzi and accessible from B. (Plan from S. Rasmussen, *Experiencing Architecture*, 1959, reprinted by permission of M.I.T. Press.)

from expected behavior that it called into question all rules, including those of architecture. The change was not from order to disorder but rather from a consensus of what was architecturally desirable to varying individual attitudes about what might be interesting.

The Massimo Palace, a fine example in the Mannerist style, is one of a pair of palaces for brothers, set together on a curved lot on a narrow street (see Figs. 16-4 and 16-5). This was the first Renaissance palace to have a curved facade. Peruzzi countered customary expectations that the facade would be flat and created surprise or even shock by this difference. He then compounded the sense of the unexpected by punching a hollow into the very center of the facade, where the solidity of the entrance door and its frame was expected. Here a pair of columns, which actually supported the upper wall, is on the same plane as the exterior wall. The columns were set off by the sun, standing out most dramatically from the entranceway behind, which is seen as a dark, shadowed void. The windows in the wall above the columns were treated almost as pictures, with heavily scrolled frames and horizontal oblong proportions, a far from common treatment. A strong cornice finished the facade. Beyond this entrance portico a corridor leads to the always-present courtyard. Here too Peruzzi has played with customary expectations, for the usual colonnade does not extend all around it. Above the partial colonnade runs a loggia; and between the two Peruzzi has cut slits into the wall to bring unexpected light into the corridor space.

The various elements encountered at the Massimo Palace were no cause for surprise were it not for a body of recognized formal patterns. A Renaissance palace should have a strong flat facade, interrupted only by a large doorway and the necessary windows. Windows at mezzanine level could be square or horizontal, but other windows were upright rectangles. Noticeable deviations constitute a formal device for which the viewer has both emotional and intellectual responses. Mannerism thus depends for its success upon the existence of formal tradition as well as public awareness of that tradition.

Formal traditions in Venice were more sensual and less intellectualized than were those in Florence. The ancient Roman forms that Venetian architects drew upon during the Renaissance were likely to be from the rich building traditions of the imperial period rather than from those of the austere republican period.

In Venice, where the main avenues are canals, the palaces lining them are seen in light reflected up from the moving water. Approach to the palaces on these canals gave a broader vision than did the narrow twisting streets of Florence or Rome. Architects responded to these challenges by making facades richer looking—more ornament, closer together, more fully developed in three dimensions in Venice than in Florence or Rome at the same period. Palaces as well as churches are discussed and photographed in McAndrews's book, *Venetian Architecture of the Early Renaissance*.

VENDRAMIN PALACE

In an early example, the Vendramin Palace, probably built in 1509 by Coducci and Lombardo (and famous as the house in which Wagner died), the formal requirements of a Venetian palace are clear (see Fig. 16-6). Business was conducted on the first floor (ground level) just as in Florence, with the numerous family groups having suites on the upper floors and all sharing the reception rooms. The entrance had wide steps onto which people could step from gondolas and goods could be unloaded. The doorway had to be wide enough to receive merchandise which would be stored within. Here the doorway was notable for its size and central placement. The prominent windows have their upper edges set at the same level as the top of the door. Tall arched windows flank the door, and pairs of small windows in turn flank these. Between the openings, the wall was punctuated with pilasters, in a regular pattern: a pair of pilasters, a window, a pair of pilasters, a bigger window, a single pilaster, the door, another single pilaster, another large window, a pair of pilasters, the small window, and a final pair of pilasters. The vertical strokes of the pilasters carried the eye to an entablature into which were set consoles supporting the balconies of the middle story. The formal elements of the middle story responded to but did not repeat exactly those of the water-level story; there were five openings, all windows, grouped as an outer window on each side and a set of three at the center, set apart by attached columns rather than pilasters. Pairs of columns framed the outer windows, whereas the central windows were separated by single columns. A decorative pattern of carved wreaths enriched the second level with its independent rhythm. The third story was more like the middle than the lower

Figure 16-6   Drawing of the facade of the Vendramin Palace in Venice. Built by Coducci and Lombardo in 1509. This drawing from the Visentini workshop reduces the palace to a formal pattern of lines on paper. From waterline to top of cornice, the square block of the building is divided horizontally by entablatures into three equal bands, each supported by a classical colonnade attached to the facade. These supports divide the facade into five bays. The outer bays are flanked by pairs of columns; the inner three are separated by single columns. On the middle and top floors the windows are all the same shape; this shape is repeated in the pair of windows that flanks the central door. (Drawing reproduced from Cott. Aug I.52, courtesy of the British Museum.)

one but did not repeat it exactly. The third level was distinguished by the richest sculptural decoration, with family emblems such as circles and the lion's head symbolic of Venice set into the frieze at the top. The whole was crowned by a cornice.

CORNER DELLA CA'GRANDE PALACE

With full knowledge of this developing tradition for palace facades, by 1525 Sansovino could build the palace called Corner della Ca'Grande (Fig. 16-7). [The name seems to be a pun: The patrons were the Corner family. The house is at the corner (the same word in Italian and English) of the Grande Canal;

Figure 16-7 Facade of the palace called Corner Ca'Grande. Built by Sansovino for the Corner family beginning in 1537. Into the heavily rusticated bottom story he has inserted a triple doorway, set between pairs of long windows, each topped by a square mezzanine window rather like the upper windows of the Massimo Palace. The two upper stories are treated similarly: seven windows, each separated by pairs of attached columns and opening onto a balcony. A subtle increase in central emphasis is obtained by uniting the three central balconies into a single long strip. Oval windows at the attic level and a heavy cornice complete the facade. (Photo by Alinari.)

Ca'Grande is Venetian dialect for "great house" but can also be taken as an abbreviation for "grand canal".] Sansovino was the major architect in Venice at this time, putting up many important public buildings. Again we find the major entrance being a flight of stairs to the water—but this time flanked by two other doors, which are in turn flanked by windows, with heavily rusticated frames. A set of small mezzanine windows is inserted above the level of the doors. On the middle story, the pattern of ornament and fenestration is a pair of half columns and then a window, repeated in seven bays evenly across the facade and ending in a pair of half columns, a pattern repeated also in the upper story.

Figure 16-8   Grimani Palace at S. Luca in Venice, begun in 1557 by Michele Sanmichele. Culmination of the experiments in design of palace facades, this one is slightly taller than it is wide. The three stories have become three and a mezzanine above the ground floor. Using the triumphal arch motif, the central door is flanked by smaller doors of the same shape. Rectangular windows fill up each bay over the smaller doors and are then repeated above larger windows in the outer bays. Tall slender Corinthian pilasters separate these bays, a single one on either side of the central door and pairs on each side of the outer bays. The entry stairs are widened along the facade to accommodate the traffic of all three doorways. Along the middle and top stories, paired and single attached columns repeat the pilaster pattern—2, 2, 1, 1, 2, 2. The entablature above the ground floor includes a balcony, so that the proportions of this "string course" are properly tall enough; between the middle and upper story no such balcony is used. The upper cornice is tall enough to dominate the whole facade and heavy enough to outweigh the lacy balcony below. The outer and central windows of the two upper stories are round-headed like the doors, but the four other windows have rectangle above rectangle, echoing the outer bays of the lowest story. Altogether, this is a facade of high intellectual and aesthetic interest. (Photo by Douglas Lewis.)

Sansovino uses not only half columns but also three-quarter columns for enrichment. Likewise he varies the treatment of the wall surface from relatively heavy rustication for the lowest story to smoother surface for the upper stories. Because the occupants were very rich and prominent, their house had not only the most prominent location but also a garden—a very rare commodity in Venice. Within the palace there was a courtyard, the facades of which had the same kinds of rustication as that of the outer facade. Its colonnades carried an open loggia above.

By careful thought for details of fenestration and ornamentation, for surface treatment of individual stones and whole walls, for ratios of wholes to parts and the incidence of holes to solids, the Renaissance architect elevated palaces into the realm of architecture. The formal qualities of this kind of building have remained the source of many later palaces and government centers. The intellectual fascination of tracing the use of a particular motif such as the golden section or pairs of attached semicolumns continues high, and may even be higher than before now that psychologists are studying how aesthetic interest is aroused and satisfied.

BIBLIOGRAPHY

Aryton, M., *Golden Section,* Metheun, London, 1957. A book on the Golden Section.

Borissavlievitch, M., *The Golden Number and the Scientific Aesthetics of Architecture,* Tiranti, London, 1958. Proportional geometry, important to the Greeks, was "rediscovered" by Renaissance architects. (cf. the Millon article and Wittkower book listed in Chap. 15).

Goldthwaite, R., *The Building of Renaissance Florence: An Economic and Social History,* Johns Hopkins, Baltimore, 1981. Considers many of the questions ignored by this chapter.

McAndrews, J., *Venetian Architecture of the Early Renaissance,* M.I.T., Cambridge, Mass., 1980. Copiously illustrated, this is a perfect example of the formalist school of architectural history.

Mack, C. R., "The Rucellai Palace: Some New Proposals," *Art Bulletin,* vol. 56, December 1974, pp. 517–529. Reply by K. Foster in vol. 58, March 1976, pp. 109–113. Inspection of both documents and building led Mack to some surprising conclusions about this famous palace.

Martines, L., *Power and Imagination,* Knopf, New York, 1979. The role of Florence in Renaissance Italy, and the role of power and status in Florentine life.

Murray, P., *Architecture of the Italian Renaissance,* Schocken, New York, 1972. A good first book for students unacquainted with this material, but it holds its interest even for the mature scholar. Well written.

INTERLUDE C

I n the past five chapters, we considered pairs of buildings and questions: Castles and safety, Romanesque monasteries and religious motivation, Gothic cathedrals and structure, early Renaissance buildings and the individual architect, and Renaissance palaces and formal qualities. As an intellectual exercise, let us now recombine the topics and consider castles and structure, monasteries and safety, cathedrals and formal qualities, early Renaissance buildings and motivation, and palaces and individual architects. By doing so, we may understand how each question might be applied to each kind of building to enrich our understanding of it.

12 For castles to achieve the safety they were designed for, their structure had to embody the ultimate in the principle of firmness, as Vitruvius would have understood it.

When the chaos of the Dark Ages evolved into a more organized medieval society, new structures were erected. Methods of handling stone and mortar were rediscovered and applied to the full range of architecture. Castles were part of this building process. So successful were their builders that the strongest castles have lasted through various bombardments and lack of maintenance until today. They do not merely give the appearance of strength, their structure actually makes them strong.

Shapes of castles were related to the strategy of attack and defense. Many were round, a shape which can withstand bombardment by stones from catapults and even by the more modern cannonballs. The central keep in Coucy-le-Chateau is a good example of this shape. So thick were its walls that without loss of strength they could be pierced by passageways. The cylindrical form and the thickness together made such a castle nearly impervious to undermining. Because the designers at that time lacked the mathematics to analyze how the various configurations worked when subjected to different kinds of stress, they based their calculations on experience. If a square keep got its corners knocked off during a bombardment, then a round one was better; or a square one with rounded corners such as the Tower of London. If a thin wall could be easily pierced or undermined, then it was made thicker. However, their rule-of-thumb methods did not allow for fine distinctions between, say, an 18-foot-thick wall that would be strong enough in 95 percent of the battles as opposed to a 20-foot-wall that would survive 99 percent of the time. Most castles were built over several generations, thereby showing evolving structural systems, such as the early keep and the later hall and boudoir in Coucy.

The slit windows found in castles were partly designed as such for safety, as we have seen, but partly for structural reasons as well. For the strength of the walls, they were kept as narrow as possible on the exterior, splaying inward to allow as much light as possible inside. Interior spaces had stocky piers topped with spreading capitals to support arches and vaults, sometimes wooden as those in Coucy but more often stone as those of the Tower of London. Since the same structural principles and elements were used in towers, churches, city walls, and the more important houses, the same aesthetic effects were achieved along with the same structural integrity.

13 If we consider the monasteries of the Middle Ages as havens of safety for their inhabitants, we must realize, first, that the safety we are talking about was both metaphysical and physical. Metaphysically, the monks and nuns were safe from the temptations and sins of the world, living among a community of individuals who were united in a quest for spiritual goodness and devotion. Special laws protected religious persons from war and other kinds of violence. Any attack on clergy was subject to the penalty of excommunication, the worst form of punishment. In a metaphysical sense, the monastery was a sanctuary from the world.

The physical arrangements of the monastery reflected the metaphysical ideas. As early as the plan of St. Gall, there could be a wall around the monastery, just as there was around the town or the castle. Placing the church at the very center of the composition not only symbolized religious withdrawal, but also provided maximum buffering between the church, as place of last refuge, and the outer world. More worldly needs, such as orchards or pigsties, occupied the outer corners of the complex. Later, in Cluny, the Romanesque church was ringed by buildings set around their own courtyards, focusing inward. When Cluny was rebuilt to house the enlarged community, it was also walled in for safety.

Perhaps the ultimate expression of the safety found in religion is the fortress church exemplified by Albi in south central France. The cathedral here was tall and strongly built, with slit windows in the lower level like those in castles. Should the town come under attack, the townspeople could take refuge in the church, hoping the enemy would spare them out of religious respect; if necessary they could fight from the church, using it as a fortress.

14   In an earlier discussion of cathedrals, we concentrated on their structure; now we will consider their formal aspects. The most perfect, formally, of the French cathedrals of the high gothic period is Notre-Dame de Paris. Its facade is divided regularly into nine parts; its towers are identical; and its overall unity is well demonstrated in the restraint with which the transept arms do not extend beyond the outer walls of the church. By contrast, the cathedral in Chartres is much less perfect, being a pastiche of Romanesque and Gothic elements by some miracle transformed into one of the greatest buildings of all time. The western facade is composed of Romanesque (and therefore rounded) portals from the mid-twelfth century under a turn-of-the-century rose window that is slightly askew from the central axis and flanked by towers that are very different from each other, revealing the 200 years or more that passed from the beginning of one to the completion of the other. Approximately 75 to 100 years separate the carving of the sculptures of the west facade from those of the north and south, but the courtesy of the later sculptors was so great that they deliberately modeled theirs after the earlier ones, so the difference is less obvious and the unity of the whole is thereby greater. Another subtlety in the composition is that of the material of the sculpture, which is a different stone from that of the masonry of the walls, but a stone of the same hue and grain; it is merely finer and thus more suitable for carving intricate detail. Once again the visual unity is emphasized. We have already noted the subtle variation achieved by making the piers alternately round with octagonal colonettes and octagonal with round colonettes—variety within unity, which could be the theme of this cathedral.

Turning now to Notre-Dame d'Amiens, another high gothic church, we find less symmetry than that of Notre Dame but more than that of Chartres. Its facade is quite unified, though crowded with detail. The very fine figures are set above a band of quadrifoils (flower-like patterns with four lobes) with reliefs of the months, virtues, etc.; and in the second half of the century brackets were added which contribute to the rich effect. The towers are as open as lacework, but since they both date from the same building period, they have the same form. Most notable asymmetry is in the transepts. Since the south transept would have opened into existing buildings, it was truncated and completed without a door; in decoration, however, it agrees with the rest of the building. Inside, the formal effects of the dimensions of bays and height of vaults are much altered today by the many gifts and alterations that have come to enrich it over the years, as well as by a German bombardment in a battle of World War I in which most of the medieval glazing was destroyed.

Dating from the same period is the cathedral in Reims. As a result of its cleaning around 1970, its beautiful creamy-rosy limestone is now apparent. Like Notre Dame and Amiens, its towers are nearly identical; like Amiens the facade boasts a row of statues of the kings of France, but here they are placed above the rose window. The row thus acts as a base for the towers as well as designating the height of the nave. The kings are visible in less detail than those in Amiens because they are farther from the ground, but they do not obscure the rose window here as they do in Amiens. As usual, the portals are richly sculptured, but the architect has introduced a unique feature—a replacement of the reliefs of the tympana (the space within the arch of the doorway, above the lintel) above the doors with larger and smaller roses of stained glass, set in spherical triangles of the glass. In a distinctive way, this glass brings more light into the interior. The architect immediately took advantage of this by designing another unique feature—the interior of the west wall as richly carved as the exterior of most gothic churches.

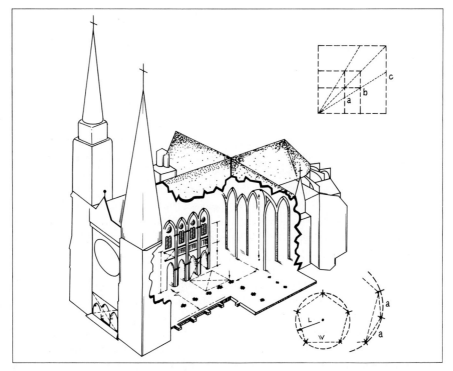

Figure C-1 Use of a chain of measurements for the principal features of Chartres Cathedral. These measurements relate to each other as the sides and diagonals of a golden rectangle (one of such proportions that if you subtract a square the size of the shorter side, the remaining rectangle has the same proportions as the original one), a pentagon of nearly the same module, its circumscribing circle and its inscribed decagon. A particular length occurs again and again, such as Z for the diagonal of a square double bay of the nave, the same Z as the height from floor to windowsill of the clerestory. Similarly the width of the nave is the same distance as that from the floor to the string course below the triforium. Use of such measurements ties the gothic interior to the Romanesque facade, where the west portal is set in another golden rectangle. (Drawing by J. Parker.)

Figure C-2   Facade of San Lorenzo, Florence; wooden model by Michelangelo, 1516 (project never built). Like Chartres Cathedral (Fig. C-1), this facade uses the golden section—but to a somewhat different result. The architectural elements such as string course and entablature are used to demarcate the geometric divisions. The geometry is expressed three-dimensionally with classical columns, and so on, in a series of interlocking and repetitive patterns. (Photo from Murray, *Architecture of the Italian Renaissance*, 1963 & 1972, by permission of B. T. Batsford Ltd., publishers.)

At each cathedral, the relation of forms between the nave and the side aisles is formal as well as structural. Von Simson, in *The Gothic Cathedral,* describes the use of the golden rectangle in Chartres, which sets up relations that are both tense and elegant (see Figs. C-1; cf. C-2). All the cathedrals use the same vocabulary but with different nuances. Amiens, the structure of which is more complicated than the others, seems to have had more influence than the others from English gothic, in which the experimentation was largely in decoration rather than in the structure of the French gothic.

This quick comparison of four French cathedrals, all built under the influence of the French monarchy, shows that different formal qualities distinguish these churches from one another, giving each a unique character within a common period style.

15   These medieval buildings also yield fruitful discussion when examined with respect to religious motivation. Other kinds of motivation have spurred other kinds of architecture. In the early Renaissance period of palace building for instance, there was competition between families to flaunt their strength and wealth in an attempt to acquire more of both. It was better for the citizens and the city when families channeled their energies into building rather than raising private armies and attacking one another directly. Moreover, families that added noble houses to the cityscape received public praise and accrued status. One could read the changing relations of the Medici family to their city in the changes made to the ground-floor level of their palace. It began as a loggia, open to the street and plaza through large arches, but after the upheavals in the life of the family and of the city in the early years of the sixteenth century, the arches were walled up to become doors and windows, and the family was safely separated from the passing throng.

The cathedral of Florence was not merely the great opportunity the architect Brunelleschi (see Fig. C-3) was waiting for to make his individual impact; it was also the religious center of the city of Florence. As such, it was the focus of attention of the city's guilds. The wool guild in particular expressed its dominance over the economic life of the city by taking responsibility for and making decisions about the erection of the great church through an executive committee called the Overseers of the Works of the Cathedral. They wanted to increase their own political and economic importance and to win the cooperation of the other guilds for this work. But they were also individuals of personal piety, so that the motivation for completing and adorning the cathedral was more complicated. It is as important to acknowledge and understand such webs of motivations as it is to recognize that motivation is one among many interesting questions with regard to this or any major structure.

16 From the Renaissance on, one important motivation was the expresssion of the individuality of the architect. In the Middle Ages, the architect had been so subservient

Figure C-3 Portrait of Filippo Brunelleschi from his monument in the Florence Cathedral, placed under his great dome in 1447, following his death in 1446. This portrait shows the mature architect as intelligent and self-possessed, but also as unpretentious. (Photo Alinari, courtesy Editorial Photocolor Archives.)

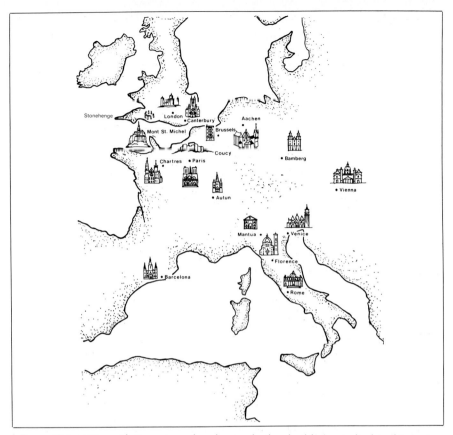

Figure C-4   Map with European churches and other buildings studied in this text.
(Drawing by J. Parker.)

to the client that sometimes the architect's name is not even recorded. You will remember that the Abbot Suger thought of himself and was considered by his contemporaries as the builder of the new parts of St. Denis, even though to him the structure was an insignificant consideration. By the time of Massimo Palace in the 1530s, the role of the architect had changed radically. He now had much more effect on the building, being hired because of his individuality as well as his competency. This individuality enabled him to create a palace different not only from previous Florentine or Roman examples but also from the brother's palace next door—even though both were made of the same material and by the same architect during the same period. Individuality has continued to be highly valued in architecture. Today it is a condemnation to say of architects that they merely copy and express no individuality of their own.

At this point, we have dealt with sixteen questions and monuments. For the student who has been faithful about considering each monument in the light of each question, the total of interactions is 256. If the student compounds the interaction by considering groups of questions with each monument (safety and motivation and structure and the individual architect and formal qualities as they pertain to a Renaissance palace, for instance), the number of possible interactions quickly soars into the thousands. We have not presented enough information to carry all these reflections to any depth, but the suggested readings and whatever picture books come to hand will possibly supplement by stimulating further thought.

17

ST. PETER'S, ROME

THE DESIGN PROCESS

In every architectural commission, there are many factors that influence the design process. Usually the process is fairly rapid and is only sketchily documented, if at all, by a few drawings or records, such as contracts. Rarely does the patron or the architect stop to write down all the problems that were addressed and the many possible solutions put forth before the one that was finally adopted. For the student, this state of affairs makes it very difficult for understanding how the design process works.

Fortunately, the design of St. Peter's in Rome extended over a very long period of time (Fig. 17-1). Moreover, the patron and architects involved realized that they were working on a major monument not only of the Christian faith but also of architecture. Careful and abundant records were kept. Like a

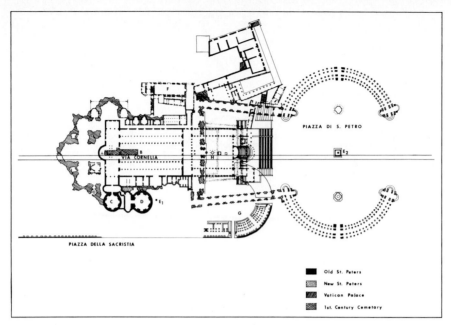

Figure 17-1   Plans of old and new St. Peter's Basilica, Rome, Italy, superimposed.
Old St. Peter's was built around 330 and its replacement was begun around 1500
and completed some 250 years later. In this plan, the original cemetery next to the
Circus of Nero can be seen; it still exists under the lowest level of the basilica. The
relative sizes of the two churches are evident, with the east end of the new church
dwarfing the apse of the old one. The original and present location of the obelisk
can be seen, as well as the juxtaposition of the Vatican Palace to the basilica.
(Redrawn by L. Dearborn from a plan of C. Fontana, *I Tempio Vaticano e Sua
Origini*, Rome, 1694.) A, Shrine of St. Peter. B, Roman cemetery. C and D,
Mausoleums from late Roman era. E1, Early site of obelisk. E2, Present site of
obelisk. F, Sistine Chapel with Vatican Palace to its right. G, Circus of Nero. H, Pine
cone in early Christian atrium.

slow-motion moving picture, the action has been slowed down for us, so that it
can be more easily comprehended. Decisions correspond to specific physical
elements in the existing structure. The decisions themselves thus have a kind of
visibility that even the uninitiated can discern.

Old St. Peter's basilica of the early fourth century was by the mid-fifteenth
century not only old but also decrepit. Some walls were leaning more than a
foot from the perpendicular, possibly because the structure had, as we have
seen, been built partly on filled land. Lack of maintenance while the papacy
was lodged in France during the fourteenth century added to the fact Rome
was nearly depopulated meant that shabbiness increased the effects of age.
The papacy returned to Rome under Eugenius IV, but it was Nicholas V who
first planned to improve the condition of St. Peter's.

THE FIRST STEP

The first step in design is an analysis of the givens (the unavoidable circumstances) of the site, the program (that is, the functions for which the building is to provide), the climate, and other unalterable factors. In the 1450s, Nicholas V had plans drawn up for the enlargement of the transepts and apse of the old basilica. His scheme of remodeling and enlarging the old building was relatively modest . Both his plan and all subsequent efforts were limited by the site of the old church over St. Peter's grave, an unalterable factor. Pope Nicholas realized that the knowledge of new church building in Rome could be a significant propaganda statement about the renewed energy of the church in Rome, but he died before his plans were carried out. Possibly his friend Alberti may have influenced him in making plans for St. Peter's, even though Bernardo Rossellino is officially credited with the design.

The period 1450–1500 may be thought of as a long period of analysis of the problem of replacing Old St. Peter's. We have already seen that in the closing years of the fifteenth century, new architectural ideas were coming from Florence to Rome. Many of the new ideas were associated with Bramante, who was building the small church called the Tempietto in Rome and beginning the elaborate garden court at the Vatican called the Belvedere. Bramante's patron Pope Julius II was first to set the goal of completely replacing an old building with a new one that would be bigger, stronger, and generally more impressive.

In the early years of the sixteenth century, Bramante drew up for Pope Julius the plans for a basilica of Greek cross plan (with four equal arms) and a great domed crossing. The dome was to be supported by large piers, quite unlike the simple colonnades and plain wall surfaces of old St. Peter's. His plans were presented to Julius II in 1506 (see Fig. 17-2).

From then until at least the middle of the century, the process of setting goals and priorities for the church was influenced by a number of actual constraints: First, there was the necessity of continuing to use the old nave with the new choir while building the new nave. This was facilitated by the custom of beginning from the west—then a fairly open site—and working toward the east. Second, there was the method of financing, to be discussed below. Third, the influence of papal power on the artistic vision of the architect was significant. Fourth, there were wars, such as the Sack of Rome in 1527, and other interruptions.

In the Christian tradition, centralized churches were preferred for martyr's shrines and elongated ones for congregational worship. Since St. Peter's basilica was both, it was necessary for the plan to include both ideas. After the fall of Constantinople in 1453, the papacy more than ever felt itself to be the head of a far-flung religion, so the premier church building of this religion must be both magnificent in detail and charged with specific symbolic meaning—the focus of faith, embodied in a centralized building, as seen, for instance, in

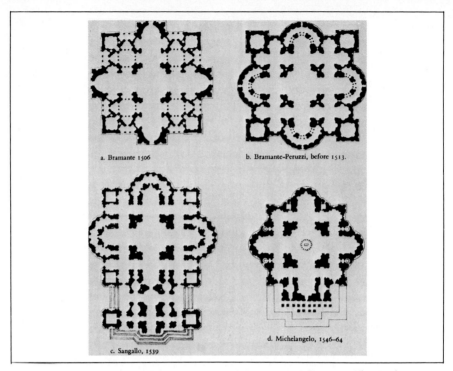

a. Bramante 1506   b. Bramante-Peruzzi, before 1513.

c. Sangallo, 1539   d. Michelangelo, 1546–64

Figure 17-2   Plans for St. Peter's. (Reprinted from J. S. Ackerman, *The Architecture of Michelangelo,* by permission from A. Zwemmer. Ltd.)

a drawing now at the Uffizi, which reveals Bramante's first scheme for St. Peter's. It shows a complex and sophisticated space with a large central cross-shape nave and transepts and with smaller crosses filling in the corners, providing an interrelation and repetition of parts. The beveled piers made the central space larger than the arms. This plan did not provide for the congregation, however, so a second scheme was called for in which the same kind of centralized plan was modified by an extended nave along the east-west axis, also preserved for us in drawings.

The early design stage of any building project results typically in a number of schemes which are evaluated for their relevance to the givens of the problem, the stated priorities, and other constraints. Discussions of the form of the church could continue while the work began on tearing down the old east end of the church, but not the apse and altar, and laying the foundations of the new piers at the crossing. A portion of the old nave was left standing, to be used while the new east end was built (Fig. 17-3, Fig. 9-5).

Neither Bramante nor Julius lived to see more than the main arches of the crossing finished, nor did they live to partake of the havoc wrought by the clever scheme for financing it. In order to finance the building Julius II sent preachers all over Europe to proclaim that by donating money to this building fund, a person could obtain an indulgence. This act of financial sacrifice ranked equally with other forms of doing the penance required of repentant sinners; so the idea was a great success and money came flooding in. There was an unfortunate by-product of the scheme, however—the Protestant Reformation. Martin Luther and others claimed that Julius's indulgence peddling was selling God's forgiveness, which could not be sold. It would be simplistic to declare that the entire Reformation could be explained by this one

Figure 17-3 St. Peter's under construction. The artist, Martin van Heemskerk, stood in the nave of the old basilica. He drew the colonnades and suggested the aisles on either side. In the center he showed the temporary sanctuary that protected the shrine of St. Peter during the construction of the piers, drum, and dome. Above that shrine rises the arch connecting two of the central piers, and behind it is the semidome over the main apse of the new building. Compare with Fig. 9-5 (Drawing reprinted by permission of Staatliche Museen Preussicher Kulturbesitz Kupferstichkabinett, Berlin.)

matter, yet it might be claimed that this was the spark that set it off. Once again, as with the pyramids, construction of a major monument had a major effect on human history.

Since patron and architect could not be certain how much money this new funding method would raise, they had strong incentives to leave some questions about the design open. Whether St. Peter's would be in the form of a Greek cross as Bramante had first suggested or in that of a Latin cross (one arm, the nave, longer than the other three) was one such open question.

THE NEXT STEP

The next phase in building is detailed development of the design. Again at St. Peter's we see this process in slow motion. While Bramante was supervising the work on St. Peter's, until his death in 1514 and that of Julius II in 1513, several people worked in his studio who would eventually take over the direction of the project. The painter Raphael, though not an employee of Bramante, was close enough to the project to be named coarchitect from 1514 to 1520. To us it may seem odd to place a painter in charge of a big architectural project, but since the late Middle Ages any kind of artist could be placed in charge of any large project that called for taste and judgment; and moreover Raphael at least had the advantage of having been Bramante's protégé. His ideas about St. Peter's may be evident in his famous painting *The School of Athens,* which depicts a large group of ancient philosophers gathered in a great vaulted space. In the painting, where we expect a dome, we look instead through to the sky—which seems a lovely painterly incorporation of the unfinished state of St. Peter's at that time. Raphael's ideas are known more directly from plans, though these may reflect also the final ideas of Bramante.

Another Bramante pupil who worked with Raphael on St. Peter's was Giuliano da Sangallo, a very late follower of Brunelleschi. Some of Bramante's ideas are supposedly preserved in drawings by Giuliano for St. Peter's. But Giuliano died in 1516, and the next architect to be placed in charge of the project was Peruzzi (Fig. 17-2).

We have already discussed Peruzzi as having been the architect of the Massimi Palace. In 1520 he succeeded Raphael as architect of St. Peter's, working on it until the Sack of Rome in 1527. Peruzzi's work, also known from plans, was a simplified and rather static version of Bramante's, with separate zones at the corners. Peruzzi returned to the purely centralized space of Bramante's first plan, where masses were distributed relatively freely about the vast central area. His work continued that continuity of design ideas stemming from the collaboration of older and younger architects in Bramante's studio. In the work of this "school," the design and hence the construction began at the core and moved uniformly toward the periphery. This "box system" contrasts markedly with the gothic system of construction by bays. At St. Peter's, conceptual development went hand in hand with construction.

The Sack of Rome disrupted work on St. Peter's as it did much of life in Rome from 1527 on. When work resumed on the building in the late 1530s, the new architect in charge was Antonio da Sangallo, nephew of Giuliano, who had already been working with Peruzzi. Antonio's connection with Bramante's studio allowed him to continue the design process easily. His work is best known to us from a surviving 1539 model. His concept of the exterior was that of parts and pieces—in this case columns—piled and added up to make a wall surface that was intended to be tall enough and rich enough in ornamentation to express the great interior volume. By the time of Antonio's death in 1546, he had strengthened the central piers, vaulted two arms of the Greek cross, and finished most of the lower vaults between the crossing piers and the outer buttressing piers. Judging from his model, the exterior would have been both "sweet" and "busy"—quite the wrong effects for an imposing capital of Christendom.

This model and Michelangelo's changes from it demonstrate the range of solutions possible at the design level. In 1547, Michelangelo reluctantly became the architect of St. Peter's, devoting himself to the task for the remaining years of his life (until 1564). As a designer, Michelangelo was first and foremost a sculptor. To him, the interior volume and the exterior wall surface were reciprocal, the wall being a carved envelope for a space at once complex and unified. The addition of parts that had motivated Sangallo's design was revised by Michelangelo in the direction of rich unity. He specifically won permission to erase the outer ring of hemicycles and chapels, although he kept the inner ring. Some of the already finished walls had to be torn down to accomplish this change of concept. Instead of repeating the form of the Greek cross crowned by a dome in the four corners, his simplification was to repeat the dome but not the cross in the corners. A semicircular apse was to be repeated at each end of the transept. Since the interior space was now single rather than doubled by an extended ambulatory, as in Sangallo's scheme, the interior lighting was now also simple and direct and the interior volume more intensely illuminated as a consequence. On the exterior, each facet of the volume was represented as a shift in wall plane. The walls became active sculptural masses rather than neutral backgrounds for small columns. Where the surface needed greater articulation, Michelangelo used giant pilasters with richly carved Corinthian pilaster capitals; the giant scale of this order both reveals and symbolizes the sculptural unity that Michelangelo was attempting to give to the huge basilica.

That unity began from the plan, an interpenetration of cross and square, in which all circulation leads back to the core. The four great crossing piers mold the central space as well as support the dome, which is 137 feet across, on the inside. The crossing of the nave and transept spaces is nestled within four smaller domed spaces, themselves bracketed by secondary piers with diagonal exterior faces. These buttressing piers bond the hemicycles of the arms to the angles of the superimposed square (see plan, Fig. 17-1), so that the exterior walls bulge and ripple as they mirror the structure within. Such heavily carved wall masses revive the ancient Roman and Byzantine structural systems, fusing them with gothic structural ideas of the late Middle Ages. In this, Michelangelo was truly a pupil of Brunelleschi. His intentions may best be seen by looking at the exterior of the apse, where the wall is divided into broad and narrow bays, articulated by the giant pilasters. Windows divide the elevation into three parts, and a plain attic was planned to top the composition. Equilibrium was desirable to contain the vertical surge of the pilasters and to offset the weight of the great dome above.

As Michelangelo saw the effect of the verticality of the pilasters, he revised his plans for the shape of the dome (see Fig. 17-4). Many features of this dome are derived from that of the Florence Cathedral, such as the double shell

Figure 17-4   Model of Michelangelo's dome for St. Peter's, 1560s. This wooden model preserves some of his ideas but when built later by della Porta, the heightened dome had ribs of the same width throughout, giving a dynamic result more in keeping with the taste of the late sixteenth century. (Photo by W. Connor of model in Museo Petriano, Rome.)

construction, the raised profile, the ribbed construction, the octagonal lantern, and the great scale. This architect, painter, and sculptor had originally planned a rather elongated profile for the dome, which reiterated the vertical thrust of the colossal pilasters and utilized rib construction for its secure and calculable means of controlling the great loads of so huge a structure. However, as his style matured, he came to prefer the sort of gravity that he built into designs for the church of San Giovanni dei Fiorentini; to achieve this effect, he changed the profile to something closer to a hemisphere. This profile, with internal chains as in the Florence Cathedral, would have achieved equilibrium without loss of vigor. Michelangelo's work on St. Peter's illustrates the culmination of the design process that integrates structural necessity, material and financial resources, adequate program, skill, and relative control over the ideas of patron and architect.

When Michelangelo died, the task of finishing the dome was turned over to his follower Giacomo della Porta, who obscured and softened Michelangelo's clear transitions. He did this by thinning the ribs of the dome and their supports, eliminating the perspective diminution that Michelangelo had planned for the ribs, elevating the dome profile again but lowering the height of the lantern, and adding rich decoration. The difference between the dome as built and as planned by Michelangelo can be seen by inspecting the large wooden model that incorporated Michelangelo's last ideas. Della Porta's dome is more like the Florentine Cathedral's dome, corresponding to an earlier stage in his predecessor's thinking.

Early in the seventeenth century, the old debate about whether the basilica was to be in the form of a Greek cross with arms of equal length (i.e., a centralized building) or a Latin cross with one long arm was finally resolved. Carlo Maderna ended that discussion once and for all by adding to Michelangelo's central area a long nave and a facade (see Fig. 17-5). While this nave was eminently satisfactory as a solution to the liturgical problem and as a means of providing much extra space for erection of honorific chapels and tombs, it had a negative effect upon Michelangelo's dome. The facade is pulled so far forward of the central space that from the plaza in front of the church one cannot clearly perceive the dome or ascertain its true relation to the volume that it covers.

Whereas Maderna repeated Michelangelo's wall treatment along the sides of the nave, on the facade he used a more elaborate and ornamental three-dimensional wall treatment. Beginning at the outer edges of the facade and using a giant order of the same proportions as Michelangelo's, Maderna built from pilasters through half and then three-quarter attached columns that flank the central door. Thus the facade bowed out toward the visitor, reaching out into the plaza as if to interact with those who stand there. The rich plasticity of this facade and its interactive mode tell us that this part of the building was done in the Baroque era. Both the nave and the facade were built between 1607 and 1626.

St. Peter's was dedicated by Pope Urban VII in 1626. Even after that,

Figure 17-5   Facade of St. Peter's Basilica, Rome. Built by Maderna between 1607 and 1614, this facade uses the same stone and same elements in the same proportions as do Michelangelo's walls on the other sides of the building, but Maderna joins them as a stage designer rather than a sculptor might. Beginning at the outer edges with giant pilasters like those on the rest of the basilica, Maderna gradually increases the three-dimensionality of his supports until the four central columns are almost free standing. From the balcony of the central window, the pope bestows solemn blessings on the crowds in the plaza. The roof is crowned by enormous statues designed by Bernini. Behind them, the lantern and only the top of della Porta's dome are visible; the nave was so elongated by Maderna that the effect intended by Michelangelo and Bramante—of a great dome dominating the building and the plaza—has been lost. (Photo by J. Null.)

however, more work was done, including major design decisions about the setting and the decoration of the interior that affect the way we experience the building today.

THE FINAL STEP

In 1629, Giovanni Lorenzo Bernini was appointed architect of St. Peter's. For nearly thirty years he worked on additions to the interior, not only tombs with decorative marble sculptures, but also the architectonic baldachino (permanent bronze canopy) over the main altar and the Cathedra Petri in the apse, a great bronze shrine enclosing what was thought to be the original chair of St.

Peter (see Fig. 17-6). So well does the baldachino focus attention on the center of the central space, that it is now impossible to imagine the basilica without it.

Beginning in 1656, Bernini worked on creating a plaza in front of St. Peter's that would be a worthy setting for it (see Fig. 17-7). Already in 1586 the

Figure 17-6   St. Peter's Basilica, interior with baldachino over the shrine of St. Peter and the Cathedra Petri visible through it. Both were designed by Bernini, as were the statues in the pier niches. The baldachino is a permanent canopy of bronze; its twisted columns reiterate the shape of some ancient ones preserved from Old St. Peter's and popularly supposed to have come from Solomon's Temple. The Cathedra Petri, also of bronze and also enriched with statues, encloses a wooden chair believed then to have been the original seat of Peter when he was bishop of Rome. It is located in the main apse, ending the long axis of the church. The two quasi-architectural sculptures were designed to work together in the vast interior. The coffered arch above the baldachino is the same shown as that in Fig. 17-3.
(Photo by W. Connor.)

Figure 17-7   Aerial view of St. Peter's Basilica and its plaza. The plaza was designed and built by Bernini from 1656 on. The spine connecting the plaza with the Castel St. Angelo (once Hadrian's Tomb) and the Tiber River was not opened until after World War II. The plaza consists of two parts, an inner trapezoid with its long side near the church facade and an outer elipsoid. Around the plaza runs an open colonnade of four rows of columns topped by more of the huge statues from Bernini's studio. A fountain by Maderna and a matching fountain by Bernini serve as foci for the elipsoid, while the ancient obelisk was moved in 1596 by Fontana to stand on axis with the main door of the basilica. The fountains were placed flanking the obelisk, and the plaza with its colonnades eventually completed the spatial experience. (Joseph H. Aronson Aerpicfoto, Ellipsoid(X2))

architect and engineer Domenico Fontana had moved the ancient Egyptian obelisk from its old site, on the spine of Nero's circus on the flank of St. Peter's to the front of the new building, on line with the main doorway. (You may read in Giedion, *Space, Time and Architecture* and in Bacon, *The Design of Cities,* about obelisks as generators of plazas in the Roman cityscape, especially in the baroque period.) Bernini also found in the plaza area a fountain by Maderna, placed to one side of the obelisk. Using the fountain as one focus, he laid out an oval plaza centered on the obelisk. Connecting that plaza with the facade of the church, he inserted an inverted trapezoidal plaza with its broad edge along the facade of the church and its narrower edge opening into the oval. The total open space thus expands and contracts as you move through it. Bernini seems to have taken the "message" implied in Maderna's facade and made it explicit in the plaza. The plaza is rimmed with rows of columns set four deep and topped, as is the facade, with larger-than-life statues of saints, designed by Bernini and executed by his studio.

Fontana had intended this oval plaza to open to the Tiber River and thus across to the rest of Rome. Under the Fascist rule in Italy before and during World War II, a monumental way was opened along the axial street that led to the river. In effect, this street imposes a late-nineteenth–early-twentieth-century idea of scale and of the relation of a major building to its urban context. This solution makes us realize that in the case of St. Peter's, the design process is essentially dynamic and will keep changing as long as both are still alive.

BIBLIOGRAPHY

Ackerman, J., *The Architecture of Michelangelo,* Zwemmer, London, 1966, chap. 8, "The Basilica of St. Peter," pp. 89–102. Clear, understandable writing.

Bacon, E., *Design of Cities,* Viking, New York, 1976. The illustrations and Bacon's commentary on them are endlessly stimulating in understanding urban design.

Giedion, S., *Space, Time, and Architecture,* 5th ed., Harvard University Press, Cambridge, Mass., 1967. Read especially pp. 79–106, 146–162, about the planning of baroque Rome, and study the pictures.

Heydeurich, L., and W. Lotz, *Architecture in Italy 1400 to 1600,* Penguin, Baltimore, 1974. Consult Contents for entries about St. Peter's.

Lehmann, K., "The Dome of Heaven," in E. Kleinbauer, *Modern Perspectives in Western Art History,* Holt, New York, 1971.

Millon, H., "Michelangelo and St. Peter's-I: Notes on the plan of the attic as originally built on the South Hemicycle," *Burlington Magazine,* vol. 3, August 1969, pp. 484–501.

Wiltkower, R., *Architectural Principles in an Age of Humanism,* Norton, New York, 1971. Part 1, chap. 5 concerns centrally planned churches.

Zevi, B., *Architecture as Space,* Horizon, New York, 1957, pp. 46–53. Ways of thinking about the space of St. Peter's.

18
BAROQUE CHURCHES

THE EMBODIMENT OF EMOTION

Renaissance art and architecture had been characterized by stately reserve and balance. In contrast, baroque art which followed it was one of deliberate emotional involvement and expression. This artistic change was partly a result of political and religious differences between the earlier and later periods. The Christian religion after the Reformation was much more a matter of individual commitment than it was during the Middle Ages. Art and architecture in the service of religion were expected to involve the individual personally in the events of the Christian drama. Post-Reformation art thus had more explicit emotional content. From the relative austerity of a painter such as Piero della Francesca we come to the relative richness of, say, Rembrandt, and from the architecture of Santo Spirito to that of San Carlo alle Quattro Fontane.

RENAISSANCE AND BAROQUE

The contrasts between the Renaissance and the baroque in art are pointed out succinctly by Heinrich Wolfflin in his *Principles of Art History*. Although his references are mainly to painting, the same sort of dichotomy can be observed in sculpture and in architecture. He notes five pairs of contrasts (in each case, the earlier period's characteristic is stated first):

llnear	palnterly
planar	in depth
closed	open
multiplicity	unity
absolute clarity	relative clarity

The equivalent in architecture could be:

austere	rich
articulation of relations	illusionism
integrated and abstract	complex and allusive
equality of parts	subordination of parts
light sources clearly shown	light sources hidden

Because the baroque was so dependent upon individual reactions and specific local history, there are important variations in baroque architecture from country to country. Nonetheless, the baroque was a truly international style in the same way that gothic and Renaissance had been, flowing forth from its origins in Italy to affect not only the architecture of such receptive neighbors as France and Germany but also that of the churches and palaces as far away as Spanish and Portugese colonies in the New World. The formal message of the baroque was received best in France; the emotional message was better received in Mexico, Brazil, and Germany.

BERNINI

We have already touched on the work of Bernini, one of the two architects whose Italian buildings became the source of the baroque. You may read about Bernini's work and intentions in Irving Lavin's masterful study, *Bernini and the Unity of the Visual Arts*. The baldachino that he designed and built for St. Peter's during the second quarter of the seventeenth century was fully baroque in its intended and actual emotional effect. In the baldachino, as in his sculpture and buildings, Bernini used what may be called extra architectural means to make his point: intellectual content and religious content are layered upon a firm structural and aesthetic base to achieve the effect Bernini wanted.

He relied heavily on story telling and associative messages to induce the effects he wanted.

CORNARO CHAPEL

That point may be clearer if we study one architectural work of Bernini in some depth. The example chosen is the Cornaro Chapel, set in the left transept arm of the church of Santa Maria della Vittoria in Rome (see Fig. 18-1). At the request of Cardinal Federico Cornaro, Bernini built a funerary chapel for him and his family, in the church of the Discalced (barefoot) Carmelites, a group of monks under the cardinal's protection (around 1650). The program (that is, set of requirements) called for memorials to six other cardinals of the Cornaro family, to the patron, and to his father who had been doge (governor) of Venice; in addition, the chapel was to honor St. Teresa of Avila, reformer of the Carmelite order, by depicting her transverberation, the moment when she was pierced by an angel with the arrow of God's love. Moreover, the chapel was to harmonize with the rest of the church which had been built during the first decade of the century. Bernini's solution to these requirements was a chapel that is unified visually and conceptually. Lavin calls it, "his most explicit and total unified work," in which Bernini made a visually and conceptually unified statement which greatly enhances the emotional impact.

Each element of the chapel contributes to this unified effect, through subordination to the whole. The architecture of the chapel repeats elements such as columns and pilasters from the architecture of the whole church, but Bernini inserted into this reiteration a pedimented altar tabernacle. Flanking the altar tabernacle along the side walls of the chapel are relief sculptures of the eight members of the Cornaro family (see Fig. 18-2). Each group of four is shown as if the individuals were in a box at the theater watching and talking to each other about the ecstacy taking place over the altar. They seem like real people in an actual space where the three realms of communication come together: Teresa with God: the Cornaros with each other, unhampered by the more than 100 years elapsed time during which they lived; and we the spectators with them.

Both the Cornaros and ourselves are witnesses to the unusual event of Teresa's transverberation. Tradition says that the event took place in the convent chapel during the mass, so that by putting the statues in another chapel, Bernini has increased the illusion of a real-time event. Bernini helps us to concentrate on the statues by the way they are lighted. The niche in which they are placed was originally lighted from above by a window with yellow glass; its light was emphasized by gilded wooden rays suspended above and behind the figures.

Within the niche of the altar tabernacle, Teresa and the angel appear as white life-size marble statues turned toward one another. Teresa is swooning backward on her cloud and the angel is standing before her, holding one corner of her robes very delicately between the fingers of his left hand, ready to

Figure 18-1 Cornaro Chapel in Santa Maria della Vittoria, Rome; by Bernini; ca. 1650. Beneath the floor of the chapel, the patron Cardinal Federico Cornaro is buried. He and seven other Cornaros (seven cardinals and a doge) gaze from their boxes along the sides at the central tableau of St. Teresa of Avila being transfixed by an angel with the arrow of God's love. (The Cornaros, Teresa, and the angel are all sculptures by Bernini.) In the vault, scenes of Teresa's life are painted and shown in reliefs of gilded stucco, while angels line the framing arch. Architecture, sculpture, and painting were all designed by one person, the unified effect of which makes a powerful emotional impact. (Photo reprinted from I. Lavin, *Bernini and the Unity of the Visual Arts,* by permission of Central Institute for Cataloging and Documentation, Rome.)

pierce her again with the arrow in his right hand. He smiles enigmatically, appreciating that the wound of the arrow will be at once painful and blissful. Teresa's expression and pose reveal an internal metaphysical event—an ecstasy like death, a passion as physical as that of a bride's, and a physical levitation symbolic of her spiritual elevation. The emotional content of the chapel is concentrated in this sculpture but reinforced by every other element as well. It

Figure 18-2   Cornaro Chapel. View of one group of the Cornaro family, showing their reaction to the miraculous incident between St. Teresa and the angel. From this angle, the carved representation of architecture behind them seems to continue the lines of the architecture of the chapel, suggesting that they share the space the viewer is in, inducing the viewer to join their awed response. (Also from Lavin, reprinted by permission of the Central Inst. for Cataloging & Documentation, Rome.)

is as if the statue sets up a dominant chord that reverberates in the architectural frame, in the reliefs of the Cornaros, in the other sculpture and painting, and in the lighting.

The interpenetration of imagery is well shown in the relief that forms the altar frontal. It is a scene of the last supper of Christ and his disciples. The relief is a smaller version of a life-sized scene in the Lateran church of the bishop of Rome. It is also a reference to the fact that Teresa's levitation took place at mass after she had (like the disciples) received communion and by it had been lifted into higher unity with Christ. This symbolism is meant to intensify the emotional impact of the chapel and to make the visitor desire the same experience.

Other scenes of Teresa's life are shown in gilded stucco on the lower parts of the vault of the chapel. Her spiritual matrimony to Christ is alluded to in the fresco at the top, where the dove of the holy spirit is painted with angels holding instruments and flowers. On the archway that separates the chapel from the church are white stucco angels with floral wreaths and open books, a reference to Teresa as author. This ceiling decoration mingles two traditions, that of illusionistic painting and that of three-dimensional reliefs, in a way that was to become common during the rococo era. It was a composite of architecture, sculpture, and painting, combined for maximum emotional and intellectual effect upon the viewer.

The pavement of the chapel combines and reinterprets realms in a new way also. To the left and right, skeletons are shown as if they were emerging from the floor, which is to be thought of as the upper limit of the underworld in which Federico Cornaro is buried and which here intersects our realm.

The final image used by Bernini to convey the mingling of realms is that of the symbolic doorway. On either side of the chapel, below the "boxes" in which the groups of Cornaro dignitaries are gathered, appears a pair of doors carved from alabaster. In each case, the outer door is ajar and the inner one is closed. This image was well known from ancient Roman sarcophaguses. Death's door, in effect, is the gate of heaven, closed to some but open to the elect.

If we read the messages of the chapel from floor to ceiling, they are as follows: the dead rise eagerly; Christ institutes the eucharist; St. Teresa in glory is transverberated, communicant, dying and espoused; the Cornaros bear witness; the Holy Spirit descends; and the angels and cherubs celebrate. The process of salvation is shown to be an existential event, taking place now for us. Should we miss the point of this appeal to our emotions, intellect, and faith, Bernini has painted on the apex of the framing arch the words of Christ to Teresa: "If I had not created heaven, I would create it for you alone." The chapel is then Bernini's echo of God's creative actions—acts which lure us to become involved in them and teach us to emulate them, by being presented in this emotionally satisfying way.

BORROMINI

Unlike the overt and verbal messages of the Cornaro Chapel, Francesco Borromini's work relies on intrinsic architectural means to make its points about emotion. Borromini's work is well photographed and intelligently written about in two books by P. Portoghesi: *Roma Barocca* and *The Rome of Borromini*. Rather than using events from the Christian drama or the lives of the saints, Borromini uses line, volume, light, color (though perhaps less than Bernini), and rhythm. In Bernini's work, these architectural qualities are subordinated to the intended message, whereas in Borromini's work they speak to us so directly that they may be said to *be* the intended message. For this reason, modern architects more easily relate to Borromini. His work appeals directly to their sense of aesthetics and need not be mediated by any extrinsic message. It is analogous to music without lyrics.

SAN CARLO ALLE QUATTRO FONTANE

The example of Borromini's work to be studied here is the church of San Carlo alle Quattro Fontane in Rome (see Figs. 18-3 to 18-5). Borromini began work on this complex of monastery and church in 1635, completing the church facade in 1667. In the previous century, Pope Sixtus V had placed four fountains at this intersection, then in the open country, in an attempt to draw urban development in this direction. One of the four corners was now occupied by a monastery; it was Borromini's task to fit the necessary

Figure 18-3   San Carlo alle Quattro Fontane, Rome; built between 1635 and 1667; Borromini. The facade of the church of this monastery was built at the end of this building period. The moving, swinging lines of the facade prepare us for movement within, but otherwise the facade is totally distinct from the interior, quite the opposite of San Andrea at Mantua (cf. Fig. 18-5). (Photo by J. Null.)

Figure 18-4   San Carlo alle Quattro Fontane; interior with view of the dome. The oval floor plan is repeated in the oval dome, topped by a lantern. The coffering of the dome includes Christian symbols as well as octagons and hexagons, all in exaggerated perspective to increase the apparent height of the dome. Pendentives support the dome. (Photo by J. Null.)

conventional buildings and spaces into a tight urban lot without disturbing the existing fountain.

Construction began with the dormitories and other living areas for the monks, of which the most notable is the courtyard. The complex spatial rhythms of the church are foreshadowed here in what appears at first glance to be a simple rectangular courtyard with a covered walkway around it. Second glance tells us that the corners of the rectangle are sliced off by gently curved segments of entablature that span from column to column near the corner. The architect quietly plays with our expectations that courtyards have 90° corners. A third glance indicates that the rhythm of openings and supports around the courtyard is syncopated.

The courtyard connects with the street through a relatively modest

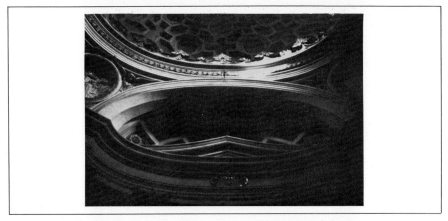

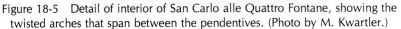
Figure 18-5   Detail of interior of San Carlo alle Quattro Fontane, showing the twisted arches that span between the pendentives. (Photo by M. Kwartler.)

doorway which is quite a contrast to the elaboration of the doorway into the church next door. The monks and their architect held to the tradition that monks who vowed poverty should live simply, but that the best and most elaborate decoration was appropriate for God. The church doorway is set in a richly developed ensemble of curved wall planes, and is emphasized further by being lined up with the tabernaclelike niche above it and the great cartouche inserted into the curving pediment above. This facade is like that of Notre-Dame de Paris in being divided into nine segments that are bilaterally symmetrical. But unlike the earlier church, movement and light are stressed. Borromini very deliberately took into account the play of light on protruding and receding surfaces as well as the inevitable accumulation of dirt in recesses to emphasize his architectural forms. As the light changes—and as the dirt accumulates and as the building weathers—it becomes more and more what the architect had in mind. On the first level on either side of the doorway, the frames of niches for statues bulge forward as if to counter the recession of the doorway. On the second level, the sides recede and the center protrudes in the shape of a tentlike tabernacle. Into the convex curve of the tent an opening is set back, but not as far back as the door of the level below. Each opening and niche is enriched by attached columns that carry entablatures that swing in and out across the facade and are further enriched by carved ornamentation. At the top of the whole composition is a huge coat of arms; the slanted edges of the pediment curve upward to enclose it, but it seems to want to break free from the wall plane.

The facade of San Carlo alle Quattro Fontane was the final work of Borromini on this set of buildings. The church within had previously been finished. We might expect the facade to indicate the shape and arrangements of the space within, but it does not. In medieval and Renaissance times, the facade was frequently built in a separate building project from the interior.

Earlier architects, however, matched the facade directly to the interior arrangements. Alberti's facade for Santa Maria Novella in Florence, for example, has prominent scrolls on the upper corners of the facade which function as an important transition between the high nave and much lower side aisles. After Alberti, the church facade became more independent from the interior, beholden only to its own organization. In this it reminds us of the facades of Venetian palaces, which were composed as strong statements in their own right.

In still another sense, Borromini does use the facade to suggest the arrangements within. In both interior and exterior he has used the same kinds of ovoid curves and arranged them in complex juxtapositions. We have already seen the use of the oval for the tabernacle of Bernini's Cornaro Chapel; ovals were also being used in the plans of whole churches, such as St. Agnese on the Piazza Navona. At San Carlo, Borromini massaged the oval to yield a new solution to that old puzzle of centralized-versus-longitudinal church. The long axis of the oval runs from the doorway to the main altar opposite it. By squeezing the corners of his oval, that is, by indenting the oval symmetrically near the altar and near the door, he created an undulating shape that has a cross axis at midpoint. In the niches at the ends of the cross axis, he placed subsidiary altars. Then he used the corner spaces between the undulating oval of the church and the rectangular wall at lot line for auxiliary services such as stairs and sacristy.

Within a relatively small volume, and without the aid of aisles or galleries, Borromini thus made a strong architectural statement—one that could be anticipated by virtue of the arrangement of elements of the facade. Both exterior and interior play directly upon our aesthetic and emotional sensibilities. Their vocabulary is volume, line, and rhythm. Borromini uses light and color to reveal to us what he is doing with these elements. The interior of San Carlo is pale in color. Much of the architectural articulation is in white against white walls, distinguished only by form from the walls or ceiling against which they stand, protrude, or thrust. We can see clearly that pediments over the niches curve upward much like the huge pediment over the entry door. Coffering within niches is distorted from the purely rectangular to accommodate itself to the oval shape of the niche. Arches twist into new shapes called torsion S curves. Walls undulate to form that pinched oval, but their entablature comes forward to form a consistent base for the oval dome above. The coffering of the dome includes crosses and elongated hexagons, so that it can more easily swell and diminish as it surges toward the lantern which brings light into the whole unified interior. It is as an architectural whole that the church of San Carlo affects our emotions. The aesthetic experience is so intense that our entire subconscious being is involved and thus our conscious understanding of the sublime—for example, God—is heightened emotionally.

Compared with Michelangelo's Medici Chapel (the new sacristy in San Lorenzo, Florence) and even more compared with Brunelleschi's old sacristy for the same church, both the Cornaro Chapel and San Carlo are rich rather than austere, illusive rather than explicit about relations, complex and allusive rather than rationally integrated; achieve their effects through subordination of parts to whole rather than by an assemblage of equal parts; and use light mystically rather than clearly. In short, both are fully baroque in their emotional and effective use of the vocabulary available to them.

THE CHURCH OF THE INVALIDS

Somewhat different emotional effects were attempted and achieved in the other two buildings that we will look at very briefly for their revelation of national variation during the baroque era. The first is the church of Hôtel des Invalides in Paris. Between 1680 and 1691, Mansart added a new domed wing to an already existing church of the veteran's hospital. The new church was later to be used as the funerary chapel of Napoleon. Although it is unique in its mastery of the baroque vocabulary, it is also typical of French use of that vocabulary—a use that was always highly intellectual. It is as though the intellectual ferment of the High Renaissance came directly to France with the baroque development of the formal possibilities of allusion to and incorporation of classical motifs, but without the emotional content that was so important in Italian baroque. One is tempted to wonder whether the French experience as the first modern nation state, so different from the Italian experience of fragmentation into many tiny sovereign principalities, did not also make a difference in the emotional climate, affecting both patrons and architects.

The church of the Hôtel des Invalides was built in the shape of a rectangular cube free stranding on three sides but attached to the old church of the veteran's home on the fourth side (see Fig. 18-6). Out of this strong and rich base, with attached columns and cornices, springs a tall drum with windows, again enriched with attached columns. Out of that in turn springs a tall dome with a tall lantern. It is interesting that even in this new vocabulary, the French retained enthusiasm for tall buildings that was so important a part of the French gothic style. Within, the space is complex, especially in that the center of the floor was lowered to receive the huge porphory sarcophagus of Napoleon. The light is almost Renaissance in its clarity and in the straightforward way it illuminates the features of the interior. The experience at Les Invalides suggests that for the French, emotion must be and is always under the pervasive control of the intellect.

OUR LADY OF GUADALUPE CHURCH

Quite a contrast is the church of Our Lady of Guadalupe in Mexico City (see Fig. 18-7). Here the emphasis is on the interior, which is richly decorated to the

Figure 18-6 Hôtêl des Invalides Church, Paris. Jules Hardouin-Mansart,
1680–1691. Baroque in its richness, French in its clarity and rationality, the cube of
the base makes a strong platform for the tall drum and dome and lantern above. At
each story attached columns support rich cornices. (Photo supplied by Caisse
Nationale des Monuments Historique et des Sites, Paris.)

point of satiation. Every inch of wall surface seems to be carved, gilded, and
then darkened by the smoke of several hundred years of devout candles, which
reveal the richness but only by glimpses. In a Spanish baroque church such as
this one, the emotional content of the architecture is its most obvious feature.
The facade is relatively simple, leaving most of the emotional impact of the
church to the interior. In the baroque architecture of the Spanish new world,
emotion is given free rein and cold intellect is kept under strict control. This
basilica, designed by Pedro de Arrieta, was built between 1695 and 1709.

If architecture is indeed a symbolic ordering of human experience, then its
emotional impact can be expected—enhanced sometimes and lessened at
other times according to the viewer's reception of it. When the emotional
impact is manipulated by a master—Bernini or Borromini—the result is an
aesthetic statement as well as a commentary on what it means to be human.

Figure 18-7   Basilica of Guadalupe near Mexico City; 1695–1709; Pedro de Arrieta. A view of one of the highly decorated altars. In Spanish baroque and its Latin American versions, the decorative richness indicates emotional involvement taken to its fullest manifestation. (Photo courtesy Mexican National Tourist Council.)

BIBLIOGRAPHY

Lavin, I., *Bernini and the Unity of the Visual Arts,* Oxford, New York, 1980. Beautifully written and well illustrated, Lavin's book sets the Cornaro chapel in the context of Bernini's creative development and in the wider context of the architecture of Rome in the seventeenth century. Highly recommended.

Millon, H., *Baroque and Rococo Architecture,* second edition, Braziller, New York, 1967. From Renaissance to baroque to rococo, this short book helps one actually see the developing differences.

Portoghesi, P., *Roma Barocca,* M.I.T., Cambridge, Mass., 1970.

Portoghesi, P., *The Rome of Borromini,* Braziller, New York, 1967. Study the pictures. You'll never see baroque architecture the same again.

Scott, J. B. "S. Ivo alla Sapieuza and Borromini's Symbolic Language," *Journal of the Society of Architectural Historians,* vol. XLI, no. 4 (December 1982), pp. 294–317. A well-argued essay that credits Borromini with including many of the same nonarchitectural meanings as Bernini.

Wolfflin, H., *Principles of Art History,* Dover, New York, 1950. Or see his essay of the same title reprinted in E. Kleinbauer, *Modern Perspectives in Western Art History,* Holt, New York, 1971.

19
ROCOCO
BUILDINGS
ARCHITECTURE AND ART

Architecture is often austere, its power and impact being derived from sparse structural form—an expanse of flat plain wall; unobstructed arches or girders arranged with imposing repetition; the drama of vast vault or massive truss. Just as often, architecture can be saturated with astounding artistic display, luxuriant in color and materials and resplendent, rich, lush, and fully embellished with inclusion of other arts. Even though architects and patrons often assume a high moral tone about their choice of the austere over the elaborate, we will focus our attention on the architectural aspects of embellishment rather than the merits of their choice.

Social and political contexts oftentimes contribute to public opinion about architecture. In France during the third quarter of the nineteenth century, the self-confidence, exuberance, and naiveté of the newly rich classes was directly reflected in the abundance of decoration as well as a certain crudity in the Second Empire style. At other times, such as in Athens in the last quarter of the fifth century B.C., art and decoration seem rather to reflect on something that was missing in the citizens' lives. The elegant lightness of the little Nike Temple on the Athenian Acropolis suggests that there was a yearning for joy and ease rather than what the population was having to endure during those years of defeat, famine, and plague.

Even if we cannot always or with certainty explain a public taste for embellishment, we can still describe it and reflect on its meaning with respect to our feelings and opinions about art and architecture.

SAINT SOPHIA AND CHARTRES

Some buildings that we have studied already may serve as good models of the kinds of differences of ensemble and of effect. An effect may be derived solely from the architecture of the building. Saint Sophia's interior was originally paneled with rich materials such as veined grey marble, dark red porphyry, green marble, and later on figured mosaics were added too. Originally the entire structure was aniconic (without pictures), its impact arising entirely from the proportions of the spaces and the richness of the materials. The exterior, now plainly stuccoed, may have originally shown a brick and stone patterning. Architectural forms decrease in complexity as the building rises higher and higher, and at the very top, they are relatively simple. In contrast, the cathedral of Chartres was designed and built to be an integration of color (in the stained glass) and texture (in the sculptures and in the very surface of the stone) with the architecture. It is virtually impossible to imagine Chartres without its imposing sculptured portals and stunning glass. Art here was subordinated to but an integral part of the architecture.

These two buildings exemplify the fact that the effects of art and architecture upon each other and on the viewer depend largely on whether the art is located on the exterior, interior, or both. Like the Pantheon before it, Saint Sophia's greatest effects are in the interior. The effects are abstract and architectural and affected very little by later additions of pictorial art. Chartres, on the other hand, has exterior sculpture, both figures and reliefs, that lure us inside, wherein we can be overwhelmed by the interaction of the spaces and the imagery of the stained glass, at once representational and abstract.

The effects of the combination of art and architecture depend also on the materials used and how they are handled. At the Parthenon, for instance, the entire building and its decoration were made of the same materials, although the decoration was set off by having been painted. In Chartres, the sculptures are made from a limestone very similar to that of the masonry in color but of a finer grain so that it would take finer detailing. The color here comes partly from the glass of the rose and lancet windows but also from some of the painted sculpture. Difference of color without that of material can promote unity of the ensemble.

CORNARO CHAPEL

A difference between the materials of art and those of the architectural setting is much more evident in the Cornaro Chapel in Rome. Within a plain, almost unappealing, exterior and a satisfying interior decorated in the usual baroque style of columns, capitals, arches, etc., we find the Cornaro Chapel by Bernini, where the same baroque is employed but with richer materials—paintings and stuccoes in the vault, marble inlays in the floor, marble reliefs on the sides, and fully modeled white marble statues in the niche. The contrasts between the richness of the architecture here and the other worldly white of the marble is skillfully played upon.

Being both in time and in sympathy close to the baroque era, architects of the rococo period built upon the ideas of rich complimentarity when they created the palaces and churches of the eighteenth century, so extremely different from the severe contrasts of late-twentieth-century modernism. (Rococo is a word that seems to derive from the French word for shell, and indeed in rococo architecture many shell-like forms are used, especially asymmetrical ones.) Explanations of architecture have relied upon metaphor ever since Vitruvius compared the Doric order with the masculine and the Ionic order with the feminine. Since baroque was heavier, richer, and darker compared with the gracefulness, elegance, and pastel colors of the rococo, the same anthropomorphic designations have customarily been given to them: baroque being considered masculine and rococo, feminine. (Such designations may seem less obvious in the late twentieth century than they did earlier on.) The scale of rococo architecture differs from that of the baroque in being less grand and hence more intimate. More attention was paid to both interior embellishment and landscape architecture, as settings for human activities. Many palaces with their accompanying grounds were erected in the rococo manner during the mid-eighteenth century, especially in France and the German lands. Rulers and nobles vied with one another in employing the finest artists and architects to produce elegant and well-decorated buildings.

THE CHURCH OF THE VIERZEHNHEILIGEN

If rococo art in general can be characterized as being light, elegant, and graceful, what specific ways were art and architecture integrated to make these effects? We can see this very well in the church of the Vierzehnheiligen, begun by Balthasar Neumann in 1743 and finished after his death in 1772 (see Fig. 19-1). (The first study of Neumann's church architecture in English is Otto's *Space into Light*.)

After some success as an architect, Neumann, who was a military officer, was sent abroad to France to study architecture; when he returned, he designed many churches and palaces. The work of Bernini and Borromini was known in Germany both from information brought back by travelers to Italy and from material published in books. So it is not surprising that the facade of

Figure 19-1   Vierzehnheiligen, begun 1743 finished 1772, near Bamberg, Germany, by Balthasar Neumann. Outward bulge at center of facade reflects oval plan within. (Photo by D. Gardner.)

Vierzehnheiligen is developed in a series of curves that flow and interact, like Italian baroque church facades, and that the doorway is emphasized by a window above it and a cartouche above that. Every element of this facade ripples. The forward bulge of the facade shows on the exterior the effect of the first oval of the interior plan pushing outward. The sandstone walls are interrupted by no less than three rows of large windows all around, preparing us for a flood of light on the interior.

The subtle but monochromatic facade is little preparation for the exuberant color of the interior (see back cover). The center of focus in the space is the huge altar to the fourteen saints. It does not stand in the apse or under the crossing but is pulled forward into the nave. The position of the altar tells us immediately that the space here is manipulated differently from what we expected. The altar is mounded up with twisting, flickering arches that connect the outer railing to the central high point. The altar seems to reiterate the surrounding architecture, acting as a focus of vision as one moves through the space. Statues of the fourteen saints are placed prominently around and amid the arches of the altar. The statues are made of marble of different colors and are gilded for emphasis. Also gilded are the elaborate Corinthian capitals of the columns and piers. Other figures of marble at the lower levels and stucco at the higher levels are placed before the piers. All are approximately life size.

Farther up, to mark the transition from wall to ceiling, smaller stucco figures of cherubs seem almost to spill out of the painted illusions on the ceiling. In these, drastically foreshortened figures are painted against an intensely blue sky, as if to dissolve away the ceiling into the heavens. The architect creates the spatial framework for the vision created by the painter and heightened by the sculptor.

All this artwork is bathed in a great amount of light from the large windows (see Fig. 19-2). Unlike Chartres, where the sculptures at the doorways receive the full benefit of the light from the sky, in Vierzehnheiligen careful provision had to be made to bring maximum light into the interior. Since the artwork in Vierzehnheiligen is equal to the architecture, the same kind of care was taken to ensure its visibility. Filled with clear glass, the windows do not so much carry the message (as they do in Chartres) as illuminate it. Windows are arranged in three tiers, above and below the balcony and in the clerestory. Light from the windows plays off the white walls and picks up the pastel surfaces, reflecting them in the gilding and silvering for a rich shimmering effect.

In this church, as in so many of this era, about half the total budget was spent on the structure and half on the furnishings and decoration. It was the architect's task to design the shell, supervise construction, and select and coordinate the artists and artisans who finished the church. Neumann was a genius at managing this cooperative work.

Figure 19-2 Vierzehnheiligen, wooden model from Neumann's workshop, showing three tiers of windows. (Permission to reprint granted by owner of the model, Historischer Verein, Bamberg, Germany. Photo courtesy Christian F. Otto.)

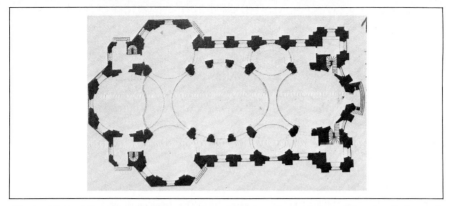

Figure 19-3   Vierzehnheiligen, plan from Neumann's workshop. The plan is formed by circles and ovals, with the main altar centered in the largest oval. A narrow envelope of space undulates between the ovals and the conventional exterior wall. (Plan reprinted by permission of Mainfrankisches Museum, Wurzburg, and by courtesy of Christian F. Otto.)

Working with Neumann were the artists of the ceiling paintings; the sculptors who did both the statues of the fourteen saints for whom the church is named and the other marble statues within the church; the stucco workers who did the less important figures, reliefs, and picture frames that were either gilded or left white; the gilders who covered figures and the irregular frames of the ceiling paintings as well as the metal work; wood carvers, metal workers, and layers of patterned floors. An enormous attention to detail, from Neumann and from all these artists, made possible the integrated effect of this church. The church was not considered finished until all the artwork was completed.

The interior of Vierzehnheiligen, where the liturgy takes place and where the artwork is located, is separated from the outer walls by a layer of space that is relatively barren of decoration but brightly lit. This space is almost too small to walk in. Its effect is mainly visual and psychological; that is, it is a buffer zone between the difficult outer world and the serenity of the interior of the church. This outer layer envelopes the ovals that make up the nave; a minor cross axis is formed by two small ovals partway into the nave and a major cross axis by two large circles that form the transept arms (see Fig. 19-3). The perimeter is articulated by pilasters and the framing of the windows. The highly perforated outer layer and the skeletal inner layer of columns, balustrades, and "ribs" that spring from the imposts above the columns define the two separate layers of space. The ovals of the interior are tangent to one another, sliced off as "torsion edges" (as Otto calls them) that are made to look like Borromini's twisted ribs. The vault of the central oval is slightly higher than those to either side of it, emphasizing the great altar and shrine set below it, and enhanced by an illusionistic painting set in an irregular shell-like frame. Thus the inner and outer layers of structure interact and contrast, as do the layers of decoration and structure with each other.

Vierzehnheiligen copies and surpasses the baroque period by using ovals in both plan and decoration. Where in an older church there would have been a crossing tower or other high space to mark the intersection of the main volumes of nave, choir, and transept, here there is rather an edge—a compound edge where the ovals come together. This intersection is not above the main altar but is displaced eastward, since the altar is pushed westward. Additional altars are placed in the apse and attached to the piers on the apse side of the crossing. The altars are set up on platforms and draw attention by such placement to the oval spaces that house them. The ovals are also made apparent by the shape of the ceiling paintings, by the paving on the floor, and by the positions of the piers.

Two major baroque concepts of space—the oval as an amalgamating longitudinal with centralized focus, and the undulating movement of surfaces and spaces—are united in Vierzehnheiligen in a manner unprecedented and rarely equaled. The intricate spatial arrangement is a perfect foil for the sophisticated integration of art and architecture. Vierzehnheiligen shows the same degree of subtlety as does the Parthenon. Each detail, such as the twisted ribs adopted from Borromini, has been considered worthy of intense thought. The whole space is filled with life and movement.

The answer that Vierzehnheiligen gives to the question of the proper relation of art and architecture is that they are integral. By having large quantities of art integral to the architecture, the combination produces an intense experience. Churches and public ceremonies were the only place where most people ever encountered art. Compared with present-day people, they lived with minimal aesthetic stimuli in their everyday lives. (We tend to be supersaturated with images from television, magazines, books, museums; and hence have a need for visual quiet.) The church in the eighteenth century, which had been caring for widows and orphans and in other ways nurturing people for centuries, went on doing so by providing havens that were at once safe and beautiful to alleviate the sensual deprivation that was otherwise all too common. The German people had suffered greatly in the mid-seventeenth century during the Thirty Years War; by the 1680s, much rebuilding was going on throughout the country, with special emphasis on the churches as havens of refuge. Vierzehnheiligen was part of this movement to rebuild. The task of architects and their associated artists and artisans was to provide an environment that would enrich a whole lifetime of attendance at this church. The interior was deliberately too much to take in at one visit. Neumann was able to understand fully what the cloistered monks and the laypersons of all classes who would come to the church would need. One of the things they would need was a highly integrated sensual and aesthetic experience, modeled after those pioneered by Bernini, which could lift them out of the everyday and into the realm of the transcendent. In a building where art was thoroughly integrated with architecture, and long before the idea was succintly stated, Balthasar Neumann discovered that art is indeed the "indispensable superfluity."

BIBLIOGRAPHY

Eames, C. and R., *Two Baroque Churches*. Brilliant film on Vierzehnheiligen and Ottobeuren. Made from a series of still shots and accompanied by Bach's music, the film shows the integration of art and architecture in a way that no book possibly can.

Otto, Christian F., *Space into Light,* Architectural History Foundation, New York, 1979. The first study of Neumann's churches to appear in English. Well illustrated.

20
NINETEENTH-CENTURY TECHNOLOGY

NEW BUILDING TYPES

When the process of building is so carefully thought out that the product is thereby raised above the utilitarian, we call the product architecture. During the nineteenth century, many types of buildings were given careful thought for the first time—some because the type had not previously existed (such as train sheds) and others because there was now sufficient money to allow for creative inventiveness in their construction (such as middle-class houses). Such an extension of the realm of architecture came about because people had new ideas about what was needed, what was useful, and what was proper. In this chapter we will examine the role that technological advances played in that expansion; and in the next chapter we will discuss the significance that new historical knowledge about architecture from past time had in the style of the expansion.

Both the new technology and the new historical knowledge contributed to a *zeitgeist* (world view) in the nineteenth century that we are now inclined to find touchingly romantic. Because of the very real advances being made in science and engineering, there grew up a belief that reason and analysis were preeminent human activities. Carried far enough, this belief suggested that science and technology would inevitably solve all the problems of humanity. Rational planning would extend these benefits to all human beings. Machines would relieve individuals of all burdensome labor. Change and speed were thus inherently beneficial and good.

THE USE OF IRON

One manifestation of this view was the construction of new buildings without architectural pretension—train sheds, for instance—that did their job simply and economically. Structures like these were made possible and necessary as a result of the Industrial Revolution, one of the primary results of which was an increase in the production of iron as well as a decrease in its cost. So iron was now available as a building material. Already in the eighteenth century, experiments in building with iron were going on at places such as Coalbrook-dale in England, where in 1779 Thomas Pritchard designed the first iron bridge. Since the concept "bridge" was then so indissolubly tied to the use of stone, Pritchard's new bridge was in the form of the traditional stone bridge, with a round arch to support the roadbed but with the elements of the arch made of iron and not solid stone. It was to be more than a century before architects and engineers were able to construct bridges that corresponded more closely to the characteristics of iron or its stronger replacement, steel. Even when the Roeblings built the Brooklyn Bridge, finished in 1883, public wariness about untried materials forced them to mask the novelty of their suspension structure by hanging it from traditional-appearing masonry towers. The strength of their bridge lay not in the solid masses of stone (see Fig. 20-1), but in the combined tensile resilience of many thin strands of metal wire twisted together to make the great cables that support the roadbed. The Roeblings had not only to design the bridge and oversee its construction but also to invent the concept and then the machinery to spin and twist the cables. This kind of invention was going on everywhere throughout the nineteenth century, as ferries were replaced by bridges, low buildings by high ones, and the slow pace of horses by the speed of railroads.

The first railroads, in England, were built in direct response to the Industrial Revolution, to move coal to factories, where it was the fuel used for the steam engines that powered the machinery. From 1836 on, the London-Birmingham line connected the two major centers. When complete, it was described as "the greatest work of civil engineering in human history, greater than the Great Wall of China" in the cost and number of hours taken to build it. On such railroads, first goods and then people could whiz along at dizzying

Figure 20-1 Brooklyn Bridge, New York, opened in 1883. Designed by John Roebling and built by his son Washington Roebling. Work on the bridge was supervised by Washington's wife Emily after he became bed-ridden as the result of a severe case of the bends, contracted when inspecting underwater work in the cassions where the bridge footings were hewn from the river bed. When it opened, the Brooklyn Bridge was the tallest structure in the city, as this contemporary photo shows. The comforting visual strength of the granite towers with their gothic arches contrasts with the suspension cables of many thin strands of wire twisted together in a process invented by John Roebling. (Photo from Anthony's Photographic Bulletin for 1883, from the Rensselaer Polytechnic Institute Archives.)

speeds of 30 miles per hour. For such railroads new kinds of buildings were necessary: stations for passengers and sheds for the trains. A good example is the Euston Station built between 1835 and 1839, for which Phillip Hardwick, an architect, did the station facade in the form of gateways and Robert Stephenson, an engineer, did the shed (see Fig. 20-2). The sheds, being constructed of iron in the form of slender columns and trusses to span the width of the tracks were much more advanced in their technology than was the station, which was more traditional in appearance, with a facade of stone and historical references in the form of capitals, columns, Roman bath windows, and so on.

THE USE OF GLASS

The other major new material that became widely used was glass. New manufacturing processes made large, transparent sheets of glass much less expensive than ever before. Experimentation with the combination of iron (later steel) frames and large glass windows made new building configurations possible. Reduction of previous taxes on glass also contributed to expanded use of this material.

Perhaps the most dramatic of these new configurations was the conservatory (greenhouse). First developed for growing exotic plants in northern climates, the conservatory was designed and built by landscape architects,

Figure 20-2   Euston Station, London, built between 1835 and 1839; Phillip Hardwick, architect, and Robert Stephenson, engineer. This was the climactic decade of the Greek revival style, employed here to clothe this unprecedented building type in newly familar imagery. The sheds, not visible here, used iron trusses and columns to span the great width of the track. The railroad station thus combined new technology with historical revival. (Compare with Chap. 21.) (Photo reprinted by permission of The Royal Institute of British Architects.)

another group (like the engineers) unconstrained by the traditional rules of architecture. The conservatory frequently had an iron frame with walls and roof of glass to maximize heat gain.

This new building type came to unexpected prominence in 1850 and 1851 during construction of the Crystal Palace for exhibiting the new "manufactories" and arts of the century. The program for the exposition building called for it to be a mile long and constructed within one year. Joseph Paxton, a landscape gardener, produced the design that made such fast and extensive construction possible: a giant prefabricated conservatory. For 6 months, iron columns and trusses were manufactured to standard specifications in factories all over England. Then for another 6 months they were assembled on the site; the columns were set on concrete footings, the trusses were fastened in place, and the glass walls and roof were set into prepared grooves (see Fig. 20-3). Existing trees on the site were incorporated into the building. Even in the mild

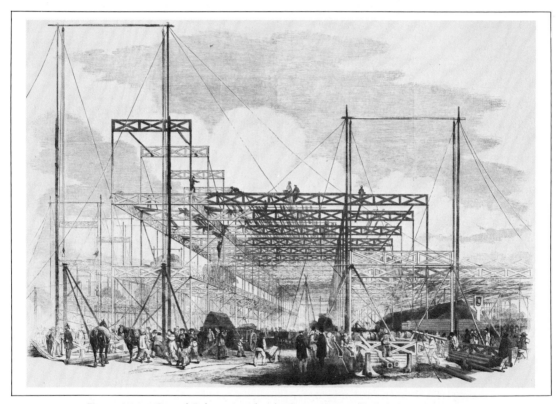

Figure 20-3   Crystal Palace, London built in 1850 and 1851; Joseph Paxton, designer. A scene during the process of construction. Paxton, a landscape gardener, used his experience in building greenhouses to design a huge exhibition hall of iron and glass that could be prefabricated in 6 months and then constructed during another 6 months. (Photo courtesy *Illustrated London News* Picture Library.)

Figure 20-4   Crystal Palace, view of interior (as reconstructed at Sydenham, 1854).
The hall was designed to be demountable and reconstructable and to enclose living
plant materials. In this view we sense the indeterminate space that was developed in
the nineteenth century and has become typical of modern architecture and urban
design. (Reprinted from A. M. Voght, *Art of the 19th Century*, by courtesy of the
Institut fur Geschichte und Theorie dur Architektur, ETH Hongenberg, Zurich.)

English climate, the light proved to be so intense inside the building that the
interior was draped with cheesecloth to cut down the glare. So vast was the
Crystal Palace that it seemed a new kind of space had been created—an
indeterminate space that would become characteristic of the next century, a
space whose inception and closure seemed totally arbitrary rather than
determined by internal necessity (see Fig. 20-4). At the end of the nineteenth
century, the German politician Friedrich Naumann wrote, "Buildings in iron
are the greatest artistic experience of our time . . . all our notions of space,
weight, and support are changed."

    That all notions could be so changed indicates that reality itself was in a
basic sense newly organized during the nineteenth century. Not only were

materials and structures different, but also the function and the financing of architecture. Joint-venture companies, holding companies, and other financial innovations made possible the aggregate investment of wealth that brought about not only the development of railroads but also the emergence of a whole network of industrial development in western Europe and the United States. The savings of sea-captains' widows and prosperous doctors in England were added to the profits of the cotton industry and the resulting capital was invested to build, for instance, the railroads of the United States and to return to the investors an ample yield on their money. Factories, office buildings, and speculative housing could be financed with these new funds.

OTHER NEW TYPES OF STRUCTURES

New arrangements of society required and found new architectural expression. In addition to the railroad structures, other new types of structures were found generously scattered throughout western society. Impermanent exhibition buildings and permanent museums open to the public and lit by vast expanses of glass were alike in being new building types. Some of the other new types were the following:

Department stores   Many different kinds of merchandise gathered together under one roof, usually in tall buildings equipped with elevators, telephones, and electric lights.

Covered markets   Like the department store, the covered market was a nineteenth century development which owed much to the availability of iron for columns and trusses and glass for infill. Early covered markets of importance were Les Halles in Paris and that at Covent Gardens in London, both now destroyed. For convenience to shoppers, many small merchants—especially those selling fresh produce—gathered together in a central area under a roof to protect them from the weather. Shopping arcades, such as the famous one at Milan, remain to this day.

Oil refineries   Beginning with the first oil wells in Pennsylvania in 1859, the extraction and refining of petroleum products has become a major industry. Oil refineries add their fantasy architecture to many cityscapes, especially at night when they are lit up, inasmuch as the process of refining goes on day and night.

Gas works   Natural gas was the most common source of lighting during the middle of the nineteenth century, for both private houses, industry, and streets. Cylindrical "gas houses" to store the fuel are still to be seen in towns of the northeastern United States.

Workhouses   Charles Dickens dramatically recorded the horrors of the workhouses, or almshouses, that were grudgingly provided for the destitute. These were very much like prisons in their layout and functioning.

"Housing" As nineteenth century cities doubled and redoubled in size, providing even a minimum of living accommodations for the immigrant populations was a huge problem. Whole families might have only one room or even have to share that room with others. People had previously lived in cottages, town houses, or manors. Housing for the lowest classes was now being built as five- or six-story tenements, provided with neither indoor plumbing nor amenities such as playgrounds for the children.

Schools A new perception of the importance of mass education meant that schools now required permanent structures rather than ad hoc arrangements in the professors' homes. Elementary schools, academies, seminaries, high schools, colleges, vocational schools, universities, kindergartens—the very proliferation of names indicates the proliferation of the school as a building type to fill the new needs of society. Most were several-story buildings fitted tightly onto urban sites.

Office buildings Government bureaucracies had been housed in palaces, but the new armies of clerks and managers for industry and finance required a multiplicity of individual "cells" in which to perform their jobs. Early pioneers in the development of the office building were Robert Mills, who designed the U.S. Treasury Building in Washington, D.C., as a series of repeated cells; Sir Charles Barry, who designed the Houses of Parliament in a conceptually similar way. Both these buildings were horizontally extended to achieve maximum light and air; but in the second half of the century the use of steel frame, curtain walls, elevators and other equipment, made taller and taller buildings structurally possible and economically feasible.

Sewers Major cities had had sewers at least since Renaissance times, but the enormous expansion of urban populations made expanded and improved sewer systems essential for public health (see Benevolo, *The Origins of Modern Town Planning*). Better design of both system and component pipes provided better service at lower cost. Possibly the most famous of these new systems were the sewers of Paris, greatly expanded by the planner Haussmann in the third quarter of the century. Improved sanitation and purer drinking water drastically lowered the incidence of cholera, which had previously raged as a frequently recurring epidemic.

Dams The new technology of reinforced concrete made higher and wider dams feasible, leading to new ways of controlling rivers (and flooding) and to new sources of electric power when that was developed after 1870. The Niagara Falls Project completed in 1895 was the first major hydro-electric project. Advances in the civil engineering of dams so impressed Le Corbusier (in the early twentieth century) that he chose them as powerful symbols of the simple, functional, yet elegant architecture of the new age.

Grain storage elevators The modern form of tall cylindrical towers (usually lined with glass) was already well-defined before 1920, ready to serve (with dams and ocean liners) as models for the necessarily simple modern architecture of the machine age. Grain elevators were necessary because of the organization of agriculture on a national and even international basis, with collection and shipment points at ports and railroad junctions.

Steamships The application of steam power and steel for material made possible ocean-going ships of a completely new configuration and much larger size than before. The simplicity of the form and its rigorous adaptation to function made the steamship a perfect symbol of the speed that so fascinated the nineteenth-century mind.

Many of these new types of structures were made possible by the use of some new inventions that facilitated communication and increased comfort. For the first time, architects had available elevators, which made tall buildings feasible. Otis invented the elevator in 1853, but it was at first used only to raise goods. After it was improved by the addition of a safety catch and a cage around the platform, it began to be used for people as well as goods (see Fig. 20-5).

Figure 20-5 Elisha G. Otis demonstrating the first safety elevator, which he invented in 1853. At first used only to lift goods (as here), it was improved by the addition of a cage which made it safe for people. Buildings taller than six stories, dependent on the invention of the elevator, followed immediately during the third quarter of the century. (Photo courtesy Otis Elevator Co.)

Equally important for the development of tall buildings was the telephone, developed by Bell and patented in 1876 and 1877. Communication between tall buildings and even between cities was made as easy and convenient as had been face-to-face meetings in the Greek agora. Conducting modern business and government affairs is unthinkable without the telephone, which greatly facilitates the flow of information. Buildings have come to be routinely designed with telephone wiring and with the telephones themselves placed in all the offices. Public telephones are also frequently provided in the lobbies.

Many experiments in forced air heating and ventilating, culminating in the invention of air conditioning, were made during the nineteenth century (see R. Banham, *Architecture of the Well-Tempered Environment*). The gas used for lighting during the middle of the century was convenient but had some drawbacks. The soot produced during combustion necessitated the choice of dark colors for walls and even ceilings. The "bad air" left after much of the oxygen was burned away was a major cause of the headaches and nausea that Victorian females so often complained of, as they were the ones who were confined in the gas-lit spaces of the home. New processes of purifying the air and of lighting the interior cleanly with electricity combined to improve indoor life. The mechanical invention of the revolving door made it possible to maintain consistent air pressure and also to retain most of the expensive heat within a building. Electric lighting has made major differences in the ways buildings are used, with large interior spaces being feasible for the first time. We think of Thomas Edison as inventing the electric light bulb, but it is more to his honor and our convenience that he invented the electricity distribution system around 1880.

The lists of new building types and new building elements suggest that architecture in the nineteenth century was more than ever a cooperative effort. Moreover, it was an effort in which engineers had new importance. The split between the train sheds built by an engineer and a station built by an architect is symptomatic of the split between the two professions that developed during the century, as they differentiated themselves and their proper spheres from one another. So distinct were the responsibilities of architects and engineers during the nineteenth century that John Ruskin, the English critic, could define architecture as "decoration added to structure." Engineers controlled the new technology. Engineers built the sewers, gas and electric systems, telephones, roads and bridges, railroads,—in short, all the infrastructure (permanent installations) of modern society. Moreover, engineers built the foundations; the structural framework; and the plumbing, electric, heating, and ventilating systems for individual buildings, systems which the aesthetic design of the buildings had to take into account.

Architecture, as we will see in the next chapter, controlled the aesthetic aspects of the building. Instead of employing decorators to embellish the shell, as rococo architects had done, nineteenth-century architects found themselves forced more and more into the role of chief decorators, with structural and systematic decisions made by others. The larger and more complicated the building, the more likely that there was a split. This division was a major element in the crisis of architecture to which the polemicists of the early twentieth century, and most of the architects of the twentieth century, were responding in their writings and in their work. One of the major efforts has been the attempt to reclaim technology and structure as properly their concern, together with the totality of the built environment.

Rarely in human history have so many new building types entered the repertoire of architecture in so short a time as did during the nineteenth century. The building industry, the engineers, the architects, and the patrons handled this set of opportunities as best they could, each with his or her own skills and preferences. Intellectually, theirs was the same problem as was the invention of the Christian basilica in the fourth century A.D., but on a much greater scale, since so many new types were called for. The building types remain with us, but the process of understanding their creation and function is far from complete.

BIBLIOGRAPHY

Banham, R., *Architecture of the Well-Tempered Environment*. Architectural Press, London, 1969. A good introduction to the effects of new heating and ventilating technologies on building design in the nineteenth century.

Benevolo, L., *The Origins of Modern Town Planning,* M.I.T., Cambridge, Mass., 1967. Brief and interesting, especially his account of engineering solutions to public health problems.

Crichton, M., *The Great Train Robbery,* Bantam, New York, 1976. The introduction to this fictionalized account is the best short history of nineteenth-century railroads.

Hix, J. *The Glass House,* M.I.T., Cambridge, Mass., 1974. A well-illustrated history of building in glass. Interesting.

Hobhouse, C., *1851 and the Crystal Palace,* Dutton, New York, 1937.

Sharp, D. (ed.), *Glass Architecture* by P. Scheerbart and *Alpine Architecture* by B. Taut. Praeger, New York, 1972. Scheerbart's early-twentieth-century visions remain compelling. Taut actually built a totally glass building.

Steinman, D. B., and S. R. Watson, *Bridges and Their Builders,* Dover, New York, 1957 (reprint of 1941 edition). Comprehensive and clearly written, helpful to beginners.

21
REVIVAL STYLES

THE USE OF HISTORY

The knowledge explosion of the nineteenth century applies to history, especially the history of architecture, as well as it does to technology. We have seen that the availability of materials that were both cheaper and more adaptable (steel and glass) led to structural experimentation. The result was buildings of new configurations, in height, for example. Further variation resulted from an exuberant playing with visual elements of a wide variety of historical examples. In the eighteenth century there had been strong interest in the architecture of China and Persia. Travelers' tales and sketches were received with delight and utilized as inspiration for such exotic set pieces as the Porcelain Room in Versailles in the Chinese manner (chinoiserie).

In the nineteenth century comparative studies of many different periods of architecture were published. The earliest survey of architectural history was by Fischer von Erlach (1737), who originated the concept of beginning architectural history with Stonehenge and ending with his own work, as if all of history had been a preparation for himself. He included some very fanciful pyramids, some realistic pagodas (Chinese towers), and some accurately reported domed buildings from the Middle East, as well as Greek, Roman, and Renaissance buildings. The Roman ones were fairly accurate, but the Greek ones were presented as if they had been built by Romans. In his own architecture, Fischer von Erlach was the first of the eclectics (individuals who assemble a whole by picking details from any and all sources). He designed the church of San Carlos Borromeo in Vienna, which is a perfect example of this eclecticism (see Fig. 21-1). The interior is oval and the facade undulating, both baroque features. Flanking the central panel of the facade and extending it on either side were triumphal arches like those in the Roman Forum; one was needed to provide

Figure 21-1   San Carlos Borromeo, Vienna, Austria. Built by Fischer von Erlach between 1716 and 1737. One of the first eclectic buildings, this church combines a baroque dome, an ancient Roman temple facade with columns and pediment, triumphal arches, and two columns like that of Trajan, their reliefs twisting in opposite directions. The plan is also baroque in its use of ovals. (Photo by Helga Schmidt-Glassner, Stuttgart.)

for a pedestrian path along the side of the church, but two of them give the church a more imposing facade. In front of concave recesses in the wide facade, he placed two columns with spiral reliefs, based on the Column of Trajan in the Roman Forum. The church has a dome like that of St. Peter's, which sits up on a drum behind the pedimented facade that is based on an ancient temple front. History, for Fischer von Erlach, was a gold mine of motifs.

When earlier periods had looked to history for inspiration, they had looked at what was close at hand. In the Romanesque era, for instance, builders took notice of the Roman remains in their own particular geographical region and used only them for their models. The Roman gate in Autun inspired the nave elevation in Autun Cathedral but was totally unknown to the builders of Durham Cathedral in England. Even in the Renaissance, Florentine architects began by studying the Roman and early Christian remains in Florence or perhaps as far away as Rome (about 150 miles). They neither knew nor cared about Roman architecture in France or North Africa. This pragmatic attitude of learning from one's own immediate environment is quite different from the nineteenth-century position of having the whole sweep of history and most of the globe as potential sources for architectural ideas.

The result of such uncritical enthusiasm was near chaos in the built environment. Not only could a gothic building be erected next to a Renaissance one and across from a Greek one, but even within one building, motifs from twelfth, fourteenth, and fifteenth century gothic could be and were mingled freely. History was reduced to a series of visual formulas.

By the nineteenth century, the idea of turning to history for only the visual details it had to offer was already an old and comfortable one. At the beginning of the Renaissance, Brunelleschi studied Roman buildings for their structural ideas as well as their decoration, but after him most architects were not interested in ancient Roman structural ideas. Attention turned from historic structure to visual effect. This disinterest was possibly related to the fact that architecture became the province of a new intellectual elite rather than that of the practical master masons of the Middle Ages. Architects and clients of the nineteenth century were so fascinated by the new motifs available to them that a lot of their attention went to aligning the best possible vocabulary with the message that the architect and client wished to convey. Churches had to be gothic and government buildings baroque, for example. Such attempts in architecture were in keeping with other nineteenth-century ideas about sincerity. If a picture showed a little girl with a puppy, high approval of the subject matter led almost automatically to approval of the painting itself. So also a so-called gothic church won approval regardless of the quality of its formal aspects.

This pervasive interest in the newly expanded past led to a long series of revivals, with one past fashion quickly supplanting another. Already in the eighteenth century there were two architectural movements which we could call revivals, the neoclassical and the Gothick. Earliest of the revival periods was neoclassicism, in the eighteenth and nineteenth centuries. This period has been described by J. Rykwert in *The First Moderns*. After the exuberance and the full-blown ornamentation of the baroque period, the neoclassical architects made a conscious effort to control themselves and their architectural expression. Such a building as Soufflot's Panthéon in Paris may seem dry and hard but was the epitome of high moral purpose. Built during the last half of the eighteenth century (1764 on), the Panthéon was a collection of classical elements. Like the Roman one, it had a temple facade and a dome, but the dome was set up on a drum, in the manner of Les Invalides, with lower domes over the arms, like the Byzantine pattern. All four arms had temple facades. The dome was supported inside by rows of columns, a tour de force impossible without careful study of the structural systems of the gothic period and of St. Paul's in London, and without the use of iron reinforcing rods. At the same time, the crypt of the church had authentic Greek Doric columns, used for the first time here in a public building. The (gothic) structure of the church was everywhere "corrected" by the proper antique taste—which is why we call it neoclassical.

STRAWBERRY HILL

At the exact same time, quite another approach to the reuse of gothic ideas was visible at Horace Walpole's country estate Strawberry Hill (see Fig. 21-2). Built between 1749 and 1777, it was an astounding frolic through the medieval

Figure 21-2 Library at Strawberry Hill, Twickenham, England, built by Horace Walpole between 1749 and 1777. Very free in its use of gothic motifs in combinations not imagined even in the late gothic of the sixteenth century—a use we now consider romantic as well as eclectic. The way stucco instead of wood or stone is used for reliefs on ceiling and wall is similar to its use in neoclassical architecture of the same period. (Photo courtesy of *Country Life*, London.)

past. Walpole selected any motif he liked, combining them without regard for scale or appropriateness. His approach was essentially romantic, springing from the same attitude toward the past that made James Stuart construct a fake Doric temple on an English estate: the past was to dream about and capture a fairy-tale fragment of. To differentiate Walpole's results from later more authentic versions of medieval architecture, his is usually spelled gothick. When Strawberry Hill was built, a new interest in "our authentic English past" was the very cutting edge of the avant garde. This premise of gothic as English was to continue into the nineteenth century as a major theme.

Another romantic approach was to use the Greco-Roman vocabulary of the neoclassicists but with a softer and more poetic manner that derived in part from the elegant rococo period. A good example is the Bank of England by John Soane, built largely during the first two decades of the nineteenth century. Classical forms are used here freely and emotionally. For instance, to make an asset of a difficult angular corner on the exterior, Soane used the circular colonnade of the temple in Tivoli, Italy, and on the inside he placed severe Doric columns to support a Roman bath window. The main banking room was based on the volume of the Baths of Caracalla in Rome but drastically simplified like the interiors of some late French Romanesque Byzantine churches in Angoulême and Périgueux. Above this simple but impressive Roman volume, he placed a combination Renaissance and baroque dome on a drum, indicating that he felt free to select classical forms wherever he found them.

JEFFERSON'S CAPITOL IN RICHMOND

Partly under the influence of James Stuart's (and his partner Revett) book *The Ruins of Athens* and other publications, and partly because of enthusiasm for the revolution of the Greeks against their Turkish masters, the next revival style of importance was the Greek revival. Since the forms used were as often Roman as Greek, the style ought perhaps to be termed classical revival. A fine early example in this style was the capitol in Richmond, Virginia, built from 1785 to 1790 (see Fig. 21-3). When Thomas Jefferson was the American ambassador to France, he visited the south of France and saw the Maison Carrée in Nîmes, a Roman temple from perhaps 100 B.C. Jefferson thought this was the most beautiful building he had ever seen. Working with the French architect Clerisseau, Jefferson developed a design based on the Roman temple to serve as a new state capitol for Virginia. A major simplification was effected by changing the Corinthian capitals to the less elaborate Ionic order and reducing the depth of the porch. Other changes included inserting an upper floor for more office space and adding doors and windows, including a Roman bath window in the pediment (triangular area within the gable of the roof). Architecture of the Roman Republic and of the Greeks (where democracy was born) was considered highly suitable for structures in our fledgling democracy,

Figure 21-3   Capitol; Richmond, Virginia; by Thomas Jefferson; built from 1785 to 1789. Sometimes called the first Greek revival building, the capitol was a reworking of the Maison Carrée at Nîmes, France, a Republican Roman temple of the late Hellenistic era. Jefferson considered Roman Republican buildings perfect models for the sober architecture of the new democratic nation. The Maison Carrée's Corinthian became Ionic here, and windows and doors had to be added, but the classical inspiration was clearly manifest. (Photo, author.)

and classical revival spread through the Finger Lakes district of New York, the small towns of Ohio and Michigan, and the plantation architecture of the south.

Another ancient civilization was brought into new contact with the western European when Napoleon and his army occupied Egypt from 1798 to 1801. Traveling with the army were scholars and artists, who carried back to France much new information about Egypt. The results in architectural terms were buildings in Egyptian revival style, thought particularly appropriate for prisons and for tombs and cemetery gates—all places where permanence was intrinsic to the meaning of the structure. An example from the 1840s is the Tombs prison in New York City.

The first moderns of the eighteenth century were also first to have real knowledge of the faraway cultures of China and India, as we have mentioned. In the early years of the nineteenth century, Britain was consolidating its rule over some of these places. Exotic architecture was compatible with romantic evocation of the past and distant. When the prince regent of England decided to build a pleasure palace in Brighton, much of the interior was decorated in the Chinese manner, but the exterior eventually had (under the architect John Nash, around 1812) domes and minarets like Persian architecture. Oriental revival like this was a minor stream in nineteenth-century architecture, but its occasional results add to the visual richness of the period. A good but distant example is Olana, the house built by the painter Frederick Church after 1870, incorporating suggestions by Vaux and Withers on a hill overlooking the Hudson River. The house is described as Moorish gothic for its combination of medieval and Islamic motifs.

Gothic revivals of many sorts flourished during the nineteenth century. We have already mentioned the Houses of Parliament by Barry and Pugin as an early example of an office building. They were also an early exploration of "the authentic English past," as Pugin called the gothic period, thereby ignoring the centuries before and after. Massing of towers, Big Ben and other towers placed asymmetrically; their horizontal spread like English gothic cathedrals; and their medieval interior decoration were all calculated to symbolize the democratic process—using the imagery of the past during which it was believed that democracy slowly but inevitably developed.

Barry and Pugin worked freely within the vocabulary of the late gothic period, in a mode called "picturesque." On the other side of the Atlantic, Richard Upjohn was working in a more archeologically correct gothic in his design for Trinity Church in New York City. Upjohn and others of the ecclesiological movement tried to select details which were considered authentic by period and appropriate to the function of a structure, be it a church or a city hall. American gothic revival included both the picturesque cottages of Davis and of Downing and the "correct" gothic of St. Patricks's

Figure 21-4   Brighton Pavilion, England. Built between 1815 and 1818 by John Nash for the prince regent (later George IV), this pleasure palace combined Oriental motifs in a very free way—Middle Eastern domes and minarets on the exterior and Chinese wallpapers and furniture on the interior. The architecture alludes to England's expanding empire as well as to expanding knowledge of architectural possibilities. (Photo by D. Gardner.)

REVIVAL STYLES

Figure 21-5   Houses of Parliament, London, England. Designed by Sir Charles Barry and decorated by Augustus Pugin beginning in 1835, the government offices hide their rigid repetition of similar cells behind an asymmetrical facade with picturesque massing of towers, including Big Ben at right. Pugin considered gothic to be the "only proper style," and with these buildings set the stage for development of high Victorian gothic, which is to medieval gothic as baroque is to ancient Roman. (Photo by R. Hummel.)

Cathedral in New York. The range of variation indicates that the goal of historical association superseded stylistic considerations.

THE ALBERT MEMORIAL

After the middle of the nineteenth century, some architects realized that they were as free to compose in the gothic vocabulary as had been baroque architects in the classical vocabulary. The result was high Victorian gothic, which you may read about in Hitchcock's *Architecture 19th and 20th Century*. Being neither picturesque nor authentic, high Victorian gothic allowed builders to evoke historic associations without being confined to accurate historical copying. A stunning example is the Albert Memorial in London, built between 1863 and 1872 by Sir George Gilbert Scott (see Fig. 21-6). How ironic that the great royal patron of the futuristic Crystal Palace should be memorialized in a structure that epitomizes Victorian historic eclecticism. The memorial is a baldachino (an Italian Renaissance form) executed in reddish stone in the most decorative late gothic flamboyancy. Within it sits a classical bronze statue of the prince consort. He is surrounded by neobaroque white marble statues of the four continents, which are linked by relief panels also in white marble. The use of polychromy (many colors) and the mixture of historic styles to create a new image is typical of high Victorian gothic.

THE GRAND STAIRCASE OF THE PARIS OPÉRA

In its richness and ornamentation, High Victorian gothic was similar to Second Empire, which also flourished during the third quarter of the century. Second Empire was the baroque revival of France under Napoleon II, its most noted architect being Charles Garnier. His masterpiece was the Paris Opéra (1861–

Figure 21-6 Albert Memorial, London. This high Victorian gothic memorial was built by Sir Gilbert Scott between 1863 and 1872. In the full spirit of eclecticism, it combines a gothic version of a Renaissance baldachino with mosaics, free-standing bronze and marble sculpture of baroque inspiration, and marble reliefs that are classical in their naturalism. The park setting is purely Victorian, as is the delight in polychromy. (Photo courtesy British Tourist Authority.)

1874), famous for its grand stairway and its foyer (entrance hall) (see Fig. 21-7). In the great tradition of palatial stairways from the University of Genoa to the palace in Würzberg, this opera house stairway was designed not only to make going up and down an architectural experience but also to provide an elaborate stage setting for personal display by the patrons of the opera. Revival of the baroque suited the nineteenth-century need for public display.

THE BOSTON PUBLIC LIBRARY

Most of our twentieth century notions of Victorian taste can be traced to the architecture and decoration of the Second Empire period. By the 1890s tastes had changed. Architecture had taken a much more subdued turn, into

Figure 21-7   Grand staircase of the Paris Opera House, built by Jean Louis Charles Garnier between 1861 and 1874. Built during the reign of Napoleon III, this building carries the style designation Second Empire, which might more descriptively be termed baroque revival. The ornate and colorful architecture was a perfect background for ladies in satins, velvets, and brocades, dripping with jewels, and for gentlemen in evening dress and uniforms. (Photo supplied by Caisse Nationale des Monument Nationale des Monuments Historiques et des Sites.)

Figure 21-8   Boston Public Library. Built between 1888 and 1895 by McKim, Mead, and White, this was the first Renaissance revival building in America. Modeled after the Bibliothèque St. Genevieve in Paris, it has all the symmetrical formality of a Renaissance palace. Inside the plan is less symmetrical, however, with a tall reading room behind the upper windows at left but a grand staircase and other spaces behind the identical windows at right. (Photo courtesy of the Trustees of the Boston Public Library.)

Renaissance Revival. A good example is the Boston Public Library, built by McKim, Mead, and White, from 1888 to 1895 (see Fig. 21-8). Considered a revolutionary building then, because it was not in the Second Empire style, this library was based on French versions of the Renaissance palace (such as the Parisian Bibliothèque St. Geneviève). It had a heavy basement, Renaissance windows set in round-headed arches, and an interior court very much like those of fifteenth-century Florence. There is also a grand public staircase, beautifully decorated with colored marbles, sculpture, and murals. The builders believed the library to be a "palace of the people."

In its conceptualization and planning as well as appearance, the architecture of McKim, Mead, and White was strongly influenced by the French Ecole de Beaux Arts, where a grand way of using the classical vocabulary was taught, one that persisted well into the 1940s in the work of Pope and others (the Jefferson Monument, etc.) In the seventeenth century the French kings had set up this official school for the training of architects and artists. Its graduates were employed by the French government to do official buildings. In the nineteenth century they spread the word to America and other countries. Only the Greco-Roman vocabulary as modified by centuries of Renaissance and baroque use was considered proper; to this was added the neoclassical idea of correctness. Buildings tended to be bilaterally symmetrical and magnificent.

Drexler's book on *The Architecture of the Ecole des Beaux Arts* is informative and well illustrated.

The changing meaning of the word Renaissance is worth noting. As late as the early 1950s, the term was used broadly to denote the early Renaissance of the fifteenth century, high Renaissance of the early sixteenth century, mannerism, baroque, rococo, and neoclassicism. Only after about 1955 were later periods clearly differentiated from their origin in the Renaissance—and that differentiation happened after it was no longer a living style in architecture.

One more revival style remains to discuss—the American colonial revival. Beginning with the 1890s, there were conscious attempts to make imposing new buildings, especially houses, in the New England and Dutch colonial styles of pre-Revolutionary America. So accustomed are we to this appearance for houses and other small buildings, that most of us are not aware that it is a historical style at all. Colonial revival as a style is still living.

Stonehenge, Roman Republican and Imperial architecture, classical and Hellenistic Greek, medieval of all periods, Egyptian, Chinese, Persian, baroque, Renaissance, and American colonial, were all available to nineteenth-century architects as sources for the appearance and symbolism of their new buildings. At the same time, new materials and new technology from the Industrial Revolution were gradually working their way into the consciousness and the working solutions of builders. For our nineteenth-century predecessors, it was difficult enough to manage the greatly expanding possibilities offered by this new awareness of historical styles. No one could reasonably expect them to penetrate, in the first generation, beyond the fascinating surface of historic differences. The second generation, however, had a revulsion against all this visual richness, and it was left to the third—ourselves—to begin to achieve a new synthesis between our own needs and the possibilities offered by history—a synthesis that goes far beyond appearance, and yet includes it.

BIBLIOGRAPHY

Carrott, R. G., *The Egyptian Revival,* University of California Press, Berkeley, 1978. The definitive study by a lover of the revival style.

Clark, K., *The Gothic Revival, An Essay in History of Taste,* Murray, London, 1962. Best known for his *Civilisation* series, Clark is always worth attending to.

Drexler, A., *The Architecture of the Ecole des Beaux Arts,* Museum of Modern Art and M.I.T., New York, 1977. The book was generated from an exhibition of the same name, held most surprisingly at the Museum of Modern Art in New York.

Fergusson, F. D., "St. Charles Church, Vienna: the Iconography of its Architecture," *Journal of the Society of Art Historians,* vol. 29, no. 4, December 1970, pp. 318–326. A study of Fischer von Erlach's chief work.

Fischer von Erlach, J. B., *Entwurff einer historishen Architectur,* Leipzig, 1725; reprinted Ridgewood, N.J.: Gregg Press, 1964. The first comprehensive architectural history, this book emphasized views and deemphasized text.

Hitchcock, H. R., *Architecture 19th and 20th Century,* Penguin, Baltimore, 1958. Too many facts, not enough pictures, but the standard text for the field. See especially his chapter on high Victorian gothic.

Hussy, C., *The Picturesque: Studies in a Point of View,* Putnam, New York, 1927. First notice of Boulee and Ledoux, the poetic classicists of around 1800.

Pugin, A. W. N., *Contrasts,* 2d, Humanities Press, New York, 1969, with an introduction by H. R. Hitchcock. First published in London in 1841. The "bad" classical in architecture is contrasted with the "good" gothic in a series of paired plates. By the interior designer for the Houses of Parliament.

Rhoads, W. B., "The Colonial Revival and American Nationalism," *Journal of the Society of Art Historians,* vol. 35, no. 4, December 1976, pp. 239–254. Symbolic meaning in the style so natural to Americans that it is rarely considered a style.

Rykwert, J., *The First Moderns,* M.I.T., Cambridge, Mass., 1980. Many fascinating details of architecture and architects in the eighteenth century. Well illustrated.

Wiebenson, D., *Sources of Greek Revival Architecture,* Zwemmer, London, 1969. Crisply reasoned and beautifully written.

INTERLUDE D

In the past five chapters we have studied St. Peter's in Rome and the question of the design process; the baroque churches of Bernini and Borromini and the question of the emotional impact of architecture; rococo churches and the question of the integration of art and architecture; nineteenth-century technology and the question of building types; and revival styles of the nineteenth century and the question of the uses of history. Before we proceed to rearrange the questions and monuments for comparative purposes, we must be sure that we can state each question succinctly and that we can bring to mind the salient features of each major monument.

17 Every building that qualifies as architecture is developed through a design process that involves the same factors. The process begins with an analysis of the site, climate, and other unchangeables and a consideration of the client's stated needs. By information gained from questions, goals of the project are refined. To achieve the goals, several design strategies are worked out and the preferred one is chosen. From several schemes for the form of the building, one is chosen on the basis of the resources available. The scheme is then worked out in great detail so that construction can follow the design selected, and the building eventually exists three-dimensionally. In the process, there are many moments when different decisions will lead to a very different final form.

18 This final form may have been designed to affect the viewers' emotions very strongly, such as a baroque church might, or much less strongly, such as a housing project put up by architects of the international style probably would. Emotional effect may be the result of the narrative content of the decoration of architecture, or it may be a direct result of the abstract quality of the space and of the subsidiary details that contribute to the purely architectural features.

19 The emotional effect is often engineered by a skillful interaction between art and architecture. The building can be conceived and built as a background for art, if the art is carefully situated in a particular place in or on a building to emphasize the significance of the building. Such effects are quite different from those engendered by an art museum in which a collection of works is placed in spaces that are usually neutral and may be changed next week.

20 The public museum was one of the new building types that architects had to provide during the nineteenth century. The Industrial Revolution had made extensive differences in people's life patterns and even in the organization of society, so that many new kinds of buildings were needed. The new types posed questions of structure, decoration, and integration into the city.

21 To decorate the new types of buildings, architects turned to a repertoire of historical motifs that was wider by far than ever before in history. Their need to present new building in acceptable form was so great that it overrode any other possible uses of history for almost a century. Conscious choice of style gradually affected the architects' ideas about style and their ideas about what history was for.

17 The preceding five chapters have dealt with monuments from over 400 years. The earliest structure studied is St. Peter's in Rome, which took over 200 years to construct. It is a very large structure, with an elongated dome set up on a drum that is in turn braced by the barrel vaults of the four arms of the plan. Three end in semicircular apses and the fourth is stretched out toward the plaza in front and reaches on toward the river. Columns, attached columns, and pilasters—all of a giant order—articulate the facade and the walls. Inside, the church is richly decorated.

18 Equally rich in decoration, but more unified, are the churches of Bernini—especially his Cornaro Chapel, in which a simple rectangular space is enhanced not only by richly colored marbles and gilding but also by painting and sculpture, designed and largely executed by Bernini. In a niche at the back of the chapel he placed a statue of St. Teresa and an angel made of white marble that contrasts vividly with the polychromy of the rest of the chapel and seems to lift the two figures into another realm, possibly the spiritual.

By contrast, the Borromini church in San Carlo alle Quattro Fontane achieves its effects by architectural manipulations alone. The oval of its plan undulates so that the walls seem to be interacting directly with the viewers. Overhead the dynamics of interaction are evident in the way that the oval lantern relates to the oval dome, the dome to the truncated barrel vaults that lead to the four niches and transform themselves into shells over the altar niches. Connections between the top of the entablature and various points in the ceiling are made by twisting ribs that form the edges of arches. These arches and entablature are white against the white of the walls—a very restrained color scheme that emphasizes the moving, affective quality of the architecture.

19 Compared with the Cornaro Chapel, Vierzehnheiligen has also a restrained color scheme, with Bernini's dark rich colors replaced in the German church by pastels and a lot of white and gold. Compared with San Carlo, Vierzehnheiligen is obviously more abundantly rich in color. Neumann seems to have learned from Italian masters as well as from his study in France, because his version of rococo architecture draws from all these sources. The colors are French, the twisted arches are like those of Borromini, and the integration of art and architecture is definitely from Bernini. Vierzehnheiligen is a large church of the customary cross-shaped plan. Its two major differences from earlier baroque churches are the use of repeated ovals to form nave, choir, and transepts and the layering of these ovals within an undulating aislelike space into which the windows pour their ample light.

20 It is awesome to realize that only a century separates Vierzehnheiligen from the Crystal Palace. So great is the chasm between the hand-crafted, extensively decorated church and the prefabricated exhibition building of metal and glass that they almost seem to belong to different worlds. In a sense they do, for the Crystal Palace was a direct product of the Industrial Revolution. Its many duplicated elements were manufactured all over England, assembled at the site, and erected in a mere 6 months. Think of the 29 years for Vierzehnheiligen and the 200 or more for St. Peter's. In materials and in extension, the Crystal Palace revolutionized architecture, being a mile long and built of metal framing filled in with large sheets of glass. The roof arched up to encompass full-grown trees, and the nave and aisles of this enormous greenhouse were filled with useful and decorative objects from all over the world.

21 No more than his contemporaries could Paxton imagine his Crystal Palace stripped of every vestige of decoration, so he added decorative details to the beams of his structure. These details, in the best nineteenth-century fashion, were versions of motifs known earlier and now given new usage. From the multiplicity of images that throng to our minds from mention of the word revival it is hard to pick one; but perhaps the irony of choosing the memorial to the patron of the Crystal Palace will help us to remember and enjoy it. The Albert Memorial, built about 15 years after the Crystal Palace, shows the full utilization of the historical motifs newly available. Albert's bronze statue sits under a gothic version of the Italian Renaissance baldachino made of several colors of stone. Full scale white marble statues of the four continents where Britain had possessions were placed at equal distances outside the baldachino and lower than the prince's statue. They were linked by marble reliefs, narrations of British history. Both reliefs and three-dimensional sculptures were executed in the ideal realism that derived from the Renaissance.

Each monument could be studied in the light of each of our five questions, but also with respect to all the questions we have discussed so far. As an exercise, we discuss each of the five monuments in relation to one particular question, but the student should be aware of the rich results obtained by viewing the monuments in relation to all of them.

St. Peter's in Rome incorporates within itself several types of church, each of which can be found separately, and thus carries the meaning of each of them. From the earliest days of Christianity, shrines were set up over the graves of martyrs such as St. Peter. Usually these were centralized structures similar to Santa Costanza, originally an imperial tomb. When Renaissance architects were experimenting with schemes for the new St. Peter's, they returned to the centralized scheme because it met their criteria for ideal form. From its earliest incarnation, however, St. Peter's was a congregational church as well as a martyrium, with a nave elongated for processions and separate from the martyrium. The present St. Peter's incorporates the traditional long nave of congregational churches, even though this interferes with the view of the great dome from the plaza out in front. As previously mentioned, the long buildings for congregations were called basilicas, a word derived from a late Roman word for law court and a usage derived from the early Christian custom of building community gathering places in cemeteries over the graves of martyrs, so that the two traditions were already mixed by the fourth century when Old St. Peter's was built. Unlike the old one, the new St. Peter's has a large and imposing dome. Domed buildings had a long association with imperial power in the Roman world and were used as major churches in the Byzantine world for a thousand years before Michelangelo designed the dome of St. Peter's. Using the dome here, with its reference to the domed churches of Constantinople, may have suggested the new sense of Rome as the center of Christendom, after the mid-fifteenth century Muslim victory over the remnants of the eastern Roman Empire. The domed structure also had a particular part to play in the urban design of Rome. Like Santa Sophia and the Florence Cathedral, St. Peter's is visible from many places in the city and thus carries out its role as a monument. All the ways of examining St. Peter's helps us to realize that one building can incorporate within it many different building types and resonate with not only each level of implied meaning but also the compound meaning of the ensemble.

Compound meaning is a good phrase to describe Bernini's Cornaro Chapel. We have seen that Bernini aimed to produce a total experience. The emotional effects he wanted were to derive from an integration of art with architecture, both of which would have religious content. Starting with the rectangular arm of a transept, Bernini by skillful manipulation of colored architectural elements, paintings, and sculptures produced the effects he desired. Today, the effects are different according to different groups of viewers: The faithful are spiritually moved as Bernini intended, and their faith is thereby deepened. The art lover or art historian enjoys deciphering the meanings and relishes the aesthetic experience of the visual elements of the chapel but perhaps misses its religious significance. Finally, the unreconstructed modernist is emotionally and rationally horrified at the combination of religious display and lushness, each of which is bad enough alone.

Many of the same emotional responses, achieved by a similar integration of art and architecture can be seen in rococo architecture, but we will not discuss them now. Instead, we will consider the design process as it relates to rococo architecture, especially that of Vierzehnheiligen. We do not have the great mass of documentation about Vierzehnheiligen that is available for St. Peter's, but what we do have is fortunately sufficient for an understanding of the process. Designing such a church was complicated because the works of many artists and artisans had to be coordinated with one another as well as with the architect's scheme for the church.

In *Space into Light,* Otto discusses in detail the changes in possible plans for the church, demonstrated by the several drawings and models that have come down to us, many of them in Neumann's own hand (see Figs. 19-2 and 19-3). By taking a church type that was fairly standard because it was cross-shaped, manipulating it through several versions of a plan based on ovals and circles, and then trying it out in the three-dimensional model, Neumann won acceptance for his ideas through a dialogue with his patron. Rococo architecture was frequently influenced very strongly by the patron, since architectural judgment was thought to be a basic constituent of the aristocratic life. The French nobility were noted for their patronage of architecture (and interior design) right up to the end of the eighteenth century, as had the Italian nobility been in the fifteenth and sixteenth centuries. In Germany, the rulers and clergy upheld the tradition of insistent interaction with the architect. On the practical side of building, Neumann's architecture was influenced strongly by the local building tradition, which called for either hung ceilings of lath and plaster or shallow vaults of stone and concrete. Such vaults could for the first time in the eighteenth century be described mathematically by the newly discovered calculus, an intellectual discovery that would affect design in the long run.

Figure D-1   Portrait of Balthasar Neumann by Markus Friedrech Kleinert, 1927. Compare with Fig. C-3. Here the architect is shown as an officer and a gentleman, elegantly wigged and clothed, grasping the plan of some fortifications in his hand to signify his work as an artillery officer. (Reprinted by permission of Mainfrankisches Museum, Wurzburg, and by courtesy of Christian F. Otto.)

Another occurrence that affected the design process was the rupture between architecture and engineering during the nineteenth century. Heretofore, training for one career might emphasize engineering and another architecture, but for the most part the training was the same for both disciplines. During the nineteenth century, the professions became distinct, with profound effect upon the built environment. Different tasks were assigned to the two groups. The engineers, being considered practical, used new materials (and old materials more efficiently) to produce utilitarian structures that society needed; and the architects, being well-educated aesthetes, used newly discovered historical motifs to decorate the great numbers of buildings required by an expanding population. Sometimes the two fields overlapped, such as when machines for factories were designed in a Doric or Egyptian revival mode, or when a nonarchitect (actually a landscape gardener) was asked to design the Crystal Palace, for which his previous experience in building conservatories had prepared him. A conservatory might have the silhouette of a domed Byzantine church or that of a neoclassical palace, but it would be constructed of glass and metal, materials available and inexpensive as a result of the Industrial Revolution. The Crystal Palace went just far enough back into the past to draw on the tradition of conservatory design and to use a few historical motifs for decoration of its trusses, and these concessions were enough to make its visitors quite comfortable with even as futuristic a structure as this one.

Quite a different set of constraints governed the design of the Albert Memorial. Built by a noted architect, Scott, this structure used an historical vocabulary in a calculated way to play on the emotions of its visitors. Each historical style was thought to carry certain symbolic and associative meanings, so it was used to evoke inevitable responses in viewers. Gothic meant religious reverence, since it originated in the age of faith. You can read about this in *Contrasts* by Pugin, who helped design the Houses of Parliament; he pairs a "good" gothic design with a "bad" classical one, for a church, house, monument, etc. Gothic for the decorative form of the baldachino would thus be sure to evoke as well as symbolize reverence and faith. Renaissance allusions were meant, it seems, to reinforce the attitudes shared by Renaissance and Victorian persons about individual worth and independence. The ideal naturalism of the sculpture reminded the Victorians that their age was rushing toward perfection and improvement in every way and especially toward human mastery of the world. The use of many different colors was a way of including the multiplicity of the world into one structure. The gilding of the bronze statue of Albert reminded viewers of how precious he was to his consort, Queen Victoria, and how well respected he was by all the people. This monument was thus a highly charged emotional construct when it was new, even though it affects us much less now. What may have happened in the interval is that Scott's sincere message and clever composition of meanings no longer convince us. We have learned to look for the kind of abstract meaning that Borromini was so good at. Modern architecture has taught us that austerity is "good" and "storytelling" is bad, so we cannot approve of the Albert Memorial which is lushly decorated and explicitly narrative.

22
CA. 1900

THE CONCEPT OF STYLE

During most of the nineteenth century the delights of architecture seemed to be bound up with the use of historical vocabularies (styles) newly available in such abundance, or new materials and technology, or both. Toward the end of the century a new question arose: Could there be any way to combine iron, glass, and electricity to achieve elegant and comfortable architecture that did not depend for its validity on the utilization of historical motifs?

Appreciation of architecture was so intimately connected with admiration for traditional styles that people assumed that the style was responsible for one's enjoyment of the architecture. Ever since Vitruvius, delight was considered as one of the basic characteristics of architecture. By the middle of the nineteenth century, however, people began to wonder if the vocabulary of

Vitruvius was still relevant to contemporary architectural problems and still fresh enough to provide delight. In the hands of many revivalist architects, use of the classical vocabulary had unfortunately devolved into a mere application of formulas, and architecture by formula rarely pleases the viewer because it is ultimately commonplace and predictable. The writings of Peter F. Smith, an architect and psychologist, deal extensively with the role of arousal and satisfaction in architectural delight; see his *Architecture and the Human Dimension* and other writings.

THE ARTS AND CRAFTS MOVEMENT

The first misgivings about revivalism in architecture came from the arts and crafts movement, which had begun as a revival itself. By the middle of the nineteenth century, machine production had driven many artisans out of business. The goods produced by the machines were inexpensive but were considered by many people to be poorly designed. Poor quality is not the fault of machine production per se, inasmuch as machines are without moral scruples or aesthetic judgment and make only whatever people tell them to make; but in the nineteenth century the machines themselves were felt to be the villains. Inspired by the gothic revival and by the pre-Raphaelite painters and poets, a group of artisans with William Morris as their leader practiced a return to the careful design and artistry they believed had been intrinsic to handwork before the industrial revolution. Morris and his group set out to make new designs of high quality for the contemporary age in wallpaper, furniture, rugs, glassware, and books. Soon they had followers not only in England but also in America.

The arts and crafts movement directly influenced two major American architects—Louis Sullivan and Frank Lloyd Wright, both working in Chicago in the last decade of the nineteenth century. Sullivan was not only a fine architect, but also a designer of ornament of great originality (Fig. 22-1). Like Morris, he turned to the past to discover not what motifs to use but rather how to think through the problem of ornament anew. Wright, who had worked for Sullivan, was instrumental in bringing the arts and crafts ideas to Chicago.

From a study of the past for its ideas of procedure rather than for an imitation of its motifs came the first nonrevival building of any importance. This was the Red House that Webb built for Morris in Kent in England from 1859 to 1860. The house was without obvious historical allusions: no columns, capitals, pediments over windows, classical moldings, or even gothic detail could be seen. If style, as was commonly thought, consisted of using themes from the past, then this house was indeed a bold rejection of style. Its walls of plain red brick under high roofs of red tile are relieved only by the loose massing of the volumes that correspond to the internal plan and by the plain windows with white painted sash. The Red House incorporates such subtle architectonic solutions of the past as proportion, flow, and restraint without borrowing its ornamental motifs.

Figure 22-1   Ornament designed by Louis Sullivan for the Old Home Bank in Denison, Ohio, 1914. Both the richness and the originality of Sullivan's forms are evident even in this modest building. His combination of the organic and the geometric had a strong influence on Frank Lloyd Wright. (Photo, author.)

In a very different place and setting another masterwork of the arts and crafts movement was the Gamble House, built by the Greene brothers in Pasadena, California, in 1908 and 1909. In the same way that the Red House conceals its relation to gothic vernacular, the Gamble House does not divulge its debt to Japanese architecture. The simplicity of the interior and exterior spaces, the elegant way that pieces of wood are pegged together, and the cantilevered supports of overhanging roofs are all Japanese in forms and construction. But the soft hand-rubbed woods of the house's floors, walls, and furniture and the muted earth colors and stained glass owe much to the arts and crafts tradition. The Greene brothers had learned to do architecture in the shingle style so popular on the shores of Long Island Sound during the last years of the nineteenth century before they moved to California, where they found an appreciative group of patrons. Most of their distinctive work is in southern California. The Greene brothers' design concepts as well as the difficulty of conveying them in words are expressed well in Reyner Banham's introduction to Makinson's book on the Greenes, in which he posits that the style of the house was as far as possible determined by four conditions: climate, environment, available materials, and clients' lifestyle. "The intelligence of the owner as well as the ability of the architect and skill of the contractor limit the perfection of the result," according to Charles Greene. The Greene brothers had come so far that style for them had almost nothing to do with historical models. History might affect the habits and tastes of the owner or the methods of the contractor, but nothing in the design. In the first decade of the twentieth century, a manifesto for the new architecture of our century was inherent in the arts and crafts movement.

The Gamble House has strong horizontal lines of roofs, decks, and terraces that related it to the site. Details such as the horizontal shingles and the shadows formed by roofs and the overhang of the second story reinforces the horizontality. The house and its terraces are inserted between two large trees on the site. The informality of the terraces creates an interesting contrast to the formality of the house plan. The house is axially entered on a large central hall that continues all the way to the rear terrace. To the right are a small study, the stairs, and a large cross- shaped living room; to the left, a front bedroom, the kitchen and pantries, and the dining room that protrudes into the terrace. Upstairs the central hall is repeated, with two bedrooms on either side, three of them with sleeping porches. There are also two smaller rooms for servants. A billiard room on the third floor, with windows on every side, is essential to the natural ventilation scheme for the house, because the hot air rises up through the halls and out the third story windows. The spaces of the house are large, flowing freely into one another in the public areas. All surfaces are composed of carefully dimensioned hand-rubbed wood. The components were assembled with great craft, from the stained glass (made by Emile Lange, formerly with the Tiffany Studios) and smaller accents of metal and leather down to such

Figure 22-2   Gamble House interior, Pasadena, California, 1908–1909, by Charles and Henry Greene. In this view of one end of the living room, the careful joining of wood into wall panels and furniture and the exquisite proportions of spaces and openings are evident. Of the objects pictured, even the rugs and piano were specifically designed for the room. (Photo by R. Hummel.)

details as the electric light switches in plated metal with a soft patina. Although based on the nineteenth-century arts and crafts tradition, the Gamble House achieves a timeless quality of beauty, particularly in its interiors (see Fig. 22-3).

ART NOUVEAU

By the year 1900, in both Europe and America a new aesthetic known as art nouveau was developing that corresponded to the new structural and lighting possibilities. The dark browns and reds of the Victorian period had been a practical response to the soot of gas lighting; now with electric lighting being so much cleaner, pastels and white were practical. Decorative forms changed too. Just as the hoop skirt and the bustle of the Second Empire gave way to the

Figure 22-3 Detail of woodwork, Gamble House. The right edge of this view overlaps the left edge of 22-2. (Photo by David Crouch; published by courtesy of the Gamble house.)

Figure 22-4   Villa Tassel in Brussels, Belgium, by Victor Horta, 1893. In this art nouveau interior, Horta explored the decorative possibilities of electric lights, pastel colors, and thin iron supports which suggested the abstract plant forms in the railing and the stylized plant forms of the wall surfaces. The thin tracery of the skylight echoes the other plant forms along this stairway. (Photo by J. Null.)

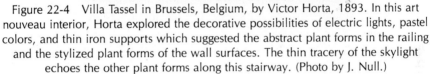

slim elegance of skirts and blouses, so the overstuffed and the deeply carved gave way to thin, lithe forms. In the work of art nouveau architects and decorators these new aesthetic ideas came to public awareness. The movement began in the 1880s, growing out of the attitudes and experience of the arts and crafts movement. By the second decade of the twentieth century, art nouveau ideals were superceded by more aggressive geometric attitudes with respect to the built environment.

Typical of the art nouveau movement was the Tassel house in Brussels built by Victor Horta in 1893. Horta was probably influenced by Viollet-le-Duc (a French architect of the third quarter of the nineteenth century) in his use of iron frankly to express the structure and by Gaudi in his shaping of exterior surfaces. He possibly also drew on English arts and crafts fabrics and wallpapers for motifs. Whatever impact these theoretical influences had on the architect, the ensemble was unparalleled in its light elegance and unity of plant forms as an astylar expression of new design possibilities (see Fig. 22-4).

This whole transitional period is thoroughly and interestingly discussed in R. Banham, *Theory and Design in the First Machine Age,* and N. Pevsner, *Pioneers of Modern Design;* and the roots of the new attitudes in the design of the nineteenth century are explored in H. Schafer, *19th Century Modern: The Functional Tradition in Victorian Design* and L. Mumford, *Roots of Contemporary American Architecture.* In *Theory and Design,* an early work by Banham, the author takes an intellectual approach to the premodern movements of the turn of the century. It was his later contact with the work of the Greenes that made Banham rethink the whole nature of modern architecture. His conclusion is that the high quality of the Greene brothers' architecture can be experienced but not readily taught, so that the architecture of Gropius, Le Corbusier, and Mies had a rhetorical and pedagogical advantage. By the time Banham came to write the introduction to Makinson's book on *Greene and Greene,* he had actually lived in the Gamble House for a time, experienced its sensual beauty, and realized that not all the pleasure derived from architecture could be reduced to cerebral formulas or mathematical analysis. Just as architects had begun—ever so hesitantly—to turn to the past for its building processes rather than its architectural motifs, so too should historians and critics take a different approach in their discussions of current aspects of architecture. Rather than ask, for example, such a typical history of architecture question as, "Was this Ionic order modeled after that of the Temple of Apollo in Didyma," one could ponder the different aesthetic and emotional effects of the use of contrasting materials—Corinthian pilasters made of white limestone as opposed to varnished oak. The historian could, in other words, explore the sensual possibilities of the use of traditional architectural vocabularies and speculate about whether or not the architect could achieve these effects using other vocabularies.

In the nineteenth century, style was viewed simply as a garment hung on the framework of the building. Architects cheerfully presented sketches of the same building done up in French chateau style or Italian villa or English Tudor for the client to choose. Ruskin, voicing the consensus of the period, said, "Architecture is ornament added to structure." There was no objection to using for a single building stone exterior walls with a Romanesque appearance, Byzantine interior decoration, and nineteenth century structure as H. H. Richardson did for Trinity Church in Boston. (The twentieth-century Episcopal cathedral in Washington, D.C., is something of an oddity in having a gothic structure as well as a gothic appearance.) The builders of the nineteenth-century St. Patrick's Cathedral or the church of St. John the Divine, both in New York City, willfully combined new structural principles with medieval visual details. Such inauthentic mixtures distinguish the revival from the original in architectural style, even if all documents about a structure are lost.

It is easy to see how the Red House or the works of Gaudi in Spain could be thought nonstylar if style involved merely consistent historical window dressing. Gaudi transformed late gothic revival vocabulary through his own ideas of a formal geometry. He transformed gothic revival through use of original plant forms in decoration that were characteristic of the art nouveau movement elsewhere. Gaudi continues to present a great challenge to analysts of architectural history, since his style is at once so personal and so much a part of his time and place (see Fig. 22-5).

Grappling with such questions about Gaudi makes us aware of the different meanings we apply to our use of the word "style." First, there is the personal touch of an architect that we think of as individual style. Rhys Carpenter has shown in his studies of Greek sculpture and architecture that just as each sculptor has a characteristic way of carving noses or ears, so that his work can be identified without question, so do architects also use small details repeatedly in building after building, such as a certain combination of

Figure 22-5   Battlo House, Barcelona, Spain. Built by Gaudi in 1905–1907. The columns from a late Renaissance facade have returned here to being "trees." Above them the facade of the next story ripples three-dimensionally, giving prominence to the reception rooms behind the large windows. The same kind of free-form window is repeated at both edges of the next level, as a sort of frame for the two simple french doors between them, and erupts into still another pair of balconies on the fourth floor. The fifth floor is relatively plain but the sixth becomes asymmetrical to give place to a whimsical tower on the left. The roof and roofline repeat the rippling effect of the second story. (Photo by S. Blatz.)

decorative moldings at the top of walls, for example. Their works can thereby be identified without doubt. The use of catenary curves, for instance, characterizes Gaudi's work and that of no one else.

Architects may also be grouped into schools by their common characteristics, such as the exclusive use of the Ionic order in the architecture of Ionia during the fifth century B.C.: or that of handcrafted materials and furnishings by all the arts and crafts builders.

Styles often have a national basis as well. Bernini and Borromini share certain Italian characteristics, such as an ease in use of Roman vocabulary and delight in rich architectural effects, that unite them despite their pronounced personal differences.

Even a whole period can show a common stylistic unity, such as the happy eclecticism of the nineteenth century.

After we delineate these aspects of style—and nowhere is this done more keenly than in Meyer Shapiro's essay on "Style"—we can postulate an updated definition: Style is the characteristic way of doing or making that goes beyond surface differences.

Freeing discussion of style from the straitjacket imposed by considering it as merely historical detail such as the orders, we can use the term in the visual arts more as it is used in literature; as being, that is, "a successful blending of form with content." It is impossible for an architect not to have a personal style, whether or not he or she consciously belongs to a group or movement. Thus we can say that Gaudi shared with art nouveau an interest in the structural and decorative possibilities of lithe plant forms, so that there was an overlap between his personal style and the group style, or school. Even Gaudi, individual as he was, could not avoid belonging to a nation and a period. It may be the hallmark of a first-rate architect that a particular work contains not only individual ideas but also several substrata of ideas from a school, nation, and period which give it universality in style.

BIBLIOGRAPHY

Clark, R. J., *The Arts and Crafts Movement in America 1876-1916,* Princeton University Press, Princeton, N.J., 1972. See also Kornwolf's book.

Cram, R. A., *Impressions of Japanese Architecture and the Allied Crafts,* New York, 1905, reprinted 1982 by C. E. Tuttle. An American architect noted for his historicizing takes a fresh look at architecture in quite a different tradition.

Kornwolf, J. D., *M. H. Baillie Scott and the Arts and Crafts Movement,* Johns Hopkins, Baltimore, 1972. Together with Clark's book, one gets a complete survey of English and American preindustrial revivalism.

Makinson, R., *Greene and Greene: Architecture as a Fine Art,* Peregrine Smith, Inc., Salt Lake City, 1977. Introduction by Reyner Banham; companion volume: *Furniture and Related Designs.* See also J. Strand, *A Greene and Greene Guide,* Pasadena, CA, 1974. The work of these architects is hard to intellectualize about but worth the trouble.

Mumford, L., (ed.), *Roots of Contemporary American Architecture,* Reinhold, New York, 1952. Nineteenth- and twentieth-century essays on architecture.

Pevsner, N., *Pioneers of Modern Design: From William Morris to Walter Gropius,* Penguin, Baltimore, 1960; revised 1974. This book begins about 1851 and closes in 1914 with Gropius's formulation of the answer to the problems of architecture in the twentieth century.

Schafer, H., *19th Century Modern: The Functional Tradition In Victorian Design,* Praeger, New York, 1970. A careful selection from the wealth of the nineteenth century to demonstrate that the aesthetic ideals of the modern movement were endemic in the design of the previous era.

Shapiro, M., "Style," *Anthropology Today,* University of Chicago Press, Chicago, 1953. The definitive essay on the concept of style.

Smith, P. F., *Architecture and the Human Dimension,* Eastview Editions, Westfield, N.J., 1979. How does architecture arouse and satisfy us? The answers discussed by someone who is both an architect and a psychologist.

23
EARLY MODERN ARCHITECTURE
SYMBOLISM AND RHETORIC

While it was still the nineteenth century, some individual architects and some groups of architects began to work in ways that developed directly into the philosophy of architecture of the early modern movement. All these architects shared an aesthetic of radical simplicity, compared with the lushness of the Second Empire or Victorian styles. Machines were making abundance possible, which was enough for most people and most architects during the first century of the industrial revolution. The forerunners of the modern movement reacted negatively against lushness and positively in favor of the elements in nineteenth-century life and technology that they considered progressive, such as speed, electricity, and freedom from historical constraint.

By the end of the First World War, a new attitude had developed that was to dominate modern architecture until the 1970s. The new attitude was that machine-made objects should be simple and direct in form. Moreover, a world cognizant of the impact of machines on the environment and fascinated by speed would tend to favor architecture that was similarly simple in form, with smooth planes and no decoration. The built environment would be made of metal and glass and concrete, with some use of stucco and brick—all manufactured materials, the potentials of which were newly realized after the industrial revolution made them much less expensive to produce.

MAILLART'S BRIDGES

This development can be seen most readily in the reception of the early twentieth-century bridges of Robert Maillart, a Swiss engineer (see Fig. 23-1). Built in the remote parts of Switzerland, his bridges were accepted by conservative local governments because they were efficient and economical. That they were beautiful too was an important goal of Maillart's, but incidental to the governing officials. (See D. Billington, *The Bridges of Robert Maillart*.) It was this beauty, however, that drew the attention of Sigfried Giedion who made the bridges emblematic of the modern position in his *Space, Time and Architecture,* first published in 1941 and quickly recognized as the bible of modern architectural thought.

Figure 23-1 Rhine River bridge at Tavanasa, Switzerland, 1905, Robert Maillart. High efficiency in use of materials resulted here in modest cost, an important value to the thrifty officials of this canton. The result was also beautiful, because of Maillart's exalted notion of successful design, a result which helped to reconcile architecture and engineering. (Photo: Canton Graubunden, courtesy of D. Billington.)

THE BAUHAUS

The economies of Maillart's designs were based on his structural innovations or, to be more accurate, on his aesthetically pleasing use of new principles of working structurally in steel and concrete. In the early twentieth century most architects were not being trained in these new structural principles. At the Bauhaus, Gropius's notable architecture school that flourished in Germany (Werner, 1919–1925; Dessau, 1925–1930; Berlin 1930–1933), the curriculum included work with hand-tools and study of painting in the most advanced nonrepresentational modes but little training in mathematics and no technical study of either materials or structure—courses that are routinely studied today in American schools of architecture. Unlike the situation of history, which was carefully excluded from the curriculum lest it corrupt the young, structures and materials were omitted because these were studied at the Techniche Hochschule (engineering school).

The Beaux-Arts tradition that architecture was a fine art continued even in the schools where the young architects were being trained to overthrow the Beaux Arts. The new architects were apt to justify simplicity and innovation on philosophical grounds. The manifestos of the various groups of early modernists sounded emotional calls for revolution rather than embodying the engineers' "intelligent, cold and calm" approach that Le Corbusier urged (but did not himself follow). Trains, ships, planes—their shapes determined by function and speed, their actions controlled by engineers—were the symbols Le Corbusier held up as examples for architects to follow. In the pages of *Towards A New Architecture,* copiously illustrated with photographs of ocean liners, grain elevators, and the Parthenon—all described as marvels of simple functional design—Le Corbusier called architecture a "pure creation of the mind." "We must clear our minds of romantic cobwebs," he urged. A world of machines demands a new aesthetic and a new manner of living. The kind of architecture that would result from this new way of seeing and living was for Le Corbusier typified by a new kind of "house as a machine for living in" (figures on his pages 222 and 223), "with walls as smooth as sheet iron, with windows like those of factories, . . . as serviceable as a typewriter."

His concepts should be thought of as being abstract rather than practical. After all, people are as often stupid, hot, and frenzied as they are intelligent, cold, and calm, so that solutions embodying only the last attributes will be at best incomplete. Moreover, the complexity of the problems of human habitation puts them at a level quite different from that which involves the design of one-task tools.

THE SCHRÖDER HOUSE AND DE STIJL

One of these houses was built in 1923 in Utrecht, Holland, by Rietveld, who belonged to a group called De Stijl (the style). Rietveld had been previously known for his modern, geometric furniture designs. The Schröder House was a symbol of the modern concept of form. Like the geometric paintings of

Mondrian (who also belonged to De Stijl) Rietveld presented an infinite series of coordinates in space rather than a closed cubic volume. Rooms seemed dispersed by centrifical force from the stair at the center. The entire upper level could open into one space, with movable walls making it possible to subdivide the large space into as many as six functional areas, for working, sleeping, bathing, etc. Walls, both interior and exterior, were flat planes. The only decoration consisted of railings of pipe painted in primary colors. The Schröder House fulfilled the demands of Van Doesburg, spokesman for De Stijl, that architecture be elementary, economic, functional, dynamic, anticubic, unmonumental and antidecorative. These terms became the catchwords of the modern movement, with the aestheticism of modern architectural forms being justified on the basis of their functionalism or thriftiness. Machine production of architectural elements was said to demand undecorated forms and to bring a newly dynamic architecture within the reach of everyman.

These new ideas came to France in the early 1920s when Mondrian moved to Paris and met Le Corbusier, who found the concepts of De Stijl quite compatible with his own understanding of architecture. Like factories, ideal houses were to have supports of steel beams, and concrete slabs for floor and ceilings. Walls were not needed for support of the floor above; and they were only minimally necessary for protection from the weather, so that architect and client had maximum freedom to arrange interior spaces according to the needs and desires of the family. Even diagonal partitions could be used. If one could only "state the problem clearly," Le Corbusier felt that it could be solved. The problems of human habitation could be resolved as "those of railway carriages, tools, etc., are resolved."

Le CORBUSIER'S VILLA SAVOYE

The kind of thinking required to design a tool is useful but not sufficient for designing a house. Le Corbusier might have been too close to the Victorian era to be able to perceive that excessive decoration was not the real problem but merely a symptom of the problem of Victorian architecture. Romantic cobwebs can be manifested in claw-footed armchairs upholstered in red plush and armored with lace antimacassars, but also in a glass house set alone in the woods—Phillip Johnson bringing to fruition Le Corbusier's basic house design of two slabs separated by steel uprights (see Fig. P-7).

During the 1920s and 1930s Le Corbusier's architecture embodied the same polemics found in his books. The Villa Savoye, a house on the outskirts of Paris built between 1929 and 1932, was a complete fusion of his five points in building form (see Figs. 23-2 and 23-3):

1 The house was set up on *pilotis* (strong piers) so that it seemed to float above the ground, which could therefore be reclaimed for pedestrians and cars. The main rooms, being thus elevated, allowed superb views of the countryside, which thereby enhanced the unity of human beings with nature.
2 Rather than having bilateral symmetry or any other formal arrangement of

Figure 23-2 Villa Savoye, Poissy, France; built by Le Corbusier from 1929 to 1932. With its severely plain white stucco exterior alleviated only by the windows, this house remains a masterpiece of the early modern movement. The pilotis (stilts) that support the main floor free the ground for multiple uses. Such supports continue above, behind the screen wall, and make possible a flexible plan. The outer shell of the house encloses a court open to the sky; the rooftop can also be used for outdoor living. (Photo by W. Connor.)

the rooms, the house had a *free plan* expressive of the new possibilities of a world enhanced by technology.

3 The *free facade* eschewed earlier conventions of facade design but was also conceptually distinct from the interior.

4 *Windows* are placed in *horizontal strips,* on all four sides. Le Corbusier wished in this manner to issue a manifesto against having the wall be a confining support. Like the plan, the elevation was to be free as never before, thanks to new technological developments with glass and steel. The strip window also lit the interior more brightly and uniformly.

5 The roof was reclaimed, like the ground, for additional use by the inhabitants; it was completed with a *roof garden,* the sod of which helped to waterproof the flat expanse. All aspects of the building could thus be seen as functional.

The Villa Savoye was conceived as a new solution to the rational problems of housing. No "local color or aestheticism" marred its purity. The house was designed to represent the "machine for living in." (However, actual services

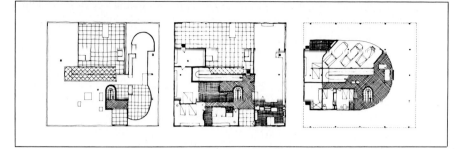

Figure 23-3   Plan of the Villa Savoye. At bottom the ground level, with garage and turnaround space for three cars, and with bedrooms for six servants. The dots represent pilotis. These show again in the middle story, as do the stairway at left center and the ramp at center; they both continue to the roof (the third plan). On the main (middle) story, the courtyard is at right, a large part of it reappearing in the upper plan. The rest of the main floor consists of bedrooms, kitchen, bath, and living spaces. A screen like an abstract sculpture crowns the roof and shelters part of the rooftop. (Plan as redrawn by Lesnikowski, *Rationalism and Romanticism in Architecture*, 1982, reprinted by permission of McGraw-Hill.)

were still provided by six servants whose rooms were located on the ground floor next to the garage. Ironically, the Villa Savoye was aesthetically but not functionally modern.)

Le Corbusier was one of an international group of architects invited to provide designs for housing to be built in Weissenhof in Germany in the 1920s. Here the ideas shown graphically in *Towards a New Architecture* were to be realized. Walter Gropius took part and Ludwig Mies van der Rohe was the director of this project. The economic restraints under which the housing was built provided an unusual challenge to the architects, who were accustomed to working with more ample budgets. The architects made a virtue of necessity, inasmuch as their concept of architecture required them to be antidecorative. Complete plainness, declared the architects, was preferable to an elaboration (perceived as immoral, wasteful, and inappropriate for the workers who were to live in the buildings). Details such as the customary elaborate door jambs and window frames were omitted from the apartments and houses. Decorative mouldings along with high ceilings and dark colors were discarded. A political and economic constraint thus led to an aesthetic and philosophical position in Weissenhof. Standards were set that influenced the appearance and meaning of modern architecture for the next 50 years. Unfortunately the houses in Weissenhof cost more than was budgeted for, and could not be allocated to simple workers.

MIES VAN DER ROHE AND THE GERMAN PAVILION

Freed from the modest economic constraints of Weissenhof, Mies van der Rohe in another context produced the German Pavilion for a fair in Barcelona,

Spain, in 1929 (see Fig. 23-4). His vision of sleek modernity—sculpture set in a shallow pool, suspended partitions of highly polished onyx, and simple chairs especially designed for the space—combined to make an unforgettable experience. James Marston Fitch called the Barcelona pavilion, "the most famous building known only from photographs" (since it was subsequently torn down). The pavilion was domestic in scale and yet totally unlike the cluttered environments most people were living in. The plan and appearance of the pavilion suggested that in the new technological age new patterns of living were likely to evolve.

Le CORBUSIER'S DESIGN FOR PARIS

Le Corbusier explored the possibilities for design of a whole new city in his "City for Three Million" (see Fig. 23-5). His designs had the ready appeal of simplicity, confirming his position as the great architectural symbolist of the

Figure 23-4   Interior of German Pavilion, International Exposition, Barcelona, Spain, 1929. (Original demolished; replica built 1983.) Mies van der Rohe used simple but expensive materials—semiprecious onyx for partitions, chrome-plated steel for supports, fine leather on the chairs, and travertine flooring. There were no decorative embellishments of any kind. Extensive use of glass permitted the space to flow freely between indoors and outdoors, and its reflective qualities were echoed in the outdoor pool enclosed with walls to form a courtyard. (Photo courtesy the Museum of Modern Art, New York.)

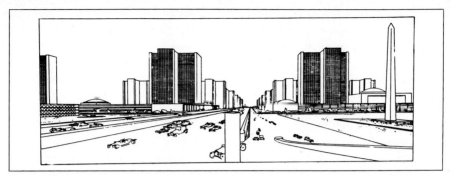

Figure 23-5 Paris as 'a contemporary city' by Le Corbusier, 1922. In this and in his "City for Three Million," Le Corbusier set forth the vision by which European and American cities were rebuilt a generation later, after World War II: office towers set in green parks, with low-rise apartments to house the workers. Cafes and playing fields were to be scattered among the trees. Some of his drawings show transportation including airplanes concentrated in a freeway-like strip sunken below ground level, in the midst of the towers. (Drawing from "Une ville Contemporaine," 1922, published by permission of Le Corbusier Foundation and Visual Artists & Galleries Assn., Inc.)

twentieth century. Towers were to be set well apart in parklike settings. The wonderful but unsanitary chaos of central Paris was to be replaced by miles of superblocks arranged in a gigantic grid pattern rather than the existing medieval irregularity. Variations of form and use were to be supplanted by clean uniformity. In *The Scope of Total Architecture,* Gropius also advocated towers set in parks as being the most appropriate modern-city form.

Archtypical modern architecture was created by Mies van der Rohe with the glass skyscraper. Already in the 1920s, he and Le Corbusier were exhibiting models of glass-walled skyscrapers. These were in effect the "machines for living in" piled up to the sky.

By the 1950s such ideas had gained so many converts that cities everywhere were being eviscerated in the name of urban renewal to be rebuilt as towers in parks. In Brazil, for example, Le Corbusier's architectural symbolism was enthusiastically received. In making the new capital Brasilia, planners and architects determined to compensate for some of the old problems of extreme density: no land for playgrounds, conflicting claims of pedestrians and cars for the same open space, and old street patterns ill-adapted to the use of the automobile, to name a few. Brasilia does indeed solve these problems by providing new street patterns around superblocks as well as car-free open space for residents. (In doing so, other problems unfortunately arise. Social classes become more rigidly segregated than ever, with the poor living in satellite communities about 30 miles from the center of the city. Even the middle-class residents have enormous distances to walk to obtain the meagerest of services. But the goal of plenty of fresh air and sunshine has been achieved.) The solution called for buildings of simple geometric form that reflect the philosophical design theory of Le Corbusier.

It was not until after World War II that Mies was commissioned to build the Seagram Building in New York City. With its urban plaza and fountains for pedestrian enjoyment, this skyscraper is symbolically similar to the huge parks of Le Corbusier's City for Three Million.

Mies articulated the philosophy behind his designing when he said, "God is in the details." It was Mies's eye for perfection of form that made modern architecture a style worth emulating all over the world, but especially in the high-technology cultures of the United States, Europe, and Japan. The rigid but exciting possibilities of modern architecture were realized not only in Europe and the United States but also in many third world countries. The term "international style" had been first applied to modern buildings in 1932 when Henry Russell Hitchcock and Phillip Johnson organized an exhibition at the Museum of Modern Art, writing a catalog for it. After World War II, because of emphasis on skyscrapers and on glass, the style was renamed the new international style. As Christian F. Otto has noted, the most interesting question about the symbolism of modern architecture is: How and why did the avant garde architecture of the 1920s become the favored mode of the international corporate world and of government bureaucracies after World War II? We may suspect that the rhetoric of the modern movement about the proper forms for the architecture of a technological age had by the 1950s become comfortably accepted. The uniformly depersonalized buildings seemed appropriate to the age of mass movements and overpopulation. The process of corporate patrons deciding to use modern architecture in preference to any historical style has been described generally but has not been well documented as yet.

All the while that Mies and Le Corbusier were winning converts to their new vision of a properly austere architecture for the modern age, another architectural monument without historical reference but with free manifestation of the warmer emotions was developing. Begun by Eric Mendelsohn in Germany, this expressionist movement emerged in the 1920s. By using the new materials, especially concrete, these buildings were richly modeled in three dimensions and highly individualistic. In abstract yet directly physical forms, this movement directly challenged the austerity of the dominant style.

Le Corbusier himself was influenced by these counterarguments about modern architecture. His church at Ronchamps and the capitol in Chandigarh show that he was able to work in the expressionist mode too, being the master he was. The planning of Chandigarh reveals the architect as being fascinated as always with grand vistas and enormous empty spaces for settings for his buildings; but the buildings themselves are richer in form and more strikingly mirror the complexity of the human spirit. This time the content of the symbols was the newly achieved sovereignity of the Punjabi people. The three major structures are carved and then poured in bulky concrete, very free in form. Having urged architects and patrons to turn from the warmed-over symbolism of high Victorian gothic and eschew Beaux-Arts Classicism, Le Corbusier was able to leave behind the simplism of his early formulations. People, he understood, need a new architecture that will not only seem to symbolize the new age but will actually embody it in new materials, new structural principles, and new ways of living in the space.

BIBLIOGRAPHY

Gropius, W., *Scope of Total Architecture,* Collier, New York, 1962. Sums up the thinking of a man who both built and taught modern architecture.

Jordy, W. "The Symbolic Essence of Modern European Architecture of the 20th Century and Its Continuous Influence." *Journal of the Society of Architectural Historians,* vol. 22, 1963, pp. 177–187

Le Corbusier, *Towards a New Architecture,* The Architectural Press, London, 1927; and later editions. For most of his life more a writer and thinker than builder, Le Corbusier remains probably the most important form-giver of modern architecture. Originally published in Paris in 1923, this book takes boats and graneries as seriously as models as the Parthenon, also cited.

Rowe, C., *The Mathematics of the Ideal Villa,* M.I.T., Cambridge, Mass., 1976. A modern architectural theorist analyses Renaissance palaces and other structures.

24
TWENTIETH-CENTURY SCHOOLS

DATE AS BENCHMARK

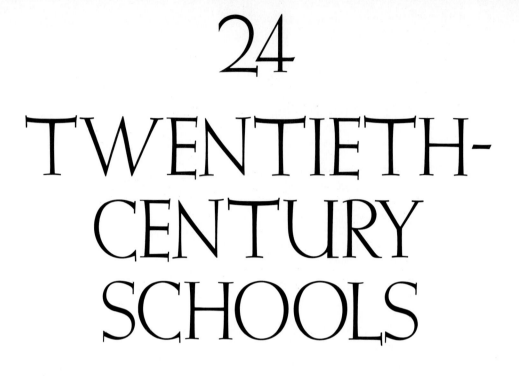

In the twentieth century, the history of architecture is not a simple matter to discuss. When Pevsner wrote his *Outline of European Architecture* in 1943, perhaps it was possible to believe that as of 1912 modern architecture had triumphed and the historical styles were dead—and truth and beauty were identical with the architecture of the international style. More recently, the ambiguities of the late twentieth century world seemed to be mirrored more truly in the "complexity and contradictions" that Venturi made us aware of (in his *Complexity and Contradiction in Architecture*). The replacement of simple conviction by cautious puzzlement is one theme of development in our times.

ORIGINALITY: THE INNOVATORS AND THE FOLLOWERS

Another important theme in contemporary architecture has been originality. According to Kubler in his *The Shape of Time*, originality is at such a premium now that we project it backward into the history of art and architecture, at least since the Renaissance, and evaluate all creative activity primarily on the basis of its originality, which is often equated with a simple priority in time. While conceding that in earlier centuries innovators were succeeded by developers and they in turn by lesser copiers, no one is willing to admit that the same process is likely in the twentieth century as well. Instead, every architect is expected to be original, at all costs, and every critic feels compelled to discover original solutions or the lack of them.

In fact, however, during the past 100 years there have been several sets of innovators and followers. The more we try to confine architectural variation to the watertight compartments of decade or style, the more bewildering the history of recent architecture becomes. Some examples may make this point clearer.

McKim, Mead, and White did buildings in the style of Beaux Arts classicism in the closing years of the nineteenth and first decade of the twentieth century. Notable among these are their club buildings in New York City (which resemble Renaissance palaces) and the Boston Public Library. If we conclude from a brief study of their work that Beaux Arts classicism flourished around the turn of the century, our statement would be correct but not complete. The San Francisco City Hall, a splendid domed building by Bakewell and Brown, was finished in 1935, and the West Building of the National Gallery of Art, by Pope, was finished as late as 1942—both very late for the Beaux Arts but by no means isolated examples. Quite apart from the demand for originality, these architects satisfied themselves and their clients with buildings of the most traditional sort.

Another example is the reappearance of the kind of house Le Corbusier was doing in the decades between wars (his white period). Richard Meier and others in the 1970s have built brilliant white houses with dramatic exteriors that set them in strong contrast to the natural setting, and interiors that continue Le Corbusier's experiments in free plan and visual interpenetration. If the experiments were completed and perfected earlier, why go back to them? Why try again to see what can be built with such ideas? Does it matter that 50 years elapsed between the innovator and the follower?

A final example: In the 1920s Mies van der Rohe made sketches and models to show his ideas about skyscrapers with curtain walls completely of glass. A glass skyscraper was technologically but not psychologically possible in the 1920s. People still expected buildings to look strong and give a feeling of security by being clad in stone or brick. Beginning after World War II, buildings were clad in metal and glass—at first enameled and finally mirrored. By the 1970s, Mies's pupils were building free-form towers clad in brown glass (for instance, on Wilshire Boulevard in Los Angeles) that looked like his early models come to life. This is another case of what Kubler calls an interrupted series. How will future historians account in theory for the gap of 50 years: will they want the copies to have been built immediately after the originals?

MAJOR INNOVATORS AND THEIR COMPETITION

A cynic might suggest that one of the great problems of modern architecture in the 1960s was that its major practitioners were very old by then. Frank Lloyd Wright died in 1959 at about 90; Le Corbusier in 1965, aged 78; Gropius in 1969 at 76; Mies van der Rohe in 1969 at 73. Each was designing and building to the very end—but only Le Corbusier in a style that had changed much from his early days. The "accident" of the long lives of these pioneers prolonged a moment, a style, a point of view—perhaps inordinately.

But it is not possible for any four men, however gifted, to dominate the architecture of a century. Indeed, many other architectural ideas were competing for preeminence during the first three quarters of the century. By noting the dates of the periods in which they flourished, we can get some sense of the diversity and coherence of the architecture of our times. At least ten schools of architectural thought and practice can be observed, enough to make the twentieth century seem to resemble the nineteenth much more than we like to admit.

Most pervasive and successful from the point of view of popular enthusiasm has been the colonial revival, which began in about 1890 and which to date shows no sign of waning. "As American as apple pie," these buildings that copy the seventeenth- and eighteenth-century architecture of New England and New Amsterdam make explicit reference to our past, seeming to validate the present by embodying it in images from the past.

Much briefer in popularity was art nouveau, which began in the 1880s but flourished at the turn of the century. Its graceful manner was no match for the rigors of World War I, which effectively terminated the movement. Always more popular in Europe than in America, the art nouveau was known here for its small decorative objects such as Tiffany glassware. The pastel colors employed by art nouveau artists were used again, notably in the 1930s, but the plant forms, especially those used for structural supports in iron, have been ignored. Decorative metal work has instead been found in the austere work of Mies van der Rohe, where it attempts to reveal the geometric structure of the building.

Running parallel to the art nouveau was the middle western style known as the prairie school. Well developed in the 1890s by Frank Lloyd Wright and others practicing in and near Chicago, the style gets its name from the way the long, low houses seem to match the horizontal extension of the prairies in which they were set (Fig. 24-1). Together with the high-rise buildings of the Chicago school, they made an original and authentically American contribution to the development of architecture. Patrons in both cases were the newly rich businessmen of this railroad, meat-packing, and merchandising capital of

Figure 24-1   Robie House, Chicago, by Frank Lloyd Wright, built in 1909. Red brick trimmed with plain bands of white stone; wide terraces and wide, cantilevered roofs; and high strips of horizontal windows made this house the antithesis of the tall, elaborate Victorian house that preceded it. The flow of space continued from the terraces into the living and dining rooms and continued around the central mass of chimney and stairs which both separated and divided the two rooms. (Photo by Hedrich Blessing, Chicago.)

the center of the United States. The tall buildings of the 1880s went on being erected in much the same mode, with load-bearing steel frames and curtain walls and large windows, until the first World War. By that date the vogue for prairie school houses had also passed. Both were superseded by a new vision—Beaux Arts classicism as demonstrated at Chicago in the World's Columbian Exposition of 1893.

The best-known architects of the United States, such as McKim, Mead, and White, were enlisted by the Chicago planner and architect Daniel Burnham to design and erect for this exposition an imposing group of large white classical buildings set around a reflecting pool in grounds at the edge of Chicago, tastefully landscaped by Olmsted's firm. Sculptural decoration was supplied by St. Gaudens and French. So much high culture completely bedazzled the American public, who turned away from the rich organic forms of Sullivan and Wright. Their originality was disturbing; the noble predictability of the Beaux Arts was flattering. For the next 50 years, most large public commissions went to architects practicing in the Beaux Arts mode.

Beginning about 1912, the intellectual rival of the Beaux Arts was the style called later the *international style,* which flourished until about 1950. Pevsner and others have often cited the Fagus Factory at Alfeld-an-der-Leine, Germany, as the first fully developed building of the new manner (Fig 24-2). This was a utilitarian building renovated inexpensively for clients who placed rigid demands on the architect, Walter Gropius. Originally a shoe factory, it had been bought by an American firm which had it remodeled in the efficient manner of industrial buildings in Buffalo, New York. Gropius found the client's program compatible with his own developing aesthetic sense and produced a metal-frame building with a thin skin of glass and masonry. The large windows met at the corners with only a thin strip of metal between them, so that the corners were nearly invisible. No decoration was added to the simple form.

From that building to the grand gesture of the Lincoln Memorial is the measure of the distance between a monument and an everyday building (Fig. 24-3). It is also the measure of the rhetorical gap between Beaux Arts architecture and the new functionalism. That both were built during the same decade (1911–1917) indicates the overlap in intellectual history between the old and the new forces in architecture. The Lincoln Memorial, by Bacon, is based on the mid-nineteenth-century work of the German architect Schinkel, who in turn combined a rather romantic use of classical forms with an early nineteenth-century enthusiasm for giantism. With its beautiful marble and impeccable craftsmanship, with its noble content, simply and sincerely

Figure 24-2   Fagus Factory, Alfeld-an-der-Leine, Germany, by Walter Gropius, built in 1911. This factory for making shoe-lasts was modeled after the industrial architecture of Buffalo, New York. It had a steel frame and the walls of the section at right were glass curtains (not load-bearing). (Photo reprinted by permission of the Gropius archive at The Museum of Modern Art, New York.)

Figure 24-3   Lincoln Memorial, Washington, D.C., by Henry Bacon, completed 1917. The noble simplicity of the large Doric columns and blocky attic story seem appropriate for the moral stature of the man commemorated in this building. The photo suggests the lively use visitors make of this monument. (Photo, author.)

expressed, the Lincoln Memorial continues that passionate enjoyment of the past that was typical of the nineteenth century. The Fagus Factory reacts against such architecture. In spite of their common dates, the factory seems a much "younger" building than the Memorial.

After the first World War the traditionalist architects continued to get the commissions, but the modernists gradually won the battle of ideas. By 1950 no more classical buildings were going up. Instead, the international style had triumphed and was being used everywhere to repair the ravages of war and to house the new expansion of industry and government. The metal-framed windows, arranged in simple geometric patterns with no ornamental embellishments, had literally *become* the building. Followers of Mies and Le Corbusier and students of Gropius were at work from Nairobi to Tokyo putting up the skyscrapers of commerce, the medium- and high-rise buildings of government, and many sprawling college campuses, like one "city for three million" after another. Many shabby urban cores were leveled to be rebuilt in the image of Le Corbusier's rational dream.

Meanwhile, the triumphant international style had all along been challenged by at least two other styles of building. The first—expressionism—had an intellectual effect on late twentieth-century architecture far out of proportion to its few early monuments. Examples are the Einstein Tower of Eric Mendelsohn, built in 1920 and 1921, and the Goetheanum of Rudolph Steiner, 1925–1928, the first located in Potsdam, Germany, and the second in Dornach, Switzerland (Fig 24-4). Both exploited the plastic qualities of materials that can be poured and moulded (concrete and plaster) rather than those such as wood and stone that must be hewn into rectangular pieces. With

Figure 24-4 Goetheanum, Dornach, Switzerland, by Rudolph Steiner, built from 1925 to 1928. Built after fire destroyed the first Goetheanum, this hall is a prime example of expressionist architecture, a deliberate rejoinder to the austerity of the international style. Steiner took advantage of the plasticity of concrete to achieve dynamic sculptural forms. (Reprinted by permission of the Philosophisch Anthroposophischer Verlagam Goetheanum, Dornach, Switzerland.)

materials responding eagerly to the personal ideas and manner of a particular architect, the style was known as expressionist. (Compare with the expressionist movement in painting of the same years.) Economic pressures for standardization to reduce costs and social pressures for clarity, logic, and precision even at the cost of ignoring other aspects of human nature meant that expressionism was outnumbered by the international style for many years. The ideas involved, however, went underground rather than disappearing completely. It is not too radical to suggest, I think, that both the new brutalism and the post-modernist movement (both post World War II) in architecture owe a great deal to these early pioneers and pick up those disturbing ideas about the nature of human beings and the kinds of architecture we need. More about these movements later. They are further examples of interrupted series.

The second contender for favorite status against the international style was that called moderne architecture, or sometimes art deco, when its association with the decorative arts is stressed. Always given the French spelling, moderne was the most successful architectural school of the late twenties and thirties, as measured in number of buildings and assessed in terms of quality. Some of the ideas of the modern movement were by the thirties beginning to affect traditionally trained architects, who responded by building streamlined classical structures with the old elements simplified into geometric forms; a Doric column, for instance, became a rectangular strip crowned by a slightly protruding rectangular block. Modernistic versions of many historical styles were built everywhere, such as stripped-down gothic, Egyptian revival revival, and other hybrids. Probably the best-known and, best-loved moderne structure is the Chrysler Building in New York City (Fig. 24-5). The materials are rich and elaborate, including marbles, onyx, and zigzag ornament in stainless steel. The ways of using ornament here grew out of art nouveau experiments, but the idea of selecting the automobile as theme for the decorative motifs was entirely that of the architect and the patron who headed Chrysler Motors. Like many other moderne structures, the Chrysler Building satisfied the taste for a building at once up-to-date, rich, and sensual. Most of the public was not ready for the

Figure 24-5 Chrysler Building, New York City, by William Van Alen, built in 1930. Briefly the tallest building in the world, this remains a favorite because of its distinct spire, glittering stainless steel surface, radiator-cap gargoyles, and art deco lobby in African marbles and chrome-plated steel. (Photo supplied by the Chrysler Building, owned by Mr. Jack Kent Cooke.)

austerity of the modern movement. World War II, with its demand for patriotic austerity, however, sent moderne into a permanent eclipse.

After the war, the task was to rebuild a shattered world. The purity of the forms of the international style was considered appropriate and was intensified by their translation into the symbolically effective materials of glass—everything clear and simple—and aluminum, a new framing material developed for use in airplanes during the war. The glass box was the distinctive architectural form of the 20 years following 1950. Phillip Johnson, who with Henry Russell Hitchcock had defined the international style in 1932 by an exhibit and catalog at the Museum of Modern Art, now in 1949 had become an architect and built himself a glass house in Darien, Connecticut. This house carried out Le Corbusier's ideal of the early twenties, being flat roofed, steel supported, and completely glass-walled (see page 359). Two other buildings of the new international style were skyscrapers: the Lever House by Skidmore, Owings, and Merrill, of 1952 (Fig. 24-6), and its neighbor, the Seagram Building by Mies van der Rohe, of 1958. Lever House, which used blue-green enameled glass, popular during the 1950s, set the fashion for using only part of its tremendously expensive site to build on. Seagram follows that pattern, leaving part of its site for a pedestrian plaza, and also copies the form of a glass curtain wall. Perhaps because of the quality of its materials and fine detailing, the Seagram Building seems to be aging very gracefully, which is quite appropriate, inasmuch as it was Mies who asserted, "God is in the details."

No more than its predecessors could the new international style exert its sovereignty without challenge. By the mid-sixties, a reaction against so much slick geometric architecture was underway. This reaction came to be called the new brutalism, because of its customary use of concrete cast in very rough forms. Marcel Breuer, once a partner of Gropius, was a pioneer (1953–1961) with the St. John's Abbey Church in Collegeville, Minnesota. Another surprising drop out from the modern movement was Le Corbusier, whose last works at Chandigarh, India, were dramatic free structures in concrete left without decorative finishes. A fine ensemble of the international style buildings enclosed in a second row of new brutalist buildings is in Brasilia, where the early ministry buildings, set along the main axis, are all sleek glass boxes, and where their later enlargements, set in a more irregular outer row, are all in rough concrete. Perhaps the most famous building of this school is the Berlin Philharmonic Hall built in 1962 by Hans Scharoun (Fig. 24-7). The old ideas of the expressionists, the new science of accoustics, and some innovative concepts about the kind of architecture needed for the complications of modern life were united here in a hall whose sound is brilliant. The natural tendency of concrete to assume any shape designed into its formwork was utilized in producing a hall of great originality. The orchestra is placed at the center, and the audience surrounds it on all sides and at many levels, sitting in irregular banks of seats or in suspended balconies.

Further competition against the new international style came from a countermovement organized around Robert Venturi who has both written and built in a mode called postmodernism. Perhaps it is only to be expected that

Figure 24-6   Lever House, New York City, by Skidmore, Owings, and Merrill, built in 1952. First to set aside a large portion of its expensive lot as public outdoor space, Lever House was also a very early example of the use of blue-green enameled glass in the curtain wall. This view reveals the transparency of the glass skyscraper, since it was taken at dusk when lights were turned on throughout the building and yet some curtains were drawn in several of the middle stories, against the brilliance of the setting sun. (Photo, author.)

the twentieth century could not close without reexamining the question of the uses of history in architecture. The house Venturi did in Chestnut Hill, Pennsylvania, in 1962, was the first to incorporate historical motifs used in a thoroughly unhistorical way—a collage of broken pediments, Roman bath windows, and clapboard siding, which is an improbable agglomeration (Fig. 24-8). At the same time, Venturi's book *Complexity and Contradiction in Architecture* encouraged architects, patrons, and users to look again at components of historical architecture and assimilate them to human needs. (Significantly, this book was published by the Museum of Modern Art, which had earlier brought out the Hitchcock and Johnson book on the international style and would later publish the Drexler book on *The Architecture of the Ecole des Beaux Arts*.) Venturi and his associates, the postmodernists, have contin-

Figure 24-7 Berlin Philharmonic Hall, Berlin, Germany, finished in 1963, interior view. The orchestra is placed at the center and the audience surrounds it at different levels. The psychological intimacy is enhanced by the acoustical brilliance of the hall. The old expressionist architecture became the new brutalist school, and here achieved an original and highly successful embodiment. (Photo by Reinhard Friedrich, Berlin.)

ued to incorporate witty allusions to history, whether in the "ugly and ordinary" buildings that are Venturi's trademark, or in the elegant houses by Richard Meier that seem to be a series of editorial comments on the houses of Le Corbusier's white period.

THE USEFULNESS OF DATES

If dates were not important, perhaps it would not matter that Le Corbusier came first and his commentator Meier later on. After the survey of architectural history we have made in this book, we may be at last ready to consider just how important dates are in the study of architecture.

Dates are certainly far from being the only important issue in architecture. They establish precedent, allowing us to credit originality where it belongs. More than that, dates provide the thread of continuity that enables us to find our way through the labyrinth of architectural complexity. Dates are to history as the alphabet is to literature—necessary, but not sufficient.

Dates help us to recognize the different meanings and uses associated with similar forms. A column with a capital remains always a shaft and a block, but the meaning changes with associated changes in the society that uses the form. A column and a capital in fifth century B.C. Athens are the only possible structural support, honed to an elegant simplicity. A column and a capital in Ravenna in the sixth century A.D., in San Vitale, for instance, are optional, since vaulted construction is a very real possibility; they are therefore decoration even though they in fact give structural support. Purely aesthetic and highly political meanings unite in the carved basket capital with its intertwined initials of the rulers Justinian and Theodora. A column and capital in the eighteenth-century church of Vierzehnheiligen in southern Germany, with gilded capital and smooth white shaft, are part of an interactive whole in which every part is both art and architecture, contributing to an experience of the sublime that lifts the visitor out of the everyday world. A column and capital at the Lincoln Memorial are giant in scale, as carefully crafted as the early Doric example, but anachronistic in their use in an age of steel framing and poured concrete. Their symbolic meaning tells us something about the recent past that we may not yet be ready to accept and assimilate.

These few examples remind us that date is related to the rhetoric or symbolic meaning of the structure, to the way art is used, to the originality or commonplaceness of a particular structural system, and finally to the delight we take in a particular work. Which came first? Which came later? Is there any causal relationship between the two? These questions of date continue to be useful.

Figure 24-8 House at Chestnut Hill, outside Philadelphia, by Robert Venturi, built in 1962. Originally built for Venturi's mother and now occupied by Thomas and Agatha Hughes (who supplied the photograph), this house was a forerunner of the post-modern movement. The facade includes stock windows in assorted sizes juxtaposed with traditional clapboard siding and a broken pediment that alludes to Roman and baroque prototypes.

BIBLIOGRAPHY

Banham, R., The New Brutalism—N.Y. 1966 (book not article of 1955).

Bletter, R. H., "The Interpretation of the Glass Dream—Expressionist Architecture and the History of the Crystal Metaphor," *Journal of the Society of Art Historians,* vol. 40, no. 1, March, 1981, pp. 20–43. The idea of glass as architectural material depended on its availability, but the imagination of architects has soared far beyond what was merely practical.

Condit, C., *The Chicago School of Architecture,* University of Chicago Press, Chicago, 1964. The authoritative study of development of high-rise structures during the last third of the nineteenth century.

Drexler, A., *The Architecture of the Ecole des Beaux Art,* Museum of Modern Art, New York, 1977. The shock of this museum sponsoring this study has scarcely abated years later.

G(lobal) A(rchitecture), no. 21, Berlin Philharmonic Concert Hall by Hans Scharoun. A picture book about the preeminent new brutalist building.

Hitchcock, H. R., *In the Nature of Materials 1887–1941: The Buildings of Frank Lloyd Wright,* Duell, Sloan and Pearce, New York, 1942.

Hitchcock, H. R., and P. Johnson, *The International Style,* Museum of Modern Art, New York, 1932. Catalog of the show that forcibly brought the modern movement in architecture to the public attention.

Kostof, S., "Architecture, You and Him," *Daedalus,* Winter 1976. This thoughtful study of Giedion's impact on the history of modern architecture is an early revisionist work.

Kubler, G., *The Shape of Time,* Yale University Press, New Haven, Conn., 1962. Brief, but one of the three or four books of a lifetime that might change one's understanding of reality.

Loftin, K., III, "The Loss of History and the Rediscovery of Origins," *Journal of Architectural Education,* vol. 33, no. 3, Spring 1980, pp. 14–18. Revisionism applied to the history of the modern movement.

Pehnt, W., *Expressionist Architecture,* Praeger, New York, 1973. Well-illustrated study of the personal architecture that does not fit the mold of the international style.

Pevsner, N., *An Outline of European Architecture,* Penguin Books, Baltimore, 1975. Beginning in the fourth century A.D., Pevsner brings his history to the early twentieth century, with later postscripts.

Pevsner, N., *Pioneers of Modern Design: From William Morris to Walter Gropius,* Penguin, Baltimore, 1974. A valuable study.

Reps, J., *Monumental Washington,* Princeton University Press, Princeton, New Jersey, 1967. Planning and architecture in Washington, D.C., in the grand manner; copiously illustrated.

Venturi, R., *Complexity and Contradiction in Architecture,* Museum of Modern Art, New York, 1966. Not to be missed for its thoughtful reappraisal of the intellectual base of modern architecture.

25

NONWESTERN ARCHITECTURE

FURTHER QUESTIONS

All the monuments studied so far have been part of the western tradition of architectural history. We have followed the flow of this history without asking some searching questions, such as when and where does this tradition actually begin. If we insist that the intellectual and hence the architectural world that we live in began with the Greeks, what are we to do about the Egyptians and the Mesopotamians? Human history is certainly older in those lands than it is in Greece. We have a tendency to incorporate their history into ours because of the prominence of both areas in the biblical history from which western cultural history derives.

When Pevsner wrote his *Outline of European Architecture,* he began with the early Christians, asserting that the culture and hence the architecture was not European before that. For some American schools of architecture, the history of architecture begins in the late nineteenth century: all architecture predating that of the United States as well as some twentieth-century European developments that contributed to it is prelude. The history of architecture, and architecture itself, may be seen as either discontinuous, or continuous from the first tentative experiments to the efforts of today.

Moreover, as we come to know more about other people with whom we share the globe, we are forced to see architecture as a human activity, rather than simply a western one. Growth in our understanding of nonwestern architecture has been hampered by the unevenness of the materials available to study it. Nonwestern architecture has up to now been largely the concern of archeologists or ethnographers. In all too many cases nonwestern architecture has not been studied at all by architectural historians.

Some nonwestern societies have rich and complex written histories, such as that of the Chinese. Others, such as the Polynesian, have a predominantly oral tradition. Information available in writing or in an oral tradition is usually not readily translatable. Not only the names of elements and concepts but also the very way of thinking about architecture are different. The difference in ways of thinking can be very useful for our own process of questioning if we let our gaps in knowledge and understanding lead us to a more fundamental problem: What questions are we to ask about architecture?

Already we have noted that some questions about architecture have been asked over and over again, such as those about the formal characteristics of architecture. Other questions, such as that of the impact of the organization of the building industry on what is put up, are just beginning to be asked.

JAPANESE ARCHITECTURE

We can begin to grapple with questions about architecture that we have not yet asked by examining Japanese architecture. When American students first see pictures of Japanese architecture, they often ask, "Are there no slums? Aren't there any dirty places in Japan?" Those are intelligent questions. Japan seems as a society to be more devoted to public cleanliness than is America. With water widely available as a cleansing agent, societies still differ widely about how much time and effort they should devote to cleanliness. Why is this? What difference does it make to architecture? Americans are often teased by other people about their excessive devotion to plumbing, to bathrooms, and to personal cleanliness, to the extent that it has become common for new houses to have one bathroom per bedroom, a decision that certainly affects architecture. Yet this American concern for cleanliness does not carry over routinely into care for the environment outside the house. In the exterior environment, the Japanese passionate interest in the aesthethic aspects of life makes a continuing difference in how buildings and spaces are used and cared for. From kindergarten on, Japanese children are taken to visit beautiful buildings and gardens, the way American children are taken to baseball games or on school field trips to visit the local dairy. With us, beauty is a private matter, with a few exceptions like the government mall in Washington, D.C. With the Japanese beautiful architecture is a matter of national pride and everyday public experience.

We are thus able through reflections such as this to put our finger on some of the architectural differences between these two cultures. But these noted differences suggest that there may be questions/differences that we cannot even imagine.

Through the work of the Greene brothers and of Frank Lloyd Wright, Japanese architecture has had great impact on American architecture. In Masuda's *Living Architecture: Japanese,* Corboz points out in his introduction that the Imperial Villa in Katsura bears a strong resemblance to Frank Lloyd

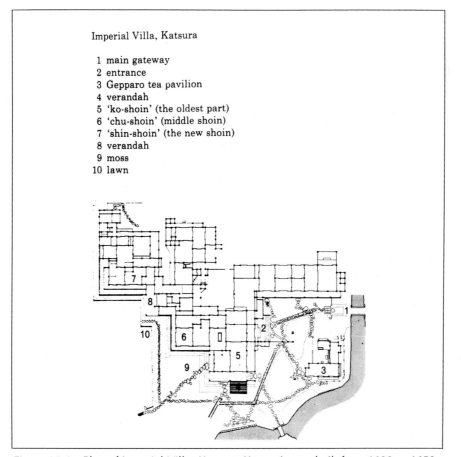

Imperial Villa, Katsura

1 main gateway
2 entrance
3 Gepparo tea pavilion
4 verandah
5 'ko-shoin' (the oldest part)
6 'chu-shoin' (middle shoin)
7 'shin-shoin' (the new shoin)
8 verandah
9 moss
10 lawn

Figure 25-1   Plan of Imperial Villa, Katsura; Kyoto, Japan; built from 1620 to 1658; Prince Toshihito and Prince Toshitada. Sliding screens subdivide the interior as needed. Rooms are edged with verandahs that make a visual and physical transition to the outdoors. The stepped-back pattern of the sections of the villa, characteristic of Japanese traditional architecture, gives each section its own relation to the gardens. (Plan reprinted from T. Masuda, *Living Architecture: Japanese,* by permission of Jean Hirschen.) Compare with Fig. 25-3.

Figure 25-2   View of Imperial Villa, Katsura, along the main facade. Smooth white panels are set in frames of dark wood; posts stand on bases of natural rock; the wide eaves shelter the porch of the oldest section at the back of the photo. A strip of pebbles is placed to catch the drip from the eaves. To the right is a "lawn" of moss, and at rear some trees are visible. The palace sits in a garden as carefully planned and detailed as the building. (Photo by Ishimoto from *Katsura*, 1960, 1972, reprinted by permission of Zokeisha Publications, Ltd.)

Wright's Falling Water house, although the first dates from 1620 and the second from 1936. Both buildings have a free plan, with broad roofs, walls used as protective screens, and a sophisticated integration of the building into the site, partly by the use of natural materials in contrast with the basic rectangularity of the structure. This similarity was no accident, inasmuch as Wright had been studying Japanese architecture since the turn of the century and had already built his famous Imperial Hotel in Tokyo. The Masuda book contains a series of fine photographs of the Imperial Villa (Plates 139–149), which reveal the careful attention to detail that was characteristic of Japanese architecture. Wright and the Greene brothers showed western architects that equally careful attention to detail and massing could be achieved in the modern mode.

The modern Japanese architect Kenzo Tange has written the introductory essay for a book of fine photographs by Y. Ishimoto of the Imperial Villa in Katsura. This essay and the picture captions should help the western student grasp something about the different ways of thinking about architecture. Our own architectural tradition has prepared us to note the formal beauty of Japanese architecture. Beyond that, the experience of Japanese architecture has provoked both tourists and western architects to reconsider the interior arrangements of a house and its relations with setting. New thoughts about architecture are conceived subliminally in an experience of a different architecture of such high quality.

It is probably not accidental that the Japanese influence was most strongly felt on the west coast, where the benign climate cooperates with attempts to integrate house and site, and where trade and immigration both pointed westward across the Pacific. Natural materials and open, adaptable plans became characteristic of the California school in the years before and after World War II, and in the work of Harwell Hamilton Harris and others, these ideas were transmitted to the rest of America.

We can also turn to California and the southwest for another nonwestern example. The architecture known as Spanish colonial was actually a compound of Spanish Renaissance and baroque style with American Indian forms and methods of building. Until recently, the Indian elements have gone unnoticed because no one was looking for them. Some studies by Norman Neuerberg have begun to concentrate on the Indian ingredients in mission architecture and church decoration in California. *Spanish City Planning in North America* suggests the use of Indian settlement arrangements in the Spanish cities of the new world. It had previously been assumed that the Spanish simply put into practice in the new world the habits they carried with them from Spain, but we now see that the matter is more complicated. The Council of the Indies (in Spain), responsible for making laws to govern the new world, was definitely influenced by Italian Renaissance ideas about ideal city form, known from several books. The actual city builders in the new world, however, saw and were impressed by the large, beautiful cities of the native Americans. When Mexico City was the Aztec capital, it had a grid plan and a

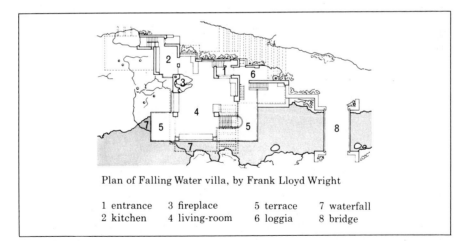

Plan of Falling Water villa, by Frank Lloyd Wright

| 1 entrance | 3 fireplace | 5 terrace | 7 waterfall |
| 2 kitchen | 4 living-room | 6 loggia | 8 bridge |

Figure 25-3   Plan of Falling Water, Bear Run, Pennsylvania; built in 1936 by Frank Lloyd Wright. Compare with Fig. 25-1. Flexible spaces that flow together and an exterior composed of setbacks align Falling Water with the Katsura villa in its effects much more closely than with either a Greek house or a Renaissance palace. (Plan from T. Masuda, *Living Architecture: Japanese,* by permission of Jean Hirschen.)

Figure 25-4   View of Falling Water from below. Superb integration with the artfully manipulated natural setting here shows that Wright was strongly influenced by his study of Japanese architecture and landscaping. His use of white stuccoed concrete is similar to that of others in the modern movement, but he goes farther than they in simultaneous use of natural materials such as local rock used for foundations and walls between the white terraces. (Photo supplied by the Western Pennsylvania Conservancy, to whom the house has been entrusted.)

large central plaza, plus smaller plazas in the four quarters of the city. This city form matched so well with the Renaissance ideas, that it was copied everywhere that the Spanish built new cities; the new cities were therefore not replications of the irregular organic plans of the medieval Spanish cities that the conquerors came from. Some of the ideas for the new cities were European and some were indigenous. It was impossible for historians to get at the real sources of these forms as long as unsubstantiated assumptions about origins were accepted instead of verified facts. This example suggests what scholars must always ask themselves: "How broad an investigation is necessary for real understanding?"

THE DEFINITION OF PRIMITIVE AND PREHISTORIC

The Indian examples also lead us to the whole question of the relation between the primitive and prehistoric cultures with their arts and architecture. In the seventeenth and eighteenth centuries, as one so-called primitive people after another was discovered and information on them brought back to Europe, it came to be widely believed that knowledge of nonliterate peoples was equivalent to knowledge of prehistoric peoples. This confusion probably arose because the word primitive was used for both groups, but the shades of meaning of the word were not clearly differentiated. Primitive has had two major meanings: (1) early in human development, before the earliest civilizations such as the Egyptians or Sumerians of Mesopotamia; (2) without reading and writing, sometimes extended to mean without modern technology. Since civilization as we know it began with the invention of writing in Egypt and Mesopotamia, and since by definition prehistoric means before the invention of written history, the word primitive was applied to both early civilizations and groups with nonwritten records. Art historians then applied the term primitive to societies in which human culture had developed apart from writing as well as those that developed before writing. From the seventeenth until about the middle of the twentieth centuries, until the emergence of the third world countries after World War II, it was common to blur the distinctions between nonliterate contemporary people and nonliterate prehistoric peoples —or more frequently to fail to observe the distinctions. A people living in the twentieth century but without writing is just as many years separated from those first stone builders in Jericho as is another but literate people of our century. The fact of literacy does not alter the length of time that either culture has had to grow and change. Primitive in the sense of nonliterate does not mean crude, unsophisticated, or simple; nor does it imply a lack of tradition. Increased knowledge of how human societies develop has forced us to realize that learning about a twentieth-century tribe of Brazilian Indians is neither more nor less helpful for an understanding of the builders of Stonehenge than is learning about the modern English. Such a shift in perspective makes it impossible for us to assume blithely, as previously, that by studying the houses of the headhunters of New Guinea we might understand Adam's house in Paradise or any other structure of the period before 3000 B.C.

This discussion of primitive and prehistoric has been expanded in order to emphasize how important it is that we ask questions which can indeed be answered by the material and methods at hand. Moreover, it also suggests that even now we may not be asking the best questions or developing useful new methods.

Many students of architecture during the period of the 1960s and 1970s found in the structures of the nonwestern world some persistent ideas about the development and use of architecture. From the tribal cultures of Africa came the idea of self-help architecture—buildings made from natural materials available on the site without cost and assembled either by the family themselves or by others as a result of a barter system of mutual assistance. Spurred by such examples, some modern architects structured their practice exclusively or largely to provide professional services to mutual-assistance groups. Historically, these efforts seem to derive from the architect-designed housing projects of the 1920s and later. One architect who has both written and practiced in this realm is the Englishman Martin Pawley. His books

Figure 25-5   Entrance to the Great Kan Ravi (men's house) at Kaimari, New Guinea. Used for ceremonies and social gatherings, a men's house of this sort was made of easily available local materials. In its height and openness, it is well-adapted to the hot and humid climate. (Photo by Frank Hurley, *Pearls and Savages*, 1924, by courtesy of the Photo Collection of the Australian Museum in Sydney.)

Architecture vs. Housing and *Garbage Housing* raise some hitherto unthinkable issues, such as the architect's responsibility for housing all the people, and the possibility of combining two problems—the deficit of housing and the surplus of empty containers produced by our throwaway society—into one solution. He suggests using the containers as building materials. His self-help housing is to be low cost because it is labor-intensive and the material for it is free. The poor could utilize their own labor rather than having to buy housing at going rates.

Others concerned about architecture became aware at new levels of consciousness that economical and political questions could not be separated from their consequences in the built environment. This was easier to see in the incongruity of one high-rise office building after another being put up in the dense but architecturally simpler urban fabric of Djakarta, Indonesia, or Ibadan, Nigeria. This new building type inserted without regard to local customs or conditions accentuated the imperial dominance of western culture over the other cultures. Such dominance began to disturb not only the local inhabitants but also at least some of the dominating Americans and Europeans. Against such imperialism, a new regionalism has begun to develop in architecture that is sensitive to local climate and materials and ways of living and promulgates local rather than international standards for architecture.

Regionalism in architecture leads us also to challenge the western assumption about the proper relation between high and vernacular architecture. In the western tradition, innovation is understood to begin at the top—in the architecture of churches and government buildings, that is—and to trickle down to the mundane buildings of everyday life. Noting how an aesthetic sense seems to run through every level of Japanese society, it is hard to believe that all architectural ideas of that culture begin at the top and trickle down in a similar way. They may instead possibly develop from an unspoken consensus in the society and from innovations of artisans. The present communist regime in China makes a point in its discussions about art objects of the past (recovered in archeological digs) that they were the work of the people, of ordinary artists and artisans, even though they were made for the rich and aristocratic. Art is defined thus as growing up rather than trickling down.

There is at least one nonwestern architectural tradition that has been extensively studied and recorded in English: that of India. Owing to the accident of British rule for over 150 years, there have been increasingly sophisticated studies of ancient, medieval, and modern architecture in India.

Something of the same expansion of knowledge is now taking place with respect to Islamic architecture. We have become recently more aware of this culture because of the economic importance of oil; Islamic cultures have similarly become aware of their participation in world culture. From their expectation of appreciation for their many fine contributions to architecture and urban design arises the question of how we are to understand which contributions are Islamic and which are earlier. Islamic architecture has all too often either been dismissed as being a mere bastardization of Roman ideas or been exalted as being totally original. Actually, a great deal of the interest comes for the student in discovering in Islamic architecture the admixture of older ideas with newer ones. The great sixteenth-century architect Sinan created the Blue Mosque in Istanbul as well as numerous other mosques in the Ottoman Empire after the prototype of Santa Sophia (Fig. 25-6). Inasmuch as Islam is a religion without a priesthood and without liturgical processions, he was not concerned with the need for a longitudinal space. The Blue Mosque could therefore be symmetrical around both axes, bringing the dominant centralizing motif of Santa Sophia to perfection. The Roman strength and clarity of the interior volumes contrasts well with the decorative oriental blue and white tile of the interior that gives the mosque its name. The building sits on one of the seven hills of Istanbul, with tall minaret towers at the four corners that reach out for the sky, setting up a tension with the large simple curves of

Figure 25-6 Mosque of Sultan Ahmed I, Istanbul, Turkey; built between 1609 and
1616 by Mehmet Aga. Like St. Sophia in having a tall domed central space
supported by smaller and lower half domes and by enormous buttress piers but
unlike it in being symmetrical around both axes, this mosque also crowns one of the
seven hills of Istanbul. The mounded shape is put into tension with its setting by the
sharp thrust upward of the minaret towers. (Photo by R. Hummel.)

the dome and supporting half domes. Built almost 1000 years apart, Santa
Sophia and the Blue Mosque raise questions about theme and variation. How
far from the original can something vary before it ceases to be a variation and
becomes a new entity? How much change from a prototype in one culture is
necessary for another culture to be satisfied with using it? How does a great
domed space affect us aesthetically and emotionally? Finally, what other
questions does Islamic architecture ask? During the 1980s and 1990s much
material on Islamic architecture should also be available in English. And since
the Islamic world is so conscious that its own value system differs from that of
the western, we may expect a whole series of questions to surface about the
nature and role of architecture.

We are also beginning to get a few works on indigenous African
architecture, such as LaBelle Prussin's book on the architecture of Ghana, but
much more needs to be done. The western prejudice that architecture is to be
taken seriously only if it is made of stone or other permanent material has
greatly hampered the study of the ephemeral architecture of both Africa and
the Pacific Islands.

In Hawaii, any casual tourist can visit several well-preserved ruins of Polynesian stone buildings, but this architecture seems not to have been studied by scholars of architectural history. Only the small objects of Polynesia, such as feather capes, have received attention as being precious items, which is analogous to the eighteenth-century treatment of rediscovered treasures of the Greco-Roman world. Perhaps the architectural history of Polynesia will be undertaken before long.

Gaps in knowledge persist even though we know how to ask a whole series of useful questions which would help us understand Polynesian and other nonwestern architecture at least as well as we do our own. In the process of learning about nonwestern architecture, our ideas of what architecture consists of may be expanded, suggesting enhancement of the numbers and kinds of questions we can ask about all architecture. The study of nonwestern architecture will then have accomplished the better (because richer) training of both the practitioners, the users, and the historians of architecture.

BIBLIOGRAPHY

Chang, A. I. T., *The Tao of Architecture,* Princeton University Press, Princeton, N.J., 1956, 1981. Essential reading for an elementary understanding of Chinese thought about architecture.

Crouch, D., D. Garr, and A. Mundigo, *Spanish City Planning in North America,* M.I.T., Cambridge, Mass., 1982. The introductory material to the section on Santa Fe deals with Indian origins of Spanish colonial built forms.

G(lobal) A(rchitecture) no. 2, *Frank Lloyd Wright, Kaufmann House "Fallingwater", Bear Run, Pa. 1937.* Stunning photos, many in color.

Hoffman, D., *Frank Lloyd Wright's Fallingwater,* Dover, New York, 1978. Many illustrations and the true architectural record of how the house came to be, according to the introduction by the patron's son.

Masuda, T., *Living Architecture: Japanese,* Grosset & Dunlap, New York, 1970. This whole series is well photographed and has good plans.

Pawley, M., *Architecture vs. Housing,* Praeger, New York, 1971; and *Garbage Housing,* The Architectural Press, London, 1975. Pawley attempts to get architects and clients to think creatively about solutions to the problems of housing human activities.

Prussin, La Belle, *Architecture in Northern Ghana,* University of California Press, Berkeley, 1969. One of the few available studies of sub-Saharan Africa. The author is both an architect, an art historian, and lived and worked for years in Ghana.

Tange, K., and Y. Ishimoto, *Katsura,* Yale University Press, New Haven, Connecticut, 1972. Beautifully photographed and poetically written.

Penguin has published the following accounts of nonwestern architecture:

Frankfort, *Art and Architecture of the Ancient Orient,* 1955 (about the Middle East).

Kubler, *Art and Architecture of Ancient America,* 1975.

Paine and Soper, *Art and Architecture of Japan,* 1955.

Rowland, *Art and Architecture of India,* 1956.

Sickman and Soper, *Art and Architecture in China,* 1956.

INTERLUDE E

Instead of the customary interlude, in which the cross comparisons are laid out for the reader, this one will give only outlines of such comparisons and leave it to the reader to think through each one.

The monuments of this group of four chapters are the Gamble House, the Villa Savoye, the Lever House, and the Imperial Villa in Katsura. We have already examined these monuments in the light of style, symbolism, date, and unasked questions.

A useful exercise is for the student to consider the Gamble House (Chap. 22) with respect to symbolism, date, and questions not asked. Then turn to the Villa Savoye (Chap. 23) and use style, date, and questions not asked. For the Lever House skyscraper (Chap. 24), try imagining questions not asked as well as questions of style and symbolism. Finally, consider the Katsura Villa (Chap. 25) in view of style, symbolism, and date. Use the pictures and descriptions in the bibliography for each chapter to gather more information and other interpretations, to enrich your comparisons. Ask some questions such as the following: "What do I already know that I can use to make these comparisons?" "What do I need to know to make valid comparisons?" "What are the features of each that could be understood only by a direct experience of the building?"

POSTLUDE

This final section is divided into two parts. In the first part, all the questions will be used to examine one monument, the World Trade Center. Some of the questions will prove to be highly illuminating; others will tend to be awkward and not very productive.

In the second part, all the monuments will be examined with respect to one aspect—that of light. More than some other possible questions, this will demonstrate our method and enable the student to deal with the complexity of architecture and be persuaded that all the constraints of architecture can sometimes simultaneously provide opportunities for innovations.

The World Trade Center was designed in 1962 by a team of architects and engineers headed by Minoru Yamasaki and was completed in 1976 (see Fig. P-1 and front cover). It was built near the southern tip of the island of Manhattan by the Port

Figure P-1   World Trade Center, New York City, 1962; by Yamasaki. These twin towers epitomize the new international style, with their sleek glass curtain walls held by aluminum framing. The structure is a steel frame. Utility floors are made visible three times by changes in the curtain-wall pattern. These towers are starkly simple and rely on size and proportion for their effect. Such surfaces reflect a great deal of light and hence heat, and have come to be recognized as powerful neighbors, ecologically speaking. (Photo, author.)

Authority of New York to be a beacon and symbol of the importance of world trade for the city. The center consists of twin towers, over 100 stories tall, resting on a base that includes plazas with sculpture and smaller buildings; within its core are such urban amenities as shops, restaurants, and mass transit stations.

1   The towers of the World Trade Center indicate approximately when they were conceived. Their outline is that of two equal shafts, each square and adorned only by a repetition of metal mullion against glass plane, except where the shafts are twice interupted by a row of opaque panels that cover utilities within. The glass has a metallic sheen, so that the towers exemplify the high-tech look that became so popular in the

1980s. Both the appearance of the buildings and the history of their erection bespeak an expansive early 1970's self-confidence in American society that existed before oil shortages and inflation caused serious reappraisal of earlier decisions.

2   Two years later the Port Authority would have had to pay more careful attention to suggestions that spending money on mass transit was a more fitting use for New York's money. (The World Trade Center was financed by surplus funds accumulated by the Port Authority as well as funds anticipated by them before there was a sharp rise in the cost of oil that caused an economic crisis.) The energy shortage turned many drivers into public transit riders, thereby putting unanticipated strain on Port Authority facilities.

There are other economic aspects involved with building skyscrapers. By the time the costs of manufacturing the components and shipping them to the site are added to the costs of construction, land, and financing, the total costs to society are greater than merely those of construction. The skyscraper has been explained as being the result of very high land value, which has led to developers crowding as many square feet onto the site as is possible. On the other hand, another motivation for building tall skyscrapers has been competition. The Empire State Building was built to surpass the Chrysler Building and other New York City tall buildings; it was in turn surpassed by the World Trade Center, which then lost out to the Sears Tower in Chicago (where tall buildings had their greatest nineteenth-century development).

The economic ramifications of building the World Trade Center involve such things as heavy demands on sewers, water supply, transportation, garbage collection, police and fire protections. If 50,000 people work in the towers and go out for lunch, for example, suppose that half buy a hot dog or cold drink and throw away the container; suppose that 25,000 buy a newspaper and half throw that away. The city is expected to collect and dispose of these trash items. The 130,000 daily visitors generate still more trash. This is an expense that the building owner usually does not incur, except in the example of Rockefeller Center where cleanliness has been shown to pay off in high rental values. The costs ultimately acrue to the public sector, according to J. K. Galbraith. (See his *The Affluent Society*.) The economic consequences of skyscrapers are more evident than those of gas stations or summer cottages, because of the large scale of the buildings.

3   These towers may initially be thought of as a complete break from tradition. However, the neighborhood around them displays a range of office buildings of many different heights, from two stories on up, that makes us realize that the tradition of building tall was by 1970 at least 125 years old.

4   The windy canyons and office buildings of Wall Street and the cemetery and Trinity Church, and the long crumbling wreckage of the West Side Highway behind the World Trade Center all made up the physical context of these towers. By being set in a cluster of other high-rise buildings, the World Trade Center is much less conspicuous than it would be in a small town. The towers are part of their context in yet another way. One has at the top a viewing area, basically the whole perimeter of that floor, from which one can get superb views of the city. The building encourages its visitors to notice and appreciate the physical context in which the World Trade Center is set. Viewers may also speculate on the social arrangements that made possible the construction and maintenance of such forms.

5   The center also made a contribution to the expanding technology that controls the use of materials in modern buildings. The use of steel and glass is now traditional, but for these buildings the task of planning and controlling what the materials would do was simplified by the use of computers. Since the buildings are so tall, they sway in the wind. The steel used at the top therefore had to be able to take tension. Because of the height and weight of the building, the steel used at the bottom had to be able to endure compression. Where and how were the engineers to change from one kind of steel to the other? With computers, the designers were able to calculate how the steel should vary as the building went up. Steels of different compositions which could withstand the particular combinations of bending, twisting, and downward thrust in each zone of the structure were required. Thus, even with modern architecture, the architects must be aware of what the properties of building materials are under all conditions.

6   The post-World War II skyscraper of metal and glass, such as the World Trade Center, evolved from the Lever House as the prototype. The World Trade Center is much larger in size and more dominant in position. All its design elements are elegant. The prototype has been brought to a kind of completion.

7   Unlike the Baths of Caracalla, or other skyscrapers such as the Ford Foundation building, the World Trade Center does not include any great spaces. It is the view from the street up past the church spire to the twin towers, or the shifting views outward from the visitors' platform that are significant. The interaction of the building with exterior space is designed in a manner reminiscent of that of Greek temples, an angular play of volumes. For all their functional uses, both temple and skyscraper are treated visually as sculptural objects rather than as enclosers of space.

8   No single person designs a skyscraper. The size of the structures, the complications of accommodating so many functions within the building, and the great number of parts that must be assembled, require the interrelated efforts of a team of designers. In an essay on architectural practice in large firms during the 1950s and 1960s, B. M. Boyle describes the organization of the firm of Skidmore, Owings and Merrill, designers of Lever House (in S. Kostof, *The Architect*). Each member of the team specialized in his or her own small area of design, and the team captain synthesized the individual elements to make the desired whole. The pattern is one of subordination and fragmentation. The results, though competent to the highest degree, have an anonymous quality, with little room for creativity. Since cooperation is necessary not only within the architectural office but also between that office and engineers, city planners, interior decorators, building inspectors, politicians, and bankers, a skyscraper is truly a cooperative effort. As such, the skyscraper speaks eloquently about how the work of building is arranged in our society, just as the Baths of Caracalla did about Roman society.

9   Though some Roman bath buildings have become Renaissance churches or present-day opera houses, it is too soon for the World Trade Center to be considered for reuse. Other skyscrapers in New York, however, have been and are being remodeled into apartments. This is particularly noticeable at the edges of the Wall Street area, long barren of residences. Social change is necessary for this kind of building reuse.

10   We have seen already that the World Trade Center was conceived and executed as a monument to the Port Authority and to the city of New York as the center of the shipping industry. In the modern period, monuments that take the form of useful structures may be termed "functional symbols."

11   The political context of the Trade Center has also been alluded to. Built to facilitate commerce, in a society that values capitalism, the World Trade Center by its prominent location in a busy port that is also the largest and richest city in the United States, alludes to its simultaneous role in international affairs. Its patron, the Port Authority, stands in a curious relation to government, having power to levy fees and taxes but not direct responsibility to any group of voters. It was exactly such independence that enabled the towers to be built.

12   The biggest dangers to the safety of a skyscraper are fires and earthquakes. Tall buildings are equipped with elaborate sprinkler systems, the intention of which is to localize any fire that should break out. As long as the water system that delivers water to the site is adequate, the system should be equal to the task. However, any disaster that affects the supply or delivery of water to the site would leave the population of the World Trade Center unprotected. Owing to the scale of the twin towers, any such shortage would lead to disaster. The municipality would be concerned inasmuch as a disaster at the World Trade Center would place excessive demands on city services. The ripple effect of any functional or structural failure of a large skyscraper extends throughout its area. It is therefore in the public interest for the technology of modern architecture to keep pace with developing safety practice.

13   We discussed religious motivation earlier as one traceable motivation for construction. The more worldly desire to impress people seems to have been important for the decision to build the World Trade Center. Not all of the motivation for building the World Trade Center was a simple desire for a unique status symbol. If others might surpass the center in height, none was likely to exceed it in the redundancy of its doubleness. There was also, of course, some honest concern for the facilitation of commerce at the international level.

14   The remarks above about materials could not help but refer also to the structure of the World Trade Center. By the 1970s, steel frame with glass curtain walls was a standard structural system for tall buildings. Among New York architects there had been competition about the address and configuration of new structures, but little conscious awareness for the most part about the aesthetic potential of the glass-filled steel-grid structure. The metal structure of these towers is not buried in their core but rather appears at the surface where it is revealed in the steel framework. (See S. Lessard, "The Towers of Light," which discusses the interplay between structure and appearance in the modern glass skyscraper.)

15   The question of the individual architect is somewhat irrelevant with respect to the huge skyscraper, as we have seen. Even the person who first sketched the concept of the design saw the ideas modified again and again by other members of the team. The architect whose name is attached to the project is the one who was in charge of it rather than the genius who conceived and executed it, as in the case of a Renaissance architect.

16   The idea of having twin buildings that make an important formal statement in the urban scene goes back at least to the baroque period. At the northern entrance to the city of Rome, there are twin churches opposite the gateway that leads into the Piazza del Popolo. These twins are fraternal, however, differing in such significant details as the plan of their domes: one has a circular, and the other has an elliptical dome. The towers of the World Trade Center are identical twins. They achieve their formal quality by the exactness of the duplication. This is the high-tech aesthetic at its ultimate, with no timid human details to distract the viewer.

17   The design process of any such building begins with assimilation of all the legal and economic constraints, goes on to the program (description of needs) of the client, and proceeds to the physical result by utilizing the team of professionals. Within the team, each member contributes his or her expertise. Within each group, the problem is discusssed until a solution mutually acceptable is reached. Out of consensus comes the design, which is then presented to the agent of the client. The process is reiterated on many levels of detail until the final design is approved. The design process for the World Trade Center differs from that of St. Peter's: the World Trade Center used more professionals, employed more technologies, and took less time to complete.

18   The rational organization of the design process is reflected also in the austere intellectual aesthetic organization of the building. By contrast with the rich complexity of the architectural environment that surrounds it, the World Trade Center makes an emotional impact by restraint and by lack of human scale. Its emotional message is that reason is all. The mind indeed delights in the purity of the design. The eye is pleased with the simplicity and elegance of line.

19   How the building was to relate to art was not a fully developed part of its design. As one comes in from the street to the plaza of several levels, some simple abstract sculpture is visible in the plaza. The scale of the sculpture to the plaza is well adjusted; and the enormous height of the buildings can safely be ignored, inasmuch as the visitor is by now too close to take in their entirety. The lobby through which visitors go on their way to the observation deck is an unornamented barnlike space. In the upper stories of the towers, the usual custom is to have decorators supply "tasteful works of art" for the reception areas of the tenants of the center; sometimes they also supply art for executive suites, but less important persons add their own calenders, family, photos, and plants—"the grafitti of all the prisoners of this world," as Alan Dugan says. In doing so, they assert themselves against all the impersonality and cold rationality of their surroundings.

20   By the 1960s and 1970s when the World Trade Center was built, the skyscraper was by far the most successful of the new building types developed during the nineteenth century. Success is judged here on the basis of how widespread the type is, how many have been built, how much money has gone into this type, and how powerful a hold the type has on our imaginations. It is no exaggeration to say that skyscrapers play the dominant role in modern architecture, equivalent to cathedrals during the gothic era. The World Trade Center is a fully developed example of the type rather than an innovative variation of it.

21   Although the World Trade Center avoids in its appearance any reference to the historical styles excoriated by the leaders of the modern movement, it cannot help being in fact part of an historical movement. Unlike the Chrysler Building or the Empire State Building, this one avoids all ornamentation—thus referring directly and overtly to such major monuments of the modern movement as the Fagus Factory or the Bauhaus.

22   In style, the World Trade Center is part of the movement called the new international style. Simplified geometric forms combined with elegant detailing and proportions characterize this style, which is further defined by its use of glass and metal skins. In these ways it is definitely a descendant of the first international style.

23   Like two great obelisks or the two halves of a pylon flanking an Egyptian gateway, the twin towers of the World Trade Center have a symbolic as well as a practical function. From the harbor, they are especially impressive as beacons of the commerce that the Port Authority fosters. Within the cityscape they dominate by their height. They also evince intelligent and proper aesthetic judgment by being set in a stepped configuration that plays them off as complimentary volumes against one another. The power and wealth that they display are thus mitigated by formal elegance of design.

24   The World Trade Center was planned during a decade when the old mood of unhesitating acceptance that the new was necessary and better was being challenged by a new mood of self-consciousness. In the eighties, we see architecture partaking of many of society's problems which make modern life ambiguous and complicated. The center remains to tell us of the very recent time when we had fewer questions.

25   Some of the questions that were not asked in the early 1970s have now been asked. Le Corbusier, for instance, supposed that air conditioning and modern building methods would make it possible and desirable to place the same sort of closed office container all over the world. The pressures of an energy shortage and the resurgence of regionalism have combined to stimulate investigation of local architectural solutions to the problems of housing modern office life in structures adapted to local conditions. What wisdom about architecture are we missing by blindly following other ideas of Le Corbusier or any other architectural predecessor? No matter what genius one person has he or she is only human and therefore limited in understanding.

LIGHT

To complete the cross comparison of monuments and questions, we will now examine each of the structures selected for major emphasis by use of the same question. This is the question of light and its effect upon architecture. What kind of light? How consciously are the effects determined? Has light changed over time? These are some of the detailed questions that occur when we begin to consider light as a design element.

1   It was possibly to keep track of the sun, the ultimate source of light for earth, that Stonehenge was designed and built in the third and second milleniums B.C. The whole complex seems to be organized around the view from the center over the heelstone to the rising sun at the summer solstice. At other times of the year, other lighting effects relate the center to different stones at the edge, thus effectively keeping track of the passage of time, of the sun's journey through the heavens. Making the wondrous understandable by showing its regularity is one function of Stonehenge.

2   The pyramids were designed to hold their own in a landscape of extremes, under very harsh lighting. Their simple volumes present one side in bright light and the other in deep shade. The simple strength of the forms appeal to the intellect, but the play of light upon them affects the emotions. Not only is sunlight involved here but moonlight as well. George Bernard Shaw's *Caesar and Cleopatra* contains a scene in which Caesar visits the pyramids and the great sphinx by moonlight, a scene which marvelously evokes the power of these structures to stir the emotions in the right light.

3   Both the traditional temples of the age-old Egyptian cults and the innovative temples of the new sun-god cult of the Pharaoh Ikhnaton made calculated use of light. In the traditional temples, such as Karnak, a basic principle of design was that the more public the area and the more people it was expected to hold, the higher the degree of illumination. Entryways and courts were fully exposed to the sun. Then came an intermediary hall with large windows. Finally, the sanctuary itself was quite dark. The sense of mystery this arrangement imposed was an important discovery, utilized again and again in the history of architecture. For propaganda reasons, the temples of the new sun god Aten were deliberately built to be open to the sky throughout, so that the sun as the god's representative could observe all that happened there. The highest ceremonies were grateful sacrifices of fruit and grains at open-air altars, rather than the secret rituals of washing and dressing and "feeding" the old god in his dark sanctuary.

4 It was partly the difficulties of lighting and airing the basement rooms of the palace in Knossos that made Wunderlich doubt that those rooms could ever have been the royal apartments as Evans had claimed. Even though enormous variation in the culturally approved proper amounts of light and air is common, he has correctly pointed out that these rooms receive too little of either to be comfortable. The Minoans used both light wells and stairways to bring light into the lower and innermost rooms of both palaces and ordinary houses, the architectural device being well attested at many sites. We know also that the entrance stairway that climbed the southern hill was covered for protection from too much sun, and included landings and porches in the form of loggias for the climbers to stop and look at the view. These elements suggest an awareness of the possibilities of light. However, neither the throne room nor the long corridor where the mural of the Lily Prince was painted had any windows, so they must have always relied on artificial light such as torches. Could the Minoans have allocated some spaces for use in the daytime and some for night?

5 What time of day it is certainly affects the viewer's perception of the Parthenon. Because the marble has oxidized, it has now a rosy glow, especially at sunset, that was not possible when it was new. The painted details and the waxy finish then must have given the whole building a sparkle that we can hardly imagine. The big simple Doric columns threw strong shadow stripes against the wall of the inner cella. The frieze that ran along the top of the cella wall and across the inner porches was never more than half lit, but even here the sparkle of color and of bronze fittings, such as spears or horse harnesses, united the frieze to the general aesthetic effect of the exterior. The great interior room to the east was different in its lighting effects (see Fig. P-2). The golden dress of the tall Athena statue and her ivory flesh were softly illuminated by three kinds of light. Direct light came from the large open doorway. Indirect light was reflected off the shallow pool at the foot of the statue, up into Athena's face. Finally, a diffused light came through the translucent marble tiles of the roof. Though this society supposedly was not interested in interior space, the spatial effect of this interior was subtle and complicated.

6 More pragmatic but equally intelligent was the control of light in a Greek city such as Olynthus. The town was laid out so as to turn its back to the north winds and open toward the southern sun. The interior courtyard of each house acted as a sun trap in winter. Most houses opened to the south, and many had upstairs bedrooms over the northern range of rooms. On the north side of the court, a roofed porch shielded those rooms from the high summer sun but permittted the low winter sun to enter with its warmth. A roofed open area tends to be 8 to 10 degrees cooler than the court next to it. These houses were thus well disposed to benefit from the sun and not suffer from it.

Figure P-2 Interior of the Parthenon, Athens, fifth century B.C. Since the roof was of thin translucent slabs of marble, the light bathing the gold and ivory statue of Athena was soft and warm much of the time. Other kinds of light added to the richness of the spatial experience: direct light from the doorway and reflected light from the shallow pool at the foot of the statue. (Drawing by P. Georges.)

Other Greek colonial cities or those rebuilt after the Persian Wars (479 B.C.) have the same north-south orientation, although Athens, developed much earlier, does not obey these principles.

One further advantage of the courtyard house must be mentioned: it gave the inhabitants private outdoor space as well as diffused lighting in all their rooms. The sun is very intense in the Mediterranean region, so that indirect lighting is sufficient and even preferable indoors.

7   Like the Greeks, the Romans used the courtyard house as their typical urban pattern and practiced turning their buildings to the south when that orientation was best for solar gain. Some of their buildings called for large sheets of glass in the windows. Not only public buildings like the Baths of Caracalla but also houses of wealthy merchants had windows with panes of translucent glass that were as much as 5 feet tall. In the baths, to light the centers of the vast domed spaces, huge windows were set into the semicircular arches, with vertical mullions dividing the windows into three upright strips, a form still called a Roman bath window. Once the light entered the space, it was bounced around from highly polished marble surfaces to glass mosaics for a lively effect that was a favorite of the energetic Romans. How different the interior of the great hall of

the Baths of Caracalla would have been if it had been painted institutional tan or grey! It was in the imperial palaces that the most elaborate experiments went on with alternations of full shade, partial shade, dappled light, and full sun, and with indirect and mysterious lighting. Many of these ancient Roman ideas were to be rediscovered again in the baroque period (see Fig. P-3).

8　Light can also serve as a useful "tool" in archeological exploration. In fact, much of what we know about Roman roads has been learned by studying photographs (information recorded on film by light) and inspecting desert areas under special kinds of light. In the 1930s when flying was still a novelty, two archeologists were flying low over the Syrian desert at sunset, after a rare heavy rain. They discovered that tiny plants, activated by the rain, were growing among rows of loose stones collected on top of the desert surface. In the low, slanting light of the setting sun, these tiny plants and the almost flat ridges they were growing on made a shadow pattern across the desert. The pattern was in the form of parallel lines about 50 or 55 feet apart. The explorers realized that they were looking at an ancient camel road—that the feet of the passing camels had thrown the small stones aside to the edge of the road. Further exploration revealed a whole network of roads in the desert, and probes at ground level showed them to be from Roman times. Light has thus revealed to us more about Roman engineering practices than we could have otherwise known.

9　A selection from the Roman vocabulary of light was carried over into the early Christian period. For instance, in Old St. Peter's and other basilicas, differences in the amount of light mark differences in function of various parts of the church. The nave was lit directly by tall windows set high in the nave walls, and indirectly by light coming in through the outer walls of the side aisles. The bema of the apse had its own semicircle of tall windows, making it the most intensely lit place in the church. It was here that the image of Christ was set up.

Figure P-3　Porch at the Getty Museum, Los Angeles, designed by N. Neuerberg, 1973. Like the ancient Roman villa after which it is modeled, this building incorporates the play of light and dark which the Romans enjoyed so much. From full dark where the photographer was standing through partial shade to full sun, the range was repeated again and again in Roman buildings. (Photo, author.)

10 In Saint Sophia, on the other hand, we find the culmination and perfection of a thousand years of experimentation with light (see Fig. P-4). The great dome and its attendant semidomes have a series of equal windows ringing their bases that seem to detach the domes from their earthly supports. More windows line the apse and both ordinary windows and huge bath windows are placed along the sides. Because the windows are filled with translucent rather than transparent material, the light within is gentle, falling as great beams diagonally across the central domed space. From the full

Figure P-4 Saint Sophia, Istanbul, sixth century. The semispherical dome was supported on pendentives. Windows were set in a ring at the base of the dome and like a screen in each of the side walls between the pendentives. Other windows pierced the buttressing semidomes and were set into the walls of galleries and aisles. From the translucent glass in these windows, rays of light fell across the interior, shimmering on marble surfaces. After gold-background mosaics were added to the walls in the tenth to thirteenth centuries, the shimmering effect was increased. (Photo by A. Dean McKenzie.)

shade of the vestibule and galleries to the partial light of the aisles, one comes to the full light of the great central space. That the viewer is awed but not overwhelmed is partly owing to the gentleness of the light and the softness of the shadows. Since the wall surfaces are in muted colors—dove gray, fawn brown, faded red, creamy white—the light sways around rather than bounces. Forms, materials, colors, and light combine to give off an effect of great subtlety. This effect is unfortunately marred at the ground level by garish nineteenth-century stained glass in the side aisles that is very distracting.

11   Since Charlemagne was attempting to revive the Rome of the Christian emperors of the fourth and fifth centuries, it is appropriate that the light in his palace chapel in Aachen is more blunt and less subtle; this sort of light seems better suited to the Franks, a people recently converted and sedentary. This church has only a few simple windows at the base of the roof and a few in the thickness of the walls, enough to provide light functionally but not enough to make any special statement about light per se. A few mosaics were placed at the top of the walls and in the gallery, but again not much was made of them as elements which might manipulate the light. If we look from Charlemagne's throne across the central space toward the apse, there is a very different lighting effect today than was originally planned. The old apse is gone, and in its place stands a gothic chapel, its walls almost completely dissolved into glass. Even though the glass is dark in tone, the gothic space delivers its message by means of the light within it (see Fig. 11-3).

12   The castles of the Middle Ages have a quality of solidness even more than do the churches. Security demanded small slit windows for safety. Primitive heating and cooking methods further darkened the walls. If the darkness had a bad effect on the psyche, little notice seems to have been taken of this factor.

13   The earliest parts of Mont-St.-Michel were heavily constructed like a castle and provided minimum light. As such a monastery survived into the gothic period, its newer buildings would have larger and larger windows, the light thereby being manipulated to enhance the feeling of awe and mystery. Romanesque churches tended to be dark because of the absence of light, whereas gothic ones were illuminated with the dark light of the deep-colored glass of many windows.

14   As a rule in gothic cathedrals the maximum amount of light was where the maximum religious and intellectual content of the building was placed. The two places were the outer side of the doorways where the sculpture was set, and in the tall and wide windows along the choir, nave, transepts, and aisles (see Fig. P-5).

A recent study suggests that if one concentrates on the stained glass, as a single panel flickers back and forth between abstract and representational, one has a spiritual experience similar to that of chanting a Buddhist mantra, the surface layer of the mind being soothed so that the innermost being may attain enlightenment.

15   Light as the ultimate symbol of God, as Abbot Suger saw it, and light as the natural illuminator of a world seem to be the two extreme ends of the continuum of philosophical positions about light. Renaissance architects, beginning with Brunelleschi, used light cleanly to reveal their forms. The light source was never hidden. Everything about the building was to be rational and logical, showing by its organization the intelligence of the beings who produced it. The creamy white of the stuccoed walls, set off by dark grey stone arches, entablatures, and other details at Santo Spirito in

Figure P-5 Sculptures of the portal of the north transept at Chartres Cathedral, around 1225 to 1250. The entrance doors to the church are at right and the piers that support the facade of the portal are at left. In the thickness of the wall, the doorway splays outward, providing wall surfaces to which the large and small figures are attached. We are standing in the right-hand doorway, looking into the wide central doorway. The light picks out edges of doorjambs and spotlights the tall figure of a saint standing at the right edge of the central doorway.
(Photo by G. Hall.)

Florence, made symbolic patterns that the light from the clear glass windows revealed easily (see Fig. P-6).

16 The way that light played on the exterior of a Renaissance palace went even more strongly to the heart of the matter. Individuality and uniqueness were valued highly in Renaissance society, so each palace had to be different from the other not only in obvious characteristics, such as the number and placement of windows, but also in the ways that light played off the surface, lingering over the bulky lowest story of the Palazzo Strozzi, and flowing freely up the surface of the Palazzo Rucellai, where all blocks were incised to the same degree. The linear quality of the Rucellai palace requires minimum light to reveal its form—an excellent decision considering the narrowness of the old streets in this area. The large windows of the facades of Venetian Renaissance palaces not only brought the dappling light reflected off the canals into the interiors, but also eased the structural load of the pilings that served as foundation for the palace, hence lowering the cost while improving the illumination of the palace.

17 At St. Peter's, Michelangelo's simplification here of the earlier structure was partly done to achieve lighting effects that were clearer and more direct. This is discussed in Zevi's book *Architecture as Space*. Earlier plans had called for an ambulatory to act as an envelope of space all around the transept and apse. Windows in the outer walls would have provided only indirect lighting for the large spaces of transepts and choir. Even though the foundations and at least parts of the walls had been built for this scheme, Michelangelo convinced his patron that the extra expense of tearing the walls down in order to simplify the space and increase the interior light would improve the building greatly. The lighting and structural effects have since been obscured by the elaborate decorations added during the baroque era—decorations that would have been nearly invisible if the previous scheme had been carried out.

18 In the baroque period, light was one of the elements of architecture that were manipulated for emotional effect. At San Carlo alle Quattro Fontane, the facade is a series of projections and recessions, emphasized by the light and dark of both highlight and shadow, with the shadow being intensified by dirt. The form is revealed by the contrast. Even if the whole facade gets dirty, more dirt collects in the recesses so that the contrast has increased as the building has aged. Both interior and exterior of this church have ranges of visibility from things that are hard to see because they are in such brilliance to elements that are hard to see because they are in such darkness. The exterior shows the most extreme contrasts; the interior has many gradations between the extremes. Borromini seems to have asked himself, "What will light do? What can I make it do?" Bernini, as we have seen, used light in the Cornaro Chapel to create an enduring drama.

19 At Vierzehnheiligen, the envelope of light separated the outer wall of the church from the interior volume. By setting the piers that support the gallery in an undulating line in from the outer wall, and by piercing that outer wall repeatedly with large

Figure P-6 Detail of Medici Chapel, San Lorenzo, by Michelangelo. Clear light enters from both sides as well as from the upper window. The architectural elements cast shadows which help to articulate the edges between wall and pendentive, window frame and wall. (Photo by W. Connor.)

translucent windows, Neumann created a special world with a luminous quality. The entering light is diffused through the interior, warmed by the pastel colors of marble and paint, reflected by the high polish of metal or marble, and diffused along the white walls. The intellect is scarcely strong enough to resist the impact of such light. (See back cover photo by D. Gardner.)

20   An abundance of light may be a mixed blessing. In the Crystal Palace, the glass roof and walls allowed so much light to enter that even in the rainy English climate, the effect was uncomfortable. Awnings of cheesecloth had to be hung inside the roof so that the light was diffused rather than direct; visitors were thereby encouraged to linger. The building being transparent, a new kind of relation was set up between the structure and its site, a relation whose potential would be explored in the whole series of major buildings during the twentieth century. The light, transparency, and great size of the Crystal Palace combined to produce an indeterminate space, another concept that was to be explored at length in the following century (see Figs. 20-3 and 20-4).

21   Better designed than the Crystal Palace for the actual conditions of light in London was the Albert Memorial. Sited in the open air, the baldachino shields the darker statue within it. The white marble of the outlying statues seems to focus the available light, whatever the weather, and the reliefs of the same marble tie them together and as it were ring the monument with light. Scott used materials and light very well and very naturally, given the climate and kind of light available (see Fig. 21-6).

22   Equally sensitive to local lighting conditions were the Greene brothers in their design for the Gamble House. The southern California sun is usually intense. The building will be in glaring sun all but 2 or 3 months of the year. The site had few trees, so that extensive roofs were needed to provide shade over terraces and sleeping porches. Nevertheless, each room has a choice of light, one side opening to a porch or terrace and one to the interior hallway. The play of textures and colors inside and out was carefully considered for the effects of light upon them. Rough exterior finishes give way to smoothly polished surfaces within. Colors inside are mostly the various neutral shades of wood and leather, with the muted tones of oriental rugs. The stained glass of all the windows of the front hall gives that space a special quality in any light, almost like being underwater—but in a placid river and not the ocean.

23   Careful attention to the quality of local light is an important feature also of the Villa Savoye. With an exterior surface of white stucco and with large windows, this house set in Spain or California would be harsh. In France, however, the effect is tempered by the greyed and moisture-laden air. The large windows of the house with little or no covering are both austerely aesthetic and luxurious: as the house sits isolated in its own meadow, the main rooms are elevated above the ground. Like the oldest Mediterranean houses, this one has its own court onto which the rooms open and from which they receive additional light.

24   Some of the same problems with light that plagued the Crystal Palace can be seen again at Lever House. Since the entire skin is glass, some parts of the building get too much or too intense a quality of light, depending on the weather and time of day. This is now regulated by movable curtains hung inside the glass. To compensate, then, for the loss of light when the curtains are drawn and to facilitate work on dark days or at night, the ceiling is laced with long strips of fluorescent lights. Such lights are usually operated by a switch that commands all the lamps of a story or a very large part of that story, so that the interior lighting is not adaptable to individual requirements. Later office design returned to personal control of lighting, in the form of desk lamps rather than overhead lighting. (See Fig. 24-6 and compare with Fig. P 7.)

25 For subtlety in lighting, the Japanese Imperial Villa in Katsura has few equals. Rooms can open directly to the garden and receive natural light or be closed off from it by a series of translucent screen walls which also thermally buffer the interior. Wide eaves cut off the direct rays of the sun, but since the inhabitants sit on the floor, they receive the benefit of whatever light there is. Interior surfaces tend to be white or light natural colors of wood, with contrasting black frames for articulation; the white reflects and diffuses the light just as do the white walls at Vierzehnheiligen. Now that we have become conscious of cultural and historical variation in how light is used, the inspection of light in the architecture of other non-Western cultures should give us new ideas for our own building (see Fig. P-8).

This review, cursory as it is, has shown that light is of great concern to architects and to the experience of architecture. It is the one element that does not cost anything, but from its use maximum results can be obtained.

Figure P-7 Glass House, Phillip Johnson, New Canaan, Connecticut, 1949. As originally built, alone on a wooded lot, the Glass House had a simple serenity that was unforgettable. Its kitchen was half separated from the rest of the space by waist-high counters; the bathroom had a solid wall of brick making a cylinder at right. The glass walls permitted visual incorporation of the changing seasons outdoors with every shift in sun, moon, and clouds immediately reflected in the ambience of the living space. (Photo supplied by Johnson.)

Figure P-8   From interior to garden at Katsura Villa, Kyoto, Japan. Like the ancient Romans, the Japanese have appreciated the range of lighting from full shade to full sun, with many subtle variations and shadings in between. We are looking here at the garden from the interior past shoji screen walls and wooden porch out into the full sun of the planted area. (Photo from Tange and Ihsimoto, *Katsura*, 1971, by permission of Zokeisha Publications, Ltd., Tokyo.)

BIBLIOGRAPHY

Boyle, B. M., "Architectural Practice in America 1865–1965—Ideal and Reality," in S. Kostof (ed.), *The Architect*, Oxford University Press, New York, 1977. Especially useful for understanding how huge buildings are designed and built by very large architectural firms.

Lessard, S., "The Towers of Light," *New Yorker*, July 10, 1978, pp. 32–58. The intentions of architects vs. inadvertent aesthetic effects, in the glass boxes that are Manhattan's new skyscrapers.

"The Tallest Steel Bearing Walls," *Architectural Record*, vol. 135, pt. 2, May 1964, pp. 194–196. How computers were used to design the framework of the World Trade Center.

GLOSSARY

The definitions of the following words pertain to their use in this text. Other possible meanings are not included.

Aggregate   Any of several hard inert materials used for mixing with a cementing material to form concrete, mortar, or plaster.

Agora   The marketplace and gathering place in ancient Greece. See *forum*.

Aisle   The side of a church nave separated by piers from the nave proper.

Ambulatory   A sheltered place to walk in (as in a church or cloister).

Amphitheater   An oval building with rising tiers of seats around an open space; an arena.

Aniconic   Without pictures (icons).

Apse   A projecting part of a building (as a church) usually semicircular and vaulted.

Architrave   The lowest division of an entablature, resting immediately on the capitals of the columns.

Articulation   The manner of jointing, marking off into distinct parts.

Atrium   The central hall of a Roman house; by extension, the colonnaded courtyard in front of an early Christian church.

Axial   Something situated along an axis, the straight line with respect to which a building or complex is symmetrical.

Bailey   The outer wall of a castle; the space within such a wall.

Baldachino   An ornamental structure resembling a canopy, used especially over an altar.

Basilica   (1) A Roman law building; (2) an early Christian church building consisting of nave and aisles and a large high transept from which an apse projects.

Bas-relief   A sculptural relief of slight projection without undercutting of the modeled forms.

Bay   A principal compartment of a building.

Beam   A long piece of heavy, often squared, timber, especially one used horizontally as a structural support; a piece of metal or stone used in the same way.

Buttress   A projecting structure of masonry (or wood) for supporting or giving stability to a wall.

Capital   The uppermost part of a column or pilaster crowning the shaft and taking the weight of the entablature.

Catacomb   A subterranean cemetery of galleries with recesses for tombs.

Catechumen   One receiving instruction in the basic doctrines of Christianity, before admission to the church.

Cella   The inner building of a Greek temple, surrounded or fronted by columns.

Chancel   The east end of a church, including choir and sanctuary.

Chevron   Two diagonal stripes meeting at an angle, usually with the point up.

Choir   The part of a church occupied by the singers or the clergy, especially the part of the chancel between the sanctuary and nave.

Circus   A large arena in the shape of an elongated U, used especially for foot, horse, and chariot races.

Cloister   A covered passage on the side of a court, especially in a monastery.

Coffer   A recessed panel in a ceiling, frequently square in shape.

Colonnade   A series of columns set at regular intervals and usually supporting a roof.

Column   A support usually consisting of a round shaft, a capital, and a base. The shaft may be constructed of one piece or made of horizontal circular drums.

Complex   A group of obviously related units, such as an ensemble of buildings.

Compression   Pressing or squeezing together. Vertical force is compressive.

Conceptual   Abstract; generalized from particular instances. In art, representation according to what is known not what is seen.

Concrete   A hard strong building material made by mixing a cement with aggregate and water.

Corinthian   A major Greco-Roman order, like the Ionic except that its capital is covered with acanthus leaves.

Cornice   The molded and projecting horizontal member that crowns a wall; a raking cornice is at an angle, like the edge of a pediment.

Curtain wall   A nonbearing exterior wall.

Doric   A major Greek order characterized by a capital shaped like a truncated inverted cone and a column shaft with no base.

Dungeon (*donjon*)   A close dark prison or vault commonly underground.

Eclecticism Selection of elements drawn from various sources.

Ensemble A group constituting an organic whole or producing together a single effect.

Entablature The part of a classical building between the columns and the roof; consists of architrave, frieze, and cornice.

Exedra An open recess, either rectangular or curved.

Expressionism The practice of depicting in art not objective reality but the subjective emotions and responses of the artist; architecture as a personal and emotional statement.

Facade The front of a building, usually given special architectural treatment.

Feudalism The political organization of Europe from the ninth to the fifteenth centuries, based on lord-vassal relations and characterized by homage, service, wardship, and forfeiture.

Flying buttress A masonry structure consisting of a straight inclined bar carried on an arch and ending at a solid pier or buttress to which it transfers the thrust of a roof or vault.

Formal Concerned with the outward form of something as distinguished from its content.

Forum The marketplace and public place of an ancient Roman city. See *agora*.

Fresco Wall painting made on wet plaster.

Frieze A sculptured or richly ornamented band, as on a building. In Greek buildings, located in the entablature between the architrave and the cornice.

Granite A very hard natural igneous rock with visible crystalline texture.

Hieroglyphs Writing in pictures, such as ancient Egyptian or Mayan writing.

Historicism A theory that emphasizes the importance of history as a standard of value. In architecture, nineteenth-century architects were overinvolved with historicism.

Hypostyle Having a roof resting on rows of columns.

Icon Picture, especially a religious picture.

Ionic A major Greek order characterized by its slender proportions and capital with volutes.

Lightwell An open shaft that brings light to the lower and interior parts of a building.

Limestone A rock made of organic remains (shell or coral), mainly calcium carbonate.

Lintel A horizontal architectural member spanning and usually carrying the load above a door or window.

Loggia A roofed open gallery in the side of a building, especially at an upper story overlooking an open court or the street.

Louver, or louvre An opening with slanted fins, fixed or movable, to allow flow of air but exclude rain and sun.

Magazine A place where supplies are stored.

Marble Limestone that has been crystallized by metamorphosis, capable of taking high polish.

Masonry Stonework or brickwork.

Mastaba An early Egyptian tomb, oblong in shape, with sloping sides, built over a tomb chamber cut in the rock beneath it.

Megaron Rectangular hall of Mycenaean times, with a central hearth and open porch, sometimes having an anteroom or vestibule.

Metope The space between two triglyphs of a Doric frieze, often with carved decoration.

Module A standard unit of measurement.

Monolith A single large stone.

Monument   Lasting reminder of someone or something notable; a memorial stone or building erected in remembrance of a person or event.

Monumental   Serving as or resembling a monument; massive; outstanding; very great.

Mortuary chapel   Where dead bodies are kept until burial; part of a church dedicated as memorial to the dead of one family, such as the Medici Chapel.

Motif   A recurring element, especially a dominating idea or central theme.

Mural   Pertaining to walls, especially paintings on walls.

Mutule   The adornment of the underside of a cornice with thin rectangular slabs with eighteen peglike forms called guttae.

Narthex   A portico of an ancient church; a vestibule leading to the nave of a church; sometimes divided into outer and inner narthexes.

Nave   The main part of the interior of a church, usually rising higher than the flanking aisles; long and narrow in a cruciform church.

Neoclassical   A revival or adaption of the classical style, especially in the eighteenth and nineteenth centuries.

Obelisk   An upright monument, four-sided and usually monolithic, that gradually tapers and terminates in a pyramid.

Order   (1) A style of building determined by the type of column and entablature forming the unit of that style. Examples: Doric, Ionic, Corinthian. (2) A group of people living together under a religious rule, such as the Benedictines.

Orientation   Placement facing the east.

Pagoda   An oriental tower (originally Chinese) which tapers upward and has roofs that curve upward at each story; erected as a temple or memorial.

Painterly   Building up a form by strokes of color rather than by drawing.

Papyriform columns   Egyptian columns in the form of stylized papyrus plants; these may be shown as open (blooming) or as a bundle of buds, or as single buds.

Pavilion   (1) A light sometimes ornamental structure in a garden, used for entertainment or shelter. (2) A temporary structure. (3) Part of a building projecting from the rest, especially in French Renaissance and baroque palaces.

Pediment   A triangular space forming the gable of a two-pitched roof, or a similar form used in decoration (such as over windows).

Pier   Vertical structural support, such as the wall between two openings. See *pillar, pilaster*. A pier is larger than a pillar or column.

Pilaster   An upright shaft, rectangular in plan, that is structurally a pier but is decorated as a column. Usually it projects one-third of its width or less.

Pilgrimage churches   Large churches placed a day's journey apart to facilitate pilgrimages in the Romanesque period. The ones in France all have similar plans.

Pillar   A post; a column or shaft standing alone; a firm upright support. A pillar is smaller than a pier, and need not be round like a column.

Piloti   A heavy column, usually of reinforced concrete, supporting a structure above an open ground-level space.

Plastic   Capable of being molded or modeled; sculptural.

Podium   A low wall serving as a foundation, as under a Roman temple.

Polar   Revolving around an axis; a straight line related to a point. Classical Greek space was organized with the observer as the pole.

Porphyry   A rock of feldspar crystals in a compact red or purple ground.

Portico   A colonnade or covered ambulatory, often at the entrance of a building.

Pozzolana   Pulverized ash that reacts chemically with slaked line and moisture to form a cement; found in Italy.

Precinct   The enclosure bounded by walls of a building or place.

Prehistoric   Before the invention of writing: In the old world, the period before 3000 B.C.; in the new world can mean before the arrival of Europeans (e.g., Pre-Columbian) or before writing which came in the early years of our era.

Primitive   Of the earliest period or stage of development. Relating to a relatively simple people or culture, one without modern technology or literacy.

Primogeniture   The exclusive right to inheritance belonging to the eldest son.

Program   Statement of an architectural problem and of the requirements to be met in offering a solution.

Properties   Qualities or characteristics.

Propylaeum (plural, **propylaea**)   In Greek architecture, a vestibule or entrance of architectural importance, before a building or enclosed space.

Prototype   Original model on which something is patterned, with essential features of a later type.

Pylon   An ancient Egyptian gateway building in the form of a truncated pyramid. Any massive gateway.

Quadrifoil   A flower-like pattern with four lobes.

Rampart   Fortification in the form of a raised wall usually surmounted by a railing or parapet.

Refectory   A dining hall, especially in a monastery.

Refinements   Contrivances or devices intended to improve or perfect.

Revetment   A facing; a veneer of a thin sheet of stone used ornamentally.

Rib   One of the arches in Romanesque and gothic vaulting meeting and crossing one another and dividing the whole vaulted space into triangles.

Romantic   Marked by the imaginative or emotional appeal of the heroic, adventurous, remote, or mysterious.

Rose window   A circular window (usually of stained glass) filled with tracery.

Rubble   Rough stone or broken bricks used in coarse masonry as filling.

Sacristy   A room in a church where sacred utensils and vestments are kept.

Sanctuary   The part of a church where the main altar is placed; a holy place.

Scenographic urbanism   Urban design based on optical perspective, such as that of stage scenery, developed in the Hellenistic period and reaching perfection in Pergamum.

Shim   A thin, often tapered, slip of wood, stone, or metal used to fill in, for leveling a stone in a building, for example.

Span   The spread between two supports, considered as either the space thus measured off or the element bridging the space.

Sphinx   A monster with the head and bust of a woman (Greek) or with the body of a lion and head of a man, ram, or hawk (Egyptian).

Stoa   A portico walled at the back, with a front colonnade and often with a row of rooms along the back.

Stucco   (1) Covering for exterior walls, made of portland cement, sand, lime, and water. (2) Fine plaster used in decoration and ornamentation of interior walls and ceilings.

Stylized   Represented according to a pattern rather than according to nature.

Tension   Stretching; the stress resulting from the elongation of an elastic body. Horizontal forces produce tension.

Terracotta   Glazed or unglazed fired clay used for statuettes, vases, and architectural details such as roofing, facing, and relief ornamentation.

Thrust   The sideways force or pressure of one part of a structure against another part, such as of an arch against a pier.

Tile A flat or curved piece of fired clay, stone, or concrete used for roofs, floors, or walls and for ornamental work.

Tracery Architectural ornamental work with branching lines.

Transept The part of a cruciform church at right angles to the nave; also, either of the projecting ends of such a part (e.g., the north transept).

Transom A window above a door.

Triglyph A rectangular tablet in a Doric frieze with two vertical channels of V section and two half channels or chamfers on the vertical sides.

Truss An assemblage of members such as beams forming a rigid framework.

Tympana The space within the arch of the doorway, above the lintel.

Vault An arched structure of masonry, forming a ceiling or roof.

Vocabulary A stock of elements employed in a field of knowledge. In architecture one can use, for example, a classical or a gothic vocabulary.

Web or webbing The part of a ribbed vault between the ribs.

Ziggurat An ancient Mesopotamian temple tower consisting of a huge pyramid of mud brick built in successive stages with outside staircases and shrine at the top.

INDEX